Europe's Growth Champion

Endorsements

'Poland's economic success over the last three decades is nothing short of remarkable. This insightful book shows how Poland owes its success to its ability to build broadly inclusive economic institutions, and traces the roots of this institutional transformation to the country's history, to its political transition driven by its middle class, to the anchor that the European Union provided, and to good political leadership. A must read for anybody who wants to understand the process of economic reform, especially today when we are witnessing the rise of an authoritarian government in Poland threatening to reverse some of these achievements.'

Daron Acemoglu
Massachusetts Institute of Technology, US

'An ambitious and successful effort at explaining the evolution of Poland from feudalism to communism and to today' success story. Full of insights, with deep lessons about development in general. A pleasure to read.'

Olivier Blanchard
Peterson Institute, US,
former Chief Economist of the IMF

'This highly readable book provides a comprehensive and novel explanation of Poland's rise to the ranks of high-income economies over the course of a single generation. The book will be essential reading for economists and economic policy-makers, including those in Poland, who face the daunting task of creating and implementing a new economic model for the future.'

Dale Jorgenson
Harvard University, US

'Based on comprehensive comparative research and rich personal experience, Piatkowski wrote a unique book on the post-communist transformation to a market-based, democratic and civic society. This is a tour de force on socio-economic changes in Poland—a country that almost 30 years ago initiated the historic process of transition and was the most successful economy to cope with its immense challenges. Piatkowski persuasively explains how this happened and what is the likely future not only for Poland, but also for the whole post-communist region and Europe.'

Grzegorz W. Kolodko
Kozminski University, Poland

'Most countries in the world are trapped in poverty or middle-income status. However, a country's destiny can change. Piatkowski analyzes Poland's recent success of ascending from a relatively poor to a high-income country in a generation's time. The book provides both inspiration and useful lessons for countries still struggling to change the fate of their nations.'

Justin Yifu Lin
Peking University, China, former Chief Economist of the World Bank

'What did Poland do to become the most successful European economy in the past thirty years? This brilliant and original book answers the question and rekindles the debate on whether successful economic development is driven by good institutions, good policies, lucky geography . . . or all three.'

Branko Milanovic
Graduate Center City University of New York, US

'No country did better than Poland after the fall of communism. This book dissects not just the specific policies that made this successful transition possible, but also its deeper roots in culture, institutions, and ideas—providing some surprising answers along the way. Piatkowski has written a deeply hopeful book that shows the way forward for Poland and other similarly situated economies.'

Dani Rodrik
Harvard University, US

Europe's Growth Champion

Insights from the Economic Rise of Poland

Marcin Piatkowski

Visiting Scholar, Harvard University's Center for European Studies;
Senior Economist, The World Bank

OXFORD
UNIVERSITY PRESS

OXFORD
UNIVERSITY PRESS

Great Clarendon Street, Oxford, OX2 6DP,
United Kingdom

Oxford University Press is a department of the University of Oxford.
It furthers the University's objective of excellence in research, scholarship,
and education by publishing worldwide. Oxford is a registered trade mark of
Oxford University Press in the UK and in certain other countries

© Marcin Piatkowski 2018

The moral rights of the author have been asserted

First Edition published in 2018
Impression: 1

Published in the United States of America by Oxford University Press
198 Madison Avenue, New York, NY 10016, United States of America

British Library Cataloguing in Publication Data
Data available

Library of Congress Control Number: 2017955748

ISBN 978–0–19–878934–5

Printed and bound by
CPI Group (UK) Ltd, Croydon, CR0 4YY

To Alex, Anais, Lily
and Beczulka

Acknowledgements

This book would not exist without support from a lot of people. I am especially indebted to Prof. Grzegorz W. Kolodko, who has been my role model for how to be creative, committed, and courageous in academic life and beyond. I feel privileged to have worked with him for almost two decades now. I could not have found a better guide. I am also grateful to Prof. Dale W. Jorgenson from Harvard University, who helped me sharpen the main ideas presented in the book. He has been generous with his time, support, and advice. I owe him a lot.

I would like to thank all those who have discussed the book with me and provided comments, suggestions, and ideas. These include Daron Acemoglu, Kaushik Basu, Olivier Blanchard, Benjamin Braun, Grzegorz Ekiert, Mikołaj Malinowski, Branko Milanovic, Robert Millward, Dani Rodrik, Gerard Roland, Michal Safianik, Martin Sandbu, Jacek Tomkiewicz, and Grzegorz Wolszczak. I also want to thank Jerzy Toborowicz for his excellent research support. Lastly, I am grateful to Harvard University's Center for European Studies for hosting me during the writing of the book.

On a personal note, I want to thank my mother, who has worked hard to raise me and my brother on her own. She had a tough life, but she never gave up. She made me who I am. I also want to acknowledge my brother, Maciej, who has always been there for me, offering support, good advice, and a sense of humour. And I want to thank all my friends—they all know who they are— who have been with me from the very beginning. And I hope will stay with me until the end.

I dedicate this book to my children, Alexander, Anais, and Lily, in hope that they will live in an ever-better world and that they will contribute in whatever way they can to making it even more prosperous, humane, and happy. Above all, however, I want to dedicate this book to my wife, Rebekah (Beczulka), who has always been my source of inspiration, introspection, and imagination. She has made me a better man.

Rights and Permissions

Table of Contents

List of Figures

List of Tables

List of Boxes

Introduction

This book is about what makes countries rich and what keeps countries poor. It tells the story of an economically backward, poor, and peripheral country that beat the odds and joined the ranks of high-income economies over the course of just one generation. Few had heard of this story, even though this country became Europe's and the world's growth champion, adding its name to the short list of global success stories. This country is Poland.

The book shares lessons from this economic success story, still largely untold, discusses the conditions that prevent countries from developing, and provides a recipe for how other economies could become high-income too. It is also about a new growth model that Poland and its peers need to adopt to continue to develop and to reach a level of true parity with the West for the first time in modern history.

The book starts by emphasizing the critical importance of institutions and culture in countries' development. I argue, based on the concept of extractive and inclusive societies developed by Daron Acemoglu, Simon Johnson, and James Robinson, that most underdeveloped countries in the world are caught in an extractive society equilibrium, where the few rule for the benefit of the few and create institutions that support the *status quo*, and that the few countries that have become rich and prosperous are those that have built inclusive societies, where many rule for the benefit of many. I assert that both the extractive and inclusive equilibria are persistent and this is why it is rare for countries to move from one equilibrium to another. This explains why fewer than fifty countries in the world have become high-income, while the rest struggle to grow.

I extend Acemoglu-Johnson-Robinson's conceptual framework to highlight the conditions, which are critical for moving from an extractive society to an inclusive society, and vice versa. I argue that throughout centuries, violence in various forms has been an unfortunate, but an inevitable component of a shift towards an inclusive society. The good news, though, is that moving from an extractive to an inclusive society seems to be a one-way street, as there are hardly any countries on record that have regressed back to an extractive equilibrium. However, growing income and wealth inequality in several developed countries today make it increasingly likely that such shifts could happen in future.

I then use the concept of extractive and inclusive societies to analyze the reasons for Poland's and—per proxy—Central and Eastern Europe's (CEE) centuries-long economic backwardness. I show that Poland was par excellence an extractive society, which failed to develop proper institutions and culture to support its development. These conditions broadly lasted for the whole period between 1500 and 1939, the beginning of the Second World War. Most other countries in CEE were similarly extractive and hence economically unsuccessful. Many poor countries in the world today continue to be in the same situation.

I go on to argue that the Second World War and—above all—communism was the external shock that helped push Poland and the rest of CEE to a new inclusive equilibrium, which laid the foundation of the country's post-1989 economic achievements. Communism took away freedom, killed and imprisoned people, and ended up in an economic disaster, but it nonetheless bulldozed the old, feudal, pre-modern social structures in Poland, which kept the country backward for centuries, and replaced it with an egalitarian, socially mobile, and well-educated society. The social inclusiveness of communism, which lifted millions of poor Polish peasants and blue-collar workers from grinding poverty, and gave them a chance to succeed for the first time in the country's history, was largely invisible under the dysfunctions, distortions, and defects of the communist economic system. But when Poles destroyed communism in 1989 and regained freedom, communist social egalitarianism was key to building a democratic, inclusive, and prosperous country like never before.

That said, at the end of communism in 1989, Poland's situation was dreadful. It was one of the poorest countries in Europe, with Poles earning about as much as one-tenth of the income of an average German. Even adjusting for the lower level of prices, Poles could buy only about one-third of what a German could buy. Poles earned less than an average citizen of Gabon, Ukraine, or Suriname. Polish incomes were also lower than everywhere else among communist CEE countries, except for Romania. It was an economic laggard even among the communist laggards. The country was bankrupt, burdened by outdated, inefficient, and environmentally destructive industry and subsistence agriculture, and buffeted by hyperinflation. There were shortages of even the most basic consumer products. Economic disaster loomed.

Yet, a quarter of a century later, Poland has become Europe's growth champion. Its real GDP per capita increased by almost two and a half times, more than in any other country in Europe. Adjusting for differences in purchasing power,

GDP almost tripled, from around \$10,300 in 1990 to close to \$27,000 in 2017 (in constant 2011 international dollars). In the same period, GDP per capita in the neighbouring Czech Republic grew by less than two-thirds; in Hungary, it increased by less than three quarters. Poland has also grown faster than all comparable countries in the world with a similar level of income. Poland has beaten even the Asian tigers such as Singapore, Taiwan, or South Korea. It has grown without interruption since 1992, registering Europe's longest growth spurt ever and one of the longest economic expansions in the world's history. It was the only economy in the European Union to avoid recession during the 2008–2009 global crisis.

I show how the remarkable growth in the last quarter of a century has led to the income of an average Pole reaching about two-thirds of the level of income in Western Europe. This is the highest relative income level in the country's history, exceeding the level of prosperity during the mythical 'Golden Age' in the sixteenth century, when Poland was the largest country in Europe, stretching from the Baltic to the Black Sea. Well-being and quality of life today is even higher because of the country's European-style welfare state. Poles now enjoy virtually the same access to the global culture, technological progress, and civilization as their Western peers. And they are quite happy about it: more than 80 per cent of Poles are now satisfied with their lives, up from only half at the beginning of transition. Poles have never had it so good before. Poland has entered its true Golden Age.

I emphasize that Poland's economic success is in many ways unique. This is because it has been achieved even though the country has no natural resources, has low debt leverage, and is part of the slow-growing Europe. More important though, Poland is one of only few countries in recent history that became high-income despite being robustly democratic, with seventeen different governments since 1989. Most other countries that caught up on the West since 1945 were not democratic for at least some part of their catching-up process. Moreover, Poland managed to combine rapid growth in income with rapid growth in the quality of life. The level of the country's well-being is higher than suggested by the level of GDP alone. According to several rankings, it is at least as pleasant to live in Poland as in the richer South Korea. Finally, it is the only democratic country in the post-communist camp where the tide of growth has lifted all boats and helped incomes of even the poorest parts of the society to converge on the West. All Poles benefited from the Golden Age, even if not in the same proportions.

I subsequently explain the sources of Poland's achievements. I analyze economic policies adopted after 1989, show how they drove economic growth, and explain what made Poland different from its CEE peers. I emphasize the importance of deep market reforms introduced at the beginning of transition, which—while far from optimal—have nonetheless laid the

3

foundations for the Polish miracle. I underline the remarkable boom in private sector development, unprecedented improvements in the quantity and quality of education, strong banking sector supervision, and robust policy making. I also explain why Poland conducted a broadly transparent and efficient privatization, which—unlike in many other countries in the region and worldwide—did not produce oligarchs. I show how the country managed to keep growth inclusive and share prosperity among all. Finally, I emphasize the critical importance of the rapid institution building driven by the prospect of the European Union membership. I conclude that, overall, Polish post-communist transition was an unprecedented success, which could have been only slightly better, but significantly worse.

If good economic policies drove good performance, then what drove the good policies? I go beyond the existing literature, which mostly emphasizes the proximate sources of growth, and focus on the ultimate sources of Poland's remarkable performance: institutions, culture, ideas, and leaders. I specifically emphasize the critical importance of Western institutions imported into Poland. As part of the EU accession process, within a mere decade or so Poland built the same institutions that took Western Europe 500 years to build. And the same institutions that made Western Europe what it is today: the most prosperous, humane, happy, and civilized continent in the world. Western institutions, supported by Western culture, values, and ways of doing things, are what made Poland successful for the first time ever.

If good institutions drove Poland's development, then what drove the good institutions? I argue that Poland wanted to adopt good institutions—democracy, free markets, robust competition, and opportunities for all—for five main reasons. First, it was because of the positive legacy of communism, which left behind an egalitarian, classless, and inclusive society, which had an interest in building an open and democratic state. Second, it developed a strong social consensus to 'return to Europe' and adopt Western institutions in the process. Third, it was governed by strong, professional, and Westernized elites, which knew where they were going and what they wanted to achieve: a full integration with the rich part of Europe. Fourth, Western Europe was open to embrace Poland on benevolent terms, using the European Union as the key instrument of institutional and financial support. Finally, adoption of good institutions was driven by the emergence of a new middle class and a new business elite. Most of these factors had not existed before and certainly not all at the same time.

Having explained the sources of Poland's economic good fortune, I move on to talk about the future. I analyze the long-term growth projections for Poland and discuss the potential upsides and downsides to growth. I claim that Poland is well positioned to converge with the West at least until 2030, supported by a super competitive economy and an inclusive society. By

2030, Poland may reach around 80 per cent of the Western European level of income, the highest relative level ever. That said, there are uncertainties about the speed of growth beyond 2030, as the country will be buffeted by the combined negative forces of population ageing, demographic decline, and slowing productivity growth. There are also substantial risks associated with the rise of illiberal politics. Lastly, I also talk about what we, economists, do and do not know about growth and discuss the importance and validity of international economic rankings.

I then argue that there is no guarantee that Poland's good performance will continue in the future unless it continues to reform. I assert that Poland and CEE need a re-adjusted growth model, which I call the 'Warsaw Consensus', to continue to converge with the West and fully catch up with it at some point in the future. I highlight how the 'Warsaw Consensus' builds on its Washingtonian older brother—the 'Washington Consensus'—but corrects its mistakes. I show in detail the rationale for ten policy prescriptions underlying the 'Warsaw Consensus'. These include stronger institutions, higher domestic savings, higher employment, more innovation, but also a competitive exchange rate, openness to immigration, and focus on well-being going beyond GDP. If the policies of the 'Warsaw Consensus' were implemented, Poland could become as rich as the West around 2040 and permanently move from the economic periphery of Europe, where it languished for centuries, to the European economic core. I argue that the success of the 'Warsaw Consensus' will much depend on the quality of its implementation and call for a new model of policy intervention. Finally, I posit that Poland is not likely to ever reach the income levels of the core of Europe, Germany, France, or the Netherlands, unless it starts to create rather than imitate the ideas of others. This will require further changes in the country's developmental DNA, including its institutions and culture.

In the last chapter I share the key conclusions, insights, and recommendations based on the Polish experience for other countries on how to shift from being poor to being rich.

1

Fundamental Sources of Growth

Institutions, Culture, and Ideas

> Third World countries are poor because [their institutions] do not encourage productive activity.
>
> Douglass C. North

> A nation's culture resides in the hearts and in the soul of its people.
>
> Mahatma Gandhi

> I believe in luck.
>
> Napoleon Bonaparte

Why are some countries poor and other rich? Why do some economies adopt good policies, while others do not? What are the fundamental sources of growth, which can explain long-term stagnation or prosperity?

In this chapter I provide a methodological framework for the rest of the book, which I will use later to explain Poland's long-term economic backwardness, its unprecedented economic success since 1989, and its prospects for future development.

I argue that most economic literature focuses on the proximate causes of economic growth—macroeconomic stability, privatization, business environment, the banking sector, and so on—and their impact on capital, labour, and productivity. But it underestimates or ignores the fundamental causes of growth—institutions, culture, ideologies, individuals, geography, and luck—that ultimately drive policies and eventually determine economic outcomes. Fundamental drivers of growth are the reasons why some countries are rich while `others are poor.

I focus on the role of institutions in explaining economic development. Following Acemoglu, Robinson and Johnson (2005), I distinguish between 'extractive societies', countries which are ruled by the few for the few, and 'inclusive societies', countries ruled by many for the many. The latter develop, the former stagnate. I argue that because of the power of the existing elites, network effects, institutional path dependence, and social norms, it is difficult and rare to move from one type of society equilibrium to another. This explains why fewer than fifty countries have become rich and developed, while the rest continue to struggle.

If being extractive or inclusive matters so much, what makes countries move from one equilibrium to another? There is surprisingly little discussion about this. I fill this knowledge gap by extending the Acemoglu-Robinson-Johnson institutional framework and analyzing the conditions necessary for the shift from extractive to inclusive institutions and vice versa to occur. I then argue that throughout history the shift from extractive to inclusive societies has almost always been accompanied by violence, especially driven by external shocks such as a military intervention. Shifts caused by internal forces were extremely rare. In turn, the shift from inclusive to extractive societies has almost never happened, at least in modern times. Finally, I introduce the interactive role of culture, ideas, ideologies, individuals, and luck.

1.1. Fundamental Sources of Growth

Why are countries poor? Is it because they do not know what to do to grow? What prevents them from pursuing good policies? Most of the existing economic literature focuses on the proximate causes of growth—changes in investment, labour, and productivity—and the role of policies in triggering them. But it largely fails to explain why growth-enhancing policies are not being implemented.

Every year, hundreds of reports, papers, and articles produced by international institutions, think-tanks, and academics re-hash the same old stories and offer the same, often trivial, advice about the need for countries to improve the business environment, enhance skills, strengthen macroeconomic stability, and so on as if the recipient countries were not aware of it. However, they never explain *why* these countries have not implemented these recommendations already (why the business environment continues to be so difficult even though it is so easy to change it?), and *what* to do in the future to make the needed reforms happen. Reading these publications, however illuminating, is like being involved in never-ending intellectual foreplay without ever taking the next step. It can be frustrating indeed.

The question of 'why' good policies are implemented or not is the fundamental part of explaining countries' performance. It is not the ignorance of policy makers that undermines growth—there has never been a shortage of

7

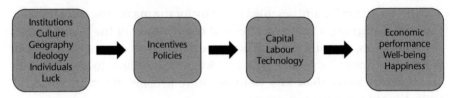

Figure 1.1. Fundamental and proximate sources of economic performance.
Source: Author's own.

good advice, especially now, where all the knowledge is effectively accessible online—but rather the policy makers' lack of willingness to adopt policies which promote development. This lack of willingness is a result of a complicated interplay of institutions, culture, ideology, and several other factors, which are the fundamental sources of growth. These factors provide incentives and drive polices which are ultimately responsible for economic performance, well-being, and happiness, as illustrated in Figure 1.1.

1.2. What are Institutions and how do They Drive Economic Growth?

Douglass C. North, an economic historian, Nobel Prize winner, and the father of institutional economics, defined institutions as 'the rules of the game' or 'humanly devised constraints that structure human interaction' (North, 1991, pp. 97–112). They include 'formal constraints (rules, laws, constitutions), informal constraints (norms of behavior, conventions, and self-imposed codes of conduct), and their enforcement'. The informal constraints, which in this book I will define as 'culture' and tackle in a separate chapter, include unwritten social norms, customs, and ways of seeing the world as well as the level of social trust, strength of political participation, or interest in transparency.

Acemoglu and Robinson (2012) differentiate between political institutions, which regulate the distribution of power among different social classes, and economic institutions that drive economic outcomes. Political institutions include democracy, dictatorships, autocracies, and mixtures of the three. Economic institutions include courts, which help secure property rights, competition watchdogs, which promote free competition, central banks, which control inflation, and many others. Political institutions affect economic institutions and vice versa (Acemoglu, Johnson, and Robinson, 2005).

Institutions provide the incentive structure, which drives the critical economic decisions among people on whether and how much to save, invest, get educated, absorb technology, innovate, and be entrepreneurial. Good institutions promote growth because they enforce property rights, create a level-playing field for everyone, allow new firms to enter the markets, lower the costs of economic transactions and support 'creative destruction'. They also provide for equality of opportunity through broad-based education, flat social hierarchy, and low income and wealth inequality. Bad institutions do the reverse. The prevailing institutions will decide what types of activities are rewarded and will flourish: productive and innovative entrepreneurs or rent-seeking politicians and criminal gangs.

Institutions, however, are not created overnight, and most often take a long time to change. This is their role: institutions are there to provide a certain degree of stability and permanence rather than change all the time. The speed and direction of the institutional change depends on a complex interaction among institutions, distribution of resources, and people's culture. Historical happenstance also matters, be this in the form of specific individuals (think Hitler or Stalin), shocks (medieval Black Death), or pure luck. The result of this interaction produces a certain set of institutions, which affects the long-term path of an economy's development.

1.2.1. *How do Institutions Drive Economic Growth?*

There is a consensus among economists that institutions are the key drivers of economic performance and societal well-being and there is a causal link between institutions and growth.[1] There is strong empirical evidence in the economic literature that differences in institutions such as secure property rights, rule of law, a level playing field, or broad-based access to education and opportunity can explain the differences in the levels of income around the world and distribution of resources, incomes, and assets within a society. There is no long-term growth without proper institutions.[2]

Figure 1.2 shows that the quality of institutions, as proxied by the rule of law, is correlated with economic development. The stronger the rule of law, the higher the level of income. There is also a strong link between changes in

---

[1] There is an abundant literature on the role of institutions. See, for instance, Rodrik, Subramanian, and Trebbi (2004); Acemoglu, Johnson, and Robinson (2001); Acemoglu, Johnson, and Robinson (2002); Acemoglu, Johnson, and Robinson (2005); Easterly (2013); Easterly and Levine (2003); North (1990); Barro (1996); Knack and Keefer (1995); Landes, (1998); Acemoglu and Robinson (2008); and World Bank (2002b).

[2] However, there is an ongoing debate in the literature about the direction of causality, that is whether better institutions cause growth or whether growth causes better institutions. On one side, Glaeser et al. (2004) conjecture that good performance helps build good institutions rather than the other way around. Chang (2011a, 2011b) shares this view and provides a long list of arguments of why it is almost impossible to tell whether growth drive institutions or vice versa. On the other side, Acemoglu, Johnson, and Robinson (2005), North (2005), and many others do not dispute the two-way connection between institutions and growth, but nonetheless underline that institutions have a causal effect on growth and sustained development over the long term.

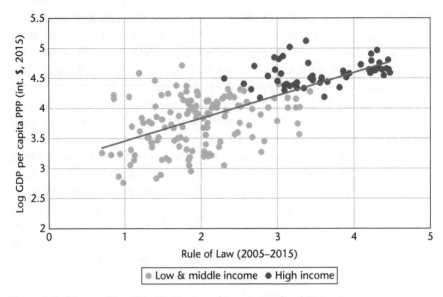

Figure 1.2. The quality of institutions and economic development.

Note: countries divided into low, middle-income and high income, as defined by the World Bank.

Source: Author's own based on the World Bank's Governance Indicators and World Development Indicators (WDI).

the quality of institutions and economic growth: Goes (2015), for instance, finds that among 119 analyzed countries during 2002-2012, a 1 per cent change in institutional quality translated into 0.35 per cent increase in the level of GDP in developed countries and a 2.6 per cent of additional GDP in developing countries. The weaker the institutions, the higher the payoff from improving them.[3]

Good economic institutions are particularly relevant for technology absorption and innovation, which are responsible for the major part of economic growth in the long term. Without secure property rights, open markets, and strong competition, absorption and innovation stagnate. Comin and Mestieri (2014) estimate that differences in technology diffusions between the West and the rest of the world account for 80 per cent of the difference in the growth rates during the last two centuries.

Good institutions not only drive growth, but also help to sustain it. Lin and Rosenblatt (2012) show that since 1950, out of about 180 developing countries only 28 countries managed to catch up by more than 10 percentage points with the US level of GDP. These were almost exclusively countries

---

[3] Of course, good institutions do not always guarantee good economic policies, especially in the short term. Good institutions only provide the potential for growth: how much of it is realized depends on specific policies and many other factors such as changes in terms of trade, technology, or political events.

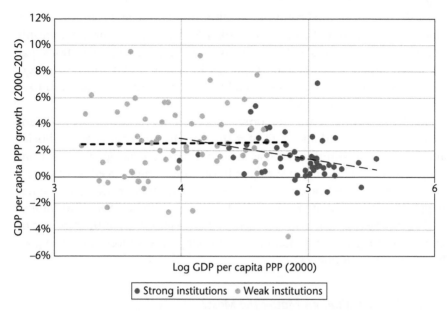

Figure 1.3. Institutions and economic convergence during 2000–2015.

Note: An index of the quality of institutions for 176 countries based on WGI and DB ranking, divided by quartiles; weak institutions defined as countries from the bottom quartile; strong institutions: countries from the top quartile.

Source: Author's calculations based on the World Bank's World Governance Indicators and the Doing Business ranking.

that got their institutions right. Glaeser et al. (2004) reach similar conclusions based on a large dataset of countries for 1960-2000. Figure 1.3 shows that institutions were important for sustaining growth also during 2000-2015 when poor countries with weak institutions grew at the same rate as richer countries with weak institutions. This was not the case for countries with high-quality institutions: there the poorer countries grew faster than richer ones. In other words, poor countries could catch up on the richer countries only when they built good institutions. Without them, there was no difference in growth.

The value of institutions shows up not only in the GDP growth rate, but also in countries' total wealth. In 2006, in a seminal study on the 'Wealth of Nations', the World Bank (2006, p. XIV) measured the value of natural, human, and institutional wealth for more than 100 countries around the world and concluded that 'rich countries are largely rich because of the skills of their populations and the quality of the institutions supporting economic activity'. In almost 85 per cent of the surveyed countries, the share of intangible capital, which includes human capital, social capital (trust and ability to work for a common purpose), and quality of institutions, represented more than 50 per cent of total countries' wealth. In high-income countries, intangible capital amounted to an astounding 80 per cent of the total wealth. Improvements in the rule of law, a proxy for the quality of institutions, had the biggest impact on intangible capital: a 1 per cent increase in the index of rule of law increased intangible capital by 0.83 per cent. Investment in fixed capital mattered much less.[4]

Finally, institutions are not only important for economic growth and wealth, but also—and above all—for the overall level of human well-being and happiness. Institutions such as democracy, free media, open markets, and many others are critical to ensuring political participation, freedom of speech, and a sense of control over one's life, the critical ingredients of human happiness and of what it means to be human (Stiglitz, Sen, and Fitoussi et al., 2008; Sen, 1999). Institutions thus matter regardless of their impact on growth, although what's good for human happiness is most often also good for economic performance.

1.2.2. Which Institutions Matter the Most?

There is an ongoing debate on which institutions drive growth and how exactly they do it. Castellano and Garcia-Quero (2012) summarize the main arguments. Among the main detractors of the key role of institutions in growth, Chang (2011a, 2011b) argues that there is much more uncertainty than the proponents dare to admit about the role of institutions in development and about their specific role in secure property rights, contract enforcement, and transactions costs. He emphasizes the importance of making a distinction between the formal shape of institutions and their functions, which can be much different depending on the specific socio-economic context. He argues that Anglo-Saxon institutions that maximize economic freedom and secure property rights are not the only way to develop.[5] In a similar vein, Tamanaha (2015) emphasizes the limits of human knowledge and the impossibility of identifying sustainable patterns of institutional development because social interactions are just too complex and unpredictable to allow this. Elinor Ostrom (2005, 2010), a Nobel Prize winner in economics, argued that it was impossible to provide an exhaustive typology of all the possible interactions between formal and informal institutions and economic behaviour and

---

[4] There was also much divergence in the impact of improved institutions of wealth: in rich countries, thanks to large stocks of good institutions, a 1-point improvement in the index of rule of law (on a 100-point scale) increased total wealth by almost $3,000; in poor countries by only around $100.

[5] He also criticizes new institutional economics, the body of economic knowledge focused on the role of institutions in development, for ignoring the often high costs of institutional reforms and the cost-benefit trade-offs. Finally, he calls for a more heterodox approach to analyzing institutions, based on a larger set of research methods and an expanded historical background.

design universal rules. Hence, we will never know how exactly institutions can affect development.

In response, the proponents of the critical role of institutions such as Acemoglu and Robinson (2012) or Rodrik, Subramanian, and Trebbi (2004), argue that it is possible to delineate the role of specific institutions in driving growth, as reflected in the empirical studies on the importance of the rule of law or open markets. Acemoglu and Johnson (2005), for instance, divide institutions into property rights institutions and contracting institutions. They define property rights institutions as institutions that limit the scope for property expropriation by the government and/or political and economic elites. Contracting institutions are institutions such as courts and public administration, which safeguard contracts and ensure compliance with regulations. They find that property rights institutions are more important for growth than contracting institutions. Countries that prevent the government and the elites from stealing income and assets from others are better positioned to grow than those that merely uphold contracting institutions. This might be because the contracting institutions can safeguard contracts, which are formally legal, but are otherwise biased towards the interest of the elites or the government.

That said, many of the proponents of the crucial role of institutions in development admit that there is more work needed to fully understand the relative importance of specific institutions and the exact mechanisms through which they affect growth. Ogilvie and Carus (2014), for example, assert that it is indeed difficult to define institutions: 'secure property rights' may be provided by different institutional arrangements and mean different things in America, France, or China. The Chinese case is especially poignant: its formal institutions have hardly changed over the last thirty years, but the way they function has changed a great deal and supported China's remarkable success (World Bank, 2017c). Similarly, the strength of contract enforcement depends not only on the formal strength of the courts, but also on the quality and efficiency of implementation, which may differ from country to country owing to different social norms. The best solution would be to find an objective measure of the quality of institutions based on the outcomes rather than inputs. But identification and agreement on what this would be is still far from clear.

The conclusion based on the existing literature is that there is clear evidence that institutions matter and they cause growth. It is also true that institutions and economic development affect one another and it is not always obvious what comes first. That said, despite the inherent and unavoidable uncertainty of what affects what, when, and how, this two-way causality can be productively studied and analyzed. In the same way that we will never be able to tell *ex ante* whether a joke will be funny or not, we will never know exactly how institutions affect development and vice versa. But this should not prevent us from trying.

1.3. Extractive Versus Inclusive Institutions

If there are so many different institutions, how can we categorize them? One way is to follow the categorization of institutions provided by Acemoglu, Johnson, and Robinson (2001, 2005) and Acemoglu and Robinson (2012), who divide political and economic institutions into 'extractive institutions' and 'inclusive institutions'.

They define extractive political institutions as institutions that 'concentrate power in the hands of a few, without constraints, checks and balances or rule of law' (Acemoglu and Robinson, 2012, pp. 74–5) and under which 'the rule of law and property rights are absent for large majorities of the population' (Acemoglu, Johnson, and Robinson 2005, p. 397). They argue that extractive economic institutions result in a weak rule of law, insecure property rights, high barriers of entry, low levels of competition, an uneven playing field, and restricted participation. In turn, they define inclusive political institutions as those that allow for 'broad participation, pluralism, checks and balances, and some degree of political centralization to enforce law and order' (Acemoglu and Robinson, 2012, p. 80). They are also accountable, transparent and responsive to citizens. Table 1.1 shows the typology of both types of political and economic institutions.

1.3.1. How Extractive and Inclusive Institutions Affect Economic Outcomes?

Acemoglu, Johnson, and Robinson (2005) propose a framework to explain how political and economic institutions affect economic performance (Figure 1.4). They argue that economic institutions result from an interplay of political institutions, which wield *de jure* political power based on the existing institutions and rules, and distribution of income among the population, with the rich

Table 1.1. Definitions of extractive and inclusive political and economic institutions

Inclusive political institutions	Extractive political institutions
Political institutions allowing broad participation, pluralism, and constraints and checks on politicians, the rule of law, and some degree of political centralization for the states to be able to enforce law and order	Political institutions concentrating power in the hands of a few, without constraints, checks, and balances or the rule of law
Inclusive economic institutions	*Extractive economic institutions*
Secure property rights, law and order, markets and state support (public services and regulation) for markets, open markets to relatively free entry of new businesses, strong contracts, access to education and opportunity for the great majority of citizens	Lack of law and order, insecure property rights, entry barriers and regulations preventing functioning of markets and creating a non-level playing field

Source: Based on Acemoglu and Robinson (2012).

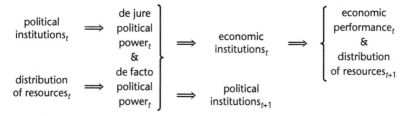

Figure 1.4. Political and economic institutions and economic performance.
Source: Acemoglu, Johnson, and Robison (2005).

elites, lobbies, and vested interests wielding a *de facto* political power. The interaction of both factors drives the design of economic institutions and decides whether these institutions are extractive—produce wealth for the few—or inclusive, sharing prosperity among many. The economic institutions in turn drive economic performance and the follow-up distribution of income from growth. The distribution of the newly generated income affects the original distribution of resources, which in turn affects the political institutions, in an ongoing feedback loop. In other words, the winning economic elites change the political system to suit their needs and then distribute the resources in such a way as to sustain the *status quo*.

1.3.2. What Makes Inclusive Societies Different From Others?

Among around forty countries around the world defined by the World Bank as high-income (excluding oil-rich countries and small island states) with GDP per capita of at least $12,475 GNI,[6] there are two overarching differences between them and the rest of the world: inclusive societies are all democracies (although the status of Singapore is open to debate) and have low or moderate inequality levels (with the Gini coefficient amounting to below or around 0.4, apart from Chile). This is clearly visible in Figure 1.5, where all high-income countries are clustered in the bottom-right corner of the chart. They are all in what could be called an 'inclusive sweet spot', where democracy and egalitarianism sustain high incomes. Other countries seem to be caught in an 'extractive trap', where the ruling elites keep societies underdeveloped.

---

[6] See the full list here: https://datahelpdesk.worldbank.org/knowledgebase/articles/906519-world-bank-country-and-lending-groups, accessed 6 Feb 2017. The countries assessed here include: Australia, Austria, Belgium, Canada, Chile, Croatia, Cyprus, Czech Republic, Denmark, Estonia, Finland, France, Germany, Greece, Hungary, Iceland, Ireland, Israel, Italy, Japan, South Korea, Latvia, Lithuania, Luxembourg, Netherlands, New Zealand, Norway, Poland, Portugal, Puerto Rico, Singapore, Slovakia, Slovenia, Spain, Sweden, Switzerland, Taiwan, Trinidad and Tobago, UK, USA, and Uruguay. Bulgaria, Romania, and Russia are upper-middle income and are likely to cross the high-income threshold soon, bringing the group to 44 countries.

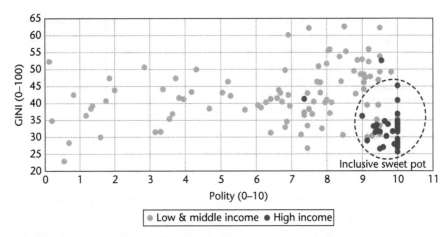

Figure 1.5. Low income inequality and democracy as key characteristics of inclusive societies, 2015.

Source: Author's own based on WDI and Polity IV database.

This finding is rather intuitive: democracy allows the whole society to participate in the political process, where one person equals one vote (although the ultimate quality of the democracy depends on the strength of the civic society and other factors). Likewise, low level of inequality is needed to ensure that everyone has a chance to succeed regardless of their socio-economic status.

Does this mean that democracy and low inequality drive growth? The literature on the impact of democracy on growth shows that both growth-oriented dictatorships and democracies can support economic development and the causality can go both ways (democracies can support growth, but also growth can support democratization).[7] The case for the impact of inequality on development is more clear, with much evidence that the level of inequality matters for long-term growth. Even the usually conservative IMF agrees (Ostry, Berg, and Tsangarides, 2014).

The bottom line is that democracy and economic growth cause each other and low inequality supports growth. All rich countries (again, except for oil-rich countries and small island states) are inclusive, democratic, and egalitarian. In contrast, most poor countries in the world are extractive, non-democratic, and unequal.

---

[7] Barro (1996) finds that overall democracy does not seem to matter for growth. Acemoglu et al. (2014) disagree and argue that new evidence clearly shows that democracy causes growth. The debate continues.

1.4. Where do the Good Institutions Come From?

Acemoglu and Robinson (2012) argue that whether countries develop extractive or inclusive institutions depends on small differences in the initial institutional conditions and a type of a shock, a 'critical juncture' as they call it, which is applied to these conditions (Figure 1.6). The resulting extractive or inclusive institutions tend to persist and explain the differences in the long-run economic performance.

The authors showed how Black Death in 1348, which cut the Western and Eastern European population by about one-third to one-half, was the critical juncture that helped gradually create inclusive institutions in the West. However, the same Black Death led to the emergence of extractive societies in the East. They argue that this institutional schism can explain the societies' further divergent development. They describe how in Western Europe the demographic shock helped peasants and merchants improve their negotiating position against the gentry and thus create a more balanced political system; in contrast, because of much weaker peasantry, smaller merchant class, and strong gentry, in Central and Eastern Europe (CEE) the demographic shock (which, as others argued, was likely smaller in any case) did not have the same effect as in the West.[8] The ruling gentry was thus able to monopolize power, weaken the monarchy, undermine merchants, and subjugate peasants. Peasantry and city bourgeoisie in CEE were weaker than in the West because of lower urbanization and population density, a legacy of delayed movement of settlers relative to the West (in turn partly driven by most of CEE not being part of the Roman Empire).[9] In the same way that boys born in the first three months of the year end up representing most NHL players because of small

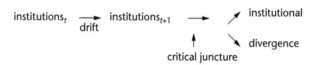

Figure 1.6. Acemoglu and Robinson's institutional framework of development.
Source: Acemoglu and Robinson (2012).

[8] Gottfried (1983) argues that Black Death affected Central and Eastern Europe, including Poland, less than Western Europe. Skodlarski (2013) claims that Poland largely avoided the epidemic.

[9] I define CEE to comprise all eleven new EU member states, from Estonia in the North, Poland and the Czech Republic in the West, Romania and Bulgaria in the East, and Croatia and Slovenia in the South. Eastern Europe starts in Belarus, Moldova, and Ukraine, and continues East.

initial differences in height, speed, and agility, small initial differences between Western and CEE led to large differences in ultimate outcomes.[10] Acemoglu and Robinson (2012) use the same framework to explain developmental trajectories of other countries in Latin America, Africa, and Asia.

Acemoglu, Johnson, and Robinson (2005) and Acemoglu and Robinson (2012) also review a large set of historical case studies to explain why some countries have better institutions than others. They emphasize three factors, which support the emergence of good political institutions. First, good political institutions arise in political systems with strong checks-and-balances. This helps ensure that political elites cannot create political institutions conducive to their particular vested interests and harmful to the rest of the society. Second, good political institutions emerge when political power is broad-based and/or when there is much turnover in political elites. This helps provide a credible commitment mechanism to political elites that if they protect property rights for all, their rights will also be protected when they are no longer in power. Lastly, they assert that good political institutions tend to develop in societies with limited rents from natural resources or monopolies because such rents enhance incentives for whoever is in power to change the political system to keep the rents for themselves.

Other scholars hypothesize about a plethora of other drivers of good institutions, including even the level of the nation's intelligence, genes, or the prevalence of parasites. Jones (2015), for instance, argues that higher average IQ, resulting from higher quality of nutrition and better access to schooling, helps countries build better institutions, because more intelligent people are prone to be more cooperative, patient, trustworthy, trustful, and focused on the long term. The resulting better institutions help increase IQ further and thus create a virtuous circle of development. Wade (2014) in turn emphasizes the importance of genes in explaining the emergence of institutions and their impact of development, although others disagree with his arguments (Ashraf and Galor, 2017). Finally, Maseland (2013) draws attention to the role of a common parasite, *Toxoplasma gondii*, in affecting cultural values and the subsequent choice of institutions.

---

[10] Gladwell (2008) claims that two-thirds of NHL hockey players were born in the first quarter of the year. He explains this puzzle by arguing that boys born early in the year were just a tiny little bit bigger, faster, and more coordinated than boys born later in the year. The miniscule differences were sufficient for the earlier born boys to be selected for a special hockey development track, leaving others behind. In time, small differences translated into yawning gaps in achievement. The same principles may apply to academic success: older kids are likely to be just a little bit smarter than the later born kids, giving them a minuscule advantage (1 or 2 points on the school test, for instance) sufficient to do better in school, all the way to Harvard. The same 'winner takes all' principle seemed to have also applied to Europe in the sixteenth to seventeenth centuries.

1.5. The Extended Institutional Framework of Development

All the remarkable work by Acemoglu and Robinson can help explain how initial conditions combined with a shock could lead to the emergence of either extractive or inclusive institutions. It can also explain how the distribution of resources affected the development of institutions. But three key questions remain unanswered: What drives the initial conditions? How does the initial distribution of resources drive the choice of institutions in the first place? And how can a country, which might have had bad luck and is stuck with extractive institutions, switch to inclusive institutions?

Acemoglu and Robinson (2012) provide only a partial answer. They argue that the emergence of political systems in colonial countries was driven by the initial density of population and mortality of European settlers. European colonial powers created inclusive political systems in countries with low population density and low mortality (United States, Australia, and other Western offshoots), because Europeans could settle in these countries and thus had an incentive to create inclusive institutions for themselves. In contrast, extractive institutions emerged in countries with high population density (because it made it easy to control and exploit them) and with high mortality rates (because Europeans did not care what institutions would rule over the locals).

So, it seems that the existence or not of the malaria-carrying mosquito can largely explain why some colonial countries such as America, Canada, or Australia are rich while others are poor. But what about the vast majority of other countries, which have never been colonial or whose historical economic performance has little to do with the mosquito?

Acemoglu and Robinson (2012) say little about the conditions for countries to move from extractive to inclusive institutions, except for their detailed discussion of the UK during the Glorious Revolution in 1688 and Botswana in the twentieth century to show how these countries have reformed internally and created inclusive societies. But there are more than forty other high-income countries today, such as Poland, and most of them did not experience the same internal revolutions as the UK or Botswana. What can explain *their* successes?

Finally, what were the roles of culture, individuals, ideas, ideologies, and geography? Acemoglu and Robinson (2012) and Acemoglu, Johnson, and Robinson (2005) consider each of these factors separately and argue that they did not matter for growth. They posit that institutions can explain everything and other factors are not important. However, such mono-causal explanation of growth is never correct, as even the three authors seem to admit in their other publications. Institutions alone cannot explain why countries are rich or poor. If so, Latin American countries, which adopted the US Constitution and copied many other institutional arrangements, would be as rich as America today (North, 2002). But they are not.

This is because institutions do not work alone. They are only as good and as effective as the people who manage them, as the ideas who inspire these people, and as the social norms, beliefs, and mental models that drive them. Institutions do not work in a vacuum, but in a complicated 'sauce' of cultural, historical, and political factors. The fact that it is difficult to model inter-actions among institutions and culture does not mean that we should ignore them. As John Maynard Keynes once said, it is better to be roughly right than precisely wrong.

Given these gaps, the Acemoglu-Johnson-Robinson institutional frame-work can be extended in three directions. First, it can be extended to discuss the drivers of the initial distribution of income and power, which decided whether countries from the beginning were more likely to become extractive or inclusive. Second, if being extractive or inclusive is likely to decide whether a country becomes rich or poor, it is critical to discuss the conditions for shifting between one set of institutions and another. Third and finally, the framework can be extended to include the interaction of institutions with culture, geography, ideas, individuals, and luck.

I present the extended institutional framework in Figure 1.7 and then dis-cuss each of my three extensions to the Acemoglu-Johnson-Robinson model in detail. Let me first explain Figure 1.7. At the dawn of the modern era around

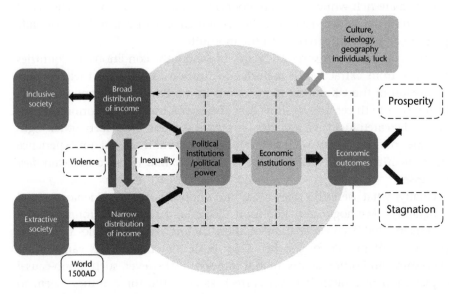

Figure 1.7. The extended institutional framework of development.
Source: Author's own based on Acemoglu, Johnson, and Robinson (2005).

the year 1500AD, virtually all countries in the world were extractive societies based on a narrow distribution of income among the ruling elites (although there were some differences among them in the initial distribution of income and power). Over the following centuries, the majority of countries that became inclusive and rich went through a period of violence (or a credible threat of violence), most often driven by external shocks or—much less often—by domestic revolutions, which broadened the distribution of income and opened the way for inclusive societies to emerge. The inclusive societies in turn created political institutions, which generated good economic institutions that drove economic performance and prosperity. The latter produced income that fed back to support good institutions and broadly distributed economic resources, creating a virtuous growth cycle. In contrast, countries that did not move to the inclusive equilibrium continued to be controlled by small elites, which appropriated the bulk of economic profits and controlled the commanding heights of politics and the economy. The whole framework is affected by the combined impact of culture, ideology, geography, individuals, and luck, which help decide whether the shift occurs between the two equilibria, and how economically efficient either of the two equilibria will be.

1.5.1. *Initial Distribution of Income and Power*

It is important to understand how widely the resources have been distributed in the distant past, at the very beginning of the modern era, and how this affected whether countries became extractive or inclusive. Distribution of resources tends to be persistent over centuries: except for a small set of countries that managed to shift from extractive to inclusive institutions (discussed below), most countries that were unequal and extractive in the distant past tend to be unequal and extractive today.

There are at least three factors that drove the initial distribution of income and power: geography, ideas and ideologies, and luck. As poignantly argued by Diamond (1997), geography matters: in the past, it was easier to accumulate income and wealth in countries with a conducive and healthy natural environment (no tropical diseases), productive sets of plant and animal species (horses), and availability of natural resources (coal), than not. Even today, there is a clear division between rich and poor countries: the former are mostly located in temperate climate zones, with the poor ones mostly in the tropics. Geography also decided the initial density of population, which was linked with the level of inequality (Sylwester, 2003). It also affected the organization of a society: nomadic societies have always been more equal than those that settled down. Finally, geography drove economic comparative advantages (wines in Portugal, wool in England, as in the eponymous example put forth by Ricardo or fertile 'black earth' lands in CEE as explained Chapter 2) and the subsequent distribution of income. It was largely conducive geography that drove Western Europe's higher density of population before the Black Death, which helped create a more powerful merchant class than in Central and Eastern Europe. It was also Western Europe's location on the Atlantic Coast that helped it benefit from the discovery of the New World. Temperate temperatures, a healthy environment, and a conducive set of available plant and animal species additionally favoured Western Europe, especially relative to other parts of the world.

Ideas, ideologies, and religions also mattered. Muslim or Buddhist societies tended to be more equal than other religions. Inequality in East Asia in ancient times was lower than elsewhere (Milanovic, Lindert, and Williamson, 2010). Even today, Muslim countries are more egalitarian than would be expected based on their level of income (Kuran, 2004). Ideologies played a role too: the ancient Inca Empire was largely a proto-socialist society, in which land was almost equally distributed among all citizens (Harris, 2017).

Lastly, luck had a role. If in the sixteenth century Queen Elizabeth had not allowed British merchants to trade freely in the open seas and appropriate most of the profits for themselves, the English merchant class might have been much slower to develop (or not develop at all) and to become strong enough to affect British politics. Luck also worked the other way: if the Spanish monarchs had taken the same decision as Queen Elizabeth, the Spanish merchants could have become strong enough to introduce an inclusive society in Spain at some point too. Yet, the Spanish monarchs decided to monopolize trade with the New World instead and undermine the growth of other social classes.

In the end, all the three factors—geography, ideologies, and luck—mattered: they created small differences in initial conditions, which subsequently helped some countries move in the direction of inclusive societies. Without a conducive geography, ideas, and much luck, the UK and many other today's rich countries could be still extractive societies, struggling to develop.

That said, it is important to remember that differences in development around the year 1500AD were not significant. All countries around the world were poor, unequal, elitist, and extractive (Milanovic, Lindert and Williamson, 2010). They were controlled by a thin sliver of oligarchs (royalty, aristocracy, clergy), which were extracting the large part of the available (low) incomes, forcing most population to live barely above subsistence. An extractive society based on a narrow distribution of income and resources was the default state of human development. However, while all countries were on roughly the same starting line, some were just slightly better prepared for the upcoming run to development. The small initial differences in conditions mattered for who eventually won the race.

1.6. Conditions for Shifting from an Extractive to an Inclusive Society and Vice Versa

Acemoglu, Johnson, and Robinson (2005) and Acemoglu and Robinson (2012) cite the UK, Netherlands, France, and Botswana as examples of countries that shifted from extractive to inclusive institutions as a result of domestic change. They also mention Japan after the Meiji restoration in the late nineteenth century as a case of a shift to inclusive institutions driven by external pressure.

Based on these examples, they argue that the shift between extractive and inclusive institutions can occur because of a threat of internal revolution or external intervention. Institutions can also be changed by shocks such as changes 'in technologies and the international environment, that modify the balance of (*de facto*) political power in society and lead to major changes in political institutions and therefore in economic institutions and economic growth' (Acemoglu, Johnson, and Robinson, 2005, pp. 392–3). But they hardly elaborate on that point and do not provide specific examples.

What about the other forty or so countries that moved from an extractive to inclusive society and became rich? The few internally led shifts to inclusive societies mentioned by Acemoglu, Johnson, and Robinson required a unique and rare set of factors to succeed: broad-based political support, critical mass of pressure on the existing institutions, and lots of persistence. All three factors had to happen at the same time for the internal change to take place. This is a tall order, which explains why internally driven revolutions are rare.

Instead, the clear majority of countries that succeeded in shifting to an inclusive set of institutions did so not because of internal revolutions but because of external shocks in the form of a direct external military intervention, a credible threat of intervention, or significant external pressure. It was the occupation of French forces under Napoleon in the early 1800s, which helped demolish old, feudal, and extractive institutions in most Western European countries. It was Stalin and his Soviet army which helped eradicate old institutions and elites in CEE, in a figurative and, alas, also often in a literal sense. It was the US occupation after 1945 that helped Germany become fully inclusive and democratic. It was the external threat in the form of renewed Russian occupation that helped change institutions in the three Baltic States— Estonia, Latvia, and Lithuania—after regaining their independence in the early 1990s. External pressure helped change Spain, Greece, and Portugal, when they emerged from dictatorships in the 1970s.

Outside Europe, external shocks were also predominant. The threat of US intervention in the late nineteenth century and then the US occupation after 1945 helped change Japan. External threat from China and pressure from the West helped drive the post-war economic success of Taiwan. Likewise, South

Table 1.2. Typology of shifts from extractive to inclusive societies

Internal reform	External intervention, threat, pressure	Other
UK, Netherlands, France	Austria, Bulgaria, Belgium, Chile, Croatia, Cyprus, Czech Republic, Denmark, Estonia, Germany, Greece, Hungary, Ireland, Israel, Italy, Japan, South Korea, Latvia, Lithuania, Luxembourg, Poland, Portugal, Romania, Singapore, Slovakia, Spain, Taiwan	Australia, Canada, Finland, Iceland, New Zealand, Norway, Sweden, Switzerland, Trinidad and Tobago, USA, Uruguay

Note: List of high-income countries based on the World Bank definition; excludes oil-rich countries and small island states; Bulgaria and Romania added as countries that should soon cross the high-income threshold.
Source: Author's own.

Korea developed because of the post-1945 US intervention and threat from the communist North Korea, which helped bring about a comprehensive land reform and eradicate growth-inhibiting feudal social structures. China, although not rich yet, could also be considered an example of an economically inclusive society (albeit not politically), which happened as a result of Mao's communist revolution, but also because of the perceived threat emanating from the West and a sense of national humiliation following China's colonial capture by Western powers in the nineteenth century. External threat from Arab societies (and lots of external pressure from the West) can also explain the emergence of an inclusive Israel. Finally, external pressure also helped Chile become (more) inclusive.

Table 1.2 lists all today's high-income countries across a typology of three possible ways of moving from extractive to inclusive societies: internal reform, external shocks, and other. The table clearly suggests that most countries became inclusive and successful because of external shocks rather than internal reforms.

There is also a group of countries that do not directly fit either of the definitions: these are the former colonies of the UK, which inherited their inclusive societies from their colonial power, or Scandinavian countries, which had their own, gradual way of shifting from extractive to the inclusive set of institutions, albeit also partly driven by external pressure and threats of social upheaval.[11]

As economics is not physics, the typology cannot be all encompassing: it is open to debate whether certain countries belong to this or to the other group. It is also true that many countries, especially in Western Europe, became more

---

[11] Denmark, for instance, abandoned absolute monarchy and adopted a new constitution in 1849 in response to the European Spring of Nations in 1848, which terrified the Danish elites and pushed them to share power.

inclusive because of the threat of internal social revolutions and threats of the same in neighbouring countries, such as the UK and most of Western Europe after the French Revolution (Aidt and Jensen, 2014; Kim, 2007). But the major point holds: most countries escaped the extractive society thanks to external shocks, not internal reforms.

1.6.1. *Why Internally Driven Shifts to Inclusive Institutions are Rare?*

Shifts from extractive to inclusive institutions are rare because the two equilibria—extractive and inclusive institutions—tend to be strongly persistent. This are several reasons for this. First, as explained by Acemoglu, Johnson, and Robinson (2005), institutions are supposed to be stable and durable, and a critical mass of political power is needed to cause the institutions to change.

Second, the incumbent elites that benefit from the existing system have no incentive to alter the *status quo*: if it ain't broke (for them), why change it? The existing system is also self-reinforcing because the elites are the ones who benefit from any growth that might occur, further increasing their advantage over the rest of the society. The costs to the elites of keeping the society repressed in poor countries are also usually low: as argued by Acemoglu (2008, p. 1067), 'in predominantly agrarian societies ... physical and human capital are relatively unimportant and repression is easier and cheaper. Moreover, ... democracy is potentially much worse for the elites because of the prospect of radical land reform'. In contrast, in more developed countries, the elites need skilled workers for the economy to function. A class conflict undermines the quality of human capital and makes social repression much costlier for the owners of capital.

Third, people become accustomed to the existing institutions, even when they are suboptimal. Changing institutions 'rocks the boat' and causes disruption, which most people seek to avoid most of the time. It is inconvenient for everyone to change a system that 'works', even if it 'works' badly. Fourth, existing societal and institutional arrangements tend to create their own supporting ideology, social norms, and beliefs, which are hard to break. The caste system in India, Samartian gentry in Poland, or the idea of 'meritocracy' and the 'American Dream' in the US are some of the many examples of such ideologies. Fifth, there are also substantial network effects involved: even if everyone agrees that there is a better system, it is costly to move towards it. To use a parable, even if we all wanted to move to a better software operating system than Windows, the large networking effects make it almost impossible or prohibitively expensive to achieve this.

Finally, even if certain societies manage to change formal institutions, for them to be effective they must be supplemented by changes in informal rules and enforcement. However, informal rules (culture) change at only a slow pace and thus the enforcement of new formal rules will have to be undertaken by the existing elites, who have no interest in enforcing the new rules (North, 1997). The story of Ukraine after it regained independence in 1991 is a good example of a formal adoption of Western institutions that was led by elites with little interest in making the new institutions effective as it would undermine the newly emerged oligarchic *status quo*.

All these various factors explain why when a country is stuck in one of the two equilibria, it tends to persist in that equilibrium, even for centuries. Extractive societies are like Segways: you need a substantial force to put them down; otherwise, they come right back up to where they were before.

The high persistence of institutions explains why internal revolutions happen only sporadically and why tens of countries today continue to languish in developmental 'black holes', where the harmful elites that control the commanding heights of politics and the economy are so strong that no one outside the elite can 'make it'. This is so despite wide open global markets, readily available knowledge on how to develop, and trillions of dollars of revenues from natural resources and from state aid paid by the West to the rest of the world since 1945.[12]

This suggests an idea for a new law of development: moving from extractive to inclusive societies and thus from poor to rich requires powerful external shocks or—alternatively—deep internal revolutions, with sufficient 'escape velocity'—a critical mass of broad societal support for reform and historical contingency—to be successful. Alas, such conditions are rare.

1.6.2. *Violence and Inequality as Drivers of Shifts Between Extractive and Inclusive Institutions*

A review of all high-income countries that shifted from extractive to inclusive institutions in the past suggests that virtually all shifts, both internally and externally driven shifts, have been accompanied by violence (a war, a rising, or a social revolution) or a credible threat of violence.

This is because, as shown in the extended institutional framework (Figure 1.7), the shift between extractive and inclusive institutions depends on the changes in the underlying distribution of resources. Such change almost never happens peacefully. As argued by Scheidel (2017, p. 8), 'across the full sweep of history, every single one of the major compressions of

---

[12] Nigeria received $50 billion in oil revenue in 2011 alone, and hundreds of billion dollars since the 1960s (http://www.resourcegovernance.org/our-work/country/nigeria). But it is still a poor country, with the level of income per capita PPP of only around $6,000, about one-tenth of the level of income in the US. Almost two-thirds of the society live in poverty (http://www.ng.undp.org/content/nigeria/en/home/library/poverty/national-human-development-report-2016.html).

material inequality we can observe in the record was driven by one or more of four levellers'. These 'levellers' or 'Four Horsemen of Levelling' include 'mass mobilization warfare, transformative revolution (which has to be "exceptionally intense if it is to reconfigure access to material resources"), state failure, and lethal pandemics (ibid, pp. 6–7). Among all the four levellers, warfare and transformative revolution were the most common.

Indeed, even the internally driven revolutions mentioned by Acemoglu and Robinson (2012) were accompanied by violence: the UK's Glorious Revolution was accompanied by a civil war and decapitation of the King. The Dutch revolution was a war against the ruling Spanish Dynasty. The French Revolution has become a textbook example of bloodshed and violence. The shift to inclusive institutions in other high-income countries was similarly violent. This is certainly the case of Poland and CEE after the Second World War and the case of Western Europe after a series of social revolutions in the nineteenth century, two wars in the twentieth century, and then a threat of invasion from the Soviet Union and its allies after 1945.

The implications of this line of reasoning are rather dismal: it suggests that a shift to inclusive societies in a peaceful manner is likely to be extremely rare. As argued by Scheidel (2017, p. 9), 'there is no repertoire of benign means of compression that has ever achieved results that are even remotely comparable to those produced by the Four Horsemen'. This suggests that changing the distribution of resources, which is key to moving to inclusive societies, will continue to be difficult. Most poor countries may therefore continue to be caught in an extractive sub-equilibrium, which they will not be able to escape on their own. They will be like a sick person lying in a hospital bed and trying to escape: she will not be able to do so unless she is helped by someone else.

What about the conditions for the shift from inclusive to extractive institutions? The good news is that inclusive societies, which combine democracy with moderate inequality and open markets, seem to be equally or even more persistent than extractive societies. It is difficult to identify countries that have shifted from being inclusive to extractive. It might have happened in Germany under Hitler during 1932–1945, but then the change was not persistent: the country moved back to being inclusive after the war (with a little help from the Americans and the threat of Soviet invasion). Shifting to an inclusive society looks like a one-way street.

That said, the fact that changes in the distribution of resources seem to happen only when violence happens, suggests that the increasing within-country inequality in today's world, as documented by Milanovic (2016a), Piketty (2014), Atkinson (2015), and many others, may continue to worsen. This implies that either we find better ways of controlling inequality or at some point in the future inequality may become so high that—short of renewed violence—some countries can become extractive again. Much, of course, depends on the definition: does the fact that in the last 30 years median incomes in the US have hardly increased, while the incomes of the top 1 per cent have skyrocketed, make America still inclusive or already extractive? The bottom line is that increasing inequality seems to be the major condition for moving from an inclusive to an extractive society.

To sum up, whether a country is extractive or inclusive largely determines whether it will be poor or rich. These two equilibria are strongly persistent and path-dependent: once you are stuck in one of them, it is difficult to get out. Such pattern helps explain why, contrary to economic theory, poor countries do not converge on the rich ones. Shifting from extractive to inclusive societies is, however, rare. The shift mostly happens because of external shocks, while inclusive internal revolutions are sporadic. Both tend to be accompanied by violence, which throughout mankind's history has been the unfortunate key driver of change in the distribution of resources. How economic resources are distributed affects the choice of political and economic institutions and the ensuing economic performance.

1.7. How to Move From Extractive to Inclusive Societies: Policy Implications

If moving from an extractive to an inclusive society in the past required an external intervention or a rare confluence of conditions for an internal reform to happen, how can we help poor countries to develop today?

If this hypothesis were true, it would mean that without changing political institutions from extractive to inclusive, any foreign aid might not be effective. In fact, to the extent that foreign aid ends up supporting the existing elites and their extractive institutions, it might indeed be counterproductive. This argument is much in line with Easterly (2002), Collier (2007), Djankov, Montalvo, and Reynal-Querol (2008), and many others, who question the positive impacts of foreign aid. Likewise, Rajan and Subramanian (2011) show that there is no evidence that public aid to poor countries affects their development (albeit it often helps poor people, especially by providing direct support to health or education).

This suggests that for foreign aid to be effective, the World Bank, IMF, and other international institutions as well as donor governments would need to link external support to changes in political and economic institutions. However, change in political institutions is often outside their mandate, while changes in economic institutions without changing political ones are not likely to persist. Alternatively, change happens only *de jure*: despite formal reforms, the ruling elites ensure that economic institutions continue to work in the same way as before, creating ever new Potemkin villages.[13] More than 70 years of foreign aid suggests that this indeed may be the case.

Even if, thanks to external pressure, it were possible to change political institutions, such change would likely not be persistent without changing the underlying distribution of economic assets and power, as highlighted in the extended institutional framework. However, it is not clear how international institutions and foreign governments could change the distribution of economic resources without an all-out intervention. Realistically, they could, for instance, insist on making the tax system more progressive, both in terms of the distribution of income and wealth. They could also insist on opening markets to competition and enhancing entry of new businesses to help create alternative elites. But the ruling elites would of course be loath to accept it; even if they did (say, during a crisis), it is likely that they would soon find other ways of recouping the losses (through, for instance, increasing their capture of public procurement).

Aside from foreign aid and the promise of support from international institutions, countries could also be helped in shifting to inclusive institutions by being offered other types of 'carrots'. For instance, developed countries could offer a large work immigration quota to developing countries that reform their institutions and widen the distribution of economic resources: in exchange for reforms, citizens of a country in question could legally work in developed countries (without necessarily being able to claim citizenship; Persian Gulf countries' model could be used, complemented with Western labour and human standards).[14] This would likely be a big vote winner in many poor countries and a boon to political elites.[15] It would also be an economic win-win for developed countries, the countries in question, and the global economy, as immigration is the most potent way to decrease global inequality, especially if it avoids undermining the institutions in the host countries (Borjas, 2015).

Other 'carrots' could also be used. Developed countries could subsidize wholesale staff replacement in poor countries' institutions most prone to corruption and state capture: police, customs, competition watchdogs, and public procurement. Staff could be recruited locally (as successfully done in Georgia, which in the early 2000s dismissed all traffic police force almost overnight and replaced them with new recruits; as a result, police corruption

---

[13] I had a personal experience of such changes when leading a World Bank project on private sector development in Ukraine in 2012–2013. The competition law was earlier changed to align it with the expectations of Western donors, but the competition watchdog was so emaciated, incompetent, and powerless that in practice nothing changed and domestic markets continued to be monopolized by oligarchs.

[14] This idea echoes a suggestion put forth by Milanovic (2016b).

[15] It would be important, however, to avoid 'brain drain'. This could be achieved by, for instance, providing time-bound work permits as well as subsidizing migrants' returns to home countries.

plummeted) or internationally (a country could hire foreign staff to take full charge of customs, for example).

Where 'carrots' will not work—because you can bring a horse to a waterhole, but you cannot force it to drink—the international community could also use 'sticks'. Could countries with extractive elites, which are not interested in a broad-based development, be forced to reform through external interventions, threats, and pressure? There is clearly no easy answer. Aside from all the moral, political, and cultural dilemmas, the historical evidence is far from unequivocal, to say the least. For every Napoleon who changed institutions in Western Europe, there are plenty of Bushes whose external interventions have failed, as exemplified by the situation in Afghanistan, Libya, or Iraq. Ditto for the track record of external threats and external pressure: for every Spain or Chile which reformed thanks to external pressure, there is a North Korea or Zimbabwe that did not. That said, there is no reason to stop experimenting with various approaches (short of Iraq-like invasions) and exerting pressure on countries to reform. An additional instrument could include barring elites of poor countries from depositing money in Western banks, requiring all companies to identify their ultimate ownership, and eliminating tax havens around the world, where the corrupt elites stock their ill-gotten money.

Finally, the last option would be to focus on engineering small and gradual changes in institutions, power coalitions, and access to information with the hope that over time they would create a critical mass of change, an approach proposed by the World Bank (2017c). However, the historical evidence presented here suggests that this might not work. This is especially so as the World Bank report assumes that (ibid, p. 4) 'all countries share a set of development objectives: minimizing the threat of violence (*security*), promoting prosperity (*growth*), and ensuring that prosperity is shared (*equity*), while also protecting the sustainability of the development process for future generations'. This, unfortunately, is not the case in extractive societies, where elites prefer to keep the *status quo* regardless of the four objectives. But perhaps I am wrong and this time it will be different. It is surely worth trying.

The bottom line is that there are few, if any, realistic ways to help poor countries to snap out from the extractive low-growth equilibrium. Short of changing the distribution of economic assets and rents, shifts to inclusive institutions will remain difficult and therefore rare. Underdeveloped countries might be here to stay.

1.7.1. *Culture, Ideas, and Individuals*

The third way in which the Acemoglu-Johnson-Robinson institutional growth framework can be extended is by including the impact of culture, ideas, and individuals.

Acemoglu, Johnson, and Robinson (2005, p. 392) argue that in their proposed framework

> the knowledge of the two variables [political institutions and the distribution of resources] is sufficient to determine all the other variables in the system. While political institutions determine the distribution of *de jure* political power in society, the distribution of resources influences the distribution of *de facto* political power at time *t*. These two sources of political power, in turn, affect the choice of economic institutions.

However, the interaction of political institutions and the distribution of resources does not happen in a vacuum, but is profoundly affected by the society's culture, ideas, and agency of individuals. All three play an overarching role across the whole institutional framework and are in a two-way interaction with each of the framework's elements. I will discuss each in turn.

1.8. The Importance of Culture

Culture has a predominant importance on growth as it affects the whole institutional framework: it affects the distribution of resources, the choice of *de jure* political institutions, the efficiency of economic institutions, and finally drives the economic outcomes.

There are various definitions of culture. North (1997, p. 1) defines culture as 'subjective perceptions people possess to explain the world around them which in turn determine explicit choices of formal rules and evolving informal constraints'. He specifies (ibid, p. 14) that 'culture provides a language-based conceptual framework for encoding and interpreting the information that the senses are presenting to the brain. As a consequence, culture not only plays a role in shaping the formal rules, but also underlies the informal constraints that are a part of the makeup of institutions'. Others define culture as 'customary beliefs and values that ethnic, religious, and social groups transmit fairly unchanged from generation to generation' (Guiso, Sapienza, and Zingales, 2006, p. 2). Merriam-Webster defines culture as 'the customary beliefs, social forms, and material traits of a racial, religious, or social group' as well as 'the integrated pattern of human knowledge, belief, and behavior that depends upon the capacity for learning and transmitting knowledge to succeeding generations'.[16]

Thus, in a broad sense, culture includes religions, mental models, mindsets, values social norms, and ways of doing things which are specific to each society and which affect how the society operates. Culture affects the way people think about themselves and others, how they perceive the world around them, and

---

[16] http://www.merriam-webster.com/dictionary/culture.

how they filter the incoming information. This affects the decisions they make about saving, education, and entrepreneurship, and contributes to whether the economy is moving forward or backwards. This is increasingly the case in a world of uncertainty, partial information, and growing complexity.

Until recently, most economists were happy to ignore culture because it is fuzzy, fickle, and hard to quantify. Culture is difficult to formalize and use in a discipline overwhelmed by mathematics. It is also controversial and any discussion about it is prone to be politically incorrect. The upside of being right is small, the downside of being, for instance, called a racist, is overwhelming. So, the incentives for economists to analyze culture are weak. Hence, they like to ignore it, finding various excuses. For example, Robert Solow, a Nobel Prize winner in economics, thought that trying to explain economic performance through culture often 'ends up in a blaze of amateur sociology' (quoted in Krugman, 1991, p. 93).

Since then, however, the economics has moved on. Today, there is a growing consensus that culture is critically important to development. An abundant literature confirms this.[17] Culture can help explain the continued economic divide between northern and southern Italy (Guiso, Sapienza, and Zingales, 2006; Tabellini, 2010), the economic activity of women (Alesina, Giuliano, and Nunn, 2013), GDP growth and social trust (Knack and Keefer, 1997), preferences for public redistribution (Luttmer and Singhal, 2011), levels of crime, or the link between 'acting white' and educational underperformance of African-Americans (Fryer, 2010). It also links economic outcomes to family ties, level of individualism, and the belief in the importance of luck versus effort in success.

Nobel Prize winner Kenneth Arrow argued that 'virtually every commercial transaction has within itself an element of trust... It can be plausibly argued that much of the economic backwardness in the world can be explained by the lack of mutual confidence'. The World Bank's World Development Report 2017 (p. 14) argues that 'A vast literature documents how social norms... govern the vast majority of human behavior. Social norms are a fundamental way of enabling social and economic transactions by coordinating peoples' expectations about how others will act'. Hirschman (1992), Putnam (1993), Fukuyama (1995), and Knack and Keefer (1997) posited that social norms, identities, and social capital are among the key drivers of economic performance, going beyond the narrow approach promulgated by standard classical economics. North concluded that (1997, p. 5) 'while the Weberian heritage of the role of the Protestant ethic in the rise of capitalism has been discredited in its crude form, cultural beliefs were an important (and at least partially

---

[17] For a useful summary, see, for instance, Alesina and Giuliano (2015), Guiso, Sapienza, and Zingales (2006), Fernandez (2010), Landes (1998) or Nunn (2012).

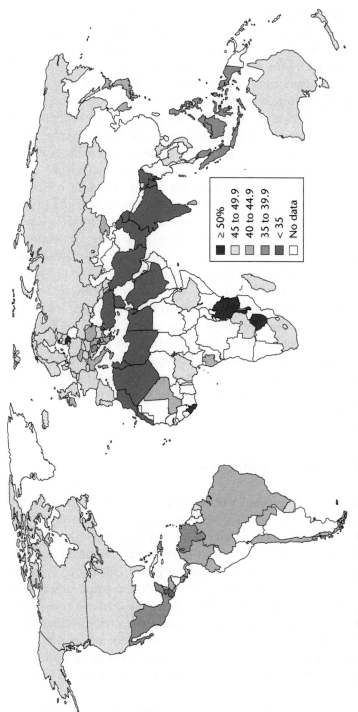

Figure 1.8. Female share of the labor force, in per cent of total, 2010–2016.

Note: Most recent year for each country.

Source: Pew Research Center based on data from the International Labor Organization; http://www.pewresearch.org/fact-tank/2017/03/07/in-many-countries-at-least-four-in-ten-in-the-labor-force-are-women/.

independent) source of the successful development of the Western world'. Finally, even Robert Solow seems to have changed his mind about culture: he admitted that financial resources are not sufficient to spur investment and they must be 'matched by the opportunity to use them... [and] the social capacity to assimilate advanced technology'(Solow, 1966, p. 480).

Indeed, without the discussion of the interaction of institutions and culture and the resulting incentives, it would be difficult to explain why Israeli scientists have more Nobel prizes than the whole Muslim world put together, why many governments around the world fail to introduce what seem like common sense reforms, or why certain ethnic groups, such as the Indian Gujarati, are so successful in business. Not all cultures are equally open to acquiring education and knowledge and to innovating. Not all cultures extol success and punish failure to the same extent. Not all cultures fight corruption in the same way.

If there is one picture to show the importance of culture for economic development, this could be Figure 1.8 on female share of the labor force around the world. The bottom line is that, for cultural reasons, in Muslim countries women are underemployed. It is difficult to become rich when almost half of society is left out of contributing to the economy.[18]

Finally, we could undertake a simple thought experiment to see whether culture matters: What would happen if, for instance, all the Germans suddenly left Germany and moved to some poor, geographically challenging, and resource barren environment? Would they succeed or fail? If you have an answer to this question, you understand the importance of culture more than many economists do.

1.9. How Culture Affects Institutions

North (1997) argues that the efficiency of institutions critically depends on the perceptions, value judgements, and 'ways of doing things' in a society. He gives an example of Latin American economies, which adopted their own versions of the US Constitution but ended up with different results than the US, to show that culture has a key impact on the credibility and efficiency of formal institutions. He goes on to argue (ibid., p. 12) that 'culture not only plays a role in shaping the formal rules, but also underlies the informal constraints that are a part of the makeup of institutions'. He adds that 'economies that adopt the formal rules of another economy will have very different performance characteristics than the first economy because of different informal norms and enforcement' (North, 1993, p. 8). In a similar vein, David S. Landes, an eminent

---

[18] Of course, women in Muslim countries, as elsewhere, contribute a lot in unpaid, household work. This, however, does not show up in GDP.

historian and the author of the magisterial 'The Wealth and Poverty of Nations' (Landes, 1998), claims that 'if we learn anything from the history of economic development, it is that culture makes almost all the difference' (Landes, 2000, p. 2).

Other research focuses on the impact of culture on specific institutions. Contract enforcement and the rule of law is much affected by social norms about what the society believes is right or wrong. If the law is at variance with the prevailing social norms, it is usually ignored (Basu, 2010; World Bank, 2015a). Religion and the social norms also affect the set up and the workings of institutions, from Sharia law to Islamic finance. It also puts limits on what is acceptable in terms of the differences in the distribution of resources (compare Scandinavian countries with the US). Institutions are also affected by implicit rules on 'what constitutes acceptable behavior within a firm or in the political arena by government officials', which 'may be as important in practice as explicit rules' (Berglof et al., 2012, p. 256). In other words, culture is also what goes without saying.

Social norms are key to keeping institutions flexible. By definition, institutions are supposed to be stable and not change. But institutions need to change together with the changing environment to remain efficient and relevant. The US Constitution is a good example: while the text of the Constitution has hardly changed since 1789 (except for some amendments), it has been re-interpreted hundreds of times by the Supreme Court in line with the changing social mores. To give an example, same-sex marriages were considered patently unconstitutional not long ago. They are fully legal now, even though the Constitution has not changed at all.

Finally, as argued by, for instance, Piketty (1995), societies differ in their assessment of what institutions are optimal to deliver economic prosperity. They differ in their views on, for example, whether success is driven by hard work or luck, which affects the choice of institutions to mitigate inequality (or not). Europe is much different from the US in its approach to inequality, largely because fewer Europeans believe that they control their own destiny.[19] Cultures also affect institutions to the extent to which economic prosperity is perceived by a society as an important goal in itself as opposed to other goals such as 'national honour', 'political prestige', or 'serving God'.

We could use another thought experiment to elucidate the impact of culture on institutions: if you took, say, an Afghani and a German and asked them to design the country's institutional framework from scratch, would they end up with the same institutions? Most likely not because people choose

---

[19] For instance, in 2014, 57 per cent of Americans disagreed with the statement 'Success in life is pretty much determined by forces outside our control' as opposed to only 38 per cent of Germans. http://www.pewresearch.org/fact-tank/2015/03/12/how-do-americans-stand-out-from-the-rest-of-the-world/.

to build institutions that most closely reflect their social preferences, beliefs, taboos, mindsets, and ways of perceiving the world.

Culture can sometimes trump the importance of institutions. Germany is an excellent example of a country that has performed well under all types of institutions in the last 200 years: under a Prussian oligarchy, during Bismarck's dictatorship, through Hitler's totalitarianism, and under the post-war democracy (Boldrin, Levine, and Modica, 2010). Likewise, it is difficult to explain the persistence of large differences in incomes between northern and southern Italy without thinking about culture: both parts have the same political institutions and the same formal economic institutions, yet these produce widely divergent results. Institutions without culture are like tigers without teeth.

In the end, culture and institutions are a two-way street: as much as culture affects institutions, institutions also affect culture. For instance, introduction of an independent central bank, which keeps prices stable, is likely to change social norms and perceptions of the value of money. Introduction of democracy can change people's perceptions about the value of political freedom versus autocracy. Opening of markets to free competition can change people's appreciation of entrepreneurship and business success, as has been the case in CEE after 1989.[20] Strong institutions can also drive prosperity despite lingering differences in culture: Wysokinska (2016) shows that Poles who emigrated from Eastern Poland to Western Poland in 1945, to territories that previously belonged to Germany, after 70 years were as prosperous as the autochthonous Poles (and more prosperous than their compatriots in the East), although in many aspects the two groups remained culturally different. Finally, East Germany provides a good example of how institutions (and ideas) can change culture: after 50 years of communism, East Germans are today much stronger proponents of bigger government and state involvement than are West Germans (Alesina and Fuchs-Schundeln, 2007).

Culture affects economic growth, but economic growth also feeds back into culture. Friedman (2005) rightly argues that economic growth makes societies more moral. Economic progress 'more often than not fosters greater opportunity, tolerance of diversity, social mobility, commitment to fairness, and dedication to democracy' (ibid, p. 15). Economic prosperity makes for better people and better societies. However, when standards of living decline and people lose hope about the future, societies can quickly regress, turning populist or even genocidal (Hitler and the consequences of the Great Depression come to mind).

But unlike institutions or business cycles, culture is slow changing: it evolves from one generation to another, building on the cultural heritage of previous generations. Culture is the mechanism through which history affects

[20] See Alesina and Giuliano (2015) and Greif (1993, 1994) for more evidence on the interplay of culture and institutions.

the present and helps determine countries' political development and economic performance today (Roland, 2010). Cultural norms are also remarkably persistent and sticky, as reflected in, for instance, the continued high circumcision rates of modern Americans.[21]

Of course, culture is not destiny. It can change. Germany, Japan, Korea, or Singapore were once believed to be unable to develop because of culture that was considered 'unfriendly' to business. For instance, in the nineteenth century the British described Germans as 'dull and heavy people' (Hodgskin, 1820: 50, cited in Chang 2011a, p. 493). Similarly with the Japanese: in the early twentieth century Americans tended to perceive them as 'being lazy and utterly indifferent to the passage of time' (Gulick, 1903, p. 117, cited in Chang 2011a, p. 493). But develop they did and joined the ranks of rich countries, mostly by adopting Western institutions, ideas, and cultural norms (World Bank, 2017c).

Not everyone agrees with the importance of culture. Acemoglu and Robinson (2012) seem to argue that culture does not matter.[22] They provide an example of Mexicans on both sides of the Rio Grande to claim that as Mexicans on both sides of the border have the same culture, but their incomes are widely different, then culture does not matter. Only institutions matter. They also argue that there is no link between Islam and lack of development in the Middle East, and that the latter is largely driven by the legacy of Ottoman and European colonialism.

Yet, they ignore the fact that the highly efficient American institutions that make immigrants in the US much more productive were built by Americans and reflect their culture rather than that of some other nation. They also do not explain why seemingly all Muslim countries, except for the oil-rich countries, have lagged behind developed economies. Turkey, one of the most economically successful Muslim countries with no oil, has arguably developed largely because of the adoption of Western institutions and values after the Ataturk revolution. In fact, Acemoglu and Robinson (2012) themselves argue that religion was one of the factors that prevented the Ottoman Empire from catching up with the West by slowing the adoption of printing presses (the first printing press in the Ottoman lands appeared only in 1727, but went bankrupt not long after because of multiple restrictions on its operations).

---

[21] In 2015, more than half of newborn boys in America were still circumcised despite there being no evidence of any health benefits of circumcision. In Europe, only 2–3% of boys are circumcised, mostly for religious reasons (*The Economist*, 2016).

[22] Although Acemoglu and Robinson nuance their opposition to the role of culture in later publications. For instance, in Acemoglu and Robinson (2016) they admit that social norms have a crucial role in building inclusive societies. Inclusive societies can develop if people believe that they can control the new institutional system. A more inclusive state feeds back into the feeling of control, starting a virtuous circle, which produces and sustains inclusive societies. Conversely, if 'societies lack informal institutions and norms that can block or discipline the accumulation of power, or they exist but are weak, they are unable to stop political entrepreneurs consolidating and centralizing power and building a [extractive] state' (Acemoglu and Robinson, 2016, p. 4).

Others like Rubin (2017) make a similar argument about the mixed impact of Islam on development, working its way through various channels.

Lastly, while rejecting the role of culture in explaining development, Acemoglu and Robinson (2012, p. 102) nonetheless admit that

> no two societies create the same institutions; they will have distinct customs, different systems of property rights, and different ways of dividing a killed animal or loot stolen from another group. Some will recognize the authority of elders, others will not; some will achieve some degree of political centralization early on, but not others. Societies are constantly subject to economic and political conflict that is resolved in different ways because of specific historical differences, the role of individuals, or just random factors.

While they do not explicitly mention culture, how they describe the origins of the institutions and their subsequent evolution seems to be much affected by a society's culture, beliefs, perceptions, and mental constructs. This is not all luck and happenstance.

1.10. Ideas, Ideologies, and Individuals

Ideas and ideologies obviously matter. It would be difficult to explain twentieth-century economic development while ignoring the impact of communism, fascism, or more recently neoliberalism à la Reagan and Thatcher.

Communism exemplifies the power of ideas and ideology. It created a totally new set of institutions, with no previous historical precedent. It was a system with extractive political institutions, but with inclusive social institutions, which provided employment, education, health services, and culture for all citizens and kept inequality at a low level (although the inclusiveness was restricted by lack of private markets, ownership, and entrepreneurship). Institutions followed the ideology, rather than the other way around.

McCloskey's trilogy on bourgeois values (2016, 2010, 2006) provides a magisterial compendium of arguments on how ideas—particularly the Enlightenment ideas of human betterment, individual rights, dignity of ordinary people, meritocracy, and liberalism—gave rise to the Industrial Revolution and the subsequent unprecedented acceleration in human progress. She rightly argues that what drove the Great Enrichment of the nineteenth century was not only institutions and material interests, but the changed ideology. Without the expansion of new ideas, it would never be possible to explain how 'in the two centuries after 1800 the trade-tested goods and services available to the average person in Sweden or Taiwan rose by a factor of 30 or 100' (McCloskey 2016; Kindle 197–8), a mind-boggling improvement relative to the stagnation of incomes for humankind before.

Mokyr (2016) makes a similar point. He emphasizes the importance of ideas in transforming Western Europe into the leading continent on Earth in the nineteenth century. He specifically focuses on the role of (technical and scientific) elites in spreading new ideas and changing ideologies. Only the power of ideas (and religion) can explain why, for instance, a poor and peripheral Sweden (and other Scandinavian countries) introduced freedom of the press in 1766, compulsory primary education in 1842, and meritocracy in recruitment for public administration in the mid-1840s way before almost anyone else, and how this helped it catch up with the Western European core (The Economist, 2013a).[23]

It is also difficult to ignore the impact of ideology on economic performance: just compare the policies of Republicans and Democrats in the US and their peers around the world. While ideology is hard to quantify and therefore is not included in mainstream growth models, any economist and policy maker ignores the power of ideology only at his peril.[24] It is in fact hard to find any economic analysis that would be devoid of the authors' ideological priors. Even seemingly objective analyses, such as those involved in a cost-benefit analysis, turn out to depend on the ideological assumptions (Klees, 2017). It is good news that at least some economists woke up to the importance of ideology and how—through storytelling and narratives—it affects economic performance (Shiller, 2017).

Finally, there is hardly anyone better than John Maynard Keynes to appreciate the importance of ideas for institutions and the whole economy. As he noted in *The General Theory of Employment, Interest and Money*:

> the ideas of economists and political philosophers, both when they are right and when they are wrong, are more powerful than is commonly understood. Indeed, the world is ruled by little else...Practical men, who believe themselves to be quite exempt from any intellectual influences, are usually slaves of some defunct economist...But soon or late, it is ideas, not vested interests, which are dangerous for good or evil.   (Keynes 1936, p. 383)

Acemoglu and Robinson (2012, p. 255) acknowledge the importance of ideas. They argue that 'institutions can change because the leading elites may want to adjust the existing institutions to the changing political, ideological or economic trends, as in the case of the abolition of slavery in the UK or Gorbachev's perestroika and glasnost in the late 1980s'. While the example of Gorbachev is far from ideal—he never meant to dismantle communism, but to save it—the moral repugnance of slavery had a large impact on mankind's

---

[23] Prussia was first to introduce compulsory education in 1763 to 'save the souls' and create a 'unified nation' (Soysal and Strang, 1989, p. 278). Sweden soon followed.

[24] See more, for instance, in Blyth (2003).

history. Slavery did not need to end—it was economically profitable and socially acceptable for most of mankind's history—but it did end, providing proof of the power of ideas whose time has come.

The role of individuals in how institutions translate into economic performance is hard to ignore either. No one needs much convincing that the world would have looked much different without Napoleon, Hitler, Mao Zedong, or Stalin. Regardless of the political and economic institutions they inherited, they single-handedly changed them to fit their own political vision. Other policy makers have achieved more gradual change (Franklin Delano Roosevelt, Mahatma Gandhi, and many others), but their individual imprint on the country's institutions and economic performance has been pervasive.

There is also empirical work on the impact of leaders on economic performance. Jones and Olken (2005), for instance, show the close interaction of the quality of the country's leaders, the country's institutions, and its economic outcomes (especially in non-democratic countries). Treisman (2014a) finds that leaders were also important to explain the divergent performance of post-communist countries in CEE.

Individuals interact with all other variables in the proposed institutional framework. They affect institutions and influence changes in culture, but culture and institutions affect them in return. For instance, only a certain unspoken set of social norms can explain why in Poland after 1989 practically all ministers of finance were chosen from among academic economists rather than from business. This stands in contrast with the choice of ministers of finance in most countries in Western Europe or, in particular, in the US, where most Secretaries of the Treasury seem to hail from Goldman Sachs.

Finally, luck also matters, of course. Was it not for the dramatic collapse in the price of oil in the mid-1980s, which almost bankrupted the Soviet Union and forced Gorbachev to announce 'glasnost' and 'perestroika', the Soviet Union could probably still be around and I would not be writing this book.[25] There are other examples galore.

Other factors also matter, although there is no space in this book to look at them in detail. Geography matters, as briefly discussed earlier, although there is no consensus in the literature on how much.[26] It matters for Poland and CEE for sure: as argued in later chapters, Poland's success in becoming a manufacturing hub of Europe has much to do with its proximity to Germany,

---

[25] A point made by Gaidar (2010). If the Soviet Union had not collapsed, I would likely still live in a communist Poland and end up as either a communist apparatchik or a political dissident. See a wonderful movie entitled 'Blind Chance' by Krzysztof Kieslowski to see how our life choices are driven by serendipity.

[26] Acemoglu and Robinson (2012) dismiss the role of geography; others disagree, such as Diamond (2012). Beck and Laeven (2006), for instance, argue that the physical distance to Western Europe can help explain development paths of transition economies.

the European manufacturing powerhouse. It would be difficult to achieve the same if Poland was located like Tajikistan.

Finally, economic performance is also driven by psychology, identity, and storytelling.[27] The decisions we take in our daily lives depend on the stories that we have been told and which we have subsequently internalized, often without us knowing. To give an idea of changing narratives, consider that back in 1945 today's neoliberal ideas would be perceived to be as absurd as state planning now. Stories and narratives change and so does the way the economy can respond to institutions and policies. This is a fascinating area for further research.

1.11. Conclusions

In this chapter, I set out the methodological framework, which will guide the rest of the book. I focused on the role of institutions, culture, ideas, and individuals, the fundamental causes of growth, in explaining economic development. Following Acemoglu and Robinson (2012), I distinguished between 'extractive societies' and 'inclusive societies'. 'Extractive societies' are poor because their elites have no interest in adopting good economic policies to benefit the whole society because it would undermine their lock on political power and economic resources. In contrast, 'inclusive societies' are those in which political and economic power is widely shared and economic policies in general aim at supporting economic growth and prosperity for all. Except for oil-rich countries, most rich and developed countries today are inclusive: they are democratic and have a low or moderate level of income inequality. Most poor countries are extractive, burdened by non-democratic (or faux-democratic) political systems and high income and wealth inequality.

I also argued that all countries in the world are caught in one of the two extractive-inclusive equilibria. Because of the power of existing elites, network effects, institutional path dependence, and social norms, it is very difficult and rare to move from one equilibrium to another. Throughout history the move from extractive to inclusive societies most often needed an external shock—a military intervention or a credible threat of such—while internally based shifts were extremely rare. Both externally and internally driven shifts were accompanied by violence. It is hard to identify examples for the shift in the opposite way—from an inclusive to an extractive society—but it could happen if today's top 1 per cent elites continue to build a system that will no longer provide equality of opportunity for all citizens.

---

[27] See, for instance, fascinating work by Akerlof and Kranton (2011), Akerlof and Shiller (2009), and Shiller (2017).

The new institutional framework offers some rather pessimistic implications for fighting poverty: if external shocks and violence are the main ways of kicking countries out from their growth-inhibiting extractive equilibrium, underdeveloped countries will be around for a long time to come. Other countries can help by providing various 'sticks and carrots' to the underperformers, but this is not likely to be sufficient. We should all keep on trying, but we should not hold our breath.

Finally, I proposed a new institutional framework of development, which extends the framework developed by Acemoglu, Johnson, and Robinson (AJR). I have shown three ways in which the AJR institutional framework can be extended to emphasize the importance of the drivers of the initial distribution of resources, the conditions for a shift between extractive and inclusive institutions, and the overarching importance of culture, ideas, and individuals for how the whole institutional framework operates.

The advantage of the extended framework over the original one developed by ARJ is that it seems to better capture reality. It explains how the whole world started from a narrow distribution of resources and extractive institutions around 1500AD and where these initial conditions came from. It also explains how some countries switched from extractive to inclusive institutions and highlights the (unfortunate) role of violence driven by external and internal shocks to make this happen. It also emphasizes how owing to increasing inequality inclusive countries could become extractive. Finally, the extended framework adds the important two-way interaction of culture, ideas, and individuals with the rest of the institutional development framework.

The extended institutional framework is self-encompassing in a sense that all interactions among the variables can be explained within the framework. Shifts in the distribution of resources affect the political institutions, which affect economic institutions, which then affect economic performance. Economic performance loops back to the original distribution of resources, strengthening the hold on power in extractive societies or supporting a broad-based political and economic system in inclusive societies. Both equilibria are self-reinforcing and any shifts between the two require substantial shocks (violence and inequality). That said, more research is needed to test alternative hypotheses to the proposed model, for instance along the lines of Tornell (1997). Further work is also needed to fully flesh out the various possible interactions within the framework (for example, how the distribution of resources affects what types of ideas and ideologies are promoted; think about the role of money in the US political system).

In the following chapters, I use the new framework developed in this chapter to explain Poland's historical backwardness, its unexpected economic miracle after 1989, and its prospects to catch up with the West in the future. I turn to the sources of its long-term backwardness first.

2

From Black Death to Black Hole

The state is the most precious of human possessions and no care can be too great to be spent on enabling it to do its work in the best way.

Alfred Marshall

History is a set of lies that people have agreed upon.

Napoleon Bonaparte

The best we can say is always partial and incomplete . . . Only by entertaining multiple and mutually limiting point of view . . . can we approach the real richness of the world.

Niels Bohr

Why have the Germans, the French, or the British have always been richer than the Poles, Hungarians, or Romanians? Why did Western Europe once control most of the world's population, while Central and Eastern Europe (CEE) hardly registered on the pages of global history? What can be learned from economic history that is still relevant today?

In this chapter I explain why Poland and, per proxy, most countries in CEE, have always lagged behind Western Europe in economic development. I discuss why in the past the European continent split into two parts and how Western and CEE followed starkly different developmental paths.

I then explain how Polish oligarchic elites built extractive institutions and how they adopted ideologies, cultures, and values, which undermined development from the late sixteenth century to 1939. I also describe how the elites created a libertarian country without taxes, state capacity, and rule of law, and how this 'Golden Freedom' led to Poland's collapse and disappearance from the map of Europe in 1795. I argue that Polish extractive society was so well established that it could not reform itself from the inside. It was like a black hole, where the force of gravity is so strong that the light could not come out.

2.1. The Rise of Western Europe and Decline of Central and Eastern Europe

In 1500AD, hardly anyone could have predicted the remarkable rise of Western Europe to the pinnacle of global power. Western Europe had no distinct advantage in technology, culture, or location relative to then powerful China or the Ottoman Empire. Yet, it was Western Europe, which prevailed and came to dominate the world for the next 500 years.

There is an abundant literature on the reasons for the rise of Western Europe. Kennedy (1987) contends that the meteoric rise of Europe was a product of political fragmentation, which spurred countries to compete against one another in embracing trade, providing conducive climate for business and promoting new, especially military, technologies.[1] North (1991) emphasizes the critical role of growth-promoting institutions. Besley and Persson (2009) underscore Europe's advantage in building efficient states with a large fiscal capacity. Following Weber (1905), Landes (1998) points to the fundamental role of culture and historical circumstance in explaining Western Europe's rise. Mokyr (2016) focuses on the key contribution of a free flow of ideas and an early appreciation of the importance of science. McCloskey (2016) explains the rise of Europe by the emergence of bourgeois values. Diamond (1997) highlights Europe's advantageous geography and the availability of productive animals (horses) and plants (wheat). In a similar vein, Morris (2010) underscores the key role of geography and the availability of fossil fuels. Landes (1969) and Mokyr (1990) focus on the critical role of technology. Finally, Ferguson (2011) emphasizes the importance of six 'killer applications'—free competition, belief in science, rule of law, advancing medicine, consumer society, and work ethic—which helped Western Europe become the preeminent political and economic force in the world. Still others focus on the role of absolutist kings, access to finance, class relations, colonialism, sex, and historical luck.[2]

Most important, however, is that while fifteenth to sixteenth century Europe was starting to take off and dominate the world, at the same time the European continent was starting to split in the middle, with the two parts of Europe going separate ways, Western Europe towards prosperity and CEE towards periphery. Europe gradually divided into economically and institutionally developed inclusive societies in the West and backward and underdeveloped extractive

---

[1] Although it is not clear why Europe became more fragmented in the first place, relative to, for instance, China and other global empires. Chiu, Koyama, and Sng (2014) argue that China was centralized because it required large resources to defend against one large enemy (the Monghols). Instead, Europe remained fragmented because it faced various sized threats from all directions. This put premium on versatility and flexibility, which smaller sized states provided.
[2] See, for instance, Jared Rubin's blog for a useful summary of the ongoing discussion on the sources of the rise of Europe. http://www.jaredcrubin.com/blog/why_the_west_got_rich_part_1, accessed 10 April 2017.

societies in the East. The former started to gradually democratize, industrialize, and trade; the latter went back to 'the second edition of serfdom' and in time became merely 'an agrarian reserve of the increasingly industrialized West' (Berend and Ranki, 1974, p. 3).

Box 2.1. ECONOMIC GROWTH TOOK ONLY 2 MINUTES ON THE 24-HOUR CLOCK OF HUMAN HISTORY

For most of mankind's history, generations after generations lived in the same conditions. Any increase in productivity translated into higher population rather than higher incomes. Productivity growth was slow and growth in population was slow too: between 25,000BC and 1AD global population grew at only 0.016 per cent per year (Kremer, 1993). It was only after the Industrial Revolution that the fast increase in productivity and economic growth started to translate into both faster population growth and rising prosperity (Figure 2.1). Today's quibbles about whether the GDP growth rate would amount to 2.0 or 2.5 per cent per year would be totally abstract to our forebears, who only knew a stagnant economy, which almost never changed (at least not much in their lifetimes, unless for the worse).

If we assume that the last 10,000 years of human history, since the first societies settled to a more sedentary life around 8000 BC, represent 24 hours on the clock, practically all the increase in the income of the world's citizens happened in only the last 200 years or 30 minutes on the clock (North, 1993). Since the appearance of homo sapiens about 150,000–200,000 years ago, economic growth happened only during the last 2 minutes of our history.

Source: Based on Jones and Romer (2009), North (1993), and Harari (2011).

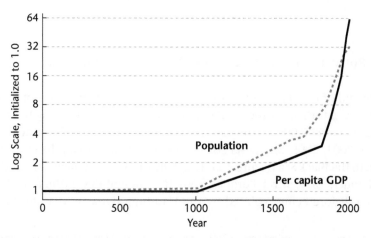

Figure 2.1. Population and GDP per capita in the very long run.

Note: Population and GDP per capita growth reflects an average for the United States and twelve western European countries, based on data from Maddison (2008).

Source: Jones and Romer (2009).

The continental split into the two parts came largely as a surprise: until the late 1500s, Poland and CEE looked, felt, and developed broadly in the same way as their Western cousins (Wyczański, 1973). The whole of Europe was predominantly based on subsistence farming, local trade, and a smothering of artisanship. Economic growth was negligible (Box 2.1). Differences in the standard of living between European countries were minimal, as large as today's gap between, say, Afghanistan and Burkina Faso. Average life expectancy from birth did not exceed 30 years (Broadberry and O'Rourke, 2010). Almost half of children did not survive until the age of 5; women got pregnant around ten times in their short lives, but they could expect only about half of their kids to survive to adulthood. Because of short life expectancy, marriages usually did not last more than a decade. Violence was rampant: the odds of getting killed were about 30 times higher than today (Pinker, 2011). People endured a back-breaking 3,200 hours of work a year, compared with about 1,600 hours today (and 1,300 hours in Germany). Ignorance, obscurantism, and sheer idiocy reigned supreme, nourished by literacy rates averaging about 10 per cent around the continent. Even intelligence was much lower.[3] And so was physical stamina: contrary to the common perception, today's white-collar workers sitting at the desk could likely easily dispatch to the other world the ill-nourished, growth-stunted, and disease-prone medieval knights, who were largely toothless, in both senses of the word (Broadberry and O'Rourke, 2010). For every European, except for the top 1 per cent of royalty, aristocracy, and church hierarchy, life in the old days was equally 'solitary, poor, nasty, brutish, and short' (Hobbes, 1651; Ridley, 2010).

2.2. Poland's Sixteenth-Century Mythical 'Golden Age'

At the end of the sixteenth century, Poland was at the pinnacle of its power. It was one of the largest and most populous countries in Europe, with a territory of more than 800,000 square kilometres and a population of around 8 million (Davies 2001, 2005; Morawski 2011).[4] It stretched almost all the way from the Baltic to the Black Sea (Figure 2.2). The Polish-Lithuanian Jagiellonian dynasty ruled much of Central Europe, from the present-day Lithuania down to Croatia, before being replaced by the Habsburg dynasty in 1526, following

---

[3] According to the so-called Flynn effect, intelligence measured by IQ has been on the constant rise during the twentieth century. It must have also been in the case in the more distant past. See Flynn (1987) and Herrnstein and Murray (1994).

[4] Poland was then officially known as the Kingdom of Poland and the Grand Duchy of Lithuania or the Polish-Lithuanian Commonwealth, established in 1569. It was disbanded in 1795 following its third partition by the neighbouring Russia, Prussia, and Austria.

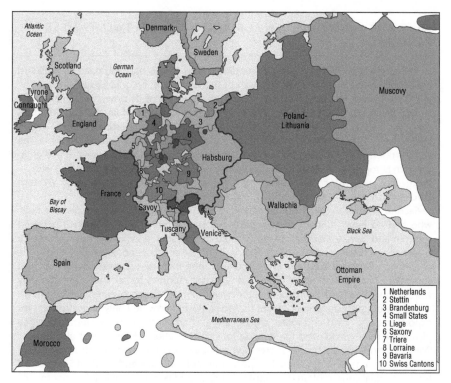

Figure 2.2. Poland's borders in 1600.
Source: http://www.euratlas.net/history/europe/1600/index.html.

the heirless death of Louis Jagiello, the King of Hungary and Bohemia, at the battle of Mohacs against the Turks. Casimir IV Jagiellon (1447–1492) has often been called the 'Father of Europe'. His children included 'one saint, one cardinal, four kings, and the matriarchs of three ruling Houses' (Davies, 2001, Kindle 5,235). Poland was considered to be an important regional power, radiating Western culture into the East.

Jagiellonian University in Kraków, established in 1364, was the second oldest university in Central Europe and one of the oldest in Europe, educating luminaries such as Nicholas Copernicus (1473–1543). Hundreds of Polish students studied abroad, most of them in Italy. Several Polish scholars and artists such as Pawel Wlodkowic (Paulus Vladimiri, 1370–1435) or Jan Kochanowski (1530–1584) were part of the European scholastic elites. Polish-Lithuanian armies were on the winning side in countless battles with Russia, Sweden, and the Ottoman Empire. Following the discovery of the New World, Poland's exports of grain to Western Europe boomed. Poland also developed the most universal democracy in the world at the time as 6–10

Box 2.2. POLAND'S GOLDEN AGE? NOT UNTIL THE TWENTY-FIRST CENTURY

Each country is prone to creating it founding myths. This is part and parcel of building national identity. Poland's national myth of sixteenth-century 'golden age' is no different. This is for a few reasons. First, even at the apogee of its power, Poland already lagged behind the West. Average level of income, productivity of agriculture, urbanization, population density—all good proxies of economic development—were much lower than in the West. Technological development was also behind. So were the literacy rates: it is estimated that only 2 per cent of peasants were literate, less than in Western Europe (Wyczański, 1973). Inequality was much higher, with the ruling elites—the gentry and aristocracy—extracting more value from the society than in Western Europe (Malinowski and Van Zanden, 2017; Malinowski, 2016a).[5]

Second, relative to the West, the majority of the Polish population were peasant serfs, who had no legal, human, and property rights. The only major difference between serfdom and slavery was that peasants could not be sold individually, but as part of a whole village (Malinowski and Broadberry, 2017). In practice, however, this made little difference.[6] Peasants lived in extreme poverty, one bad harvest away from death and starvation. Famines happened often, but were not reported by *szlachta*, although they were ubiquitous all over Europe at that time, even in much richer countries (Ridley, 2010).

Third, not unlike developing countries today, Poland provided only basic products for exports, mostly wheat and forest products. It exchanged them for Western luxuries to please the gentry's demand for 'conspicuous consumption'. Poland's was also not the West's 'breadbasket', as the Polish stereotype maintains. Polish grain exports amounted to only 1–2 per cent of total Western European grain consumption and less than 5 per cent of total individual consumption (Skodlarski, 2013). In addition, most of Polish economic life was monopolized by non-Poles: German merchants represented the elite of the merchant class in cities and most city population (for instance, according to Skodlarski [2013], Germans represented 80 per cent of the city's richest merchants in fourteenth-century Kraków). Jews monopolized most of the country's services and finance. Dutch merchants played the key role in Poland's exports of grain (as *szlachta* prohibited Polish merchants from engaging in international trade) and appropriated the bulk of value added (they reported profits of 300–400 per cent on trading grain with the Poles, as argued by Sowa, 2012, p. 191). Poland was not a banana republic, but for sure a wheat republic.

Finally, the 'golden age' sowed the seeds of Poland's subsequent humiliating demise. It was in the late sixteenth and seventeenth century that the country developed the institutional, social, and cultural cancer that killed it at the end of eighteenth century, when the country disappeared from the map of Europe. Peasants were enslaved, cities were emaciated, the royal power was undermined, and oligarchic *szlachta* took complete control of the country. Overall, Poland's international position in the sixteenth and early seventeenth centuries was strong, but much less so than what most Poles believe. Poland's true Golden Age only began in the twenty-first century (Piatkowski, 2013).

---

[5] Clark (2007, p. 14) argues that 'in preindustrial agrarian societies half or more of the national income typically went to the owners of land and capital, in modern industrialized societies their share is normally less than a quarter'.

[6] To digress, it is somewhat strange that today's scions of the enslaved serfs, who were routinely demeaned, raped, beaten, tortured, and killed by their masters, not unlike slaves in America, are proud of that period in Poland's history. It is as if African-Americans were proud of the pre-Civil War Southern States in America.

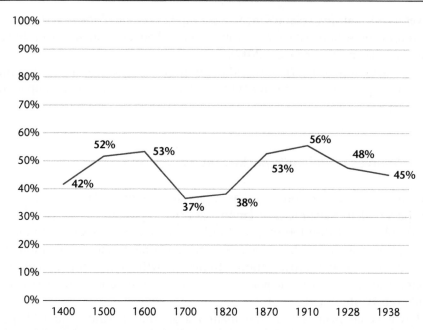

Figure 2.3. GDP per capita in Poland relative to Western Europe, 1400–1938, Western Europe = 100.

Note: Data for Poland for 1410, Voivodship of Cracow. The 1400–1820 Western European average calculated as average for the United Kingdom, Netherlands, Northern Italy, and Germany based on Malinowski and van Zanden (2015); 1870–1910 represents the average for 12 Western European economies based on Bukowski *et al.* (2017), 1928–1938 based on Bolt and Van Zanden (2014).

Source: Author's own based on sources in the Note.

per cent of the society (the gentry) was entitled to participate in the regional and national parliamentary process and—since 1572—in elections of the King.[7]

Although most Poles consider the sixteenth century to be the country's 'Golden Age', which is not necessarily in line with historical evidence (Box 2.2), the Polish success nonetheless did not last long. After 1600, Poland increasingly lagged behind Western Europe in the level of economic development. Poland's income per capita—after peaking at slightly above half of the Western level of income during 1500–1600—throughout the following 400 years hardly ever exceeded 50 per cent of the Western income again (Figure 2.3).[8] In the

---

[7] There are various estimates of the size of the Polish gentry: older estimates suggested that *szlachta* represented about 8–10% of the society. Davies (2005) puts the number closer to 6%, but compares it with France or England where fewer than 2% of the society belonged to nobility. Only Spain was comparable with Poland in terms of gentry's size. Hungary and Scotland was not far behind.

[8] Historical data on GDP in Poland from Malinowski and Van Zanden (2017) are 'as good as it gets'. If there are any errors, these are applied consistently among all the countries, making economic comparisons possible. Other sources of data similarly show that Poland has been perenially underdeveloped: Allen (2001) estimated that average wages of Polish construction workers in the sixteenth century in Kraków, Gdańsk, Warsaw and Lviv ranged between 60 and

seventeenth century, Poland's income per capita was one of the lowest among countries for which data are available, lower than even in Japan or India (Malinowski and Van Zanden, 2017).

So, what happened? What caused the split in the middle of the continent, which has persisted until today? Why was Poland never able to catch up with the West?

2.3. Sources of Poland's Backwardness

The literature focused on CEE has a laundry list of explanations for the region's underdevelopment. It emphasizes the importance of its peripheral geography, growth-inhibiting institution of serfdom, weak technology absorption and innovation, lack of capital, frequent wars, occupation by foreign powers, low urbanization, stunted growth of the non-agricultural sector, bad governance, unequal and exploitative international trade system, and even Western 'girl power'.[9]

I will argue instead that the main reason that Poland—and CEE per proxy—was economically backward during the whole period between 1500AD and 1939 is because the Polish gentry, or *szlachta*, monopolized power in the sixteenth century and proceeded to use it to enslave peasants, destroy city bourgeoisie, and create a par excellence extractive set of political and economic institutions.[10] In line with the institutional framework presented in the previous chapter, the resulting extractive society undermined economic development, thwarted civilizational progress, and kept Poland deep in the European periphery. The extractive society was supported by bad institutions, harmful culture, and inimical ideologies.

2.3.1. *Extractive Political Institutions*

Poland developed political institutions, which stood in stark opposition to the idea of inclusive institutions, which should be built on broad political participation, free interplay of social interests, and abundant checks and balances.

---

70 per cent of wages in London and Amsterdam. Wójtowicz and Wójtowicz (2009) argued that at its peak in 1580, Poland's income per capita amounted to 71 per cent of Western Europe, although these estimates were never published in referred journals and the sources of the estimates are not known. Baten and Szołtysek (2014) show similar results.

[9] See, for instance, Chirot (1991), Berend (2003), Berend and Ranki (1990), and De Pleijt and Van Zanden (2016). In addition, Wallerstein (1974) argues that the international trade system was biased against CEE, with the Western European 'core' exploiting the peripheral East; de Moor and van Zanden (2010) discuss the Western 'girl power' and its effect on fertility.

[10] I will use the Polish word *szlachta* interchangeably with gentry, nobility, and a landowning class.

Such institutions ensure that the society is organized for the benefit of the whole society rather than only its elites. Inclusive institutions limit rent-seeking of the elites, provide a level playing field for everyone regardless of their socio-economic background, and protect property rights for all, not just for the elites.

In Poland during the long period between the 1500s and 1795, the year when Poland disappeared from the map of Europe following its partition among the neighbouring countries, only *szlachta* had the right to participate in the political process. This was not unusual, of course: in other countries in Europe at that time only gentry had some modicum of political rights, if at all (absolutist kingdoms were the norm in Europe, with little input from other social classes). What was exceptional in Poland, however, was that gentry represented almost 6–10 per cent of the society and was by far one of the largest electorates in Europe. It had full rights to take part in the political process (acting through local and national parliaments), elect kings (from 1572 onwards), and enjoy full personal liberty (they could not be imprisoned without a court's decision). Unlike in many Western European countries, where there were legal differences between upper and lower segments of the privileged society (there was aristocracy and lower-status gentry), all Polish *szlachta* had the same rights regardless of their economic status or ownership of land. The privileges, rights, and obligations of a billionaire magnate were in principle exactly the same as that of an indigent, landless gentry. Poland was then by far the most democratic society in Europe from the sixteenth century until the country's partition in 1795. It was not until the electoral expansion in the mid-nineteenth century that the size of the electorate in the UK, for instance, was as large as in Poland during the sixteenth century.[11]

In practice, however, among millions of eligible gentry, very few leveraged their political rights. The poor, landless *szlachta*, which represented the majority of the privileged class, did not have an interest or means to participate in the political process. Thus, throughout the sixteenth to seventeenth century, not more than 200 gentry routinely took part in the work of local parliaments (Sejmiks). The numbers started to dwindle as time wore on. In the end, only the top 5 per cent of *szlachta*—the aristocrats—had an active interest in the political process. This allowed them to assume a *de facto* full control over all political decisions, using sticks and carrots to guide the political involvement of the poor majority (Beauvois, 2014).

---

[11] The UK achieved a similar level of democratic participation to Poland only after political reforms in 1832, which doubled the voting franchise to about 16 per cent of the adult male population, or about 4 per cent of all the population (Acemoglu and Robinson, 2012, p. 306). See also Davies (1998).

The most astonishing feature of the Polish political system and its focus on individual rights taken to the anarchic extreme was the institution of *liberum veto*. Based on the principle of full equality among the landowning class, *liberum veto* gave each member of the gentry the right to individually veto each parliamentary decision. This translated into an effective requirement of unanimity on all decisions. While *liberum veto* was used for the first time only in 1652, when a minor gentry bribed by an aristocratic oligarch shouted 'liberum veto' during the parliament's proceedings, it soon became a permanent feature of the political process. Not surprisingly, it effectively paralyzed the parliament. In the seventeenth and eighteenth centuries, fewer and fewer parliament sessions ended with any decision, as the emerging neighbouring powers—Russia, Prussia, and the Austrian Empire—bribed the willing members of *szlachta* to stop the proceedings. In the eighteenth century, Sejm met for not more than 40 days per year (Konopczynski, 1948). During the whole region of Augustus III (1734–1763), only one parliamentary session concluded with passing new laws (Davies, 2005). Because of *liberum veto*, the legislative process effectively ground to a halt (Malinowski, 2017).

Other social classes—nascent city bourgeoisie and peasants—had neither *de jure* nor *de facto* political rights (Bogucka and Samsonowicz, 1986). Unlike in Western Europe, cities were not represented in the parliament (although a few large cities such as Kraków could participate in the parliamentary sessions as observers). Their influence on the political process was largely negligible, as *szlachta* actively worked to suppress it. Economic influence of the city bourgeoisie was also small, as their income and wealth paled in comparison with aristocratic landowners. Peasants had no political rights whatsoever. They had hardly any rights, in fact, as discussed below.

Polish kings were hereditary until 1572, as in the rest of Europe. However, following the death of the last king from the Jagiellonian dynasty, *szlachta* introduced a unique system that gave it the right to elect kings. The system functioned until the country's demise in 1795. All gentry had the right to elect the King of Poland from a number of candidates.[12] While in Western Europe and Russia monarchs enjoyed a largely absolutist power, in Poland the monarchs increasingly became just *primus inter pares*, with prerogatives not that much different from today's presidents (or company's CEOs).[13] Polish gentry did not owe total allegiance to the King. It had a legal right to revolt against the King, whenever he—in *szlachta*'s own view—was perceived to have broken the rules of his 'employment'. *Szlachta* used this right to mount several military revolts, which contributed to further limiting the

---

[12] The French Henry Valois won the first elections in 1572, although he soon escaped back to France and a new election had to be called.

[13] See, for instance, Davies (2005) for further details.

royal power. Uniquely in the absolutist world, at each election, the new Kings had to sign a contract with *szlachta*: the so called *pacta conventa* bound him to deliver on the electoral promises, while Henrician Articles committed him to respecting (and often expanding) *szlachta*'s privileges and constraints on King's powers.

Whatever was left of the King's formal powers was in practice mitigated by the astonishing wherewithal and wealth of aristocratic magnates, which often rivalled that of the King. In the sixteenth and seventeenth centuries, the Radziwill family, for instance, the most powerful oligarchic family hailing from today's Lithuania, owned 23 palaces, 426 large and small towns, 2032 estates, and 10,053 villages, and operated a private army larger than that of the King (which in peace time numbered fewer than 3,000 soldiers).[14] In 1620, another Eastern magnate, Konstanty Ostrogski, left an inheritance worth twice as much as the country's annual budget (Sowa, 2012). They and other oligarchs created *de facto* autonomous private countries within the Polish-Lithuanian Commonwealth, functioning largely outside the purview of the King (Malinowski, 2017). As argued by Sowa (2012), since at least the 1650s, Poland existed mostly in theory, but hardly in practice, as it became a loose federation of largely independent oligarchic states.

2.3.2. *Economic Institutions*

In line with the predictions of the institutional model presented in the previous chapter, the monopolization of political institutions by *szlachta* also led to a monopolization of economic institutions to serve the interests of the elites. Economic institutions became as extractive as the political ones.

2.3.3. *Rule of Law and Property Rights*

The rule of law largely applied only to the gentry. They enjoyed full legal, personal, and economic rights, including security of property (even if in practice, given the large wealth inequality within the gentry, property rights of poor *szlachta* were often subject to predation of the stronger). Implementation of the law was also in the hands of the gentry, which largely managed the court system. The role of independent royal courts was limited. The whole justice system was inefficient, starved of resources, and blighted by the gentry's opposition to any restraints on personal freedom. During the seventeenth century, courts gathered to adjudicate cases only once or twice a year, leaving

---

[14] Sowa (2012) and https://en.wikipedia.org/wiki/Radziwi%C5%82%C5%82_family.

many cases un-reviewed or unresolved (Malinowski, 2017). In the rare instance when the court reached a judgement, the lack of strong enforcement made the court judgements easy to ignore.[15] In practice then, there was hardly any rule of law. Disputes among the gentry were resolved through force or by the decision of the oligarchs.[16]

Peasants originally enjoyed a set of basic legal rights, including the right to appeal against their landlords to the royal court. However, in 1518, they lost access to royal courts. From then on, landlords became judges in their own cases. They became responsible for collecting taxes from peasants, adjudicating conflicts, and policing villages. Not surprisingly, this arrangement did little to preserve peasants' rights. Beatings, rapes, and killings of peasants became rampant during the following centuries, with no punishment or due reporting. Unlike in the US, where Harriet Beecher Stowe's depiction of the atrocities of slavery in 'Uncle Tom's Cabin' moved consciences of many, the plight of Polish serf slaves was hardly ever documented.

Peasants also did not have the right to own land. They could only lease the land from the landlord. However, even this arrangement was not secure and was subject to change at the whim of the landlord. While up until the late fifteenth century many serf obligations were settled in cash, not unlike in the West, later cash payments were increasingly replaced with an ever-growing amount of mandatory paid labour. This was made easier by a law introduced in 1520, which permitted landlords to unilaterally change serf contractual obligations. Subsequently, serf obligations rose from one day per week of free work on the landlord's property in the early sixteenth century to six days per week per peasant family in the seventeenth century.[17] Serfdom became an insurmountable obstacle to economic development as it undermined peasants' labour mobility, weakened incentives for capital investment and innovation, hurt work ethos, and stymied the growth of cities.

The legal situation of the city dwellers was somewhere in between *szlachta* and the peasants. A few large cities such as Kraków, Gdańsk, or Lwów, enjoyed

[15] The memoirs of Jan Chryzostom Pasek, which are part of the standard curriculum in Polish elementary and secondary schools, reflect on the lack of judicial enforcement. The author of the memoir written during 1690–1695 was a Polish nobleman, who boasted about how he escaped unscathed from five court's judgement of forced exile for beating a fellow nobleman and a later punishment of infamy (abolition of legal rights and loss of 'good standing'). He died in peace on his own land in 1701 (Pasek, 1690/2004).

[16] Sowa (2012) reports an amazing story of how Bohdan Khmelnytsky, the future leader of a successful Ukrainian uprising against Poland in 1648, which marked the beginning of the end of the power of the Polish–Lithuanian Commonwealth, asked for an audience with the Polish King Władysław IV Vasa to plead his case against the ongoing harassment from a local Polish nobleman. In probably some of the most misguided advice ever given, the Polish King responded to Khmelnytsky: 'Don't you have your sword to use?'. He did. The history of Ukraine, Russia, and Poland was never the same again.

[17] In some cases, even 12 days per week per family, as reported by Mączak (1981) and Kieniewicz (1969).

a certain degree of a legal autonomy from the rest of the political and economic system. They were largely self-ruled and enjoyed token political rights. *Szlachta*, however, loathed their autonomy and did much to undermine it.[18] Outside the few autonomous cities, the majority of other cities were private, established by *szlachta*, and therefore subject to a changing set of rules, with no recourse to the legal system.

Because of the continued fight against the cities, the declining prosperity of peasants, and the shrinking local markets for goods and services, cities never developed. Poland had become one of the least urbanized countries in Europe. In 1600, the urban population of Poland amounted to only 0.4 per cent of the total, while the European average amounted to 7.6 per cent (and almost a quarter of the population in the Netherlands). The low urbanization rate in Poland persisted for centuries: in 1850, the urbanization ratio still amounted to only 9.3 per cent and was the lowest in Europe next only to Austria/Bohemia (Broadberry and O'Rourke, 2010). Until 1750, there was only one large city in Poland, with more than 10,000 inhabitants, less than anywhere else (Table 2.1).

The halted growth of cities restricted the size of the domestic market for agricultural products. Less demand from cities undermined incentives for increasing agricultural production, which in turn restricted growth in farm incomes that could be spent on products and services offered by cities. The vicious circle added to agricultural underdevelopment. Serfdom alone is estimated to have reduced cities' growth rate in CEE by one-third relative to cities in Western Europe (Dittmar, 2011).

2.3.4. *Market Competition*

Product and service markets were grossly uncompetitive. Owing to high transport costs, underdeveloped cities, and strong vested interests among the landowners, the domestic markets were fragmented and insulated from competition. Prices for grain, for instance, differed widely across the country (Malinowski, 2016b). Barriers of entry were high: peasants and city dwellers were prohibited from buying land; strong regulation of city professions kept prices of services high. Domestic merchants were not allowed to engage in international trade. Markets disintegrated further following the gradual decline of central state capacity in the seventeenth and eighteenth centuries

---

[18] *Szlachta* also fought cities economically, by putting restrictions on domestic and international trade. Moreover, it located Jews just outside the city walls to provide cheaper, non-regulated product and services in competition to the guild-driven city system. For instance, Kazimierz, Kraków's beautiful former Jewish quarter, was originally established as an instrument of *szlachta's* economic warfare against the city.

Table 2.1. Number of cities with at least 10,000 inhabitants, by country, 1500–1800

Territory	1500	1550	1600	1650	1700	1750	1800
1 Scandinavia	1	1	2	2	2	3	6
2 England and Wales	1	4	6	8	11	21	44
3 Scotland	1	1	1	1	2	5	8
4 Ireland	0	0	0	1	3	3	8
5 Netherlands	11	12	19	19	20	18	19
6 Belgium	12	12	12	14	15	15	20
7 Germany	23	27	30	23	30	35	53
8 France	32	34	43	44	55	55	78
9 Switzerland	1	1	2	2	3	4	4
10 Northern Italy	21	22	30	19	22	29	33
11 Central Italy	9	9	9	11	10	11	11
12 Southern Italy	14	15	20	20	19	25	30
13 Spain	20	27	37	24	22	24	34
14 Portugal	1	4	5	5	5	5	5
15 Austria-Bohemia	3	3	3	3	4	6	8
16 Poland	0	1	1	1	1	2	3
Region							
1–6 North and west	30	30	40	45	53	65	105
7–9 Central	56	62	75	69	88	95	135
10–14 Mediterranean	65	77	101	79	78	94	113
15–16 Eastern	3	4	4	4	5	7	11
Europe	154	173	220	197	224	261	364

Source: McEvedy and Jones (1978), p. 18.

and the growing divergence in regional laws (Malinowski, 2017). Monopolies abounded. *Szlachta*'s monopoly over alcohol production, which led to widespread alcoholism, was particularly shocking (Box 2.3).

2.3.5. *Social Mobility*

Social mobility was severely restricted. Peasants, who represented more than 80 per cent of the society, could not leave their villages without permission from their landlord (since 1496, only one son per peasant family was allowed to leave; in practice, this rarely happened). Later, *szlachta* prohibited peasants from choosing professions outside agriculture. Given the lack of personal freedom, no recourse to an independent justice system, and lack of mobility, there was *de facto* not much of a difference between the status of a serf peasant and that of a slave (Malinowski and Broadberry, 2017).

Merchants were free to move, but were not allowed to buy land. Their choice of occupations was constrained by strict medieval guild rules. They were also barred from occupying positions in public administration and engaging in international trade. *Szlachta* restricted international trade to foreigners only to ensure that domestic merchants could not develop and potentially become a threat to *szlachta*'s political dominance. For the same

---

Box 2.3. HOW *SZLACHTA* TURNED PEASANTS INTO ALCOHOLICS

In 1496, Poland introduced the so-called 'propination laws' (from Latin and Greek 'pro-pino', which meant to 'drink to one's health'), which prohibited peasants from consuming alcohol not produced in their landlord's distillery or pay a fee to the landlord for the right to distil their own alcohol. Even teetotallers had to buy a given quota of vodka. Many peasants were paid for their work on gentry's land with bottles of alcohol.

The propination laws became widespread in the eighteenth century and were lifted only by the foreign partitioning powers in the mid and late nineteenth century. Throughout this time, profits from propination were one of the key sources of income for landlords, often exceeding income from agricultural production. Forced consumption of vodka led to widespread alcoholism in the countryside and had negative impacts on health and development. In addition to malnourishment, alcohol consumption is likely to have contributed to the stunted growth of Polish peasants: in nineteenth century, Polish recruits in the Austria-Hungarian army were on average almost four centimetres shorter than their Austrian peers (Komlos, 1985).

Propination laws also likely contributed to anti-Semitism, as Jews operated most local taverns where the monopoly alcohol was served to the peasants. It combined the image of a hated monopoly with their enforcers.

Source: Author's own based on Lech (1965), Bobrzynski (1888), and Dubnov 1918 (2000).

---

reason, what we what call today the 'service sector' such as petty trade, restaurants, and artisanship, was outsourced to Jews, who did not have any political voice and thus presented no danger to *szlachta*'s political monopoly.

Social mobility within *szlachta* was also low: the clear majority of the wealth and income was concentrated in the hands of relatively few aristocratic families and was transferred from generation to generation. Given the lack of standing armies, weak public administration, and stunted cities, career prospects for poor gentry outside agriculture were limited.

2.3.6. Public Administration and State Capacity

Public administration hardly existed, especially in the seventeenth century and onwards. Unlike in Western Europe, the royal court never developed administrative capacities; its role was restricted to providing direct services to the King. Local administration was managed by *szlachta*, but its role was limited. Diplomacy was done *ad hoc*, with no permanent diplomatic postings in other countries. Lack of funds and lack of interest from the gentry, which was keen to keep the markets fragmented, meant there was also hardly any investment in public infrastructure. The road network in pre-1795 Poland was one of the least developed in Europe (Davies, 2005). Furthermore, because of the fierce opposition of *szlachta* to any strengthening of royal power, and in contrast to most countries in Europe, Poland had only a minimal standing army during the whole sixteenth-to-eighteenth-century period. Larger armies were summoned *ad hoc* whenever needed and financed with a special, one-off tax pre-agreed with *szlachta.*

There was hardly any permanent tax system to speak of. The gentry was exempted from paying all taxes, except for a token real estate tax; they were also exempted from import and export customs duties on trade 'for their own consumption', a privilege which was widely abused. Income from the royal lands, salt mines, and duties on internal trade was the only major source of income for the King. In 1584, there was no single stable source of tax revenue from *szlachta* (Figure 2.4). Thus, up until its partitions in 1773–1795, Poland had by far the lowest public tax revenue in Europe. In 1700, the whole revenue of the royal treasury amounted to a shockingly low 3.2 per cent of the tax revenue in France. In 1788, the level of revenue continued to stagnate, while every other country in the regions expanded its tax revenue considerably (Figure 2.5). Lack of funds undermined the delivery of even the most basic state functions, including an army, court system, and a public administration. Weak state capacity also increased financing costs for the private sector: an average interest rate in the private markets oscillated around 6.5 per cent during most of the seventeenth century, about double the rate in the leading countries of the West (Malinowski, 2017).

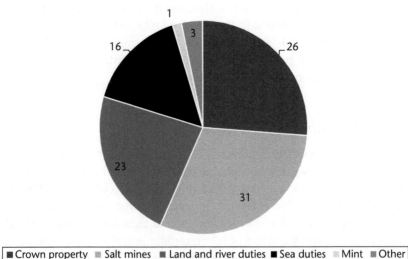

■ Crown property ■ Salt mines ■ Land and river duties ■ Sea duties ■ Mint ■ Other

Figure 2.4. Structure of the revenue of royal treasury in 1584 during the reign of King Stephen Bathory (does not include *ad hoc* additional tax revenue voted in by the parliament from time to time to finance wars).

Source: Author's own based on GUS (2014).

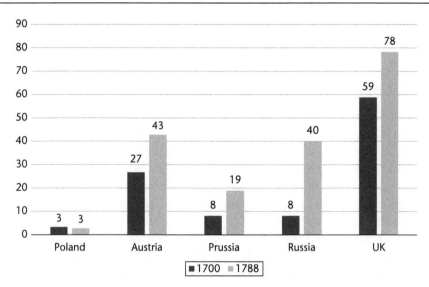

Figure 2.5. Revenue of the central treasury, in silver, 1700 and 1788, France=100.
Source: Author's own based on GUS (2014).

Ironically, it was only after Poland disappeared from the map of Europe, following three stages of its partition among Russia, Prussia, and Austria during 1773–1795, that the occupying powers introduced a modern tax system (and other modern institutions). The tax system was later inherited by the newly independent Poland, which after 123 years under foreign occupation re-appeared on the map of Europe after the First World War. But the old elites had not disappeared: they continued to oppose higher taxes and a strong state. By the end of the 1930s, Poland persisted in having one of the lowest tax revenues per head in Europe, amounting to less than 10 per cent of the tax revenue per capita in the UK (GUS, 2014). It also failed to fully merge the taxation systems bequeathed from the three partitioning powers: even in 1939, three different parts of Poland continued to pay partly different taxes (Leszczyński, 2012).

Finally, the growing paralysis of the Parliament because of *liberum veto* and the increasing power of oligarchs led to *de facto* elimination of the central state as a functioning authority, as reflected in, for instance, the declining number of days when the parliament was in session or the dwindling number of central state decisions regulating the country's tolls (Malinowski, 2017). The Polish state also lost a monopoly on violence, a fundamental feature of any well-functioning state. Rule of law, if any, was increasingly delivered by the powerful aristocratic oligarchs. The state also provided hardly any public goods and routinely failed to enforce laws and regulations. By most definitions of the state, the Polish state ceased to exist sometime in the seventeenth century.[19] It became a failed state, a Somalia in the middle of Europe, *toutes proportions gardées*.

2.3.7. Technology Absorption and Innovation

Extractive institutions undermined technology absorption and innovation. Data on the expansion of the printing press, the 'Internet' of the fifteenth and sixteenth centuries, suggests that even during its supposed 'Golden Age' Poland was already well behind the West in technological development. In 1500AD, there were only three printing presses in Poland, as opposed to twenty printing presses in the similarly peripheral Spain and many more in France, the Netherlands, or Italy (Figure 2.6). The expansion of printing presses in Poland was also much slower than in the West. The technological divergence deepened during the subsequent centuries as the Polish gentry blocked technological progress out of fear that it would undermine the *status quo*.

Serfdom, a key extractive institution, did not provide incentives to innovate. Peasant serfs all over CEE had 'few incentives to innovate, since it was their masters, not they, who stood to benefit from any innovation' (Acemoglu and Robinson, 2012, p. 166). Given that labour was abundant and for free, there was also no economic incentive to invest in labour-saving machinery, without which there was no innovation and technological progress. Serfs were cheaper than machines (and sometimes cheaper even than horses).[20] As a result, Poland has been technologically backward throughout all its modern history, providing another example of the remarkable persistence of initial conditions and their impact on technological progress (Comin, Easterly, and Gong, 2010).

The bottom line is that the old Poland failed to build most of the institutions necessary for economic development. Narrow elites controlled the commanding heights of politics and economy and acted exclusively for their own benefit. They supported institutions that were designed to sustain their lock on power rather than provide the right incentives and opportunities for the population to engage in productive business. In many ways, Poland's extractive institutions were not different from the growth-inhibiting institutions in Latin America (Box 2.4). Politics were controlled by the nobility,

---

[19] The point also made by Sowa (2012).

[20] Ridley (2010, Kindle 2,709) argues that until the Meiji revolution the same lack of incentives for capital investment prevailed also in Japan as 'people were cheaper to hire than draught animals'. Lack of incentives for capital investment was also the case in Southern US before the Civil War: because of cheap slave labour, American slave owners had no incentive to increase capital intensity and promote technology absorption (Acemoglu and Robison, 2008). As a result, the South has always been behind the North in technological innovation. It is true even today.

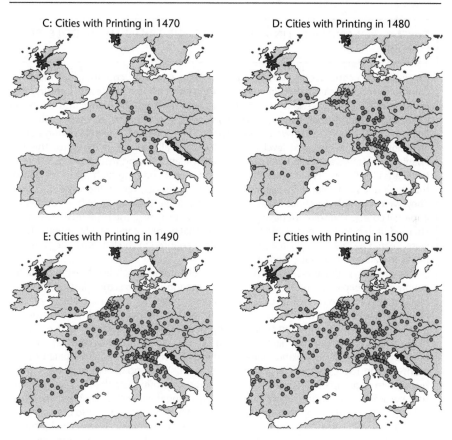

Figure 2.6. Location of printing presses in Europe between 1470 and 1500.
Source: Dittmar (2011).

peasants were *de facto* enslaved, and business was in the hands of foreigners hired by the nobility to prevent the domestic merchants from flourishing. Public administration hardly existed. The state had almost no tax revenue. It is hard to imagine how such an institutional set-up could promote growth.

More modern institutions were built on the Polish territories only after the three neighbouring powers partitioned the country. Prussia, Austria, and—to a lesser extent—Russia, introduced the rule of law, secure property rights, and a (relatively) well-functioning state. They also eliminated serfdom (1807 in Prussia, 1848 in Austria, and 1864 in Russia), often against the wishes of the Polish gentry, who wanted to keep the *status quo*.[21] While many members of *szlachta* opposed the partitioning powers and fought them in several uprisings,

---

[21] Sowa (2012) and Leder (2014) argue that the abolition of serfdom on the Polish territories of Russia was the Czar's punishment for the active participation and support of the Polish elites for the 1863–1864 uprising. *Szlachta* was against lifting serfdom.

Box 2.4. POLAND: A LATIN AMERICAN COUNTRY IN THE MIDDLE OF EUROPE

Up until the Second World War, Poland and Latin American countries had much in common. Until the elimination of serfdom in the mid and late nineteenth century, the situation of Polish serf peasants was quite similar to the Spanish colonial institutions of *encomienda, mita, repartimiento,* and *trajin,* which—according to Acemoglu and Robinson (2012, p. 12–13)—were developed to 'force indigenous people's living standards down to a subsistence level and thus extract all income in excess of this for Spaniards. This was achieved by expropriating their land, forcing them to work, offering low wages for labor services, imposing high taxes, and charging high prices for goods that were not even voluntarily bought'. Polish serf peasants were in the same situation. They were not able to choose their occupations, leave their land, or have access to impartial courts. They did not have personal immunity against the landlords. They were charged high prices for goods, such as alcohol, that were not voluntarily bought. They were treated as *szlachta's* private property, often counted in the landlord's accounting books as part of the overall (fixed) assets.

In many ways, the pre-Second World War Poland was much like Mexico. In both countries, the exploitation of people, power of monopolies, and strict class distinctions blocked the economic incentives and entrepreneurship of the vast majority of the nation. Thus, both countries largely missed out on the Industrial Revolution. A striking parallel is how the elites in both countries appropriated frontier lands. In Mexico, newly developed lands were appropriated by the incumbent elites, further strengthening their hold on power. Ditto in Poland: following the creation of the Polish-Lithuanian Commonwealth in 1569, all new frontier lands in today's Belarus and Ukraine were taken over by the narrow group of oligarchs. In time, buffeted by profits from their new properties, they became *de facto* independent from the king, ruling their land empires on their own.

Inequality and lack of opportunity inherent in an 'extractive' society also bred chronic political instability. Much reminiscent of Poland's partition among the three neighbouring powers during 1773–1795 and disappearance from the map of Europe, political instability in Mexico in the nineteenth century—there were fifty-two presidents in Mexico during 1824–1867—weakened the central state and resulted in a loss of more than one-third of its territory to the US. It could be argued that if the US had been more imperialistic and Mexico's other neighbours were a bit more powerful (Guatemala and Belize do not exactly fit the bill), Mexico could likely have been partitioned too, much like Poland.

Sources: Based on Acemoglu and Robison (2012).

others seemed to care more about their own interest—there were relatively few opposing voices to the partition of Poland as long as *szlachta's* class interests and property rights were secured—than about national interests (in any case, *szlachta* did not consider peasants to be part of the 'nation'; peasants themselves perceived themselves to be more 'local' rather than Polish). Because of the imposition of better institutions, Polish territories flourished for the first time since the sixteenth century. In 1910, on the eve of the First War World, GDP per capita of the population on today's territories of Poland reached about 56 per cent of the level of income in Western Europe, more than in the sixteenth century 'Golden Age' and only slightly less than Poland's relative income in 2016 (Bukowski et *al.*, 2017).

However, the catching up fizzled out after the First World War. The newly independent Poland, which re-emerged on the map of Europe in 1918 after 123 years under partitions, undertook a gargantuan work to put the country back together from three different pieces with different educational systems, laws, institutions, measurement systems, and even the width of train tracks.[22] The task was especially difficult given the massive destruction of infrastructure and enormous human losses during the First World War.

Yet, because of the long dark shadow of old, extractive institutions, growth-inhibiting culture, and wrong choices in policy making, including over-appreciation of the zloty and fiscal austerity during the Depression, on the eve of the Second World War, Poland's relative level of income amounted to only 45 per cent of the West, lower than in 1913. Despite the high rent of backwardness, reflected in the structure of the economy where more than half of the population was still employed in agriculture, the interwar Poland failed to catch up. Extractive institutions continued to keep the country poor, backward, and peripheral. Poland was a perfect example of Acemoglu and Robinson's (2012, p. 38) dictum that 'different patterns of institutions are deeply rooted in the past because once society gets organized in a particular way, this tends to persist'.

2.4. Why did Poland Create Extractive Institutions?

This is a key question with relevance for Poland but also for many other countries today, whose extractive institutions keep them underdeveloped. I will focus on the three likely reasons for the emergence of extractive institutions: the long-term implications of the Black Death, political monopoly of the landowning class, and economic specialization.

2.4.1. *The Impact of Black Death*

As discussed in Chapter 1, Acemoglu and Robinson (2012) and many others argue that the institutional and economic divergence between Western and CEE was largely caused by the impact of the Black Death epidemics in 1346–1351, which cut Western European population by about one-third to

---

[22] Some of these partitions are even visible today, almost 100 years later, in infrastructure, political voting patterns, and even student performance. See, Bukowski (2016) and Grosfeld and Zhuravskaya (2015).

one-half and slightly less in Eastern Europe (Gottfried, 1983). As a result, in Western Europe the Black Death increased the negotiating power of the surviving peasants and merchants to wrest the remnants of feudal control from the landlords. The latter, devoid of labour to till lands, had no choice but to acquiesce to demands. They had to eliminate serfdom or replace serf obligations by money rents. When they disagreed, peasants revolted. Western Europe was overrun with peasant uprisings. In the end, a new, 'copyhold' contract emerged, which regulated the details of the tenure agreement and set a fixed annual rental payment for peasants.

City merchants and the nascent bourgeoisie did not let the disaster go to waste either: they revolted, protested, and fought the feudal landlords until they gained enough independence to set themselves on a path to eventual full political and economic emancipation. At the end of the process, the peasantry and merchants gained a critical mass of basic political power, which it sustained going forward despite later attempts of feudal lords to thwart it. Emancipating peasants and rising bourgeoisie had an interest in supporting strong, often absolutist, and centralized royal power to protect their newly acquired rights against the landlords. In time, a new political system developed, with a strong central state and three separate economic classes, landowners, bourgeoisie, and peasants (as well as a small class of priesthood).

Such social process has never happened in Poland and CEE. One reason may be that because of a less deadly strain of the bacteria, lower population density, and sheer geographical isolation, the Black Death seems to have affected CEE less than the West (Gottfried, 1983). More important though, peasants never achieved a critical mass of power to jockey for an improved political position. Hardly any peasant revolts occurred in Poland and CEE during Middle Ages. A tipping point of change had not been reached. Ditto for the Polish nascent bourgeoisie, which was much smaller than in the West to start with and just did not have enough time to grow enough to matter politically. The fact that most of the cities' elites were foreign did not help either.

All over CEE neither peasants nor the bourgeoisie had enough power to force the landowning elites to change political institutions. Unlike in the West, the two social classes were just a bit too small, too young, and too inexperienced relative to the landlord class to fight for their own interests, especially to strengthen the royal power to act as an arbiter of class conflicts. Faced with the risk of a class revolt, the landowning elites counterattacked and eventually fully monopolized the political process. Political competition died.

As argued by Acemoglu and Robinson (2012), small differences in the initial institutional conditions when confronted with an external or internal shock, a 'critical juncture' such as the Black Death, translate into a much different institutional development path. This leads to an institutional divergence, which tends to persist and explain the long-run economic performance.

This is exactly what happened in Europe. Hit by roughly the same shock—the Black Death—but because of slightly less powerful peasantry and bourgeoisie, CEE developed extractive institutions, which prevented it from developing, while Western Europe gradually developed inclusive institutions, which spurred its development.

2.4.2. *Political Monopoly of Szlachta*

The alternative argument to the impact of the Black Death is that CEE would have developed differently regardless of the effects of the epidemic. This is because from the very beginning its institutions—by sheer historical accident—were set up differently from those of the West. In Western Europe, feudalism developed in its 'classic' form, where there was a strict vertical hierarchy of social positions among peasants, landlords, upper-class aristocracy, and the king. Each one was vertically allegiant to the next. This created differences in the landowning class: there was a lower class of the gentry and a higher class of aristocracy.

CEE was different. Partly because of the lack of Roman heritage, its feudal system was developed more horizontally, where the ruling prince or king would bestow full ownership of land on knights in return for military service. Land ownership was hereditary. All landowners were vassals directly reporting to the King. There was no hierarchy within the gentry class. All members of the gentry had the same legal rights regardless of their landowning or income status. This class egalitarianism and homogeneity, sheer power of numbers, and—as we would say today—a flat management structure (direct allegiance to the king) strengthened the political position of the gentry against other social classes.

This arrangement mattered when the kings needed support to change the rules of the political game. In Poland, the long process of the political monopolization of the country by *szlachta* started in 1374 when the ruling king Louis the Hungarian agreed to cap real estate tax rates for *szlachta* in return for a change to the hereditary rules to allow Louis' daughter to become the Queen of Poland. This so-called 'Koszyce privilege' set a historical precedent. Emboldened by its success, *szlachta* now demanded new privileges from each new king. The process soon snowballed into an orgy of privilege making. Between 1388 and 1573, the Polish nobility wrested from the King more than twenty different privileges (Table 2.2). The privileges solidified gentry's power and diminished influence of everyone else. In the early sixteenth century, the gentry capped its successful run by turning Poland into an elective monarchy, with kings elected in free elections by all (male) *szlachta*, a unique arrangement in Europe and the world.

The ability of *szlachta* to fully monopolize power suggests that even without the impact of the Black Death it would have subjugated other classes and

Table 2.2. Expansion of privileges of Polish szlachta between 1374 and 1572

When	Where	Who	What
1374	Koszyce	Louis the Hungarian (Louis I the Great)	Lowering of land tax on *szlachta*; introduction of a maximum rate of lad tax, prohibition for foreigners to serve in public positions, elimination of obligation to serve in the army only to defensive wars (and payment for foreign expeditions)
1388	Piortrkow	Władysław II Jagiełło	Confirmation of the previous privileges; payment for participation in foreign military expeditions
1422	Czerwinsk	Władysław II Jagiełło	Full protection of *szlachta*'s property rights
1423	Warta	Władysław II Jagiełło	Rights for *szlachta* to replace village heads (*sołtys*) and assume their rights, limits on peasants' mobility, fixed prices for artisan products sold by cities, restrictions on city jurisdiction over *szlachta*, equal legal treatment for all *szlachta*
1430–1433	Jedlnia/Kraków	Władysław II Jagiełło	Habeas corpus (personal liberty for *szlachta* without court order)
1454	Cerekwica/Nieszawa	Casimir IV Jagiellon	Elimination of *szlachta*'s obligation to participate in wars; commitment not to raise taxes without the agreement of local parliaments, expansion of penalties for escaping peasants
1456	Korczyn	Casimir IV Jagiellon	Confirmation of the voting rights for *szlachta*, peasants to leave villages only after paying off all his obligations to the landlord
1496	Piotrkow Trybunalski	John I Albert	Elimination of customs duties for *szlachta* (for personal use); only one peasant per village to leave per year, prohibition of merchants to buy land, new taxes on city goods
1501	Mielnik	Alexander Jagiellon	Expansion of powers of the Senate; King to only preside over its proceedings, legal right for *szlachta* to remove allegiance to the King in case of breach of laws
1504	Piotrkow Trybunalski	Alexander Jagiellon	Control of Senate and Sejm over allocation/lease of royal lands
1505	Radom	Alexander Jagiellon	Constitution 'Nihil Novi': new laws need approval of Sejm and Senate
1518	Torun	Sigismund I the Old	Elimination of royal prerogative to adjudicate conflicts among *szlachta*, Church, and serf peasants
1520	Bydgoszcz	Sigismund I the Old	Serf obligation to work at least one per day week; restriction of city courts' jurisdiction over *szlachta*; right to sail on rivers restricted to *szlachta*
1532	Piotrkow Trybunalski	Sigismund I the Old	Peasants cannot leave village without landlord's permission; prohibition on hiding escaped peasants in cities
1538	Warsaw	Sigismund I the Old	Elimination of the royal prerogative to remove *szlachta* from public posts
1543	Warsaw	Sigismund I the Old I	Lifting of limits on the amount of serf labour
1573	Warsaw	King Henry of Poland, Henry III of France	Henrician Articles: a *de facto* constitution, which established the principle of an elective monarchy based on free election of kings by *szlachta*, imposed restrictions on the power of the king; confirmed full religious freedom and tolerance, affirmed *szlachta*'s existing privileges; authorized *szlachta* to disobey king's orders when in breach of the law; *pacta conventa*: king's written commitment to fulfilling electoral promises

Source: Author's own based on Davies (2005), Skodlarski (2013), and Tazbir (2007).

imposed serfdom. Brenner (1976) explains that in CEE nobility could subjugate peasants because the latter were much less organized, solidarity-driven, and aware of their class interest than peasants in the West. Peasants in CEE had not managed to develop into a cohesive social class, which would '"struggle for commons rights" against the lords which was so characteristic of western development' (Brenner, 1976, p. 57).

Why was the social capital of peasants in CEE lower than in the West? This was likely because of different timing and history of settlement. The peasant class in CEE developed much later than in the West, because the region was settled later than Western Europe. In addition, most new peasants were settled in brand-new villages established by the landlords, who offered incentives to attract an immigrant workforce. Peasants in such villages were easier to control than in villages in the West, which were settled before landlords assumed power over them. Tighter control weakened the need for peasant collaboration and shared governance. Finally, peasants also had weaker contacts with the city bourgeoisie, which by itself was not sufficiently strong and did not have enough time to achieve critical mass to be able to check *szlachta*'s power. Consequently, peasants in CEE were much less resistant to landlords' pressure than their peers in the West (Brenner, 1976). The relative power of landlords was much higher in the East than in the West.[23]

2.4.3. *Wrong Economic Specialization*

The final reason for why Poland and CEE built institutions that were different from those in the West was their economic specialization. Countries specialized in agriculture tend to have different institutions from those specializing in trade, manufacturing, or finance. There is no *ex ante* guarantee that the institutions that will result from different economic specialization will be growth-friendly and support development. That was the case in Poland during the sixteenth and seventeenth centuries, when it built institutions supportive of its comparative advantage in agriculture.

Discovery of the New World by Christopher Columbus in 1491 was the critical historical juncture. It led to a rapid growth in international trade, declining costs of transport owing to improvement in shipping technology (transport of wheat to distant markets by land was uneconomical), and integration of hitherto largely separate domestic markets. The discovery of new markets gave Western Europe, which was already slightly ahead of the rest of the continent in development, an additional boost. The West's conducive geographical position, availability of skills, and access to capital pushed it to

---

[23] See Aston and Philpin (1985) for a debate on Brenner's argument.

specialize in trade, finance, and proto-manufacturing (Pamuk, 2007). However, the slightly less developed Poland was better positioned to leverage its fertile land and cheap and abundant labour, and shift towards agricultural production (Berend and Ranki, 1974; Berend, 2003; Chirot, 1991). Market forces and comparative advantage helped split the continent into two.

The economic division of the continent was accelerated by the quickly rising prices of wheat generated by high inflation resulting from the inflows of the New World's silver: in the fifteenth and sixteenth centuries food prices in Western Europe increased four to five-fold, while artisan products and wages increased only by two to three-fold (Skodlarski, 2013). In response to the improved terms of trade, landlords had the incentive to intensify serfdom to increase agricultural production. As Berend and Ranki (1974, p. 13) put it, 'the most important reason for the renewal of serfdom was to secure the labor required by the large estates'. In the late sixteenth century, at the same time as Poland reverted to serfdom, its grain exports increased more than ten-fold (Skodlarski, 2013). Economic specialization drove economic performance (Box 2.5).

Somewhat paradoxically, the process of 're-feudalization of Central Europe' accelerated when wheat prices started to decline after 1580. They did so in response to increasing productivity in Western agriculture, availability of

---

Box 2.5. ECONOMIC SPECIALIZATION AND ECONOMIC PERFORMANCE

David Ricardo in 1871 was the first to develop a theory of comparative advantage, which explained why international trade incentivized countries to produce what they could do best—the famous example of wine in Portugal and cloth in England—and why trading with each other was in everyone's interest. He argued that even countries that are less productive in every sort of production or service in absolute terms, can productively engage in trade if the relative differences in productivity are smaller than among trading partners.

Although this theory suggests that free trade based on comparative advantage should benefit all trade partners, it matters what economic activity a country chooses. There is a fundamental difference in whether a country specializes in high-end finance à la Wall Street, trade, manufacturing, or in wheat, potatoes, and carrots.

The problem is when you specialize in agriculture. Much unlike manufacturing, where the level of value added is high and there is a large scope for fast productivity growth, the potential for productivity improvement in agriculture is much smaller (Rodrik, 2013). In addition, once you specialize in agriculture, it is difficult to move to another type of production because of increasing returns to production (you get better and more productive in what you do the more you do it), economies of scale (you get cheaper the more you produce) and agglomeration effects (you benefit from all similar producers, suppliers, and clients located in the same place). Most important though, economic specialization spawns supportive political and economic institutions, which are almost impossible to dislodge without a powerful shock. Many poor countries find themselves in such a pickle today, especially in Africa, South Asia, and Latin America.

Russian wheat exports through the new port of Archangelsk, and appearance of rice as a wheat substitute (Morawski, 2011). To sustain profitability, *szlachta* moved to cut labour costs even more, intensifying serfdom and personal bondage further. It also continued to build institutions that would support the existing system.

In the end, market-based economic incentives drove building of institutions, which supported the economic specialization. The more Poland specialized in agriculture, the more it had a reason to strengthen institutions that supported it. The newly built institutions provided additional incentives for further specialization, creating a vicious circle, which Poland was never able to escape until its disappearance from the European map in 1795.[24]

In summary, Poland built different institutions from those in the West because of the weaker impact of the Black Death on class relations, much stronger initial position of *szlachta* that allowed it to achieve a political monopoly, and the region's comparative advantage in agriculture. Which of these three factors were the most important? It is difficult to pinpoint one critical factor. All three factors were closely intertwined and supported one another. It seems though that the stronger initial position of *szlachta* relative to peasantry and bourgeoisie—driven by lower density of population, patterns of settlement largely based on immigrations from abroad, and a different legal basis of the power of nobility than in the West—was the most important driver of Poland's re-feudalization. It was given an additional boost in the form of rising demand and increasing prices for grain exports following the discovery of the New World. Monopolization of political institutions by *szlachta* would have likely happened even without the differential impact of Black Death on both parts of the continent.

2.5. Why Poland's 'Democracy' did not Lead to Economic Development

An important question is why Poland, which developed the largest (even if distorted) democracy in Europe and the world in the early sixteenth century, failed to develop. Should not the fact that almost 10 per cent of the Polish society was (at least formally) included in the political process, have guaranteed the emergence of 'inclusive institutions' and good economic outcomes, in line

---

[24] Unlike Wallerstein (1974) and others who developed a 'dependency theory', I am not arguing that there was an inherently biased trade system, where Western Europe 'exploited' CEE. But I am arguing that the normally functioning markets can produce similar results without anyone's explicit intent.

with Acemoglu and Robinson's framework? In addition, why did the noble-cratic (a combination of nobility and democracy) Poland end up with the same extractive society and the same humiliating economic decline after the sixteenth century as the absolutist Spain?[25] Why did it lag in development behind the much less democratic UK? If it was not the level of (formal) political inclusivity that mattered for development, then what was it?

Three factors can help to explain the difference in development between the two groups of countries: the extent of political competition, initial conditions, and state capacity. First, Spain and Poland were politically monopolized (although by different social classes), while the political power in the UK, the Netherlands, and many other successful Western European countries was much more broad-based. In Spain, the profits from the discovery of the New World were taken over by the monarchy and used to develop a political monopoly to the exclusion of every other social class. In Poland, profits from international trade and colonization of today's Ukraine and Belarus were monopolized by aristocracy and used to emasculate the monarchy. However, it turned out differently in the UK (and other Western European countries): the expansion of the global trade in the sixteenth century strengthened the British merchant class and added to the already pluralistic political and economic landscape. The UK ended up with a broad-based society and a robust degree of political competition among the royal power, landed aristocracy, and emerging bourgeoisie. What seems to have mattered then was not who monopolized the power—it was the King in Spain, but nobility in Poland—but whether other social groups had any say in the political process.

Second, initial conditions mattered as they decided how countries reacted to external shocks. The relatively weak initial position of the nobility and merchant class in Spain allowed the King to monopolize the revenue from external expansion. In contrast, in Poland the weak position of the King allowed *szlachta* to monopolize profits and eliminate tax payments on sizeable revenue from exports of grain and—following the establishment of the Polish-

---

[25] Poland and Spain shared many similarities during the sixteenth to eighteenth centuries. Despite an economic bonanza in the sixteenth century, fuelled by the inflows of American silver in Spain and high grain prices in Poland, both countries wasted the accumulated resources and declined economically from the seventeenth century onwards. They urbanized at a similarly low pace: at the end of the seventeenth century, only 10 per cent of the society was urbanized in Spain and Poland (Acemoglu and Robinson, 2012, p. 215). The two countries also followed a largely similar path of stunted development. In 1960, the incomes of both countries were similar. Both countries also developed similarly dysfunctional political systems: parliaments in both countries (although for various reasons) ceased to operate effectively in the seventeenth and eighteenth centuries (after 1664 the Spanish Cortes did not meet again until the early 1800s, in Poland, under the rule of Augustus III (1734–1763), the Polish Sejm has managed to complete its proceedings only once). Lastly, Spain and Poland had similarly large nobilities, which in both countries amounted to almost 10 per cent of the society. Molinas (2013) provides a useful analysis of the extractive structure of the Spanish society throughout the ages.

Lithuanian Commonwealth—on large revenues from farmland in today's Belarus and Ukraine. In the UK, the relatively weak position of the King (as well as a historical accident that Queen Elizabeth agreed to allow the private sector to profit from international trade) helped the private sector flourish and create a viable competition to the royal power.

Third and finally, the degree of political and economic centralization and administrative capacity were also important. The UK developed a strong and a smooth-functioning state, whereas Poland and Spain did not.[26] Unlike the UK, both Poland and Spain lacked an efficient tax administration. This constrained financing of public administration and undermined the provision of critical public goods and institutions, including the rule of law, property rights, basic infrastructure, and education.

The interplay of these three elements can be seen in Table 2.3. Political monopoly, a low initial level of broad-based political and economic power, and weak state capacity seem to have been the key drivers of the rise of extractive societies in Poland, Spain, as well as—by proxy—Portugal, Greece, and most countries in CEE. In contrast, the UK, the Netherlands and—to a lesser extent—France, represented the opposite case. Of course, the three elements do not exhaust the list of drivers—many other things mattered such as access to natural resources, geographical location, and culture—but they seem to have had an important impact on the path of European development in the modern era.

2.5.1. Why Didn't Polish Szlachta Support Growth-Promoting Institutions and Policies?

The last important question is why the Polish gentry did not want to promote growth to increase its own incomes? Why didn't they have a stake in building

Table 2.3. Drivers of extractive and inclusive institutions in Europe after 1500AD

	Low	High
Political competition	Poland, Spain	UK, the Netherlands, France
Initial conditions: broad-based political and economic power	Poland, Spain	UK, the Netherlands, France
State capacity and degree of centralization	Poland, Spain	UK, the Netherlands, France

Source: Author's own.

---

[26] Grafe (2012) shows how Spain's decentralization and regional fragmentation undermined the fiscal capacity of the state, trade in internal markets, and growth. Only the violence unleashed during the Civil War in the 1930s managed to free the country from regional separatisms and ubiquitous internal trade barriers.

stronger institutions and a stronger state? Why, given that they controlled the parliament and thus the way the money was spent, did *szlachta* not agree to allow higher taxes to sustain good institutions and fund defensive wars, as was the case in the UK and elsewhere? The simple answer is that they did not have to: the political monopoly allowed *szlachta* to extract full rents from fragmented competition, weak property rights, and onerous regulations to sustain political and economic predominance. Monopolists have no interest in supporting competition if it undermines their own monopoly. Opening up of the society would directly undermine *szlachta*'s political, social, and economic dominance—by reducing the scope for rent-seeking—but also in an indirect way, by supporting growth that could undermine the *status quo* and spur emergence of competing social classes. Polish gentry faced the same trade-offs as predatory elites in many poor countries in the past and today, in Africa, Latin America or Asia. It is (almost always) better for the elites to fully control a poor country, than lose control in a rich country. Elites will do whatever is needed to stay in power, regardless of whether it is good for the country or not.[27]

But political and economic incentives cannot fully explain differences in the performance of Poland and the rest of Europe. How could one explain, for instance, that in the UK the disenfranchised social classes had a right to petition the Parliament and their petitions were often acted on, while in Poland such acts were unheard of? Or why did the rich elites in Western Europe use their large economic resources to promote science, culture, and progress, while the elites in Poland and CEE used the same large resources to fund conspicuous consumption only? Why did the Western elites engage in business and commerce, while in Poland they frowned on it? None of it can be explained without a closer look at the fundamental role in development played by culture and ideology. This is what I turn to next.

2.6. The Role of Culture, Values, and Ideologies in Poland's Backwardness

As discussed in Chapter 1, institutions alone cannot explain the difference in the levels of incomes among countries. This is because formal institutions are only as good as the cultural norms, religions, and ideologies that support them.

---

[27] Bueno de Mesquita and Smith (2014) provide an entertaining account of why political leaders do whatever is needed to keep them in power and why they do not care about the country's interests unless they are aligned with their own.

Perceptions, social norms, values, and mindsets matter. They are the foundation on which institutions are built. Just think about the different meanings of democracy in Iraq and Ireland. Without a parallel change in social attitudes and norms, an adoption of, for instance, the Swedish anti-corruption law in today's Uganda, Uzbekistan, or Ukraine is unlikely to be successful.[28]

During the long period between the 1500s and 1939, the Polish elites largely nurtured culture, values, ideologies, and mental models, which were harmful for economic development and which kept the country from catching up with the West. In general, the ruling *szlachta* had contempt for business, disparaged science, opposed intellectualism, and was suspicious of rationalism. It was also anti-urban, anti-cosmopolitan, parochial, and rustic. It buttressed conspicuous consumption, alcoholism, and sloth. Religious tolerance, attachment to personal freedom, equality (if only for the gentry), and gender relations were among the few bright spots.[29] With such culture and ideology, even the best institutions would not have functioned well.

2.6.1. Contempt for Business

Polish *szlachta*, akin to many other aristocratic cultures around the world, from Hungary and Romania to Brazil and Peru, always treated business with contempt. As early as 1505, the *Nihil Novi* quasi-constitution prohibited *szlachta* from involvement in trade, business, and other 'city activities' at the penalty of loss of nobility. The law was formally repealed in 1775, but the social stigma of business involvement remained (Morawski, 2011). A British visitor to Poland in the early nineteenth century commented that for the Polish

---

[28] For instance, Ukraine adopted a state-of-the art anti-corruption legislation in the 1990s. Yet, it nonetheless lingers in 131st place among 176 countries in the Transparency International 2016 Corruption Perceptions Index.

[29] Poland was a pioneer in religious tolerance: in 1573, the Act of the Confederation of Warsaw promulgated in the Henrician Articles confirmed the principle of religious freedom and tolerance for all. While the law lost most of its shine after 1650, as the Polish Catholic Church became increasingly successful in fighting Reformation, Poland remained one of the most religiously tolerant countries in Europe until 1795. It has become 'a land without stakes' (Tazbir, 1967). While Poles are rightly proud of this legacy, the question is to what extent the religious tolerance was purely a reflection of *szlachta*'s enlightened values and to what extent the tolerance could be explained by their enmity towards any constraints on personal freedom. As to gender relations, unlike in most other countries at that time, Poland fully recognized women's property rights and personal freedoms (albeit again for gentry women only) (Davies, 2005). This helped build cultural norms of largely balanced gender relations, which broadly persisted until today (Poland is one of the most gender-friendly countries in Europe, based on both formal and day-to-day evidence). Finally, cultural antecedents of *szlachta*'s attachment to human rights, personal freedom, and resistance against oppression help to explain why Polish society has always fiercely fought against foreign occupations (during many, albeit mostly ill-fated and foolhardy uprisings) and why it was the country—following the rise of Solidarity—that ultimately destroyed communism in 1989.

gentry the involvement in commerce 'would be treated by others as having lost their caste and descended to a lower rank of society' (Jacob, 1826, p. 79). *Szlachta* deeply internalized these values and keenly felt a sense of disgust about their Western peers' engagement in trade and production. Merchants were universally hated for 'destroying and immiserating the Kingdom and enriching foreign countries and themselves', while city-based artisans were disparaged for 'obscene physical exertion at odds with what makes an honorable man' (own translations based on Tazbir, 2013, p. 34). Instead of commerce, aristocracy thought itself worthy only of military service and administration (Turnock, 2006). Quite remarkably, *szlachta*'s contempt for business broadly persisted until 1939: it is difficult to find any examples of successful entrepreneurial activity of the Polish gentry until then. In fact, one of the reasons why the Polish state had to increase its involvement in the economy in the 1930s (and ended up owning 30 per cent of it) was the lack of Polish capitalists and entrepreneurs (Crampton, 1997). Old cultural norms proved to be unbelievably persistent (Kochanowicz, 1991).

Only anti-growth culture could explain Adam Smith's lack of comprehension why Poland, despite advantageous terms of trade, rich land, and protection of distance could not produce 'any manufactures of any kind, a few of those coarser household manufactures excepted, without which no country can well subsist' (Smith, 1776, p. 10). He understood the negative role of feudal institutions, noting that 'Poland, where the feudal system still continues to take place, is at this day as beggarly a country as it was before the discovery of America' (ibid., p. 10). But he struggled to explain why the European-wide increase in prices, which improved Poland's terms of trade for agricultural exports, 'has not, it seems, increased [Poland's] annual produce, has neither improved the manufactures and agriculture of the country, nor mended the circumstances of its inhabitants' (ibid, p. 10).

Those few Polish noblemen who wanted to be involved in business without paying the price of social ostracism, found an innovative solution: they outsourced business to foreigners, mostly to Germans and Jews. This allowed them to profit from trade and industry through various types of partnerships, while preserving the 'virgin' status of non-business involvement. The outsourcing arrangement had the additional important benefit, as discussed earlier, of preventing the emergence of an alternative business class, which could endanger the gentry's monopoly on power and social privilege.

Tellingly for such anti-business culture, the mainstream Polish literature in the whole period from the sixteenth century until 1939 provides hardly any examples of successful businessmen. Stanisław Wokulski, the main protagonist in Bolesław Prus' novel 'The Doll' studied by all Poles at school, is the only businessman widely known to the Polish public. Wokulski accumulates a large fortune on providing supplies to the Russian army (note the type of business engagement, no productive entrepreneurship here) during the Russian-Ottoman war in 1877. But he ends badly: he disappears (allegedly commits suicide) over a rejection of his love by an aristocratic woman, who despite being impecunious cannot bring herself to 'lower' her social status and marry a 'mere' businessman. This is not exactly the best example to follow.

2.6.2. Isolationism, Anti-City and Anti-Bourgeois Attitudes

Unlike nobility in the West, who congregated in cities and around the royal court to jockey for influence and social position, the Polish *szlachta* kept themselves as far from city life and the royal court as possible. They considered both to be 'nests of evil, lies and vice'. Instead, they developed a preference for rustic, isolated, and farm-oriented life (Tazbir, 2013). Today's cliché of a 'Pole-Catholic' was then a cliché of a 'noble-landowner', a 'man of earth', and of 'simple tastes', free from the debauchery of city life.

Szlachta's preference for 'splendid isolation' extended beyond their own farms; they also successfully lobbied for the isolation of the whole country. Not unlike the Chinese, who voluntarily gave up on sea exploration in 1444, following a successful voyage of Admiral Zheng He, Polish nobility ensured that Poland had never developed a strong navy.[30] *Szlachta* also ensured that Poland was never involved in international exploration or colonialization outside Europe (unlike the much smaller Sweden or Denmark, for instance, not to mention the neighbouring Russia, which expanded from a small princedom concentrated around Moscow to the largest country in the world).[31] Splendid isolation won the day.

2.6.3. Anti-Intellectualism

Szlachta disparaged the benefits of science and technological progress. They perceived progress as a danger to the *status quo*, and feared that open markets and innovation could unleash forces that they could not control. They failed to understand why their Western peers, the Isaac Newtons of the world, kept tinkering with new ideas, designing new theories, or promoting scientific experiments. The attitude 'If it ain't broke, why fix it?' reigned supreme.

---

[30] Polish history textbooks talk about only a single sea battle at Oliva in 1627, when the Polish navy beat the Swedish navy squadron. The Polish navy, however, was soon disbanded.

[31] The Polish King or *szlachta* did not show much support either for Jacob Kettler, the Duke of Courland and Semigalia, a fief of the Polish-Lithuanian Commonwealth located in today's Latvia, who during the seventeenth century attempted to colonize Tobago and Gambia (Plakans, 1995).

Thus, despite often substantial wealth, the Polish *szlachta* contributed hardly anything to global science, technology, or innovation. Thomas Hobbes' idea that 'leisure is the mother of philosophy' (Hobbes, 1651) seemed utterly foreign to the local elites. For them, leisure was leisure and nothing more. As a result, except for Nicholas Copernicus in the sixteenth century (although a son of merchants), a few poets, writers, artists, and composers, such as Adam Mickiewicz, Henryk Sienkiewicz or Frederic Chopin, and an oil engineer, Ignacy Łukasiewicz, in the nineteenth century, as well as Maria Skłodowska-Curie in the early twentieth century, the country was not exactly punching above its weight in terms of its contributions to global scientific and technological progress.

2.6.4. Lack of Technology Absorption and Innovation

The only truly creative idea ever developed by *szlachta* was a harmful ideology—sarmatism—that 'explained' why they were the ruling class. Sarmatism maintained that *szlachta* were the scions of an ancient tribe of Sarmatians, an Iranian people, who—at least according to this ideology—came to Poland and subjugated the autochthonous, 'lesser' population (Brzezinski and Mielczarek, 2002; Anthony, 2007; Davies, 2005). The alternative story said that Sarmatians were the descendants of Roman senators. The Polish elites used the newly concocted ideology to justify their freedoms, privileged position, and subjugation of the peasant serfs. Sarmatism permeated the whole culture of pre-1795 elites and was reflected in values, norms, and beliefs. It had its most visible impact on the Polish dress: Rembrandt's paintings of a Polish and a Dutch nobleman in the 1630s are worth, as usual, more than a thousand words as an illustration of the fundamental difference in culture between Poland and Western Europe (Figure 2.7).

2.6.5. Ignorance of Education

The Polish elites had only a scant appreciation for the value of education. Poland had one of the lowest rates of literacy in Europe during 1475 and 1750 (Figure 2.8). Only 5 per cent of Poles could read in 1750, while at the same time literacy in the Netherlands was close to universal. There were several reasons for the low literacy rate—lack of funding, the Catholic doctrine, which emphasized the key role of the priest in interpreting the Bible rather than direct study of the text, and low urbanization rates—but lack of interest among the elites in providing education to the masses played an important part.

Looking at the Polish literature until 1939, there are not too many examples of role models promoting the value of science and education. There was also little interaction with international scientific elites: while in the sixteenth century Polish scientists kept in touch with their Western peers and the

Figure 2.7. 'A Polish Nobleman' (1637) and 'Man with a Sheet of Music' (1633) by Rembrandt van Rijn.

Source: From the collection of The National Gallery of Art, Washington, DC, Open Access Policy.

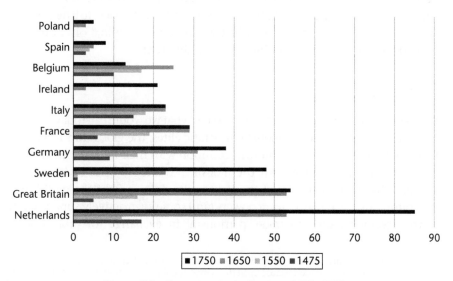

Figure 2.8. Literacy rates in Europe, 1475–1750.

Source: Author's own based on van Zanden *et al.* (2014).

gentry eagerly studied in the West, from the seventeenth century onwards this tradition largely disappeared. Polish noble youth, inspired by the Sarmatian myth, isolationism, and a megalomaniacal assumption of cultural advantage over the West, remained home. *Szlachta*'s illusions and grandiosity extended to the economy: they widely believed that without Polish grain and timber 'there would be no piece of bread in Europe or boats on the seas' (Tazbir, 2013, p. 146). The megalomania did not even die when the country disappeared from the map in 1795. Much like an alcoholic who blames his wife and everyone else for the collapse of his marriage, the Polish elites largely convinced themselves that the humiliating collapse of the country was the fault of the neighbours and that they were just the innocent victims.

2.6.6. *Rule of Law*

The gentry disrespected the rule of law, especially since the beginning of the seventeenth century. Courts hardly existed. Anarchy reigned. Polish literature provides useful evidence of the gentry's lack of respect for and trust in the rule of law. 'Pan Tadeusz', Adam Mickiewicz's most famous poem in Polish literature, nicely exemplifies the erstwhile well-established cultural norm that gentry had to 'take things in their own hands' to solve disputes and enforce their perceived rights rather than resort to external justice. At best, when *szlachta* was aware of the existence of rules, they ignored them. At worse, they explicitly acted against the law. The gentry's behaviour was remarkably like its peers in Latin American, where 'one of the most powerful social norms which still guides much of life in Latin America [and] dates back to the colonial system [was the rule] known as "obedezco pero no cumplo," or "I obey but I do not comply"'.[32] Polish nobility was no different.

2.6.7. *Patriotism*

Polish *szlachta* often preferred class interest to what we would call today national interest. Similarly to today's global plutocratic elites, the global top 1 per cent, Polish gentry seemed to have more in common with their Russian, Austrian, or Prussian noble peers than with the 'Polish' peasants.[33] Class divisions help explain why many members of the Polish elite did not fight the partition of the country by the neighbouring powers (and some even actively supported it), as they seemed happy to trade 'patriotism' in exchange for protection of

---

[32] From 'Why Nations Fail' blog, http://whynationsfail.com/blog/?currentPage=12.

[33] 'Polish' in quotation marks because until the arrival of public education in the late nineteenth century, most peasants did not consider themselves to belong to any nationality. As mentioned earlier, being 'Polish' was reserved for the gentry. Even in 1938, a large proportion of poor peasants in Eastern Poland considered themselves 'local' rather than Polish.

their class interests. The class war started to unravel only in the nineteenth century after the three partitioning powers hurt the interests of *szlachta* by imposing the rule of law, introducing public administration, promoting trade, and freeing peasants. The political power of the nobility was also undermined by a process of verification of noble titles, which in the Russian empire alone decreased the number of gentry by more than 400,000 (Demidowicz, 2010). Like the disenchanted Iraqi soldiers, who started the guerrilla war only when they were fired from the disbanded Iraqi army in 2003, Polish déclassé gentry seem to have become the fiercest opponents of foreign oppression and promoters of Polish patriotism only after they lost their privileges.

2.6.8. *Ideology*

Finally, the Polish gentry was animated by ideas, ideologies, and values that were almost the exact opposite of the middle class, 'bourgeois', protestant values of saving, hard work, and moving ahead. *Szlachta* praised the benefits of moderation in work, had an insouciant attitude about what happens 'tomorrow' (reminiscent of the Spanish *'mañana'*) and paid scant attention to the value of time. Alcohol, conspicuous consumption, and lavish parties were the only exemptions from moderation.[34]

As forcefully argued by McCloskey (2016), without such 'bourgeois' values, which promote engagement in business, innovation, and equality for all and respect for human betterment, development can hardly happen. As she puts its (ibid., Kindle 187) 'our riches were made not by piling brick on brick, or bachelor's degree on bachelor's degree, or bank balance on bank balance, but by piling idea on idea'. It was not capital that made countries successful, but the ideas that let the most talented people in the society flourish. That hardly ever happened in Poland. If James Watt, Thomas Edison, or Edmund Cartwright were born in pre-1939 Poland, they would likely never have had a chance to make it.

2.7. Conclusions

There are many explanations of the origins of the economic backwardness of Poland and CEE. Among many important factors, such as geography, initial conditions, and historical happenstance, extractive institutions played a key

---

[34] In the eighteenth century the Polish gentry drank about 20 litres of vodka and 700 litres of beer (2–3 per cent strong) per person per year (Lozinski and Lozinski, 2012; Wnuk, Purandare, and Marcinkowski, 2013). For comparison, in 2010, total alcohol consumption in Poland was about 11 litres per person per year (WHO, 2015).

role in thwarting Poland's development. The extractive institutions were designed by the elites, the *szlachta*, which monopolized political power to keep the country's politics and economy under control and to prevent the emergence of competing social classes. The extractive institutions punished productive investment by chaining peasants to land, putting obstacles to trade, privileging one social class against the others, minimizing taxes, and underinvesting in security and public institutions. The pre-1795 elites created a libertarian, American Tea Party dream: a country with no taxes, no public administration, and no constraints on the freedom of the elites, where the strongest ruled and the weakest perished. The Polish gentry developed a unique concept of 'representation without taxation' and power without responsibility. But the 'Golden Freedom' did not work well: Poland, an erstwhile regional superpower, become the first large country in the history of Europe to collapse on its own and disappear from the map in 1795.

Growth-inhibiting institutions interacted with equally harmful culture, values, social norms, and ideologies. Polish elites developed a set of norms that disparaged business, constrained social mobility, and undermined the value of knowledge, technological progress, and education. It is hard to imagine how such cultural norms could promote development rather than economic stagnation and decline. The culture of the old Polish elites was not different from their peers in the rest of CEE, especially in the similarly aristocratic Hungary and Romania. It was also not that much different from today's culture in some countries in Latin America, Africa, and Asia, where premodern, hierarchical social structures and anti-growth culture continue to thwart development.

Paradoxically, it was the foreign occupiers that after 1795 imposed on Poland the institutions that were critical for development: functioning public administration, basic education, the rule of law and respect of property rights, access to capital, and political stability.[35] Serfdom was abolished and peasants were finally free to move. New industries developed, including steel, coal, and textiles. Łódź emerged as the leading textile manufacturing hub in the region and was often compared with Manchester. As a result, Polish lands started to move forward: GDP per capita relative to Western Europe increased from around 40 per cent in 1820 to 56 per cent in 1910, higher than its previous peak in the 1500s during the country's 'Golden Age'.

---

[35] Although the adoption of the Constitution in 1791, the second constitution in the world after the US Constitution and the first constitution in Europe, was an ambitious attempt to reform Poland, including by strengthening the rule of law, enhancing access to education, and opening markets. However, its implementation was thwarted by internal opposition and external intervention. The new Constitution was revoked in 1793 and followed by the country's final partition in 1795, which ended the sovereignty of the Polish state.

However, the catching up largely stopped when the newly independent Poland re-emerged on the map on Europe in 1918. Despite a remarkable effort to stitch together three parts of the country that belonged to different empires into one nation, the country has not done well economically. The old system of extractive society would not let the country escape from poverty. Despite a substantial rent of backwardness, which should have spurred Poland's catching up, in 1938 Poland's income relative to the West was actually lower than in 1913. Like a black hole, where the force of gravity is so strong that the light cannot come out, the Polish extractive system was so well established that it could not reform itself from the inside. It needed a powerful external shock to change.

Many countries around the world today grapple with extractive systems similar to those that blighted Poland's growth prospects for centuries. They continue to be ruled by narrow elites, who often self-servingly prioritize their own interests over the interests of the society. They build and sustain institutions that help sustain monopolies, economic rents, and political power. The systems are so powerful that they are unable to reform themselves from within. It is often not true that the elites in these countries mean well, but they just do not know how to conduct a better, growth-supporting policy, as argued by many international institutions and economists, partly because it also helps justify their existence. The assumption that if we help the policy makers with better information, evidence, and advice, based on top-notch analysis, good international practice, and randomized controlled trials, they will get it right and better economic performance will follow may often be naive. The key problem is that the elites just do not want to do it. Policy makers do not get policies wrong because of their ignorance, but they get it wrong at times because of their malevolence.

They are very few countries in history which have managed to move from extractive to inclusive societies. In almost every case, as argued in Chapter 1, the reforms were driven by an explicit and powerful external threat or direct external intervention. Without such shocks, the economic and political systems tend to persist. Communism provided the shock that snapped Poland from its developmental black hole and the extractive society. This is what we move to next.

3

What Black Death was to Western Europe, Communism was to Central and Eastern Europe

Communism might have had the wrong answers, but it had the right questions.

Based on Octavio Paz

Communism will be remembered largely as the 20th century's most extraordinary political and intellectual aberration.

Zbigniew Brzezinski

Under capitalism, man exploits man. Under socialism, it's the other way around.

Anonymous

Lines to stores are better than lines to employment offices.

Władysław Gomułka, First Secretary of Poland's Communist Party, 1956–1970

How bad was communism? Could it have worked? Where would Poland and CEE be without it? Did it leave any positive legacy? How did it affect the post-1989 transition?

Communism has a bad name and deservedly so. When it collapsed in 1989 in CEE and soon after in the Soviet Union, it left in its wake poor societies, uncompetitive economies, technological backwardness, and a damaged environment. It also cost millions of human lives: during Stalin's reign alone, more than 20 million people are estimated to have died in the Soviet Union, killed, starved to death, or worked to exhaustion (Snyder, 2012). In CEE, the death toll was much smaller, but still numbered hundreds of thousands of people. Communism turned out to be a road to nowhere. Good that it died.

And yet, there were silver linings to communism. Despite its social, economic, and moral bankruptcy, it nonetheless turned out to be the key to unlocking growth potential in Poland and CEE and to be the indispensable ingredient of the region's golden age after 1989.

I argue in this chapter that despite ending up in an economic disaster, communism imposed on Poland after 1945 nonetheless helped bulldoze the old social structures of an extractive society which condemned Poland to be a perennial developmental black hole, and that would otherwise not have fallen. Communism boosted social mobility, promoted egalitarianism, and secured good quality of education for all. These elements proved indispensable in 1989 and helped Poland succeed.

I also argue that until the 1960s forced industrialization and unprecedented movement of labour from agriculture to industry in Poland supported GDP growth rates that were not much different from those in Western and Southern Europe and higher than in capitalist countries in the global periphery, such as in Mexico, Brazil, or South Korea. But growth rates started to decline in the 1970s and then stagnated in the 1980s because of diminishing rates of return on investment, lack of technological progress, and the impact of external shocks. This is when the income gap with the West opened up more than ever before.

I conclude by saying that the standard narrative that if Poland (and other CEE countries) had returned to capitalism after 1945, it would have developed as quickly as the West, is simplistic. I show that a capitalist Poland would have faced significant challenges to growth and good economic performance and convergence would have been far from guaranteed.

3.1. What Communism was all About

Humans have always suffered from a selective memory, which is a precious defensive mechanism against remembering horrors and unhappiness. We do not want to remember why many of our great-grandparents were sick and tired of capitalism, which in its original, nineteenth-century form was soulless, brutal, and inhuman. It was capitalism that destroyed dreams, careers, and lives of millions of people around the world, especially during the 1930's Global Crisis. We do not remember that many of our great-grandparents were convinced that predatory capitalism was the reason for the two World Wars, which killed more than 60 million of people.

If we remembered this, we would not be surprised how alluring communism could have been to our forefathers.[1] Communism attracted millions because it

---

[1] I refer to communism as an overarching definition of various shades of Soviet-inspired socialism. While communism, which promised to get rid of private ownership and pay to each

promised to break the vicious circle of extractive societies and political, economic, and social oppression, and to create a new, inclusive society, in which everyone would be employed, fed, and taken care of, according to their needs and abilities. Lincoln Steffens, an American journalist who was sent to Moscow during the post-First World War negotiations to engage with the new Bolshevik Russia, wrote that:

> Soviet Russia was a revolutionary government with an evolutionary plan. Their plan was not to end evils such as poverty and riches, graft, privilege, tyranny, and war by direct action, but to seek out and remove their causes. They had set up a dictatorship, supported by a small, trained minority, to make and maintain for a few generations a scientific rearrangement of economic forces which would result in economic democracy first and political democracy last.

He later famously added:

> I've seen the future, and it works. (cited in Acemoglu and Robinson, 2012, p. 119).

He was not alone. Many others shared Steffens' infatuation, including such celebrated Western intellectuals as Jean-Paul Sartre, Bertrand Russell, or Erik Hobsbawn. The disillusionment about communism came much later, and for some, never. Many believed until the very end that communism was indeed the answer to development. In his bestselling economics textbook published in many editions during the 1950s and the 1960s, Paul Samuelson, the future Nobel Prize winner in economics, projected that the Soviet Union's GDP would soon overtake that of the USA. Even in 1980, when communism was already in its early death throes, Samuelson projected that the size of the Soviet Union's economy would beat America's by 2012 (Acemoglu and Robinson, 2012). When Nikita Khrushchev, the head of the Soviet Union, proclaimed in 1956 at a party at the Polish Embassy in Moscow that the Soviet Union 'will bury the West', many believed him.[2]

3.1.1. How was Communism Supposed to Work?

The objective of communism was to get rid of the business cycle, market uncertainty, and the animal spirits of capitalism, which were believed to produce waste in economic output, leading to high unemployment and misery for millions of people, and replace it with a planned economy, which would set prices to equilibrate demand and supply, eliminate economic uncertainty and output losses from gyrations of the business cycle, and banish unemployment. Central planning embodied a strong belief in the power of

---

'according to their abilities and needs', has never been fully implemented, the name is still the best shorthand to define the socialist system to an informed global reader.

[2] https://en.wikipedia.org/wiki/We_will_bury_you, accessed 15 June 2017.

reason, science, and economic enlightenment that would triumph over the irrational, unscientific, and 'animal' instincts of the market. Economic planning would help tame the wild beast of the market and use science to spur growth and catch up with the West for poor, developing countries (Lange, 1936; Lange, Taylor and Lippincott, 1956; Kornai, 1980; Ericsson, 1991).

The gist of the communist growth strategy was to catch up with the West through industrialization. This was in line with the then-fashionable Harrod-Domar growth model, which called for a rapid capital accumulation as the key driver of growth. It was also in line with the view that industry has a much higher growth potential than agriculture, has an unlimited scope for productivity growth, and exhibits increasing returns to scale. It was not much different from today's global infatuation with manufacturing, which—in contrast to agriculture and services—arguably allows for unconditional convergence, that is increase in productivity not dependant on the overall business environment and the quality of institutions (Rodrik, 2013).

Given that communist countries were too poor to generate sufficient domestic savings and had no access to external financing to finance industrialization, Stalin and his CEE followers decided to use what was available: nationalize the existing industrial stock and take over the economic surplus produced by agriculture, the economy's largest sector, to finance further industrialization. In the absence of efficient tax systems, economic surplus from agriculture was appropriated by imposing low prices on food products, introducing systems of minimum deliveries to the state, and by collectivizing agriculture. The collectivizing of agriculture was achieved by taking over private land from peasants and combining it into large, state-run agricultural companies known by the Russian names of 'kolkhozes' and 'sovkhozes'.

The appropriation of agricultural surplus was supposed to be a transient arrangement: when the newly built industry accelerated economic growth, it would produce enough new economic surplus to feed all, including farmers (at least those that stayed on their farms; most were supposed to be absorbed into the new industries and escape the torpor of village life), and provide sufficient financing for further industrialization. A virtuous growth circle would start and carry the communist countries to modernity. All it needed was a spark.

3.2. Why Communism Collapsed

Needless to say, it did not work out this way. Lower-than-advertised rates of investment, diminishing returns from large investment into heavy industry, lack of technological progress, and distorted prices were the main reasons for the collapse of communism. However, the fundamental cause of the economic underperformance of communist countries was an extractive system of political and economic institutions (except for inclusive educational and labour markets, as discussed later), which stymied entrepreneurship, competition, and incentives for personal enrichment.

As regards investment, communist countries invested much less than commonly believed. The image of communist industrialization recalls gargantuan investment projects, high investment into heavy industry (coal mines, steelworks, and power), and mechanized agriculture with a ubiquitous Soviet tractor. However, this image is largely false, especially in CEE, as the size of investment was much lower than reported by the official statistics. New estimates, which adjust the official datasets for inflated volumes reported by communist firm managers to meet the targets of the central plan and artificial prices for investment inputs, suggest that the investment rates relative to GDP in communist CEE were lower than in Western and Southern Europe (Spain, Portugal, Greece) throughout the whole 1950–1990 period, except for the 1970s (Figure 3.1). Investment rates were particularly low in the 1980s, when they barely exceeded 20 per cent of GDP.

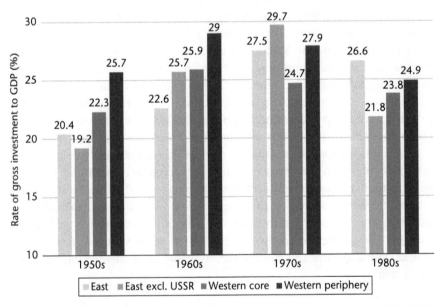

Figure 3.1. Gross investment in Eastern, Southern, and Western Europe, 1950–1989, as per cent of GDP.

Notes: East: Bulgaria, Czechoslovakia, Germany (East), Hungary, Poland, Romania, the USSR, and Yugoslavia; western core: Austria, Belgium, Denmark, France, Germany (West), the Netherlands, Norway, Sweden, Switzerland, and the UK; western periphery: Finland, Ireland, Greece, Italy, Portugal, and Spain.

Source: Author's own based on Vonyo (2016).

Along with the falling investment rates, diminishing returns to investment also kicked in: new investments into the same type of heavy industries, especially steel, heavy chemistry, or coal, were becoming less and less productive. Investment into consumer industries with potentially higher returns was limited. Heavy industry remained an investment priority until 1989, despite falling productivity of investment. Ideology prevailed over economics.

Furthermore, the underperformance of centrally planned economies was also driven by the lack of technological progress. Centrally planned economies just could not produce incentives for increasing productivity, lowering costs, or enhancing the quality of production. Meeting the production volume targets set by the planning ministry was the key objective; quality of production was not important. Innovation was frowned upon, as any efforts to improve products and services could jeopardize the fulfilment of production targets by diverting resources. The more a company invested in innovation, the more it risked missing the production targets. In any case, in an environment of permanent shortages where companies could always sell everything they produced, improving the quality or functionality of a product was not necessary. Finally, Western restrictions on sale of technology to countries behind the Iron Curtain made it even more difficult to increase productivity.[3]

As a result, innovation and technological absorption gradually ground to a halt. Total factor productivity (TFP) growth, a measure of efficiency of using capital and labour, gradually declined in all communist countries. These measures were lower than in the West throughout the whole communist period (Table 3.1). This was the case even though the communist countries were much poorer and therefore had a much bigger scope for technology absorption and the associated productivity boost. They should have developed much faster than the West.[4]

Lastly, the communist underperformance was driven by a distorted pricing system, in which prices were set by central planning committees rather than the market interaction of supply and demand. Thus, prices largely lost their relation to the inherent value or costs of production. Distorted prices led to large misallocation of resources into low-return heavy industry rather than

---

[3] Technology transfer to communist countries was governed by the Coordinating Committee for Multilateral Exports Controls (CoCom) established in 1950: in 1952, there were 400 major categories on the list of prohibited technologies and almost 200,000 items. All sales of advanced technology, including ICT and telecoms, were banned until 1989 and some even until 1991. As a result of the import restrictions, 'as late as 1987, Moscow could not receive more than six long-distance calls simultaneously, while long-distance calls to other parts of the country had to go through Moscow' (Berend, 2009, p. 25).

[4] Craft and Tonioli (2010) argue that adjusting for the differences in the initial level of income, communist countries in CEE should have grown by at least an additional 1.3 percentage points per year. Low TFP growth was the main reason for the underperformance.

Table 3.1. Comparative annual rates of productivity growth in Central Europe (log %)

	1950s	1960s	1970s	1980s
Labour productivity				
West Germany	6.6	5.2	3.7	2.6
Austria	4.4	4.9	2.9	2.3
Czechoslovakia	4.1	2.6	2.1	1.1
Hungary	3.1	4.0	2.6	2.5
Poland	2.6	2.1	2.6	2.2
TFP				
West Germany	5.5	3.0	2.4	1.6
Austria	3.6	3.1	1.6	1.0
Czechoslovakia	3.2	1.3	0.7	0.3
Hungary	2.6	2.5	1.0	1.1
Poland	3.1	2.0	1.3	0.9

Notes: Labour productivity is GDP per work hour. TFP is the growth accounting residual unadjusted for educational attainment. Capital shares are 0.3 for Western market economies and 0.4 for socialist countries.

Sources: Vonyo and Klein (2017).

high-return consumption-oriented industry. They also blunted incentives for technological progress by keeping the potential rents from innovation low. Centrally set prices also removed information inherent in market-based prices about the changing patterns of demand and ensured that the structure of production was increasingly removed from demand. Finally, distorted prices, especially of energy, led to the emergence of energy intensive and environmentally harmful industries, which became vulnerable to oil-price crises.[5]

Most of all, however, communism fell because of extractive political and economic institutions that supported growth in the short term, but failed to sustain it in the long term. Political institutions were monopolized by one single communist party; political pluralism was eliminated; elections were not contested. Economic institutions did not provide incentives for entrepreneurship, 'creative destruction', and innovation. They promoted the *status quo* and frowned upon change.

Consequently, the communist extensive growth model, based on reallocation of farm labour and investment into heavy industry, eventually ran out of steam. With no more farmers to be moved to industry (except for Poland and Romania), difficult access to financing (especially after the 1980s interest rate shocks to the cost of foreign debt), and rapidly declining TFP growth, economic growth collapsed: in the 1980s, it averaged only around 1 per cent in the three largest economies in the region (Figure 3.2). The communist growth model reached its limits.

---

[5] See, for instance, Eichengreen (2008a), Broadberry and Klein (2011), and Berend (1999).

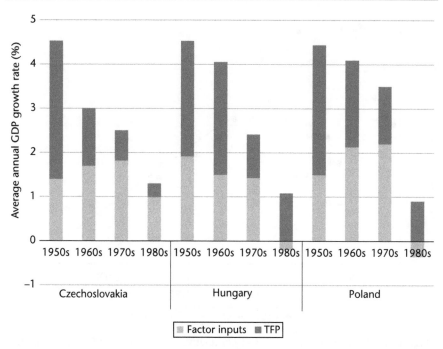

Figure 3.2. Structure of GDP growth in Poland, Czechoslovakia, and Hungary, 1950–1989.

Note: Calculations based on new estimates of capital stock to adjust for inflated official statistics.
Source: Author's own based on Vonyo and Klein (2017).

3.3. Poland was a Communist Growth Laggard

Stalin once said that imposing communism on Poland was like trying to 'fit a saddle on a cow'. He was right, as Poland never fully yielded to communism—millions of Poles sacrificed their personal freedom, life opportunities, and professional careers to oppose the communist regime, and many died fighting it—and eventually played the key role in dismantling it.[6] Stalin was also prescient that the communist economic system would never fit the country well: Poland turned out to be the worst performing European economy in the post-war period until 1989.

Poland's GDP per capita grew at only 2.2 per cent per year between 1950 and 1989, underperforming all other communist countries. It also grew much slower than any other economy in Europe, with the only exception of rich

---

[6] See, for instance, Applebaum, (2012) and Davies (2005).

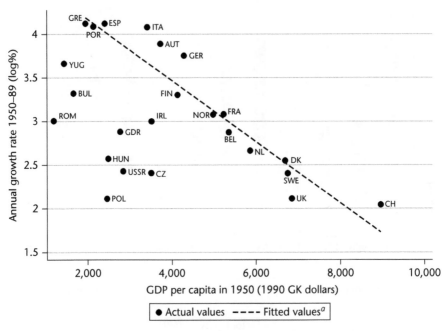

Figure 3.3. GDP growth rates 1950–1989 relative to 1950 level of GDP per capita.
Source: Vonyo (2016).

Switzerland. Southern European countries—Spain, Portugal, and Greece—which in 1950 were as poor as Poland—grew at double the rate of Poland (Figure 3.3). Poland was the European economic laggard.

Polish economic underperformance is surprising for several reasons. First, after the Second World War Poland was one of the poorest countries in Europe (with an income per capita of around 2,500 dollars in 1990 prices), which according to the standard growth convergence theory, should have helped it grow faster than its richer peers. This happened after 1989, but not before.

Second, Poland benefited from the change in its external borders: following Stalin's intervention at the Yalta summit in 1944, Poland's borders were moved about 300–400 km from the East to the West. In the process, Poland lost 80,000 square miles of territory in the East (today's western Belarus, Ukraine, and Lithuania), but gained 50,000 square miles of territory in the West, taken over from Germany (Figure 3.4).[7] This was a remarkable real estate deal, one of the best in mankind's history, economically speaking: the newly acquired territories in the West were significantly richer and more developed than the eastern territories. They had much better infrastructure, more

---

[7] https://en.wikipedia.org/wiki/Territorial_changes_of_Poland_immediately_after_World_War_II.

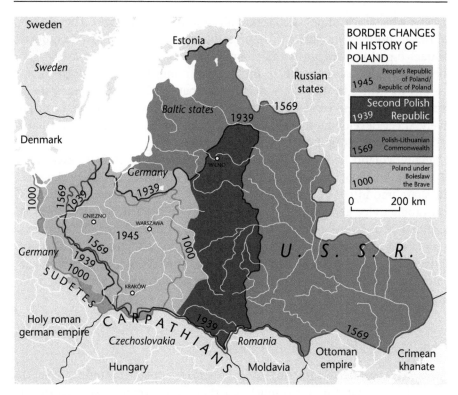

Figure 3.4. Poland's changing borders between 1000AD and 1945.

Source: https://upload.wikimedia.org/wikipedia/commons/b/b9/Border_changes_in_history_of_Poland.png.

developed industry, larger cities, and more productive agriculture. Their pre-war GDP was more than double that of Poland.[8] In effect, Poland swapped the backward, peripheral, underdeveloped, conservative, and ethnically challenged lands in the East for the prime real estate in the West.[9] Together with idle production assets left by the fleeing Germans, this should have generated fast growth with little additional investment.

Third, after 1945 for the first time in its history Poland became ethnically, religiously, and culturally homogenous. Before 1939, Ukrainian, Jewish, Belarusian, and German minorities represented almost one-third of the

---

[8] According to Bolt and van Zanden (2014), Poland's income per capita in 1938 amounted to about \$2,200 versus around \$5,000 in Germany, almost 130 per cent higher than in Poland.

[9] The difference in the standards of living between the newly acquired post-German lands and the lands in the East is well illustrated by the civilizational shock experienced by the newly arriving Polish peasants, who migrated to settle in the new lands in the West. On some occasions the shock was so large that the new inhabitants did not know how to use the sophisticated infrastructure in the abandoned German cities (Mach, 1998). See also Thum (2003).

society, which created political, economic, and social challenges. The pre-war Polish authorities struggled to resolve them successfully. Ethnic conflicts distracted political attention and complicated economic policy making. The supposed neglect of the rights of the German minority was one of the main reasons for Hitler to start the war in September 1939. The post-war Poland ceased to face these challenges. Given that ethnic diversity seems to negatively affect development and provision of public goods, this should have supported growth (Alesina and La Ferrara, 2005).

Finally, Poland had much higher share of agriculture in GDP, exceeding 50 per cent in 1945, than most other communist countries (in Czechoslovakia, the share amounted to 32.4 per cent; in Hungary, 36.6 per cent). High share of low-productivity agriculture should have driven faster growth by shifting surplus labour from farms to industry (Vonyo and Klein, 2017). Estimates suggest that during 1950–1990 a 10-percentage point higher initial share of agricultural employment in Europe translated into more than 1 percentage point faster GDP growth (Vonyo, 2016). However, Poland did not benefit from this growth bonus.

3.3.1. Why did Poland Underperform?

There were several likely reasons for underperformance of communist Poland. One reason is that it invested much less than other communist countries at the same level of development (Vonyo, 2016).[10] Somewhat paradoxically, one of the likely reasons for lower investment rates was Poland's lower level of political repression, which made it difficult for the state to take over economic surplus to finance larger investment. Poland was the only communist country that largely failed to collectivize agriculture and allowed large private ownership of land (which represented more than two-thirds of the total). Poland was also the only communist state in which the government backed down in the face of the consecutive large labour protests in 1956, 1970, and 1980. This was not the case in East Germany in 1953, in Hungary in 1956, and in Czechoslovakia in 1968. Polish communists also allowed—in response to the society's demands—higher private consumption than elsewhere, which lowered the available savings for investment. Being a bit 'nicer' than other communist countries (or among the Asian tigers) did not pay off economically.

In addition, Poland experienced much lower growth in productivity throughout the whole communist period (see Table 3.1). Although it is not

---

[10] Official statistics on investment rates under communism tended to inflate investment. Vonyo (2016) discusses the shortcomings of the official data and makes the appropriate adjustments. Orłowski (2010) makes a similar argument and calculates his own investment series.

Table 3.2. Gross external debt in US$ billion, 1971–1989

	1971	1979	1989	1989/1971
Bulgaria	0.7	4.5	9.0	1186%
Czech Rep.	0.5	4.0	6.5	1200%
Hungary	1.1	7.8	18.5	1582%
Poland	1.1	20.5	40.0	3536%
Romania	1.2	6.9	1.0	−17%
Yugoslavia	3.2	15.0	17.7	453%

Source: Hutchings (1983) and Collins and Rodrik (1991).

fully clear what drove slower growth in labour productivity, it is likely to have been affected by low productivity growth in agriculture (especially in the private sector, which suffered from excessive fragmentation, as most private farms had only a few hectares of land), a less efficient planning system, and low investment, which reduced scope for productivity growth embedded in new machinery.

Lastly, Poland's underperformance in the communist period was largely driven by the lost decade of the 1980s, during which GDP declined. There are a number of reasons for the economic stagnation of the 1980s. One was Poland's default on its large foreign debt, which had accumulated during the 1970s to finance an investment spurt into heavy industry. The country's foreign debt ballooned from $1.1 billion in 1971 to $40 billion in 1989, way above that of any other communist country (Table 3.2). Poland was the only communist country that ever went bankrupt when it stopped servicing foreign debt in 1982. In addition, energy-intensive industry suffered an oil-price shock, which undermined its competitiveness.[11] Economic growth was also disrupted by a growing wave of strikes organized by Solidarity in 1980, the first independent trade union in the communist camp, introduction of martial law in 1981, and the subsequent imposition of a Western embargo on Poland's trade.

The importance of the lost decade of the 1980s is clearly visible in charts comparing Poland's performance with that of its peers in the peripheral countries of Southern Europe and Ireland. Until 1960, they developed at a similar rate and had a comparable level of income with Poland (Figure 3.5). However, Poland's growth decelerated in the 1970s and then collapsed in the 1980s, whereas the other countries continued their fast convergence. In 1990, there was a yawning income gap between Poland and Southern Europe.

---

[11] The 1970s oil price shock affected Poland and other communist countries later than in the West because of a 5-year average price formula for oil imports from the Soviet Union, which delayed the impact.

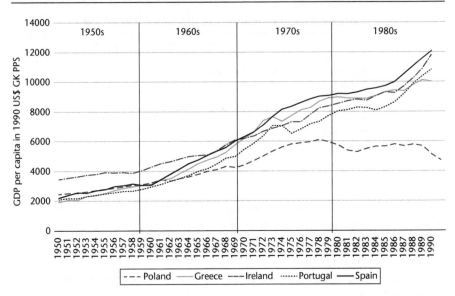

Figure 3.5. GDP per capita for Poland, Spain, Portugal, Greece, and Ireland, 1950–1990, in 1990 US$ GK PPS.

Source: Author's own based on The Conference Board Total Economy Database.

3.4. Why Communism was not all Bad

Communism was not an unalloyed disaster. Today's black-and-white picture of communism hides many important shades. Despite all its underperformance relative to Western and Southern Europe and communist peers, Poland's cumulative growth throughout the 1950–1990 period was not much different from that of capitalistic countries on the global periphery. Mexico, Brazil, Yugoslavia, India, or even South Korea (until 1980) did not perform noticeably better than Poland (Figure 3.6). Or rather they all performed equally badly, especially India. In any case, a centrally planned economy, even in its Polish inefficient version, was still capable of growing on par with global peers.

But GDP growth is not all. Other factors matter, such as life expectancy, access to education, level of inequality, social mobility, participation in culture, or the level of crime. Across all these dimensions, Poland and other communist countries in CEE were doing much better than GDP levels and growth rates would suggest.

The UNDP's Human Development Index, which measures society's well-being by looking at the level of income, literacy, and life expectancy,[12] shows

---

[12] The HDI is a relative index of development. A country with a GDP per capita of $ 40,000 international dollars (at 2000 purchasing power parity), an average life expectancy at birth of 85,

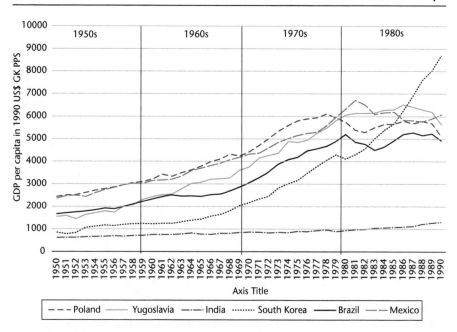

Figure 3.6. GDP per capita in Poland and the global peers, 1950–1990, in 1990 US$ GK PPS.

Source: Author's own based on The Conference Board Total Economy Database.

that in 1990 Poland's well-being was much higher than among its global peers such as Mexico, Brazil, Thailand, or Turkey. Quite surprisingly, despite the much lower level of income and the economic collapse of the 1980s, Poland's well-being was even higher than in a much richer Portugal and only slightly lower than in South Korea or Spain (Figure 3.7). Poland overperformed in well-being throughout the whole communist period (Baines, Cummins and Schulze, 2010; Crafts, 2002).

Communism was thus able to squeeze out much more well-being from its (meagre) income than capitalist countries, especially outside the West (Cassidy, 1997). This was true for life expectancy, health outcomes, or social mobility. Revolution in the access to education was particularly shocking: communist countries developed a comprehensive kindergarten and preschool system, which covered more than 90 per cent of children aged 3–5, from virtually zero before the Second World War. It also created unparalleled opportunities for older kids: around 90 per cent of youth aged 14–18 attended school during communism compared with only 5–10 per cent before the war. University enrolment increased from 1–2 per cent before the war to above

enrolment rates for all levels of education of 100 per cent and a 100 per cent adult literacy rate, would score 1. All other countries are measured relative to this benchmark.

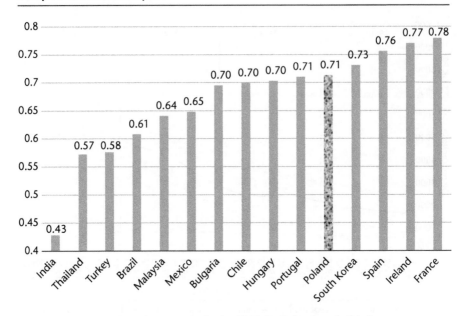

Figure 3.7. Human Development Index in 1990 for Poland and global peers.
Source: Author's own based on UNDP's HDI, http://hdr.undp.org/en/data#.

10–15 per cent under communism (Berend, 2009). Communism turned out to be much more efficient socially than economically.

3.4.1. *From an Extractive to an Inclusive Society*

The key legacy of communism was not the economic catastrophe that it ultimately brought, or—on the positive side—the high level of well-being that it produced, but the fact that communism bulldozed the old, feudal, extractive structures of the society, which thwarted Poland's (and CEE's) development for centuries. It laid the foundations for the emergence of an inclusive society after 1989, and the subsequent historically unprecedented economic miracle.

As explained in the Chapter 2, until 1939 Poland was largely an extractive society, controlled by the few for the benefit of the few. After regaining independence in 1918, it was widely expected that the newly independent Poland would get rid of the old, class structures and replace them with a new, egalitarian society, where each citizen would have an opportunity to flourish. Alas, it did not happen. The old extractive structures of the society were largely re-built. Landowning class safeguarded their vested interests; the new bureaucratic and military elites adapted to the old system. The majority of the society continued to be left behind. The extractive elites kept the country in a political lock, both during the short democratic period and then after Józef Piłsudski's *coup d'état* in 1926. The extractive society was too strong to reform itself.

The ruling extractive elites ensured that land reforms were shallow, access to education remained reserved for the few, and markets were closed to new entrants. The initially ambitious land reforms gradually fizzled out. By 1939, only 7 per cent of land was parcelled out from the large estates to peasants (Skodlarski, 2013). Structural reforms also lagged: in 1939, more than 60 per cent of the society continued to be employed in agriculture, only about 10 percentage points less than in 1918 (Leitenberg and Goertz, 2003). Most peasants continued to live in extreme poverty, which shocked foreign observers.[13] Rural indigence restricted demand for non-agricultural products, undermined the growth of domestic industry, and thwarted the development of local markets. Industrialization was slow: in 1938, per capita level of industrialization in Poland amounted to only 23 per cent of the level in the UK in 1900 (Bairoch, 1982).

Basic education expanded greatly in the interwar period, but nonetheless primary school enrolment never became universal (Benavot and Riddle, 1989). Almost 20 per cent of the society remained illiterate, more than in elsewhere in Europe except for the Balkans, Greece, Portugal, and Spain (Roses and Wolf, 2008). Enrolment in secondary education was also low and covered only 3.2 per cent of the population, less than in any other country in Europe apart from Spain and Portugal (Table 3.3). Finally, university education, which was the ticket to joining the elites, covered only around 1 per cent of the population in the late 1930s, versus 2.4 per cent in France (to put it in perspective, more than 50 per cent of young Poles studied in 2016 or 50 times more).[14]

Public administration was controlled by old elites, with positions in administration distributed largely based on social status rather than ability. It was not until the 1930s when 'a new generation of government officials who were employed because of their education and not because of their status' had a chance to find gainful employment in the public sector (Janos, 2000, p. 78). Nonetheless, old elites continued to predominate in the allocation of public positions, perks, and procurement contracts. Corruption was rampant (Supruniuk 2011, Tycner 2014). Rule of law was reserved only for the rich.

---

[13] Carl Herslow (1946), Swedish Consul-General to Poland in the 1920s, wrote in his memoirs that he was 'terrified at the sight of a Polish village'. He considered Polish peasants' plights as 'below the human level of existence'.

[14] Barro and Lee (2013), and Lee and Lee Long Run Education Dataset available at http://www.barrolee.com/Lee_Lee_LRdata_dn.htm.

Table 3.3. Rate of secondary schooling, 1910–1937

	UK	BEL	NL	SWI	GER	DEN	SWE	NOR	FRA	CZE	AUS
1910	2.4	2.5	5.7	3	5	4.9	2.3	4.9	2	n/d	2.8
1928	6.5	4.2	7.1	5.4	6.4	7.9	7.2	5.1	4.9	3.7	4.7
1937	7.1	6.5	9.7	6.7	5.8	9.9	9.6	6.3	8.2	5.4	6.5

	ITA	POR	IRL	GRE	SPA	HUN	FIN	POL	RUM	YUG	BUL
1910	1.2	1	3.5	1.4	1.3	1.8	4.1	n/d	1.1	1	2.4
1928	2	1.4	4.3	4.1	1.6	4.4	7.1	3.5	4.9	3.3	2.9
1937	3.5	2.1	6.5	5.5	2.5	4.2	7.7	3.2	5.3	3.8	4

Note: Number of students attending secondary schools for 100 children in the age group 10–19.
Source: David (2009, p. 342).

The majority of the society, the peasants, continued to be devoid of opportunities for social advancement.[15]

Finally, there was hardly any entrepreneurship and 'creative destruction'. Various barriers to entrepreneurship—lack of access to capital, segmented markets, monopolies, red tape—undermined the emergence of new firms. Quite unbelievably, two-thirds of industrial production was ruled by cartels and monopolies, one of the highest ratios in Europe.[16] The landowning aristocrats represented the bulk of only 900 rich people in the country; there were only 200 entrepreneurs and financiers among them. Virtually all of the rich people, however, made their fortunes before 1918 (Tycner, 2014). Many were immigrants, as the Polish elites continued the long-tradition of ensuring that business was outsourced largely to foreigners with little political power. Or they promoted foreign capital: in 1935, there were 209 foreign-owned companies among 244 large enterprises employing more than 500 people (Skodlarski, 2013). Shockingly, no single new large domestically owned private firm emerged during the whole interwar period. It did not bother the elites; to the contrary, it helped them keep the extractive *status quo*.

In any case, involvement in business continued to be frowned upon as 'beneath the honour' of the landowning elites. Whenever they engaged in business, the objective was not necessarily to maximize profits, develop new technology, or conquer global markets, but to earn enough to maintain consumption patterns congruent with their social status and prestige (Kula,

---

[15] Chałasiński (1938) summarizes the results of 1,500 interviews with young peasants in 1930s' Poland. The common theme of all the interviews is the peasants' despondency and desperation about their limited chances for social advancement. Not unlike 'untouchables' in India, Polish peasants saw themselves as an 'underclass', which could not break through the severe social divisions between them and the elites (aristocracy, bourgeoisie, and intelligentsia).

[16] Siegfried Tschierschky (1932), competition expert of the League of Nations, wrote in 1932 that 'there is no other country in which cartelization [of the economy] would develop so much as in Poland'.

1962). On the whole though, as in the feudal past, the Polish elites continued to steer clear of business. Roman Dmowski, the leading Polish conservative politician and nationalist of the early twentieth century, complained that 'new forms of domestic industry were created by foreign forces, free from the traditional Polish passivity... déclassé gentry and intelligentsia only wanted to benefit from the ready-made jobs created for them by the foreigners' (Dmowski, 1903, p. 88). Others such as Znaniecki (1935, p. 166) emphasized that 'gentry-type traditions of good behaviour went together with an admiration for a rigid social hierarchy, inclination to take positions in the hierarchy specific to each social class, rather than promotion of pioneering ambitions to blaze independent trails in the society'. Finally, Polish young gentry 'preferred to live in poverty in the cities rather than look for jobs'. Such an approach was considered to be 'smart' by their class peers (Wasilewski, 1934, p. 233).

The bottom line is that the aristocratic elites and intelligentsia (mostly formed by the déclassé gentry) seemed to be comfortable with outsourcing the business life of the country to foreigners, while they focused on other, non-commercial social and 'patriotic' pursuits (Chałasiński, 1946).[17] They were ready to die heroically for the country at any time, but could not spare a minute to help build the country's economy.

Extractive society also made it difficult to conduct a good economic policy. Despite its poverty, isolation, and backwardness, Poland was among the few countries in Europe that were hit by the 1930's global crisis the most (as opposed to Poland in 2009 that became the only country in the European Union to avoid a recession). Poland's industrial production in the 1930s fell by almost 50 per cent, rivalling that in pre-Hitler Germany (Janos, 2000; Eichengreen and O'Rourke, 2010). This was largely because the ruling elites decided that keeping the zloty pegged to gold for as long as possible was critical to maintaining the country's 'prestige' regardless of the economic implications.[18] Consequently, zloty became overvalued and the economic recovery started later than elsewhere.[19]

Because of all these factors, the newly independent Poland, despite many achievements, including a stunning victory in 1920 against the Bolshevik

---

[17] See also an interesting debate here: http://nowadebata.pl/2016/12/15/spoleczna-genealogia-inteligencji-polskiej/.

[18] Eugeniusz Kwiatkowski, minister of economy in the 1930s, supported the policy of the strong zloty. Yet, he is mostly known in Poland for his support for large investment projects and considered a hero and a model of economic policy making. In practice, despite his good intentions, the strong-zloty policy is likely to have cost Poland more than all the benefits of the investment projects he supported.

[19] There is a general agreement among economists that breaking the link with gold was critical to economic recovery in the 1930s (Eichengreen, 1992; Eichengreen and Sachs, 1985; Bernanke and James, 1991; Eichengreen, 2008b). Countries that maintained their commitment to the gold standard incurred overvaluation of their currencies, were forced to keep interest rates high, and paid for it with sluggish and delayed recoveries.

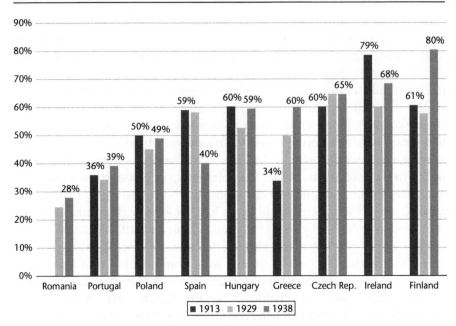

Figure 3.8. GDP per capita in Poland 1913–1938 and regional peers, France=100.
Source: Author's own based on Bolt and van Zanden (2014).

forces on the outskirts of Warsaw, which saved Europe from being overrun by communism, failed economically. In 1938, the income of an average Pole was lower relative to Western Europe than in 1913 (Figure 3.8). Derek H. Aldcroft (2006, pp. 171–2), an eminent economic historian, summarized it well by saying that '[interwar] Poland was a country with a lot of potential, but it never met the pre-war expectations for development'.

The interwar Poland failed because it reproduced an extractive society not much different than that experienced during the long period of feudalism. Serfdom was gone, but feudal structures remained. In many ways, the interwar Poland resembled the American South between the Civil War and the 1960s: while formally slavery was abolished and African-Americans were free to 'pursue happiness', in reality, up until the civil rights reforms in the 1960s, the old, slave-owning elites continued to control the South. They achieved it by restricting voting for African-Americans, maintaining segregation, restricting access to education, and using violence, whenever needed. As Acemoglu and Robinson (2012, p. 348) point out, 'the southern planters lost the war, but would win the peace'. The same could be said about the Polish elites during 1918–1939, as they restricted political, economic, educational and social access to the Polish lower classes. What the 1960s social revolution was to the USA, communism was to Poland.

3.5. How Communism Destroyed Feudalism

A German economist, Friedrich List, called for 'defeudalization' and elimination of 'parasitic nobility' as a necessary condition for development (David, 2011, p. 30). He argued that only socially mobile societies could fully develop, allowing all talents to contribute to growth. Stratified societies of the old type, controlled by a thin sliver of privileged elites, the leisure class involved mainly in conspicuous consumption (Veblen, 1899), would block development. Acemoglu and Robison (2012) made a similar argument.

In Poland, the post-1945 communism replaced the old, pre-war elites, already much diminished during the War, with new elites, chosen mostly from among the downtrodden peasants and blue collar workers. The old elite's values, social norms, and rules were replaced with new norms. Old institutions were also largely razed to the ground, in a figurative and often literal sense, and replaced with new, communist institutions. The society opened up to an extent never experienced before, through changes in ownership, education for all, and high social mobility.

Already in 1944, when most of Poland was still occupied by German forces, the new Polish communist government announced a revolutionary land reform. All landholdings above 50 hectares (100 hectares in the former German territories) were parcelled out among landless peasants and share-croppers. By 1949, the land reform covered 6 million hectares and created almost 750,000 new farms. Former landowners were given only a token compensation and were prohibited from settling down close to their old property (Skodlarski, 2013). Poland's land reforms were among the most radical in the communist camp (Berend, 1999). Following completion of the land reform, the old landowning elites ceased to exist.

In education, for the first time in Poland's history, the new communist government offered free, uniform, public, and compulsory primary education for all kids aged 7–15. By 1950, virtually 100 per cent of children were enrolled in public education. Soon after, illiteracy was largely eliminated. In contrast, before 1939 more than 10 per cent of all kids aged 7–12 did not attend primary school (and a whopping 28 per cent of kids aged 13). In the poorest regions, such as Poleskie or Wolynskie, often almost one-third of all kids aged 7–13 did not go to school (GUS, 1939).

Secondary education, in particular vocational education, has also greatly expanded. In 1938, only 36,700 pupils were enrolled in secondary education, a dismal 0.7 per cent of more than 5,000,000 kids of secondary school age. There were hardly any kids from poor, underprivileged families among the high-school pupils (GUS 1939, p. 321). In the 1960s, however, secondary education expanded to more than 20 per cent of population, an unprecedented achievement.

Improvements in access to tertiary education were revolutionary. The communist authorities introduced a radical affirmative action programme aimed at helping peasants and the rapidly growing industrial proletariat to enrol in tertiary education for free. Both also received extra points on entrance exams to ease their entry (those with privileged backgrounds received negative points). Subsequently, university enrolment skyrocketed from 1.2 per cent in 1935 to 7 per cent in 1960—a level virtually equal to that in France—and to 14 per cent in 1970 (Figure 3.9). By the 1970s, for the first in Poland's history, the vast majority of the country's educated elites had a plebeian background.[20]

Post-1945 Poland also experienced a historically unprecedented social mobility. By 1960, in one of the largest internal migrations in European history and the largest social transformation in Central Europe (Berend, 2009), millions of Polish peasants left villages and moved to cities, multiplying their productivity, wages, and quality of life in the process. More than a million of people moved during 1950–1955 alone, more than ten times more than during the 1937–1939 state industrial investment programme in the Central Industrial Zone (COP) (Dwilewicz et al., 2010). Unemployment disappeared. Between 1950 and 1975, employment in agriculture decreased from 57 per cent of total employment to 30 per cent of total employment, a decline much deeper than in peripheral countries in Southern Europe and behind only Bulgaria and Hungary (Figure 3.10). At the same time, the number of white collar workers increased from about 800,000 in 1939 (with a population of around 35 million) to 2.1 million in 1956 (with a population of only 28 million). The number of engineers increased from 7,000 in 1946 to 110,000 in 1970, the number of doctors from 7,000 in 1946 to 43,000 in 1967, and the number of teachers went up from 97,000 in 1946 to 320,000 in 1967 (Zarnowski, 2007). Such fundamental changes in the social structure of the society have never happened before.

---

[20] Interestingly, the newly minted elites did not feel indebted to the communist state for their social advancement: to the contrary, they soon showed 'ingratitude' towards their communist sponsors and largely adopted the cultural norms of the pre-war intelligentsia and together with the blue-collar workers became the foundation of Solidarity. Leszek Balcerowicz and many other economic policy makers in Poland after 1989 were among those who benefited from the communist social advancement. Balcerowicz, a son of a butcher who became an economics professor and then the key figure of Poland's transition, admits the key supportive role of communism in providing for his education, but then does not dwell on the implications (Balcerowicz and Stremecka, 2014). He is far from acknowledging that were he born 20 years earlier, during the inter-war period, his economic status would almost certainly ensure that he would have never 'made it'. It is an interesting question why the new intelligentsia adopted the attitudes of old intelligentsia. It seems that among many factors a strong appeal of old, romantic, freedom-and-glory focused historical narratives was important. Sometimes myths can therefore play a useful role. It might have also mattered that unlike in many other countries in Europe, Polish intelligentsia did not collaborate with Hitler during the WWII and thus kept its moral authority and was attractive to follow. There were no Quislings in Poland.

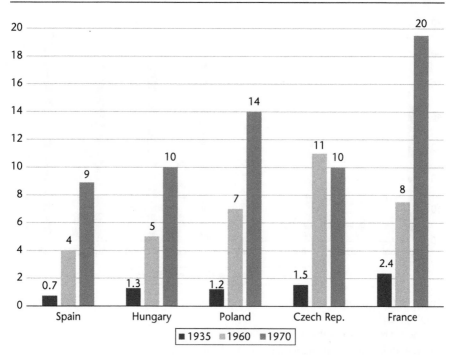

Figure 3.9. University enrolment, as per cent of the total population of university age, 1935–1970.

Source: Author's own based on Lee and Lee Long Run Education Dataset; http://www.barrolee.com/Lee_Lee_LRdata_dn.htm.

Social mobility was additionally underpinned by an unprecedented influx of peasants and workers to jobs in public administration and state-owned enterprises: in the early 1970s, people with peasant and working-class backgrounds represented 30 per cent and 26 per cent of non-manual workers, respectively (Zagórski, 1978). According to Erikson and Goldthorpe (1992), communist Poland was much more socially mobile than Western countries (England, France, West Germany, Sweden) as well as more mobile than a fellow communist Hungary. The social advancement of farmers and the working class to the ranks of intelligentsia was without comparison. As argued by Domański (2000, p. 26), '[communist] policies directed towards shaping new hierarchies and patterns of mobility in Poland did the trick, resulting in a temporary weakening of social rigidities'. Poland's social mobility during the 1945–1960 period was the highest on record (Domański, 1998; Mach 2004).

Finally, communism flattened inequality. At the end of the communist system in 1989, income inequality measured by the Gini coefficient amounted to about 0.25, at the level of today's Scandinavia. Wealth inequality (although there are

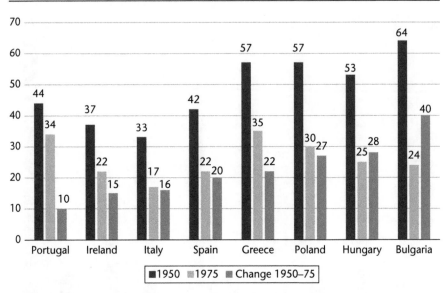

Figure 3.10. Changes in agricultural employment, 1950–1970, in per cent of total employment.

Note: Sorted by the size of the change during 1950–1970.

Source: Author's own based on Broadberry and O'Rourke (2010).

no specific data) was also likely much lower than elsewhere in the world today, lower than even in Scandinavia: during communism, most Poles hardly owned anything except for a small apartment, a small car (think of Fiat, Skoda, or Trabant) and (in the case of a lucky few) a telephone.[21] There were no billion-dollar worth entrepreneurs, no millionaire sport stars and celebrities, and no well-paid CEOs. Such low inequality stood in marked contrast to earlier periods in history, in which tiny elites controlled much of the country's wealth and income. For instance, in 1939, the top 1 per cent of the richest Poles, almost exclusively the landowning elites and a few businessmen, controlled about 16 per cent of total income. Their share in total income collapsed to about 5 per cent in 1950 (Figure 3.11). Hungary and other communist countries experienced similarly dramatic declines, reflecting the shift from extractive to inclusive societies (Mavridis and Mosberger, 2016; Novokmet, Piketty, and Zucman, 2017).

Communism also excelled in emancipation of women, culture, and sports. It helped emancipate women by providing subsidized childcare, long maternity

---

[21] To share a personal example: my own family, which solidly belonged to the Polish 1980's middle class, owned a 48 square metre apartment (occupied by my parents, my brother, and me), an old Skoda, a telephone line, and had some small savings used to chase the few products and services worth buying.

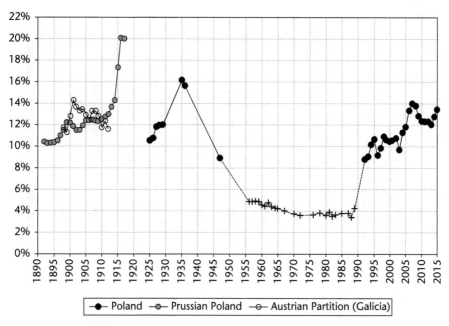

Figure 3.11. Share of the top 1 per cent of the richest Poles in total income, 1920–1995. *Source*: Bukowski and Novokmet (2017).

leave, and free health care.[22] Women's labour participation in communist Poland was much higher than in Western Europe: in 1980, almost 60 per cent of women in Poland participated in the labour force, as opposed to only 50 per cent in the US, 43 per cent in France, and 22 per cent in Spain (Figure 3.12). Following the collapse of communism, women's participation rate declined: in 2014, in Poland it amounted to only 49 per cent.[23]

To boost labour participation and promote gender equality, communist authorities provided a guarantee to women of equal pay for equal work. The overall flatness of salaries also played a role in strengthening gender equity.[24] As a result, the wage gap between men and women during communism compared favourably with most countries at the same level of development (Brainderd, 2000; Newell and Reilly, 2000).

Polish culture also punched above the country's weight. It established a strong reputation in film making, with such directors as Roman Polanski,

---

[22] For instance, in most communist countries women were entitled to up to 3 years of maternity leave and a guarantee of return to the previous job (Brainerd, 2000, p. 140).

[23] http://data.worldbank.org/indicator/SL.TLF.CACT.FE.ZS.

[24] My family's own history exemplifies the flatness of salaries: in the 1980s, the salary of my father, a CFO, was not much different from that of my mother, a schoolteacher of Polish literature. Today, it would likely be multiple times higher.

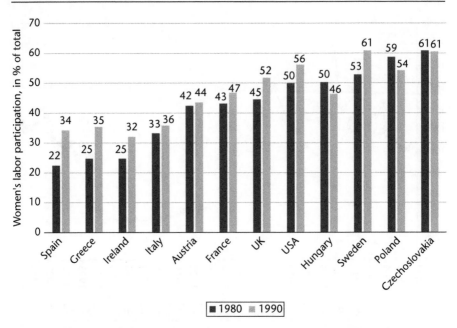

Figure 3.12. Women's labour participation rate across countries, 1980 and 1990.

Note: Percentage of economically active women aged 15 and above to total population. Sorted by the highest percentage in 1980.

Source: Author's own based on Chase (1995).

Krzysztof Kieslowski, or Andrzej Wajda. It also made a global mark in classical music, with Krzysztof Penderecki, Henryk Górecki, and Witold Lutosławski. Communist Poland also won two Nobel Prizes in literature, awarded in the 1990s to Wislawa Szymborska and Czeslaw Milosz.

What is important, culture was not reserved for the high-brow: the communist state lavishly subsidized theatres, operas, museums, and other types of cultural entertainment for the masses to a much larger extent than in capitalist countries, even in Western Europe (Berend, 2009). More Poles participated in culture in 1990 than in 2009: almost one-third of Poles went to music concerts in 1990 versus only 17 per cent in 2009 (Figure 3.13).

Finally, communist countries including Poland were quite successful in sports, performing way above what would be suggested by the country's level of income. For instance, during the 1976 Summer Olympics in Montreal, communist Poland won 26 medals and was ranked in sixth place overall.[25] Poland also did well in team sports, including two third places in the football World Cup in 1978 and 1982.

---

[25] https://en.wikipedia.org/wiki/Poland_at_the_1976_Summer_Olympics.

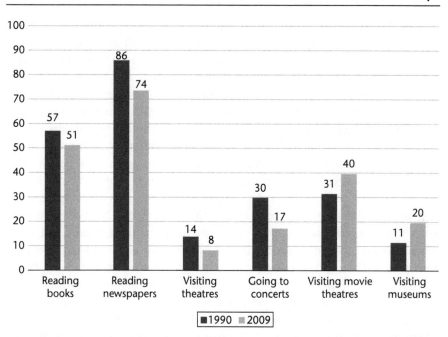

Figure 3.13. Participation in culture, in per cent of total population, 1990 and 2009. *Source*: Author's own based on GUS (2014).

Separately, communism also helped push the West to create more inclusive, more prosperous, and more humane societies. It was the threat and the fear of communism that civilized Western capitalism. The late Polish Pope John Paul II put it well, when in 1993 he argued that 'several severe social and human problems of Europe and the world are rooted in the aberrations of capitalism. Communism was a reaction to reckless capitalism. The change of the latter was due, in a great deal, to the ideas of socialism'.[26] As a result, lives of millions of Westerners improved. The collapse of communism did not spell 'the end of history', but it did help strengthen the neoliberal forces in the West, which could now claim, repeating Margaret Thatcher, that 'there was no alternative' to hard-core capitalism. Without the communist enemy, the West became less inclusive, more populist, and slower-growing.

3.6. What if Poland had Remained Capitalist in 1945?

An interesting question is how Poland and other CEE countries would have performed if they had never fallen under communism. The standard narrative

[26] Pope John Paul II, statement in *La Stampa*, 1993.

in Poland and in much of CEE is that was it not for communism and a centrally planned economy, a capitalist Poland (as well as Hungary, Czech Republic, etc.) would have flourished and become as rich as the West or at least as rich as Spain or Portugal, which in 1950 had a similar level of income.[27]

Yet, Poland's convergence with the West after 1945 under a counterfactual capitalist scenario would be far from guaranteed. First, an analysis of political and economic programs of the Polish émigré government in London at the end of the Second World War suggests that this 'Western' government, built from a likely coalition of conservative, socialist, and peasant parties, would have pushed for economic planning, nationalization of economy, industrialization, land reform, and support for agriculture. There was much agreement then among all the London-based parties that the key objective of economic policy was to move away from the anarchy and chaos of the market and shift towards economic planning, similar to the pre-war autarkic state-led development policy. The capitalist development programme would then have been not much different from what transpired under communism.[28] Ironically, the economic programme could have been even worse, as the leading peasant parties, which would have likely played a key role in the new democratic government, argued in favour of 'agrarism', a concept according to which Poland's economy should be based on agriculture and industry should only have a supplementary role. The conservative parties were also against industrialization, seeing it as a platform for emergence of industrial proletariat and the nest of communism (Dwilewicz et al., 2010). In 1945, a belief in economic *laissez faire* seemed to the London-based government to be as absurd as going back to central planning today (Leszczyński, 2015b).

In this scenario, the new democratic government would have to face the same or even sharper challenges than communists in implementing its programme. In particular, it would have difficulty in securing financing for the planned industrialization. It would have to finance industrialization by taxing

---

[27] See, for instance, Balcerowicz (2010). He compares Poland with Spain in 1950 and 1990 and Hungary and Austria and argues that the difference in economic performance was a result of communism and implies that if Poland (and other CEE countries) had been capitalist from the beginning, it would be as rich as Spain today too.

[28] In March 1944, the London-based Committee of National Unity, which represented all political parties, issued a programme on 'What is the Polish nation fighting for', which called for universalization of ownership, active state involvement, full employment, a planned economy, and 'equalization of Poland's level of economic development with Western Europe through focused public and private investment' (Leszczyński, 2015a, p. 138). Even traditionally conservative parties followed the *Weltschauung*: in its 1944 political manifesto, a conservative party of Stronnictwo Narodowe proclaimed that 'a belief in economic automatism, laying at the foundation of economic liberalism, is now a thing of the past. Experience has taught us beyond any doubt that a free play of market forces does not automatically lead to harmonization of micro and macro economy or to the appropriate coordination of the economic objectives with the general objectives of national life' (Leszczyński, 2015a, p. 144; English translation in Leszczyński, 2017). See also Kowalik (2006).

population, mostly farmers, which represented the predominant part of the society. It could also tax the landowners, but given that they would play an important role in the government, that some of their land would be parcelled out, and that the democratic government would have to pay much higher compensation than a communist one, it is not clear whether any significant revenue from taxation of the rich would be forthcoming. In the interwar period, governments representing the same elites have repeatedly failed to increase taxation of the rich. Even if the tax increase was possible, following the war the landowners were too few and too immiserated to be a source of much tax revenue. It would then leave peasants as the main source of financing.

But in a democracy, which unlike communism could not use political and economic repression, it would be immensely difficult to tax agriculture sufficiently to provide financing for state-driven industrialization. It has been tried before 1939 and it failed. The track record of the interwar Poland suggests that even under an autocratic regime of Marshall Józef Piłsudski and his followers, securing financing for industrialization proved to be difficult. It would be even more difficult under a presumptive post-1945 democracy. It is likely that the available financing sources would be smaller than under communism, which used political oppression to wrest resources from the society and keep a lid on consumption. On the whole, given the political constraints, track record of inefficient taxation, and lack of economic repression, it is far from clear whether the government could muster sufficient resources to push industrialization.

Second, the alternative scenario assumes that the new capitalist Poland, unlike the communist government, would attract foreign direct investment and large foreign financing to finance a Rosenstein-Rodan style 'big push' in industrialization. Again, it is not clear whether such a scenario would play out. Poland could likely be one of the recipients of the Marshal Plan, which helped Western Europe develop. Yet, Poland's share in the Marshal Plan, whose total value amounted to about $110–120 billion in today's money, would represent only a few per cent of the total or just a few billion dollars.[29] It would not be sufficient to make a difference. In fact, as argued by Eichengreen and Uzan (1992), the Marshall Plan had largely a symbolic significance: it is estimated to have raised the investment rate in Western Europe by only about 1 per cent of GDP and contributed to a negligible 0.2 percentage points of additional GDP growth per year (it, however, mattered more as a commitment mechanism to open borders to trade, maintain macroeconomic stability, and sustain social cooperation).

As to other sources of foreign financing, it is not clear how much would be forthcoming. Given that Poland would continue to border the Soviet Union, it

---

[29] The Marshal Plan amounted to about $13 billion (1948–1951 prices, or almost ten times more in 2016 prices, Broadberry and O'Rourke, 2010; Eichengreen, 2008a).

would thus remain in the European grey zone of security, especially if it did not change its borders and shared a long, pre-1939 border with the Soviet Union (which would additionally drag down growth, given the underdevelopment of the Eastern areas and rife pre-war ethnic conflict). As a result, the geopolitical risks would reduce the inflows of FDI, as in the interwar period, when FDI inflows were negligible. An uncertain geopolitical situation would also increase the costs of external financing, undermining both public and private investment. Separately, high security risks would lead to large spending on the military, reducing resources for public investment.

Third, even if financing was available from domestic and foreign sources, it is far from clear that the state-sponsored push would be productive. The global track record of 'big push' industrialization strategies is abysmal. The track record of interwar Poland suggests the same: the increasing state-ownership in the economy, which reached almost 30 per cent of GDP by 1939, did not help Poland avoid a 40 per cent decline in industrial production during the Global Depression in the 1930s, more than in most other countries in Europe. The largest state-driven industrialization programme, the so-called 'Central Industrial Zone' (COP) project initiated in 1937, produced only 100,000 new jobs (which pales in comparison with millions of new jobs created under communism) and could not have a tangible impact in a country with a labour force of almost 20 million. It was also not clear whether new factories were profitable and thus whether the newly created jobs were sustainable.[30] Similar attempts in other countries in CEE had a comparably limited effect (Aldcroft, 2006; Turnock, 2006).

Finally and most importantly, successful industrialization and economic development would not happen without the inclusive institutions of an open society, with good education for all, a level playing field for everyone, and a broad-based and pluralistic political system. There is little in the Polish history to suggest that such a scenario of a shift from extractive to inclusive institutions would be possible. As argued earlier, extractive institutions tend to self-perpetuate and are unlikely to change without an external shock. Poland would likely continue to be stuck in its old, growth-inhibiting equilibrium. As in the interwar period, constraints of the political process would likely ensure that the land reform would only be partial, education would remain restricted to the better off, and market competition would continue to be undermined by the vested interests. The case of the Southern USA after the abolition of slavery is instructive in this respect (Box 3.1). In the end, it is not clear whether or how much better Poland would have performed under

---

[30] The COP in Poland reached full capacity and employment only under German management during the Second World War, and after the war under communism. It never underwent a test of free market sustainability.

Box 3.1. CASE STUDY OF THE SOUTHERN USA AFTER THE ABOLITION OF SLAVERY

Polish extractive elites in 1918–1939 were remarkably like the extractive elites in the South of the USA until the 1960s. Both Poland and the South of the USA freed their serfs and slaves, respectively, at almost exactly the same time in the mid-1860s. Both were also forced to do so against their wishes, respectively by the Russian Czar and Abraham Lincoln. And both elites never let go of their power until they were forced to do so.

After the Civil War, despite far-reaching changes in the *de jure* powers and the formal enfranchisement of African-Americans, the source of *de facto* power in the South had not changed at all. Southern elites continued to control the land, the commanding heights of the economy, and the political system and legislation. They were able to sustain the *status quo* by putting restrictions on access to education, property, and voting rights of black Americans (the so-called Jim Crow laws). They also used intimidation to disenfranchise the poor. In the end, they succeeded in 'turning the postbellum South into an effective 'apartheid' society where blacks and whites lived different lives' (Acemoglu and Robison, 2008, p. 18). Despite formal freedom, the Southern US became 'an armed camp for intimidating black folk' (W.E.B. Du Bois, 1903, p. 88). Economic development suffered because 'Southerners erected an economic system that failed to reward individual initiative on the part of blacks and was therefore ill-suited to their economic advancement. As a result, the inequities originally inherited from slavery persisted. But there was a by-product of this effort at racial repression, the system tended to cripple all economic growth' (Ransom and Sutch, 2001, p. 186, cited in Acemoglu and Robison, 2008). Southern US lagged behind the North in development until the 1960s. It started to catch up only later.

Interwar Poland was remarkably similar. The role of black ex-slaves was played by peasants and—to a lesser extent—the industrial proletariat. Like the Southern US until the anti-segregation reforms in the 1960s, 1918–1939 Poland was like a large Potemkin village designed to keep up appearances, while sustaining the old extractive system. It restricted social mobility, access to education, and participation in the political system. And it failed to catch up on the West throughout the whole 1918–1939 period.

capitalism, especially in the first three decades when the growth rates of the communist Poland were comparable with those in the West.

The important question then is how capitalistic Spain, Portugal, and Greece, which in 1950 were as poor as Poland, developed so quickly? There are several crucial differences between these countries and a counterfactual post-1945 capitalist Poland. First, all three countries were dictatorships until the 1970s, which allowed them to pursue economic reforms without the burden of having to deal with vested interests and public discontent. This would not be the case for a democratic Poland (unless it too shifted to a dictatorship, a quite likely scenario given the pre-war autocratic track-record). Second, Southern Europe had a much better security situation, as it was removed from the main theatre of the Cold War and did not share a border with the Soviet Union. Third, all Southern countries received significant hard currency inflows from tourism, especially in the 1960s and onwards, which helped finance industrialization. In Spain, for example, inflows from tourism represented almost 10 per cent of GDP in the 1960s (Mills, 1965). Tourism inflows into Poland would be negligible.

Fourth, Southern Europe started to develop in the 1960s following deep trade and market liberalization (the Spanish 1959 reforms, which started its economic miracle, are a good example). It is not clear if given their statist instincts, the Polish elites would do the same. Fifth, Southern Europe had arguably more 'social capability' to absorb technology from abroad and promote entrepreneurship. Spain, for example, had two well-established entrepreneurial, bourgeois, and industrial areas in Catalonia and the Basque country, which had enough social capital, managerial know-how, and financial capital to take the lead in development (Boix, 2004). Poland was dramatically different: it did not have a Polish entrepreneurial or a merchant class (as mentioned earlier, before the war most of trade and business was in the hands of Germans and Jews) and thus little social capacity to develop.[31]

Finally, as argued by Boix (2004, p. 13),

Spain [and other Southern European countries] could count upon an extremely favorable foreign environment: for geopolitical considerations, the American and European governments were keenly interested in a stable, rapidly growing Spain; foreign capital was available and ready to invest in a potentially medium market located close to the European core; and the military ties with the United States acted as a mechanism to insure foreign investors against any policy reversals or confiscatory threats in the Peninsula.

It is far from certain that as a frontier country with the Soviet Union Poland would have received the same treatment.

3.7. Conclusions

When communism fell in 1989, it bequeathed the new, democratic Poland a bankrupt economy and an impoverished society. The centrally planned economy was doing relatively well until late 1960s, but then started to lose distance to other communist countries and—above all—to the West. Hit by external shocks (higher interest rates on the large foreign debt and higher oil prices) and internal shocks (the rise of Solidarity and subsequent social and economic disruption), the Polish economy stagnated in the 1980s.

Communism also developed, despite its lofty ideals, a new extractive class of communist *nomenklatura*, the perfect embodiment of George Orwell's famous

---

[31] In 1936, among 469,000 trade establishments in Poland, Jewish-owned stores represented almost half of the total. http://liberte.pl/splata-dlugu-po-ii-rp/.

quote that 'all animals are equal, but some animals are more equal than others', which undermined the moral appeal of communism. It also created an extractive economic system with no incentive for technology absorption and innovation. When the sources of extensive growth—shifting peasants to industry and jacking up investment—diminished, there was not enough technological progress to keep the economy going. The communist economic system achieved its limit.

But despite all its economic ills and social misery, communism also bequeathed the new democratic post-1989 Poland a society that has never been so egalitarian, open, educated, and ready to take its fate into its own hands. It created the first ever inclusive society and broke with the old, pre-modern feudal political and economic system, which kept Poland (and many other countries in CEE) backward for centuries. Communist Poland laid the foundations for a new paradigm in which the vast majority of the people could benefit from economic opportunities. In a paradoxical way, the communist Polish Republic did what the United States did at the beginning of its existence: distributed land to those in need, provided education to all, and broke the back of the old, feudal political and economic system. This made the post-1989 miracle possible. This is what we turn to next.

4

Poland's Transition Success Story

I don't care too much for money, for money can't buy me love.

The Beatles

There are three kinds of lies: lies, damned lies, and statistics.

Benjamin Disraeli

Everything that has already happened must have been inevitable.

Amos Tversky

How successful has Poland's transition from communism to capitalism been? How is this best measured? What makes this experience unique and why does it matter?

In the previous chapters I documented how Poland struggled to develop throughout hundreds of years and as a result how it has failed to converge on the West. Against this background, in this chapter I show the remarkable change that has happened in Poland since 1989, as it became Europe's and the world's economic growth champion (among its peers) for the first time in its history. I also show how in the last twenty-five years Poland has offset 500 years of economic stagnation and shortened the distance to the West in terms of the level of income and quality of life to an extent never experienced before. Poland has entered its true Golden Age.

I start the chapter by first assessing the optimal way to measure countries' economic performance. I argue that measuring changes in median income is a much better way to assess countries' economic success than changes in GDP, as the latter hides how the income is distributed among the population. I also argue in favour of increased focus on the measurement of well-being, quality of life, and happiness, which should become a key part of assessing countries' performance.

I then go on to argue that Poland has achieved historically unprecedented success since 1989. It increased its income from around $10,300 in 1990, adjusting for purchasing power parity (PPP) in constant prices, to almost

$27,000 in 2017, and moved from poor to high-income within the life of just one generation. I claim that Poland's economic success is unique, because it has been achieved despite the country's lack of natural resources, low debt leverage, and a vibrant and young democracy, with 17 governments presiding over reforms since 1989. Poland is among only a few countries in recent history that have managed to become high-income while being fully democratic.

I conclude by showing how and why Poland has been successful in creating an inclusive economy, where economic growth lifted all boats: it was the only democratic country in the post-Soviet camp where 100 per cent of society, including the poor, increased their incomes faster than in the West. Higher incomes translated into the highest levels of well-being and happiness on record. Poles have never had it better.

4.1. Measurement of Economic Performance and Prosperity

What is the best measure of countries' economic and social performance? GDP is still the key indicator of economic performance—for good reasons. Despite all its limitations, such as not measuring household work (as the well-known quip goes, GDP will decline if you marry your nanny) and that it ignores everything that really matters for people's lives aside from income, it is still the most readily available way to track countries' changes in prosperity.[1] GDP closely correlates with the quality of life, well-being, and happiness. Most often, although not always (as I discuss below), the higher the income, the higher the quality of life and the higher the overall life satisfaction. Regardless of many feelgood stories, such as those about Bhutan and its Gross National Happiness, people in poor countries live shorter lives, have lower well-being, and are less happy than their peers in richer countries.

GDP growth, however, can be shown in various ways. Countries with growing populations, such as the United States, prefer to show the overall change in GDP. Others, such as countries in Europe where population growth is much slower, or Japan, where population is shrinking, prefer to show changes in GDP growth per capita. Depending on which GDP measure you take, the results can be much different and so the accompanying narrative. What may look a great success based on growth in the overall GDP, may look much less appealing when measured on a per capita basis.

As shown in Figure 4.1, which compares economic performance of the USA and the European Union during 1995–2015, one can reach much different

---

[1] See Coyle (2015) for a nice discussion of what GDP is and isn't and why we still have not found anything better.

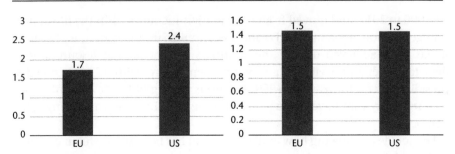

Figure 4.1. European Union vs. the US: GDP growth (left chart) vs. GDP growth per capita, 1990–2015 average.

Source: Author's own based on WDI.

conclusions as to who has performed better based on which GDP measures one looks at: on total GDP growth, the US is doing much better than the EU, having grown 0.7 percentage points faster than the EU; yet, in GDP per capita terms, 'innovative and entrepreneurial' US is doing exactly as well as the supposedly 'sclerotic' Europe. The measure one chooses thus makes a big difference to social and political perceptions.

Which GDP is better? Among economists, there is a clear consensus that GDP per capita is a better measure of economic prosperity. It is because it measures what really matters: change in income and the living standards of the country's citizens rather than an amorphous totality of the society. It is also a better target for economic policy: the main objective of economic growth is not to increase abstract 'total GDP', but to boost citizens' prosperity.[2]

However, while GDP growth per capita is a better measure than overall GDP growth, it is still far from perfect. This is because it ignores how income is distributed among the society. In an extreme scenario, average GDP per capita may grow, but if the whole increase in income is appropriated by the top 1 per cent or top 10 per cent of the society, the income of the remaining 99 per cent and 90 per cent may not change. This indeed has been the case in the US in the last thirty years, where despite much higher GDP the income of a typical American household has hardly risen (Piketty, 2014). In fact, income of the poorer half of society in the USA stagnated for more than fifty years, as most of the increased GDP accrued only to the richer part of the society (Figure 4.2).

---

[2] It can be argued that population growth that increases total GDP growth shows a country's 'vitality'. I am not sure. If this were so, given its high fertility rate, Afghanistan would be the most 'vital' country in the world. Likewise with immigration: 'attractive' countries attract immigration. But this is not a straightforward measure: today, inflows of immigrants do not reflect the countries' attractiveness, especially if they have a similar level of income, but their immigration policies. Europe, if it only wanted to, could attract a billion of migrants overnight. Would it then prove that Europe is 'more attractive' than America, if America retained barriers to immigration? That said, the overall GDP matters, for instance, as a measure of a country's ability to defend itself or participate in global policy making.

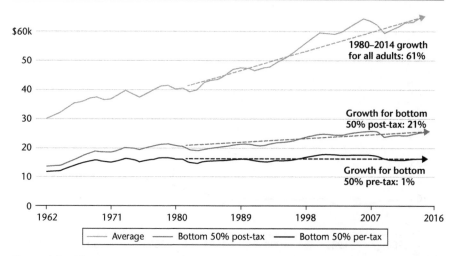

Figure 4.2. Changes in income for all Americans and the bottom 50 per cent of Americans, 1962–2014.

Source: Piketty, Saez, and Zucman (2016).

To correct for how GDP is distributed, we thus need to measure changes in individuals' income, ideally including not only wages, but also other sources of income such as income from capital, pensions, or public transfers. This can be done thanks to the growing availability of data from household budget surveys, which measure changes in household income across the whole income distribution in a society. This can tell us whether growth really 'lifts all boats' or whether it just pretends to do so.[3]

Since 1980, in the vast majority of 27 countries with comparable household survey data, GDP per capita rose faster than the median household income (Nolan *et al.*, 2016). It suggests that GDP per capita growth overstated growth in the living standards of 'typical' households. This is most often the case because the lion's share of the increasing income has been taken over by the richest households. The USA is among the countries where the divergence between GDP and income of an 'average Joe' has been the greatest. Between 1979 and 2013, while GDP per capita grew by 1.6 per cent per year, the median household income grew by only 0.3 per cent a year. At the same time in

---

[3] Data for median household incomes have been put together only recently. The most comprehensive database maintained by the Luxembourg Income Study Database (www.lisdatacenter.org), covers about 55 countries (as of March 2017) and presents data mostly since the 1980s. However, with the arrival of 'big data' and with more commitment from policy makers, it should be possible to expand household surveys to all countries in the world, conduct household surveys each year, and ensure that the results are fully credible. It will also be imperative to ensure that better data are obtained on the incomes of the top and the bottom decile, the richest and the poorest, which both for various reasons want to avoid (the rich) or do not bother (the poor) with the survey.

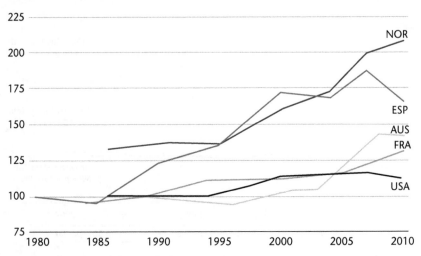

Figure 4.3. Changes in median incomes for selected countries, 1980=100.
Source: Author's own based on Roser, Thewissen, and Nolan (2016).

France, growth in GDP per capita was slower at 1.4 per cent per year, but the increase in income of an average family was three times as high as in the USA. In other words, because of high inequality in the USA, in the last thirty years most French citizens have increased their income faster than most Americans (Piketty, 2014). By 2010, the poorer half of the French society has actually become richer than the poorer half in America. And the difference in incomes has grown further since then (Piketty, Saez, and Zucman, 2016).

The picture is similar for other OECD countries: since 1980, median incomes of Americans have increased slower than in all other countries (Figure 4.3). The American poor have been specially affected: incomes of the bottom 20 per cent of US households are lower than among their peers in developed countries. Only the rich Americans are much richer than else-where.[4] These findings suggest that if shared prosperity for everyone is the goal of economic policy (as it should be), the European economic system is better than the one in America.

However, most Americans are still richer than Europeans. Is it because they are more productive or because they just work more?

The biggest part of the difference in incomes between the USA and Europe can be explained by the Americans working more than Europeans. Differences in productivity are much lower: productivity of an average Frenchman, for

---

[4] http://www.nytimes.com/2014/04/23/upshot/the-american-middle-class-is-no-longer-the-worlds-richest.html?_r=0; explanation of data: http://www.nytimes.com/2014/04/23/upshot/about-the-data.html.

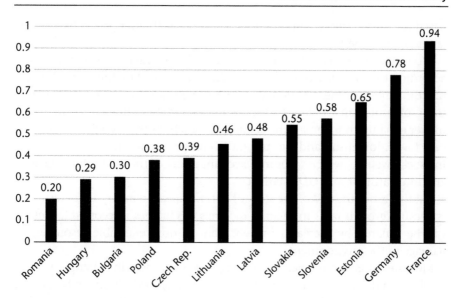

Figure 4.4. Labour productivity per hour worked in 2015, in 1990 US$ (converted at Geary Khamis PPPs), US=1.

Source: Author's own based on the Conference Board Total Economy Database.

instance, is only 6 per cent lower than in America (Figure 4.4). This suggests that the French are poorer than Americans not because they are less product-ive, but mostly because fewer of them work (the employment rate is lower) and because those employed work fewer hours in favour of more leisure time. In other words, the French like to enjoy life a bit more than the Americans do (the French have more than a month of paid vacation versus only two weeks on average in the USA). It is not clear what is wrong with that. After all, the whole point of economic growth is to produce enough prosperity so that people can work less to meet their needs and enjoy more of their free time.[5] Americans live to work, while Europeans work to live.[6]

The comparison between France and the USA suggests that when looking at changes in GDP and household incomes, we also need to look at the under-lying data on productivity and working hours to see whether growth has been

---

[5] In his famous book on 'Economic Possibilities for our Grandchildren' published in 1930, John Maynard Keynes was predicting that by 2030 people in rich countries would be on average eight times better off, which would allow them to reduce work to a few hours per day and enjoy the rest of their free time. He was largely right about the eight times increase in GDP, but was largely wrong about the work hours: we work less than in the 1930s, but nowhere close to 'three hours a day'.

[6] The example of France suggests that it could close a large part of the income gap with the USA by maintaining their lifestyle (fewer working hours), but at the same time increasing the employment rate (lower in France than in the USA largely because of much more generous retirement systems) and the level of productivity to the US level.

based on 'sweat' (more working hours) or 'brains' (higher productivity). The latter is clearly better.

We can complement this analysis with other comparisons. For instance, according to a measure of economic welfare developed by Jones and Klenow (2016), while incomes of the French are more than 30 per cent lower than those of Americans, owing to higher life expectancy, more free time, and higher equality in incomes, the economic welfare of the French is only 8 per cent lower. Jorgenson and Slesnick (2014) propose a new method of measuring social welfare, which takes into account many of these additional factors, and integrating it into GDP statistics.

But this is not the end of the story of optimal measurement of progress. This is because growth rates in median incomes or changes in economic welfare can be inflated by increases in debt, sale of non-renewable resources, or damage to the environment.

Measures of economic performance ignore the underlying changes in debt levels, even though it matters whether a country's growth is driven by a credit binge or whether it is based on real earnings. The rule of thumb suggests that debt in an economy should grow in line or slightly above (for countries with developing financial markets) the growth rate in nominal GDP. When growth in debt is much faster than the increase in nominal GDP, sooner or later it leads to financial crises. This has been illustrated recently during the Asian, American, and the euro zone crises and countless earlier examples, in which excessive debt leverage led to crises. Higher debt also tends to put drag on growth and make growth more volatile (Pescatori and Simon, 2014; Kumar and Woo, 2010). Neither is good for social welfare. It is therefore important to track income growth together with the increase in debt. Even though by itself debt is not 'bad' as long as it finances productive investments, in the long term the lower the debt, the healthier the growth.[7]

In principle, we could construct a measure of 'real GDP growth net of debt', which would show how much total (public and private) debt is needed to produce an additional unit of GDP. Figure 4.5 shows growth in GDP per capita and total private debt for France and the US since 1990. France's GDP per capita increased by 28 per cent during 1990 and 2015, while total credit increased by only 5 per cent. At the same time, US GDP per capita increased by 42 per cent, but total credit increased by 65 per cent. In other words, American growth has been more credit-intensive than GDP growth in France. Credit build up that is too rapid may undermine the economy if it enters a credit crisis, such as the one in 2008–2009, or when it has to deleverage when debt becomes too high.

---

[7] Of course, much depends on the specifics of the debt: to what extent it is foreign/domestically financed, whether it is denominated in domestic or foreign currency, or its average maturity. Details matter. But on the whole, the lower the debt leverage, the better.

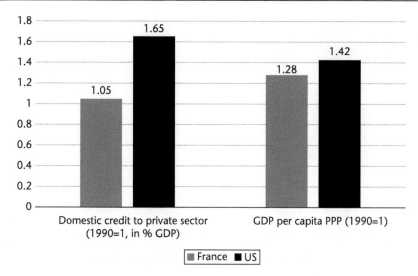

Figure 4.5. GDP growth per capita versus increase in total domestic credit for private sector for France and the US, 2015, 1990=1.

Source: Author's own based on World Bank WDI and Bank of International Settlements.

It also matters whether growth is based on rents from natural resources or hard work. It is misleading to compare GDP growth between countries that have abundant natural resources and those that do not. It is like comparing oranges and apples. The difference matters also because growth based on natural resources is 'easier' to achieve in the short term, but harder to sustain in the long term. Economic history suggests that countries that have become rich have hardly ever achieved it thanks to natural resources (with the possible exception of Australia or Norway).[8] In fact, natural resources are often a 'curse' that thwarts rather than promotes development, as has been the case in most developing countries.

Figure 4.6 shows that Poland developed faster than any other country in the last twenty years despite having one of the lowest rents from natural resources. Other countries such Brazil, Mexico, Malaysia, or Russia benefited much more. Only South Korea and Poland's neighbours in CEE had a similar 'bad luck' in being devoid of natural resources.

Finally, we need to look at economic growth adjusted for the impact on environment. There is 'clean' growth, which keeps the environment intact, and 'dirty' growth, which undermines it. There are various ways of looking at

---

[8] As to the oil-based rich countries in the Persian Gulf, it is far from clear whether they will be able to sustain their level of income when oil runs out or when renewable energy replaces oil. Historical experience (such as the case of colonial Spain) suggests that without strong institutions, high human capital and conducive culture, even substantial wealth, can quickly dissipate.

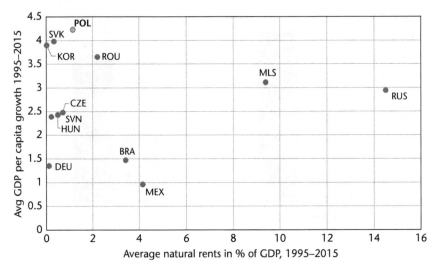

Figure 4.6. Total natural resources rents (per cent of GDP) versus GDP per capita growth, 1995–2015.

Note: Total natural resources rents defined as the sum of oil rents, natural gas rents, coal rents (hard and soft), mineral rents, and forest rents.

Source: Author's calculations based on WDI.

the impact on the environment. For example, Yale University's Environmental Performance Index (EPI) looks at countries' performance in protection of their ecosystems. Poland is classified in thirty-eighth place among 180 countries globally, behind most regional peers, but ahead of Japan.[9] There are also other rankings, which rightly assume that measuring countries' overall performance should not ignore the impact on the environment.

4.2. Measurement of Well-Being and Happiness

Measuring changes in median household income, adjusted for the number of working hours and a host of other factors as just discussed, is the best way to assess economic performance. Yet, we cannot stop there. Money alone does not bring happiness (although it surely helps). There are many other factors that affect what ultimately matters: people's well-being, happiness, and the meaning of their lives.

There is strong consensus in the economic literature about the weaknesses of GDP as the single most important indicator of human progress (Stiglitz,

---

[9] http://epi.yale.edu/country-rankings.

Sen, and Fitoussi, 2008). GDP fails to measure all the things that affect people's well-being and happiness, especially in more developed countries whose citizens have already met all their basic needs. Probably no one has better encapsulated the weakness of GDP in measuring our lives than Robert Kennedy, who argued that:

> Too much and for too long, we seemed to have surrendered personal excellence and community values in the mere accumulation of material things. Our Gross National Product...counts air pollution and cigarette advertising, and ambulances to clear our highways of carnage. It counts special locks for our doors and the jails for the people who break them. It counts the destruction of the redwood and the loss of our natural wonder in chaotic sprawl. It counts napalm and counts nuclear warheads and armored cars for the police to fight the riots in our cities. It counts Whitman's rifle and Speck's knife, and the television programs which glorify violence in order to sell toys to our children. Yet the gross national product does not allow for the health of our children, the quality of their education or the joy of their play. It does not include the beauty of our poetry or the strength of our marriages, the intelligence of our public debate or the integrity of our public officials. It measures neither our wit nor our courage, neither our wisdom nor our learning, neither our compassion nor our devotion to our country, it measures everything in short, except that which makes life worthwhile.   (Kennedy, 1968)

So, the quest began to find other ways of measuring what really matters to people. The most established measure is the UNDP's Human Development Index, which looks at income, life expectancy, and educational attainment as the key sources of well-being. However, it is far from perfect: it ignores many important aspects of well-being, such as political freedom, work–life balance, commute time, quality of environment, or the level of crime. Moreover, given that in recent decades life expectancy and educational attainment have reached almost maximum levels and there is not much space left for further improvement (one cannot educate more than 100 per cent of population), the ranking's explanatory power has diminished.

The alternative indicators such as the OECD's Better Life Index corrects many of the weaknesses of the HDI index, although it covers only the rich thirty-four OECD member states. When building the Better Life Index, the OECD rightly argued that 'there is more to life than the cold numbers of GDP and economic statistics'.[10] Its Better Life Index therefore looks at social well-being across eleven dimensions, including the dimensions missing in HDI plus measures of subjective well-being, housing conditions, social

---

[10] Quite interestingly, the Index allows users to change the relative weights for subindicators and thus alter the ranking. For instance, raising the weights for 'education' and 'safety' to their maximum (while keeping other subindicators in the default position) raises Poland's ranking to twenty-second place, beating Spain and Italy. See the index's website at: http://www.oecdbetterlifeindex.org/.

connections, and availability of jobs. There are also other useful indexes, such as the Social Justice Index or BCG's Sustainable Economic Development Assessment (SEDA).

Happiness is harder to measure than well-being: it is more fickle, not surprisingly. As we all know from our own daily experience, people's happiness depends on so many factors that can easily escape measurement. Yet, there is a growing strand of economics that strives to measure happiness, most often titled as 'subjective well-being'. In particular, there is an ongoing debate about whether there is a point at which increasing income stops to increase happiness. One group of economists claims that once the basic needs are met, people's happiness increases at an ever smaller rate and at some point stops growing altogether (this phenomenon is known as 'Easterlin paradox' after Richard Easterlin who noted it back in the 1970s). Richard Layard, a prominent proponent of this view, argues that 'once a country has over $15,000 per head, its level of happiness appears to be independent of its income per head' (Layard 2003. p. 17).

However, other economists vehemently disagree: in a well-publicized paper, Stevenson and Wolfers (2013) argue that there is no satiation point for happiness: it keeps on increasing indefinitely, although at a diminishing rate (Figure 4.7). Other research results tend to support this view (Deaton, 2008).

However, other economists question whether you can even compare happiness to changes in GDP. In particular, the way that happiness is measured— ranked on a 1–10 scale—automatically implies that there is a limit to how much happiness can increase. But this obviously is not the case for GDP,

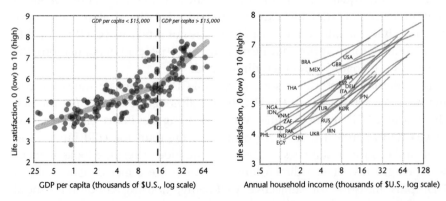

Figure 4.7. Income and life satisfaction: cross country and within country comparisons.

Note: Data from 2008–2012 waves of the Gallup World Poll. GDP per capita is on a log scale: each additional unit represents a doubling of income. GDP per capita PPP from the World Bank's WDI.

Source: Brookings (https://www.brookings.edu/interactives/you-can-never-have-too-much-money-new-research-shows/) based on Stevenson and Wolfers (2013). Data for charts: http://users.nber.org/~jwolfers/data.php#satiation.

which can increase without a limit. Diane Coyle (2015, Kindle 703–11), one of the key experts in the debate, argues that there is no reason to

> expect happiness to rise fully in line with GDP in the first place—not least because the fall in GDP associated with a recession always causes great unhappiness. Of course, higher incomes should make us happier on average but why would anyone expect GDP and happiness to rise in proportion to each other? Higher incomes make us taller on average too, but nobody would expect height to continue rising at the same pace as GDP.

Nonetheless, Coyle does not dispute that fact that higher income increases happiness, but points to the many inherent pitfalls in the debate.

Aside from GDP, there are many other, non-monetary sources of happiness. Extensive literature suggests a number of factors. For instance, having a job is the most important ingredient of happiness, as it seems to uphold people's sense of self-worth and meaning of life. Not having one makes people deeply unhappy, across all races and all countries. So does a long commute time. Happiness increases for those who are married (although that in itself does not prove the direction of causality), healthy, religious, and social. The larger the circle of family and friends, and the longer the time spent with them, the higher the level of happiness. Finally, political freedom and human rights matter. Living under a dictatorship makes people less happy.[11]

The bottom line from the discussion here is that GDP is far from the best way to measure a country's performance. It is much better to use changes in median household income (as well as changes in income across all income groups) and productivity per hour. Both variables should be put in the context of the evolution of debt, changes in the stock of natural resources, and the impact on natural environment. We also need to go beyond GDP and focus on the well-being and happiness. I will now use this framework to assess Poland's recent track-record.

4.3. Poland's Economic Performance Since 1989

In 1989, Poland was one of the poorest countries in Europe: an average Pole earned less than $50 a month or less than one-tenth of an average German income (Gomułka, 2016). Even adjusted for the much lower level of prices in Poland, Poles' purchasing power was less than one-third of that in Germany.

---

[11] For the background papers, see Stevenson and Wolfers (2013); Easterlin (1974); Deaton (2008); Frey and Stutzer (2002); Kahneman and Deaton (2010); see also Inglehart and Welzel (2005); Helliwell, Layard, and Sachs (2017).

Poles were poorer than an average citizen of Gabon, Ukraine, or Suriname.[12] Poland's income lagged behind even its communist peers: its GDP per capita amounted to only half of the level of income in Czechoslovakia.

On the inauguration of the new Solidarity-led democratic government in August 1989, the economy was undergoing what could be described as an economic cardiac arrest. Despite earlier attempts at reforms undertaken by the communist government during the 1980s (Bąk, 2009), Poland was the only country in the Soviet camp that went bankrupt. It was also the only country in the Soviet camp that experienced rampant inflation, exceeding 260 per cent in 1989 and more than 400 per cent in 1990. Finally, it was the only country in the Soviet camp that faced such prevalent shortages of even the most basic consumer products: at some point in 1988–1989, stores carried only bread, milk, and vinegar. Poles needed coupons to buy even the most basic foodstuffs (Figure 4.8).

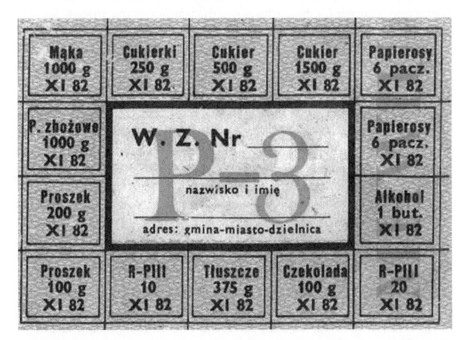

Figure 4.8. Shortages in communist Poland: 1982 coupons for flour, sugar, cigarettes, alcohol, chocolate, fat, washing powder, and wheat products.

Source: Open Source Access; from: https://commons.wikimedia.org/wiki/File:Kartka_P3_11-83.jpeg.

---

[12] World Development Indicators, GDP per capita, PPP (constant 2011 international $), https://data.worldbank.org/indicator/NY.GDP.PCAP.PP.KD, accessed 20 August 2017.

Polish industry was outdated and inefficient, managing to export only around $16 billion worth of raw materials, steel, coal, and ships, mostly to other Soviet camp countries (for comparison, in 2016 Polish exports amounted to almost $250 billion). The largely subsistence agriculture employed a quarter of the workforce. Its industry was one of the least competitive and most environmentally unfriendly even among the communist peers. And it had one of the worst infrastructures in the region, with less than 200 kilometres of old, mostly post-German highways for a country in the middle of Europe with 38 million people.

In 1989, most experts expected Hungary, which had reformed the most before 1989, as well as Czechoslovakia and East Germany, which had the strongest industry and the lowest macroeconomic instability, to do well during the transition. Slovenia, the richest communist country, was also expected to thrive. No one expected Poland to do so (Blanchard, 2010).

Yet, twenty-five years later it is Poland that has become the unrivalled leader of transition and Europe's and the world's growth champion. Since the beginning of post-communist transition in 1989, Poland's economy has grown more than in any other country in Europe. Poland's GDP per capita increased almost two-and-a-half times, beating all other post-communist states as well as the euro-zone (see Figure 4.9). The runner-ups, Slovakia and Estonia, lagged much behind. In PPP terms, Poland's GDP increased by almost three times, to almost $27,000 in 2017, placing Poland firmly among high-income countries.

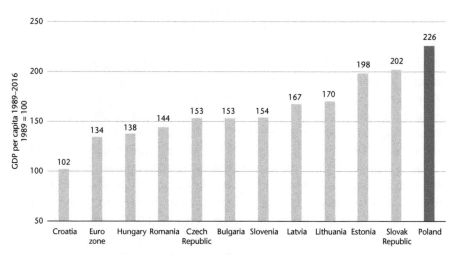

Figure 4.9. Changes in real GDP per capita, 1989=100.
Source: Author's own based on the Conference Board TED.

127

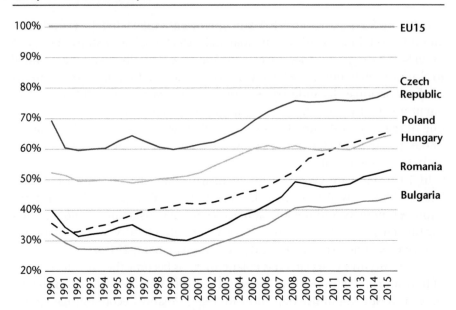

Figure 4.10. Changes in GDP per capita, PPP, 1990–2015, EU-15=100.
Source: Author's own based on IMF WEO.

As a result of fast growth, Poland's level of income relative to Western Europe increased from less than one-third of the average level of income in the EU-15 to 65 per cent in 2015 (Figure 4.10). Poland was the fastest converging economy in Europe in that period. Interestingly, it also beat East Germany, which despite more than a trillion dollars of subsidies received from West Germany after the unification in 1990, improved its income relative to the West by much less than Poland did.[13]

Poland's relative distance to the West in terms of income has never been shorter. Throughout the last 600 years, Poland has always lagged behind the West by a significant margin. Polish level of income per capita stagnated at around half of the level of income in the West, even during the mythical 'Golden Age' in the sixteenth century (Figure 4.11). It is only after 1989 when Poland truly converged on the West. In 2015, GDP per capita relative to the West equalled the highest level of GDP per capita reached in 1910. In 2016, it exceeded it. The country has begun its true Golden Age (Piatkowski, 2013).

The gap in income relative to the West is actually even smaller when adjusted for the availability of free public services, such as health and education. Thanks to a relatively large welfare state, in 2016 Poland's 'actual individual consumption' (AIC) amounted to 70 per cent of the euro zone, above

---

[13] In 2014, East Germany's GDP per capita PPP amounted to about 80 per cent of the level of income of the ten leading Western countries, up from around 75 per cent in 1989; in Poland, it grew from around 37 per cent in 1989 to 60 per cent in 2014 (Darvas, 2015).

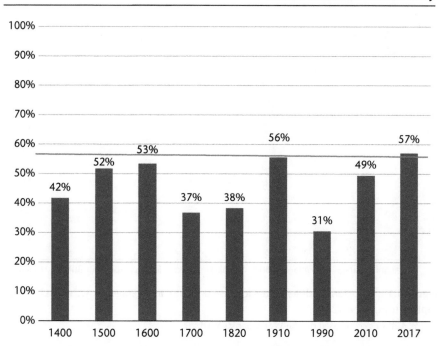

Figure 4.11. Poland's income relative to Western Europe, 1400–2017, PPP.

Note: Malinowski and van Zanden (2015) for years 1400–1820, Western Europe calculated as unweighted average for the UK, the Netherlands, Northern Italy, and Germany. Bukowski *et al.* (2017) for 1910; Bolt and van Zanden (2014) for 1990–2010; own projections for 2017.

Source: Author's own based on sources listed in the Note.

65 per cent based on income per capita (PPP) alone.[14] Poland's distance to the West has never been closer.[15]

4.3.1. *World Growth Champion*

Poland did well in the global perspective too. Its average GDP per capita growth calculated since 1995, when the post-communist statistical offices adopted new international statistical standards and started to fully account for the growth of the private sector, was among the highest in the world, behind Estonia, Latvia, and Lithuania, and the highest among large middle-income and high-income

[14] For definition of actual individual consumption, please refer to http://ec.europa.eu/ eurostat/statistics-explained/index.php/Glossary:Actual_individual_consumption_(AIC). For current data, see http://ec.europa.eu/eurostat/documents/2995521/7489718/2-15062016-BP-EN.pdf/ 28dcdd85-11ec-49c5-9410-0376bea53913.

[15] There is a discrepancy in the level of Poland's income relative to Western Europe depending on the source of data and the used set of fixed prices. Poland's income according to Bolt and van Zanden (2014) based on 1990 prices is lower (57 per cent of the West when extrapolated to 2017) than Eurostat's most current estimates (65 per cent of the euro zone-18 in 2016). I use the first source to keep historical data comparable, which are calculated with the same set of prices.

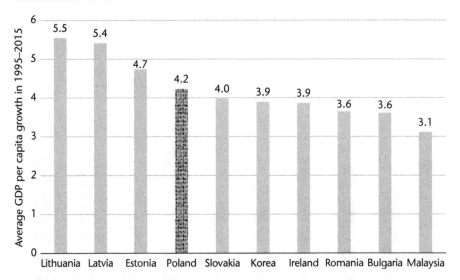

Figure 4.12. Top ten middle/high-income countries in average growth in GDP per capita during 1995–2015.

Source: Author's own based on the World Bank's WDI.

economies (Figure 4.12). Poland has grown faster than all the Asian Tigers, including Korea and Singapore, faster than Malaysia, a fast-growing emerging market, and faster than Ireland, the 'Celtic Tiger'.

Poland, next to Slovakia, also achieved high-income status the fastest among global peers, just behind the previous record of South Korea. After crossing the upper middle-income threshold of $10,000, as defined by the World Bank, it took just fifteen years to achieve high-income status. It rushed through the so-called 'middle-income trap', a concept according to which it is difficult for middle-income economies to break to the ranks of the most developed countries.[16] In the post-war period, only a handful of countries made it to the rich world: Japan, Singapore, Taiwan, South Korea, and more recently all post-communist new EU member states (although in 2017 Bulgaria and Romania were still a bit away from crossing the high-income threshold). But with the exception of South Korea and Slovakia, they all did it at a slower pace than Poland.

---

[16] Gill and Kharas (2007) came up with the idea of a 'middle-income trap'. Following their publication, which attracted much interest, especially from the media, a vigorous academic debate started on whether the trap truly existed. The detractors argue that if the middle-income trap existed, more and more countries would be trapped in it. Yet, the number of middle-income countries has not changed in recent decades. My view is that the middle-income trap does not exist, but the concept is useful as it helps concentrate minds on the reforms needed for middle-income countries to continue to converge. The authors themselves admit that the concept is open to debate. They also argue that a new theory is needed to explain what middle-income countries can do to become high-income (Gill and Kharas, 2015). This book provides one of such possible new theories.

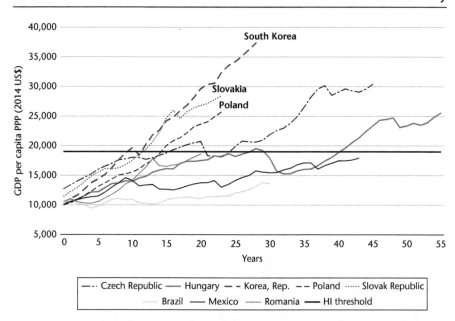

Figure 4.13. Time needed to cross the high-income threshold after reaching the upper middle-income threshold, in years.

Note: X-axis: time in years from when the economy crossed the upper middle-inome threshold, as defined by the World Bank.

Source: Author's own based on World Bank (2017a).

Poland's growth has also been less volatile than in other countries: since it joined the upper middle-income group in late 1990s, the standard deviation of growth has been much lower than among the European and global peers. Only Hungary experienced a more stable, albeit slower growth (Figure 4.14). Lower volatility is good for growth, as it reduces the risk premium for investment. More generally, there is evidence that countries that become high income enjoy a more stable growth than others. In particular, they almost never experience deep economic crises (Piatkowski, 2009; Balcerowicz and Rzońca, 2010). In other words, less volatile, even if slower growth, is more likely to produce better long-term results than high, but volatile growth, with intermittent periods of fast growth and crises.

Poland is close to beating the world in the persistence of economic growth: it has grown without interruption from 1992 until 2017, twenty-five years in a row, beating the historical records of South Korea, Singapore, and Japan. It has also equalled the Netherlands' record of twenty-five years of uninterrupted growth between 1983 and 2008 and is projected to beat it in 2018. Among middle- and high-income countries, only Australia, whose economy has been continuously expanding since 1992 until the present, can match Poland's growth record (although Australia grew at a slower rate in that period) (Figure 4.15).

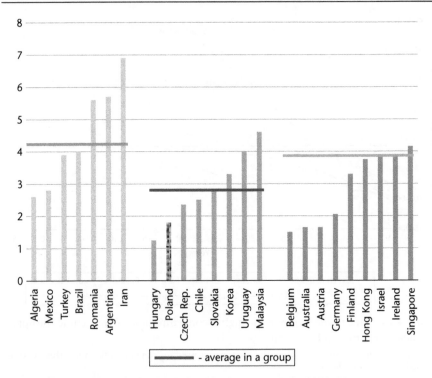

Figure 4.14. Growth volatility in Poland and among peers, 2000–2014.

Note: GDP growth standard deviation when a country was upper middle-income. Period: year of joining the high-income or upper-middle income group until 2014.

Source: Author's own based on World Bank (2017a).

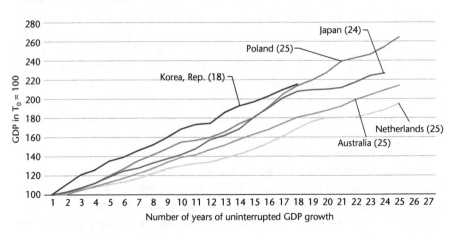

Figure 4.15. Duration of growth spurts and change in GDP for middle-income and high-income countries.

Note: Change in GDP since a country started growing until a first recession.

Source: Author's own based on the World Bank WDI.

4.3.2. Growth in Productivity

As discussed earlier, it matters whether growth has been based on long working hours or on fast improvement in productivity. For Poland, although the working hours are still much higher than in the West, most growth has been driven by progress in productivity. Since 1995, Poland's productivity per hour worked has grown faster than in all other regional peers except for Romania (Figure 4.16).

Fast growth in productivity has been largely driven by reallocation of resources from the low productivity sectors—share of agriculture in employment declined from almost 30 per cent in 1990 to around 11 per cent in 2016—to the higher-productivity manufacturing and service sector (World Bank, 2017a). Productivity has also been driven by improved within-firm productivity owing to enhanced skills, improved management practices, and technological catch-up (Albinowski *et al.*, 2016). FDI inflows in particular played a big role in increasing productivity: they established new, high productivity companies and positively affected performance of domestically owned companies.

Productivity growth has also been helped by the large manufacturing sector, which has much higher productivity growth rates than other sectors of the economy (Rodrik, 2013). Thanks to the geographical proximity to Germany, high quality of human capital, and low labour costs, Poland has become a Central European manufacturing hub and one of the key actors in the European value chains (Stöllinger, 2016). The share of manufacturing in

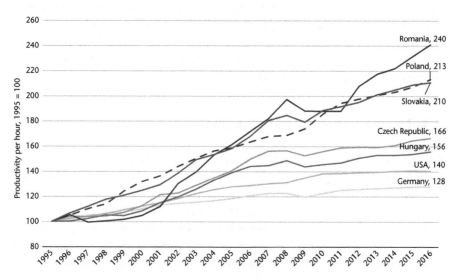

Figure 4.16. Changes in productivity per hour, 1995–2015, 1995=100.
Source: Author's own based on the Conference Board Total Economy Database.

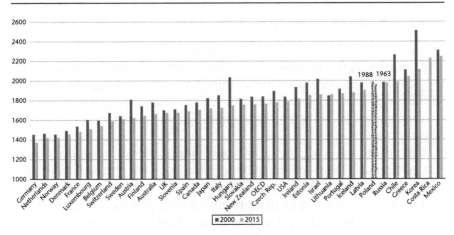

Figure 4.17. Hours worked in OECD countries, 2000 and 2015.
Source: Author's own based on OECD database.

GDP has increased since 2000, bucking the trends in most other EU and OECD countries.[17]

4.3.3. *Long Working Hours*

Poland combined fast growth in productivity with long working hours. In 2000, an average Pole worked almost 2,000 hours per year. In 2015, the working time has hardly changed, amounting to 1,963 hours per year, one of the highest ratios among high-income countries (although Greeks worked even more than Poles did, apparently). Poles worked about 300 hours more per year than the average in Western Europe and an astonishing almost 600 hours more than in Germany (Figure 4.17). Poles were one of the most hard-working nations in the developed world.

4.4. Uniqueness of Poland's Success

Poland has achieved its remarkable economic success despite the odds. First, unlike many other countries who have become rich because of oil, gas, and other natural resources, Poland has few natural resources. It is a net energy importer, which imports almost 100 per cent of its oil and more than 40 per cent of its natural gas. It has no other major natural resources, except for copper, which however represents only a negligible share in total exports. It also has coal, but this is more of a burden than a benefit, as it is loss making

[17] Based on: http://data.worldbank.org/indicator/NV.IND.MANF.ZS/. Accessed 15 June 2017.

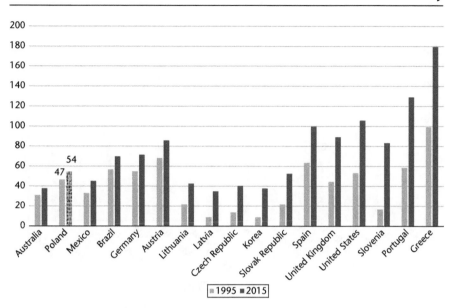

Figure 4.18. Public debt in per cent of GDP, 1995 and 2015.

and has cost the Polish taxpayer more than 150 billion zloty (or more than $40 billion) since 1990 in subsidies and negative spillovers on infrastructure and the environment (Bukowski and Śniegocki, 2014).

Second, Poland's growth has not been artificially enhanced by increase in debt. In 2015, Poland's public debt amounted to about 54 per cent of GDP and was lower than the EU average (Figure 4.18). Private debt was even lower: in 2016, the Polish household and corporate sector was among the least leveraged among all peer economies, both middle- and high-income (Figure 4.19). Poland's overall debt also has been more slow-growing in the past two decades than elsewhere. Debt steroids have not fuelled Poland's success.

Third, unlike the Asian Tigers and many other emerging markets, Poland's success has not been driven by the rise of China: more than 80 per cent of its exports have been directed towards the slow-growing EU markets rather than the fast-growing markets in Asia. In 2014, Poland's direct exports to China represented only 1.2 per cent of total exports, compared with a whopping 24 per cent for South Korea.[18] Despite this apparent geographical handicap, Poland's exports since 1989 have nonetheless increased more than 15-fold, from $16.5 billion in 1989 to almost $260 billion in 2016, exceeding the growth rate in any other large country in Europe as well as in South Korea and among other emerging markets (Figure 4.20). Poland's share in global exports tripled from 0.4 per cent in 1990 to 1.2 per cent in 2016 (World Bank, 2017a).

---

[18] http://atlas.media.mit.edu/en/visualize/tree_map/hs92/export/pol/show/all/2014/.

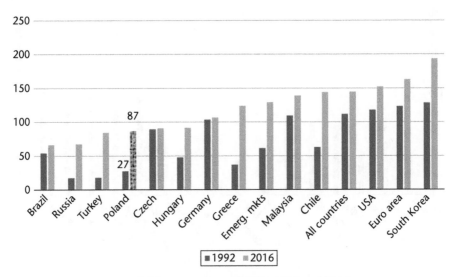

Figure 4.19. Private total debt, in per cent of GDP, 1992 and 2016.

Note: Private debt defined by BIS as private non-financial sector, all sectors. Emerging markets: data for 1996; Brazil: data for 31 March 1996; Russia: data for 1995; euro area: data for 31 March 1999.

Source: Author's own based on IMF and BIS.

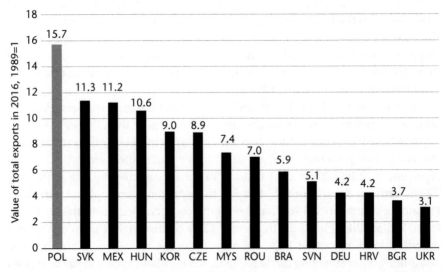

Figure 4.20. Exports of good, services and primary income in 2016, in current US$, 1989 or the earliest available year=1.

Source: Author's own based on the World Bank's World Development Indicators.

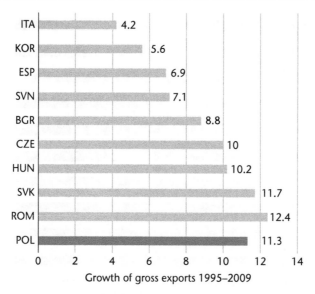

Figure 4.21. Growth of domestic value added embodied in gross exports, 1995–2009 (CAGR).

Source: World Bank (2015) using OECD-WTO TiVA data.

However, gross export numbers could be misleading because they hide the fact that value added in exports can be produced elsewhere than by the final exporter (for instance, a Volkswagen assembled in Slovakia increases its gross exports by the whole value of the car, even though most value added is produced in Germany). The domestic value added embodied in gross exports in Poland during 1995–2009 increased at a faster rate than among most regional and global peers (Figure 4.21). This was the case even though the slow-growing EU markets represented 72 per cent of final demand for Polish value added embodied in exports, while East Asia represented only 4 per cent (Figure 4.22).

Finally, and most importantly, Poland achieved success despite being a vibrant, young democracy, with seventeen different governments wielding power since 1989. While there is no consensus on whether democracy is good for growth or not,[19] among countries that have joined the ranks of rich countries after 1945, only Japan (although it was ruled by just one party for most of its post-1945 history), Ireland, Italy, and (after 1989) a few fellow countries in CEE (Slovenia, Czech Republic, Slovakia, and Hungary) have been consistently and robustly democratic. Most other success stories in Asia

---

[19] An informative survey of literature about a link between democracy and growth concludes that 'the net effect of democracy on growth performance cross-nationally over the last five decades is negative or null' (http://blogs.bu.edu/jgerring/files/2013/06/DemogrowthWorldPol.pdf). See also Barro (1996) for a similar view. However, a more recent paper by Acemoglu *et al.* (2014) argues that there is a link between democracy and growth.

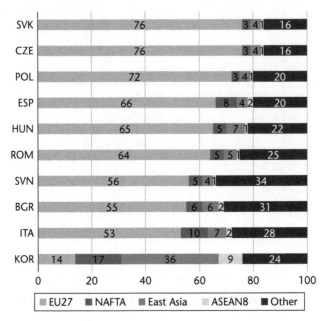

Figure 4.22. Final demand for Polish value added embodied in gross exports by destination (per cent), 2009.

Source: World Bank (2015) using OECD-WTO TiVA data.

and Southern Europe had a chequered history: there has been either little democracy (Singapore) or a significant part of catching up happened under dictatorships (Taiwan and South Korea until the late 1980s, Spain, Greece, or Portugal until the 1970s). Poland proved that a robust democracy, an important value in itself, does not make it impossible to achieve economic success. To the contrary, if done right, it is a key driver of prosperity.

4.5. Poland's Inclusive Growth

Poland's growth story since 1989 is also unique because it was the only large and democratic country among all post-communist economies, where economic growth benefited all households: during 1989–2015, the incomes of 100 per cent of society grew faster than incomes in the richest G-7 countries (Figure 4.23). In contrast, in the vast majority of other post-communist countries, large parts of the society failed to converge. According to EBRD, even in Estonia, which next to Poland is often referred to as another post-communist growth champion, incomes of more than half of the population grew slower since 1989 than in the West. In Hungary, income of the whole population has apparently grown at a lower rate than in G-7

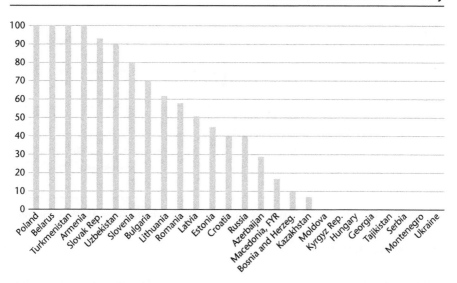

Figure 4.23. Percentage of population with a higher growth in income than the G-7 average, by deciles, 1989–2016.

Source: Author's own based on EBRD (2016a).

countries.[20] In general, a remarkable 56 per cent of the population in all post-communist countries experienced a slower growth in income than the average for G7 countries (EBRD, 2016a). Contrary to initial expectations, transition failed to improve the (relative) lot of millions of people. Poland was an exception.

Poland's growth has lifted all boats, but not by the same amount, however. Since 1989, the richest 10 per cent of Poles increased their incomes by about 135 per cent, while the average income increased by 100 per cent (Figure 4.24). However, the bottom 10 per cent of poor Poles augmented their incomes by only 40 per cent and incomes of about 70 per cent of Poles grew slower than the country's average, suggesting that growth could have been shared better.[21] Nonetheless, Poland still did better than others. For instance, average incomes

[20] The data on incomes during the transition, however, must be treated with caution. Data for the early transition period are patchy and not fully compatible with later series; often guess estimates must be made. More importantly, the data on incomes alone do not account for the overall large increase in social well-being, including personal freedom, democracy, ability to travel abroad, or access to global technology and knowledge.

[21] The EBRD data based on household surveys are different from data from national accounts, which show that Poland's real GDP per capita increased by almost 2.5 times since 1989, as discussed earlier in this chapter.

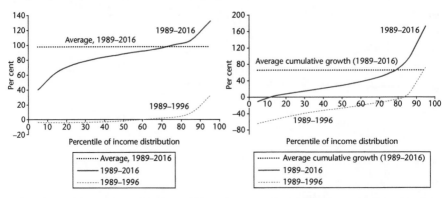

Figure 4.24. Poland versus Russia: cumulative income growth since 1989 by income decile, 1989–2016.

Source: Based on EBRD (2016a).

in Russia increased by about three-quarters since 1989, but incomes of the richest 10 per cent increased by almost 180 per cent, much more than in Poland. In addition, incomes of the poorest 10 per cent in Russia declined.

Growth in Poland has been inclusive throughout the whole post-1989 period. Data for 1999–2013 show that the median household disposable income increased in Poland by 39 per cent, while in the Czech Republic or Hungary the median incomes increased by 34 per cent and 20 per cent, respectively. However, in Germany and the USA, median incomes stagnated (Figure 4.25).

4.5.1. *Impact on Poverty and Inequality*

Poland's inclusive growth helped keep inequality low. While inequality, reflected in the Gini coefficient, increased from 27 in 1989–1990 to about 30 in 2015, the increase was smaller than among most other transition economies. The level of inequality was also much lower than among global peers such as Mexico or Brazil (Figure 4.26). Policy changes introduced in 2016—a child cash transfer, more progressive taxation, and a higher minimum wage—are likely to reduce the level of inequality further (World Bank, 2017a). Wealth inequality is also lower than in most countries in Europe, amounting to 0.59 Gini (Figure 4.26). This is largely because of the legacy of communist egalitarianism, but also partly because most Poles own their homes (76 per cent relative to less than half in Germany), which helped them benefit from an increase in real estate prices (NBP, 2015; World Bank, 2017b).

At the same time, relative poverty declined to 3.3 per cent in 2015, the lowest level in the post-1989 period, and a level not much different from that in Western Europe (Czapinski *et al.*, 2015). The new child cash transfer program initiated in 2016—a $130 monthly cash payment to the second and each

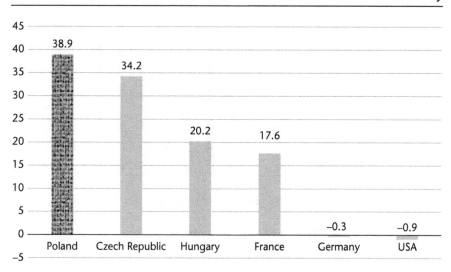

Figure 4.25. Change in median household disposable income, adjusted for price differences between countries (PPP), 1999–2015.

Note: LIS counts after-tax cash income from salaries, interest, and stock dividends, and direct government benefits such as tax credits. Czech Republic: 2002–2010, Poland: 1999–2010, Hungary 1999–2012, USA, France, Germany: 2000–2010.

Source: Author's own based on Roser, Thewissen, and Nolan (2016).

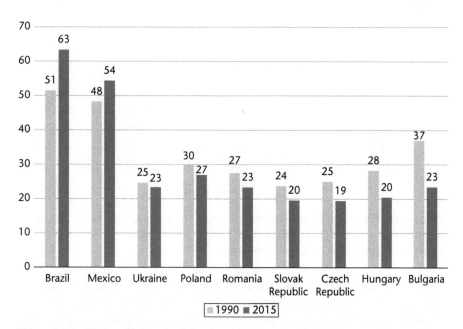

Figure 4.26. Gini coefficient for Poland and European and global peers, 1990 and 2015.
Source: Author's own based on the World Bank's World Development Indicators.

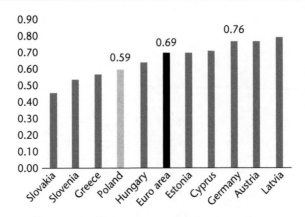

Figure 4.27. Gini of wealth inequality.
Source: NBP (2015).

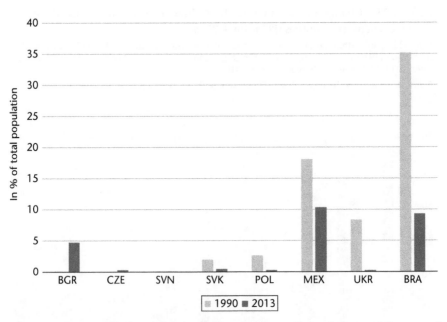

Figure 4.28. Poverty in Poland and among peers, share of population with income of less than \$3.1 a day, 1990 and 2013.
Source: Author's own based on the World Bank Database.

consecutive child in families with at least two children (and to all children in poor families)—will reduce that ratio further. Looking more globally, the share of Polish population living in extreme poverty, or on an income of less than \$3.1 a day, which was never high to start with because of the strong welfare state under communism, declined to zero in 2013 (Figure 4.28).

4.6. Drivers of Inclusive Growth

Inclusive growth in Poland has been driven mainly by a broad-based access to high-quality education, increasing employment, and broadly efficient public redistributive policies, including a relatively high minimum wage. High social mobility and egalitarian culture also played a role.

First, Poland experienced a remarkable educational boom after 1989. While primary enrolment ratio was already universal before 1989, secondary enrolment increased from 80 per cent to close to 100 per cent. At the same time, tertiary gross enrolment ratio increased from 20 per cent in 1989 to more than 70 per cent in 2015, among the highest levels in OECD countries, next to South Korea (Figure 4.29). At the same time, the share of the labour force with a university degree has more than tripled from 10 per cent in 1989 to 31 per cent in 2014.

The quality of education also improved substantially, especially in primary and secondary schools. According to the OECD PISA ranking of functional literacy of fifteen-year-olds (based on tests in science, maths, and reading), covering 540,000 pupils in seventy-two countries, Poland's quality of

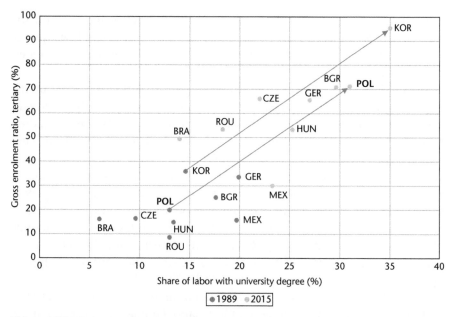

Figure 4.29. Gross enrolment ratio, tertiary, both sexes (per cent) and share of labour with university degree, 1989 and 2015.

Note: Total enrolment in tertiary education, regardless of age, expressed as a percentage of the total population of the five-year age group following on from secondary school leaving.

Source: Author's own based on the World Bank's World Development Indicators.

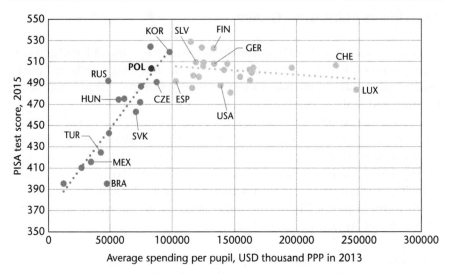

Figure 4.30. OECD PISA 2015 score and spending per pupil.

Note: PISA test score represents average from mathematics, science, and reading.

Source: Author's own based on the OECD PISA database.

education is much higher than suggested by its level of income and the amount of spending on education (Figure 4.30). Despite much lower public investment, young Poles are better educated than young French, Swedes, or Americans.

Poland does especially well on social equity in education measured by the extent to which parents' social and economic status affects the children's school performance. In 2015, the gap in science scores between children from the poorest 20 per cent of household and the richest 20 per cent amounted to about two years of schooling and—while far from ideal—was nonetheless lower than in most other EU member states. Also, the number of kids without basic skills was lower than the EU average (Figure 4.31).[22] Looking globally, Poland also scored well on the proportion of 'resilient students'— students that are in the bottom 25 per cent of the index of socio-economic status, but perform in the top 25 per cent of peers with the same socio-economic background globally—where more than 30 per cent of Polish poor students have top scores in education (OECD, 2016a). It also had the smallest regional differences in educational attainment among peers (OECD, 2016e). OECD (2016b, p. 225) concludes that in Poland 'families can expect that, no

---

[22] The PISA index of social, economic, and cultural status (ESCS) 'places students on the same scale and allow a comparison of performance of student groups from similar socio-economic contexts across countries and economies'. (OECD 2016b, p. 218)

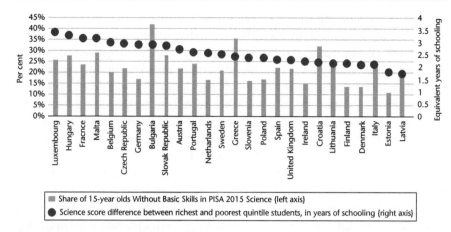

Figure 4.31. A gap in cognitive skills between rich and poor students in the European Union.

Source: Bodewig and Gortazar (2016).

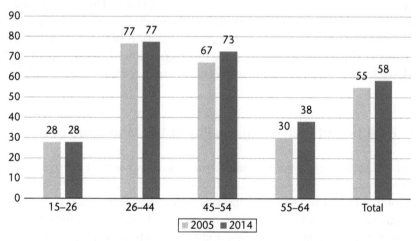

Figure 4.32. Employment rates in Poland for different ages, 2005 and 2014.

Source: Author's own based on Myck and Najsztub (2016).

matter which school their children attend, they are likely to achieve high levels'.

Second, inclusive growth has also been driven by increasing employment, especially among the lower-skilled older generation. Since 2005, owing to rising demand for labour, improving skills, more flexible employment rules, and reduced access to early retirement, the employment rate increased from 67.2 to 72.5 per cent for Poles aged 44–54 and from 30.0 to 37.9 per cent for Poles older than 55 (Figure 4.32).

145

Third, public policy also helped keep growth inclusive. While taxes are only mildly progressive, social transfers helped redistribute income to the poorest households (World Bank, 2017a). Public policy was largely pro-social even in the early 1990s, in the throes of the post-communist transition. In addition, free public services, especially health and education, also played an important role. Finally, legislation on minimum wages helped by providing a floor for the lowest incomes. Nominal minimum wage was raised from about 40 per cent of the median wage in 2005 to almost 50 per cent in 2016, above the average for OECD countries (World Bank, 2017b).

Fourth, social mobility has been high. A series of large sociological surveys on more than 30,000 respondents conducted during 2011–2015 found that more than 40 per cent of households from the bottom 20 per cent of households moved to higher group levels, while 40 per cent of households in the top 20 per cent moved down to lower income levels (Czapinski *et al.*, 2015). These are higher social mobility rates than in America, for instance (Jerrim and Macmillan, 2015).

Finally, growth has been kept inclusive owing to an egalitarian culture, which does not accept excessive disparities in income. The average salaries of CEOs of Polish banks, both foreign and domestically owned, amounted to below one million dollars per year in 2016, a fraction of the incomes of their peers in the USA or in Western Europe (even after adjusting for differences in bank size).[23] Management salaries in other industries were similarly subdued.

4.7. Evolution of Well-Being, Quality of Life, and Happiness

Rapid and inclusive growth has helped increase the quality of life in Poland to the highest levels on record and to a higher level than expected based on the level of income. In the OECD Better Life Index, one of the most comprehensive measures of countries' well-being, Poland is in twenty-seventh place among thirty-five OECD countries, above its position based on the level of income per capita. Relative to the OECD average, Poland excels in personal security, education, and work–life balance. It lags in income, subjective well-being (happiness), and housing (size of apartments) (Figure 4.33).

According to another index of well-being—the Social Progress Index, which measures how countries are performing in meeting social, economic, and environmental needs of their societies—Poland also 'punched above its weight': its position in the index is higher than its relative income

---

[23] http://samcik.blox.pl/2017/03/45000-zl-dziennie-Tyle-zarabia-najdrozszy-prezes.html, accessed 10 June 2017.

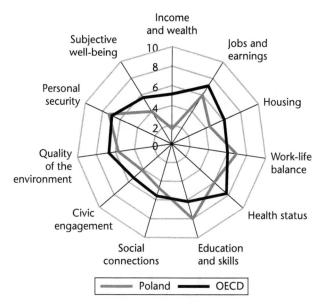

Figure 4.33. Well-being in Poland versus the OECD average, 2015.
Source: OECD (2016f).

(Figure 4.34).[24] Poland 'squeezed' as much well-being from its GDP as, for instance, much richer South Korea or Israel. These findings are confirmed by BCG's 'Sustainable Economic Development Assessment (SEDA)', which, similarly, shows that Poland's quality of life is much higher than expected. In 2015, Poland was the best performing economy in the world in converting its growth in income into improvements in well-being.[25] The results of all the rankings imply that the gap in the quality of life between Poland and the West is actually smaller than that suggested by the difference in income levels alone. Poles' quality of life is likely closer to three-quarters of Western Europe than two-thirds based on income alone.

One of the reasons for the much increased level of well-being is a dramatic improvement in the quality of the environment. Communism was one of the most environmentally destructive economic systems ever developed. Artificially low energy prices, lack of incentives for technological progress, primacy of growth at whatever price, and blocked channels for public dissatisfaction made Poland and other Soviet camp countries the paragons of environmental disaster. In 1980, the amount of energy needed to produce one unit of output and the corresponding pollution was almost eight times higher in CEE than in

---

[24] http://www.socialprogressimperative.org/global-index/, accessed 11 June 2017.
[25] https://www.bcgperspectives.com/Images/BCG-The-Private-Sector-Opportunity-to-Improve-Well-Being-Jul-2016.pdf, accessed 26 March 2017.

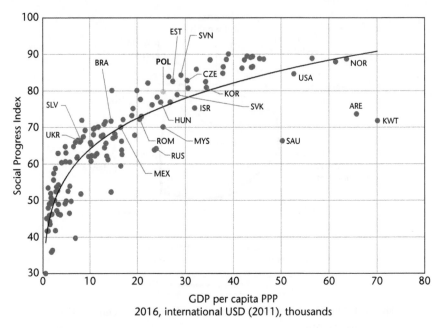

Figure 4.34. Social Progress Index versus level of income, PPP, 2016.
Source: Author's own based on the Social Progress Imperative database and IMF WEO.

Western Europe (Berend, 2009, p. 21). In Poland's industrialized region of Silesia, the concentration of benzopyrenet in the air was ten times higher than in the West, leading to respiratory diseases and premature death (Berend, 2009). The transition saved the environment. Energy intensity, a ratio of energy consumption to GDP, in Poland and among its regional peers declined at a globally unprecedented pace, from 12,910 Btu per dollar in 1990 to just 6,000 Btu in 2011, only 20 per cent higher than in Germany (Figure 4.35). For comparison, in Russia the energy intensity was two and half times higher.[26] The much improved structure of the economy has resulted in Poland's growth becoming decoupled from CO_2 emissions (Figure 4.36). It was exactly the opposite twenty-five years ago.

4.7.1. *Quality of Life*

The improved quality of the environment has helped to enhance the well-being of the population and further bridge the gap to Western Europe in terms of quality of life. The gap is even shorter if we consider that, thanks to the

[26] https://knoema.com/atlas/Poland/Energy-intensity?compareTo=CZ,HU,DE,SK,RU, accessed 15 June 2017.

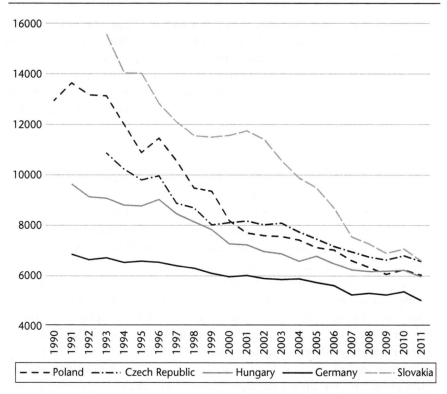

Figure 4.35. Energy intensity calculated in constant prices of 2010 (Btu per US dollar).
Source: Author's own based on Knoema database.

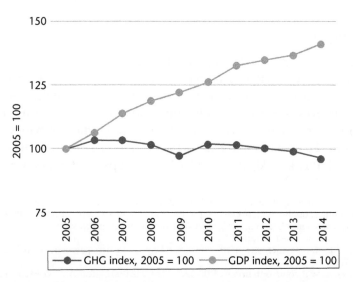

Figure 4.36. Economic and GHG emissions in Poland, 2005–2014.
Source: World Bank (2017b).

internet and open borders, Poles now enjoy almost the same access to global technology, culture, and entertainment as an average German, Frenchman, or Spaniard. Poles use the same smartphones, watch the same movies, listen to the same music, download the same apps, and watch the same sports programmes. They drive smaller cars, live in smaller apartments, and have smaller incomes and savings, but their access to the global civilizational bounty is largely the same, even if GDP fails to measure it.[27]

In some ways, Poles have even leapfrogged the West. This is especially the case with modern technologies, in which Poland did not have any sunk costs so could move directly into frontier technologies. For instance, thanks to large investments in mobile telecommunications, Poles now enjoy better and cheaper access to mobile internet than in Western Europe.[28] They also use the most modern payment technologies: in 2015, Poland became Visa's largest market in Europe in contactless card payments.[29] Poles also use online banking more often than in Germany.[30]

Finally, Poland has also closed much of the gap to the West with respect to life expectancy and child mortality. In 2014, an average Polish man could expect to live almost seventy-four years, up from sixty-six years at the beginning of transition. At the same time, life expectancy of a Polish woman reached almost eighty-two years, up from seventy-one years in 1990. Despite an income almost twice as high as in Poland, an average German woman could expect to live only two years longer.[31] Poland's life expectancy also compares well globally (Figure 4.37). Statistics on infant mortality tell the same story (Figure 4.38).

4.7.2. Happiness

The ultimate objective of development is to make people happy. Poles are now happier than ever before, an amazing feat given Poles' tendency towards gloom and moroseness. In 2015, more than 80 per cent of Poles were satisfied with their lives, up from slightly above 50 per cent at the beginning of transition (Figure 4.39). This was the highest proportion of happy Poles on the record. Poles have never lived better, although few of them seem to recognize it (Piatkowski, 2013). Indeed, only 22 per cent of Poles are satisfied

---

[27] Coyle (2012) is right to argue that GDP severely underestimates the benefits of growth in consumer choice, quality enhancements, product safety, and aesthetics (think of iPhone).

[28] http://www.spiegel.de/netzwelt/gadgets/datentarife-in-der-eu-wo-mobiles-surfen-guenstig-ist-a-1122608.html, accessed 15 June 2017.

[29] https://letstalkpayments.com/10-countries-riding-contactless-payments-wave/, accessed 10 June 2017.

[30] https://www.ft.com/content/5e9c5f08-52c9-11e4-9221-00144feab7de, accessed 15 June 2017.

[31] http://ec.europa.eu/eurostat/statistics-explained/index.php/File:Life_expectancy_at_birth,_1980%E2%80%932014_(years)_YB16.png, accessed 22 March 2017.

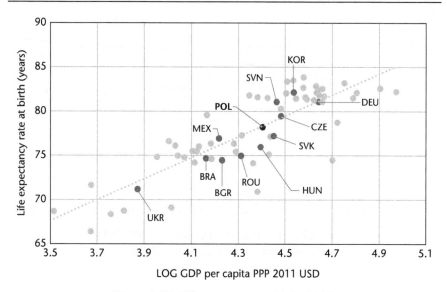

Figure 4.37. Life expectancy at birth, 2015.
Source: Author's own based on the World Bank database.

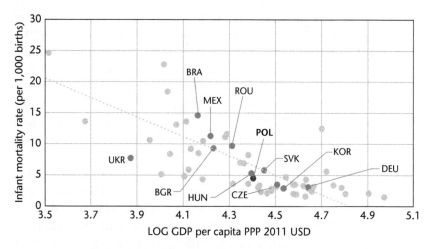

Figure 4.38. Infant mortality rate, 2015.
Source: Author's own based on the World Bank database.

with the country's situation, a somewhat schizophrenic view given the high level of happiness in their private lives.

Poland has also increased the happiness of its citizens (defined as life satisfaction) more than elsewhere in the region. In 2015, happiness of Poles was among the highest in post-communist countries and higher than suggested by its level of income. Almost 60 per cent of Poles expressed satisfaction

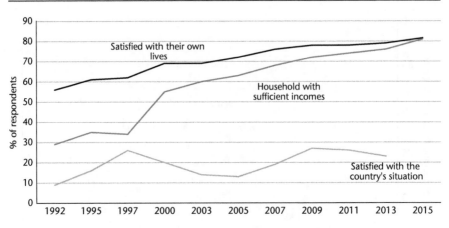

Figure 4.39. Life satisfaction in Poland, 1992–2015.
Source: Author's own based on Czapiński *et al.* (2015).

in life, more than in other post-communist countries except for the Czech Republic, Latvia, Slovenia, Estonia, and Kazakhstan (Figure 4.40).

The level of happiness of Poles is also not far behind that of Western Europe: 88 per cent of Swedes, 72 per cent of the French, and 71 per cent of the British were satisfied in life in 2010, not much higher than in Poland. EBRD (2016a) argues that the previous 'transition happiness gap'—the fact that happiness in Poland and other post-communist countries relative to the West was lower than suggested by the level of income—disappeared.[32] EBRD's Life in Transition survey (EBRD, 2016b) additionally compares Poland with Italy and Germany and finds that Poles are now more satisfied with life than Italians (58 per cent in Poland versus 42 per cent in Italy), although less so than in Germany (75 per cent).

That said, there is a large generational difference in the level of happiness: the older, post-communist generation is much less satisfied with life than the new generation. Only half of Poles sixty years and older are satisfied with life relative to more than two-thirds of young Poles aged eighteen to thirty-nine (EBRD, 2016b). The difference in life satisfaction is driven by educational attainment, income, and urbanization (all three are lower for the older generation). Income, in particular, plays a big role: among the bottom one-third of the poorest Poles only 28 per cent were satisfied with life in 2016 versus 75 per cent for the top one-third. Domestic surveys such as the one conducted by

---

[32] EBRD (2016a) argues that in post-communist countries the 'happiness gap' was previously driven by a perceived low quality of government, corruption, and high inequality. Improvements in these factors as well as increases in education, urbanization, and income helped eliminate the gap.

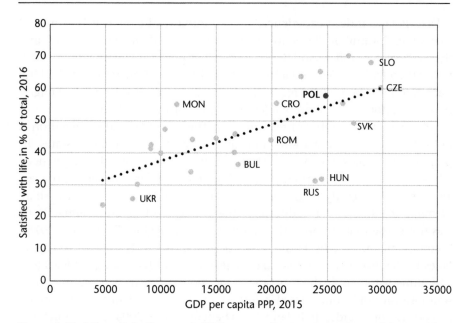

Figure 4.40. Life satisfaction and GDP per capita in post-communist countries, 2015–2016.

Note: The vertical axis shows the percentage of respondents who agree or strongly agree with the statement 'All things considered, I am satisfied with my life now'.

Source: Author's own based on EBRD (2016a).

Czapiński *et al.* (2015) confirm the findings of the cross-country studies. However, educational attainment, income, and urbanization on their own cannot fully explain the negative perception of the world among older Poles. Some other factors, such as the influence of communist experience, seem to play a role in lowering the level of happiness among the older generation. But this discrepancy will not last forever.

4.8. Failures of the Polish Transition

There are three common criticisms of the Polish transition. First, Poland experienced a large wave of emigration following the 2004 EU accession, which—as some people argue—undermines the perception of success. Second, Poland has built its success on excessively low wages and precarious labour contracts. Third and finally, it witnessed a dramatic fall in the fertility rate. The resulting demographic decline may thwart Poland's growth in the future. Let's take these three criticisms in turn.

First, Poland indeed experienced a large outflow of labour. It is estimated that about 2.4 million Poles now work abroad, mostly in the UK, Germany, the Netherlands, and Ireland (GUS, 2016). They produce somebody else's GDP rather than Polish GDP. Detractors of the Polish transition argue that had the transition been better managed, all these Poles would not have left. Emigration is therefore a reflection of a failure of the Polish transition.

I disagree, for a number of reasons. First, the size of Poland's emigration is not different from emigration from most other new EU member states. In proportion to its population, Estonia, Latvia, and Lithuania experienced a higher emigration rate than Poland despite a faster growth rate in the last 15 years and a slightly higher level of GDP per capita. In terms of the share of migrants with tertiary education, the structure of Poland's emigrations was not worse than among other countries in the region (Rhee *et al.*, 2016). Second, emigration reflects the basics of economics: it is difficult to expect Poles to stay home if they can take a cheap flight to London, get a legal job, and immediately triple their incomes. One thousand years of economic backwardness cannot be fully erased in just twenty-five years. Third, Poles working abroad are not a burden to Poland, but a benefit: during 2004–2013, emigrants remitted back home almost 42 billion euro or one-third of inflows of EU funds. In 2013 alone, Polish emigrants sent remittances worth more than 4 billion euro or 1.1 per cent of GDP. This supported economic growth and well-being (Chmielewska, 2015). Fourth, the wave of emigration did not undermine Poland's competitiveness—wage growth remained subdued after 2004 and there were no shortages of labour—suggesting that most emigrants would not have found a job back home.[33] Fifth, emigration is part and parcel of labour mobility that underpins the foundation of the European Union and its freedom of capital, good, service, and labour movements. It not only benefited the emigrating Poles, but also the host countries, in a classical win–win (Rhee *et al.*, 2016). Finally, if we look at the overall level of income and the quality of life of all Poles, not only those that live in Poland, emigration has boosted both and helped close the income gap for many relative to the West. In other words, we should not judge Poland only by the prosperity of its residents, but by the prosperity of all Poles, regardless of where they are located.[34]

---

[33] This was largely because the opening of the EU labour market to Polish emigration coincided with an arrival of a large demographic wave into the labour market—a demographic echo of an early evening curfew and electricity shut downs during the martial law in 1981–1982—which the labour market could not absorb.

[34] No one, for instance, would demand that Robert Lewandowski, the star striker of Bayern Munich, return to Poland to score goals there rather than in the Champions League and earn millions in return. The same applies for another Robert Lewandowski, who works in a good restaurant in London, enjoys his work, and earns much more than he would earn back home.

Of course, it would be ideal if all Poles stayed home and did not emigrate. But it is way too early to tell whether these Poles are 'lost' forever: with the rising incomes and quality of life in Poland, many of the Poles are likely to return. When they come back, emigrant Poles will bring back with them precious human, financial, networking, and cultural capital that will support the country's further catching up. If they had never left, Poland would likely have to pay them to leave to acquire Western skills. Rather than a bane, emigration could then turn out to be a big boon for Poland's future.

Second, it is true that much of Poland's success has been based on low wages. Growth in wages has been much slower than growth in productivity throughout most of the transition period. Since 2000 labour productivity increased by half, but labour income grew by only one-third (Word Bank, 2017a). In the same period, Poland's unit labour costs, which reflect changes in productivity and wage costs, declined precipitously, while those in Germany, in itself one of the most wage-stringent economies in the EU, increased (Figure 4.41). As a result, Poland's competitiveness boomed, but wages, consumption, and quality of life increased at a slower rate and the gap with the German wage level remained large (Figure 4.41).

Much of the slow growth in wages has been caused by a decline in labour unionization and increasing political power of capital, two factors that have been felt globally (Milanovic, 2016a). However, Poland also experienced an unprecedented rise in temporary employment contracts (so called 'junk contracts'). In 2014, more than a quarter of the working population in Poland was employed on temporary contracts. This was the largest share in the EU and the second largest among OECD countries, just behind Chile (Figure 4.42). Such a high use of temporary contracts increased job market uncertainty, weakened incentives for investment in skills, and likely slowed productivity growth. The increased flexibility, however, helped Poles survive the difficult times during 2003–2004, when unemployment hit 20 per cent, and then prosper

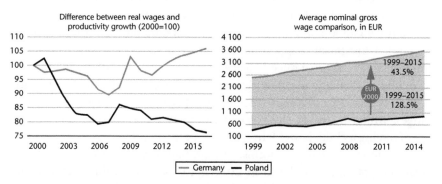

Figure 4.41. Wages and productivity in Poland and Germany, 2000–2015.
Source: World Bank (2017a).

155

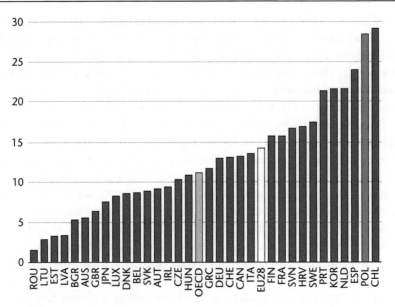

Figure 4.42. Temporary employment in OECD countries, 2014.

Note: Prime-wage workers (25–54 years old) as per cent of total employment.

Source: OECD (2016c).

during the global crisis in 2009. Nonetheless, 'junk contracts' are a clear failure of policies, which needs to be corrected (I discuss what needs to be done in Chapter 9).

Lastly, the success of Poland's transition has been marred by an unprecedented decline in fertility, which collapsed from the replacement rate of around 2.1 children per woman in 1989 to only 1.3 children in 2015, one of the lowest ratios in Europe and the world (World Bank, 2017a). The fall in fertility worsens the impending demographic decline, accelerates population ageing, and undermines Poland's chances to catch up with the West. It is not fully clear what drove the decline in fertility, but it is likely it has much to do with the increased uncertainty about jobs and the future (the rise of temporary contracts is one of the culprits), insufficient support from the state in the form of child care (under communism, Poland guaranteed a place in a crèche and a kindergarten to almost every child, particularly in cities; the system was largely dismantled in the early 1990s; only recently has it started to be re-built again) and—above all—cultural changes, which increased the perceived monetary and lifestyle opportunity costs of having a child. Lower fertility is one of the few downsides of importing Western values and cultural norms. The primary objective of the child cash transfer programme introduced in 2016 is to increase fertility, but it is not clear how large the impact could be. The government's own projections assume an increase in fertility rate to 1.6 children per woman within the next decade.

This would be welcome, but still far from the 2.1 replacement rate. To stem the demographic decline and continue to catch up with the West, Poland will thus need to open up to immigration, as discussed in Chapter 9.

4.9. Conclusions

There are small lies, big lies, and statistics, as Benjamin Disraeli, the UK's erstwhile prime minister once said. Indeed, there are a various ways of measuring economic performance. Looking at GDP growth alone can be misleading. It is because it ignores changes in incomes for different segments of the society, the rich and the poor. Without knowing who actually benefits from growth, we can hardly know whether our policies have worked well and what to do in the future. In the USA, for instance, despite fast growth in the overall GDP, in the last thirty years incomes of the majority of Americans have largely stagnated. Changes in median incomes should become the primary target of policy making, not GDP growth alone.

GDP also fails to show whether growth has been artificially supported by increase in debt, which—if it expands at an excessive pace—almost always ends up in a crisis. It also fails to inform whether growth has come at the expense of non-renewable resources or the quality of the environment. Finally, it does not show us whether growth has been driven by 'perspiration' (more working hours) or 'inspiration' (more productive working hours). The whole point of economic growth is to give people more leisure time, not more work time.

Finally, GDP is not made to measure changes in human well-being and happiness. It should not be criticized for it: it has not been designed to do so. But what we measure matters for policy. Well-being and happiness should become the key targets of policy-making. GDP growth has no meaning if it does not increase happiness. It is only a means to an end, not an end in itself.

Poland is an excellent example of a country that achieved unprecedented success in boosting GDP and using it to achieve the highest levels of well-being and happiness on the country's record. Despite a dramatic point of departure in 1989, when the country was bankrupt and in the throes of an economic crisis, in the subsequent twenty-five years Poland moved from being poor to high-income. After more than 400 years of (mostly) languishing at the European periphery, it has suddenly become Europe's and global growth champion (among countries with a similar level of income). This has never happened before.

In the process, Poland created an inclusive economy, where the benefits of economic growth have been shared with all citizens (even if to varying degrees). Poland is the only democratic country in the post-Soviet camp where the incomes of the whole society, including the poor, grew faster than in the West. Since 1989, real median incomes more than doubled, productivity skyrocketed, leisure time increased, and natural environment improved by leaps and bounds. All this together translated into high levels of well-being, which are higher than suggested by Poland's level of income. Rapid growth in incomes and improvement in well-being made Poles happy: more than 80 per cent of them are now satisfied with their lives, up from only half at the beginning of transition. Poland's true Golden Age has arrived.

This success was unusual because it has been achieved despite the odds: Poland's growth was not based on natural resources, debt growth steroids, or lucky positioning close to the booming markets in China and Asia. It also suffered from 'messy' democratic politics, which made the reform process difficult. Indeed, outside the West, there are only a few countries in the world that became high-income while being democratic throughout the whole catching up process.

That said, Poland suffered a number of failures during the transition. Wages increased slower than productivity, 'junk' labour contracts proliferated, and fertility declined to one of the lowest levels in the world. These are real failures that need to be corrected for Poland to continue to grow at a fast pace and fully catch-up with the West.

In addition, more than 2 million Poles emigrated, although—unlike the negative view of the detractors—this was largely inevitable. After long centuries of economic underdevelopment, twenty-five years of economic success cannot fully erase the yawning gap in wages between Poland and the West. No amount of patriotism could have kept Poles at home if they could multiply their income by simply hopping across the border to Germany or taking a low-cost flight to Dublin. What matters though is what happens next: will these Poles ever come back?

Much will depend on the policies that Poland adopts in the future. These will follow the policies that made Poland's remarkable success in the last twenty-five years possible. This is what I turn to next.

5

Drivers of Poland's Successful Transition

We are pioneers. We are venturing along the tracks that nobody else before us followed. The transition from capitalism to communism is easy, one decree on nationalization solves the problem. However, the transition from communism to capitalism is a totally different matter. It is easy to make fish soup from the aquarium with living goldfish, but just imagine what challenge it is to try to make the aquarium with living goldfish out of the fish soup. And this is precisely what we are trying to do.

Lech Wałęsa

Bitter medicine is easier to take in one dose than in a prolonged series of doses.

Leszek Balcerowicz

Poland's transformation can be seen as a success, but only to the extent of achieving two-thirds of its potential.

Grzegorz W. Kolodko

Why did Poland succeed during the last twenty-five years for the first time in its history? What were the main drivers of growth? What was different from other countries? What went right and what went wrong?

In this chapter I explain the proximate sources of Poland's unprecedented success since 1989, including the importance of initial conditions, transition policies, and the impact of EU funds. I start by dividing the transition into two periods: the initial period of 'shock therapy' during 1989–1991 and then the second period of economic recovery after 1992. I first discuss the ongoing debate on the 'shock therapy' versus 'gradual' approach to post-communist transition. I use the example of Poland's 'shock therapy' to analyze the pros and cons of both approaches. I conclude that the differences in actual policies were much smaller than the rhetoric used by both sides of the debate would suggest.

I then go on to explain why Poland was more successful than other transition economies. I focus on the importance of initial conditions, policies in the early 1990s and onwards, and a number of other factors such as the size of the domestic market and changes in educational attainment.

I conclude the chapter by discussing whether Poland could have grown even faster. I argue that it could have, as is always the case for any country, but on the whole the Polish transition was almost 'as good as it gets'. I then draw the lessons learned and policy insights from Poland's transition for other countries.

5.1. 'Shock Therapy' Versus Gradualism

Did it make more sense to transform communist economies from a centrally planned to a free market economy 'overnight', in what came to be called 'shock therapy', or rather adopt a more gradual approach?[1] In hindsight, what should have been the optimal speed, sequence, and policy content of post-1989 reforms? Answers to these questions are important to how this transition is marked in history and to what lessons can be drawn from this experience by other countries.

What were the arguments behind the 'shock therapy' adopted in Poland, the Czech Republic, and a few other countries in the region?[2] The proponents of this approach such as Leszek Balcerowicz, the architect of Poland's reforms, or Vaclav Klaus, his Czech peer, put forth a number of arguments.

They argued that fast and decisive reforms to liberalize, stabilize, and privatize communist economies were indispensable to create a critical mass of change and thus to prevent the return of communism. The key idea was, as Vaclav Klaus, minister of finance of Czechoslovakia during the critical early post-transition period, put it 'not to give the opponents of reform time to organize and block change' (Klaus, 2014, Kindle 1392). Only radical change could also credibly change expectations and ensure that people and businesses quickly adjusted to the new, capitalist reality. It did not make sense to 'cut the cat's tail in pieces' or 'take bitter medicine in doses'. Only rapid policy reforms could leverage the rare period of 'extraordinary politics' (Balcerowicz, 2014) when everything was possible. Speed was also needed to stem the macroeconomic crisis: countries such as Poland, which in 1989 was in the throes of hyperinflation, had no choice but to move fast. Rapid reforms were also needed to help convince Western Europeans that CEE deserved to be welcomed into the European community. As Bronislaw Geremek, one of Poland's leading

---

[1] The term 'shock therapy' was coined by Jeffrey Sachs in the mid-1980s to describe reforms in Latin America. It was then used to describe Polish reforms in 1989–1990 led by Leszek Balcerowicz, Poland's Deputy Premier and Minister of Finance. See Lipton and Sachs (1990) and Sachs (1993).

[2] Or rather Czechoslovakia until it was dissolved on 31 December 1992.

policy makers of the transition era, noted: 'we must move very quickly...
because Europe had no intention of waiting for us' (Kowalik, 1994, p. 122).

They also claimed that post-transition reforms had to be not only rapid, but
also deep and comprehensive. As 'it is impossible to cross a chasm in two
leaps' (Vaclav Klaus quoted in World Bank, 1996, p. 9), reforms had to go far in
liberalizing, deregulating, and demonopolizing the economy to kick-start the
growth of the private sector, eliminate monopolistic rents, and reduce scope
for corruption. Comprehensive reforms were also needed to improve allocation of capital and harden budget constraints on state-owned enterprises
(SOEs). All reforms had to go together to maximize their impact. There was
no place for cherry picking.

Furthermore, 'shock therapists' believed in the virtues of fast privatization,
the last part of the 'stabilize, liberalize, and privatize' triad of the 'Washington
Consensus'.[3] The objective of privatization was to spur the development
of the private sector, enhance productivity, and limit potential fiscal liabilities. Privatization was also meant to build ownership, create capitalism,
and banish the spectre of communism. Public revenues from privatization
were only of secondary importance. As Vaclav Klaus (2014, Kindle 1612–14)
said: 'we were not interested in the size of privatization proceeds, because
our goals were different. Our aim was structural change—to privatize the
whole economy'.[4]

Leszek Balcerowicz and others also argued that a post-transition 'shock' and
subsequent recession was inevitable.[5] This is because of the accumulated
deficiencies, distortions, and absurdities of the communist system, which
could not be fixed overnight. The structural distortions included uncompetitive heavy industry, which was largely sustained for military reasons and
could not compete in international markets, and consumer industry, with
low-quality products no one wanted to buy anymore. The resulting 'creative
destruction' had to produce a temporary economic dislocation. A recession
was inevitable also because of accumulated macroeconomic distortions—high

[3] The 'Washington Consensus' is a set of policy principles, which guided the policy of
international institutions and developed countries in the 1990s. In its original version, the
Consensus was not overly controversial (Willamson, 2004). Over time, however, it came to be
associated with all the evils of the neoliberal agenda that extolled the primacy of markets and
denigrated the public sector.

[4] Klaus also argued that it was not useful to try to identify 'optimal' owners. On the contrary, 'it
was vital to get the privatization done so that the market rather than the state could sort out who
the best owners really were' (Klaus, 2014, Kindle 1629–31).

[5] Although, initially, many experts assumed that the transition would immediately spur
growth because removing distortions and liberalizing prices should immediately improve
resource allocation and lead to growth (Blanchard, 2010; Shleifer 2012). Others were less
sanguine, but still optimistic: for example, Leszek Balcerowicz projected that following the
introduction of his reform plan in 1990, Poland's output would decrease by only 3 per cent
and start growing again within a year. In practice, Poland's GDP decreased by 18 per cent and
growth resumed only in 1992.

excess money demand, unrealistic exchange rates, and high budget deficits. The post-transition recession, at least statistically speaking, also reflected reduction in waste prevalent in the centrally planned system, including excess use of energy, raw materials, and labour. Elimination of the most wasteful production was economically justified, but it shrank GDP even more.

Finally, the proponents of 'shock therapy' argued that the fast approach to reforms bore fruit: countries that were reforming faster such as Poland or the three Baltic States started the post-communist recovery earlier and then grew faster than countries that reformed at a slower speed.[6] They point to the large empirical evidence that links early transition reforms to subsequent strong economic performance (IMF, 2014).

The other side of the debate, the 'gradualists', vehemently disagree with the 'shock therapists' and argue that the 'shock therapy' provided much shock, but little therapy (Kolodko, 2000; Stiglitz, 1999; Berend, 2009; Roland, 2000).

They argue that because of erroneous policies modelled on the ill-advised 'Washington Consensus', the post-communist transition was largely a failure. Despite high expectations at the beginning—Olivier Blanchard, the former chief economist of the IMF and one of the key Western experts on the post-communist transition, spoke for many when he noted in his 2010 speech that 'when transition started, there was a wide belief that output could only increase' (Blanchard, 2010)—after twenty-five years of transition, half of post-communist countries have failed to catch up on the West (Darvas, 2015). Most countries developed at a much slower pace than expected. Some countries such as Ukraine or Moldova hardly developed at all. Even among the biggest winners of transition—the new EU member states—in 2016 the average level of income was only about 50 per cent higher than in 1989, implying an average annual rate of growth of less than 2 per cent a year. As a result, in 2016 the share of most post-communist countries in global GDP was actually *lower* than in 1989 (Figure 5.1). Poland, Slovakia, and Lithuania were the only exceptions. Mundell (1995, paraphrased in Kolodko and Nuti, 1997, p. 20) concluded that 'the Black Death is the only appropriate comparison to the deep [post-transition] recession—except that in that case income per head did not fall'.

'Gradualists' also point to the fact that however little economic growth there has been, the growth has been unequally distributed. Because of increased inequality, not everyone benefited from growth in the same way. After twenty-five years, incomes of large segments of population in most

---

[6] Hungary is considered to have adopted a gradualist approach after 1989, although this is largely because it had implemented many pro-market reforms already before 1989 under the so-called 'goulash communism'. It thus had much less scope for dramatic reform breakthroughs (Bokros, 2014). Hungary's example shows that the distinction between 'shock' and 'gradualism' may not always be sharp.

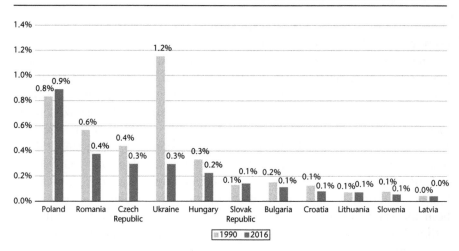

Figure 5.1. The share of ten post-communist new EU member states and Ukraine in global GDP, 1989 and 2016, PPP.

Source: Author's own based on the World Bank WDI database.

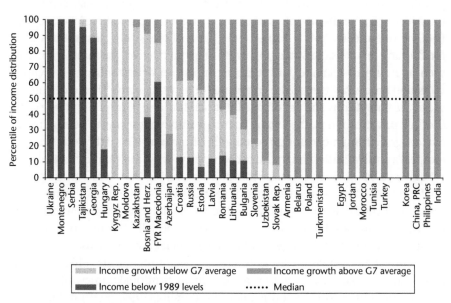

Figure 5.2. Changes in incomes in transition economies and selected emerging markets, by deciles of population, 1989–2015.

Source: Author's own based on EBRD (2016a).

transition economies have failed to catch up on the rich G-7 countries. Most transition economies have done much worse than many developing and emerging markets, from Egypt to India, where the whole population benefited from economic growth (Figure 5.2). In Ukraine, the whole society (with the exception of oligarchs, of course) is now apparently poorer than in 1989.

Why shift from communism to capitalism if the new system leaves people even more behind the West than before?

'Gradualists' also criticize the sequencing of post-transition reforms. They point to the downsides of the headlong rush to 'liberalize, stabilize, and privatize' without paying sufficient attention to the importance of institution-building and market regulations. This led, among other things, to disorganization of markets, supply chains, and production networks, which contributed to the much deeper than expected post-communist recession (Blanchard, 1997). Slow market and institution-building also led to slower economic recovery. Given the lack of well-functioning markets under communism, it is the institution-building, not liberalization, stabilization, and privatization, which should have been the key focus on reforms (Kolodko, 2000). Without good institutions, informal institutions took over, oligarchic capitalism developed and market capitalism was derailed.

Privatization policy based on the concept of 'privatize now, regulate later' is a good illustration of incorrect sequencing. 'Shock therapists' assumed that rapid privatization on its own would help restructure SOEs and maximize economic impact even in the absence of secure property rights, a competitive level playing field, or free media. Yet, it turned out that without strong institutions and functioning markets, privatization was often ineffective. In some countries such as Russia or Ukraine, privatization ended up delegitimizing the whole transition process as it led to the emergence of new oligarchy. This undermined social trust in reforms and encouraged state capture and corruption. In the end, botched privatization pushed some countries into what seems to be a permanent low-growth-high-corruption equilibrium, from which it might be difficult to escape. Fast privatization might have been penny-wise, but pound-foolish.

Stiglitz (1999, p. 5) emphasizes this point by saying that 'while those pushing for privatization pointed with pride to the large fraction of state enterprises that were turned over to private hands, these were dubious achievements. After all, it is easy to simply give away state assets, especially to one's friends and cronies'. Instead, the challenge is not to give property away for close to nothing but to privatize in such a way as to create a well-functioning, efficient, and competitive market. However, this 'requires an institutional framework, a set of credible and enforced laws and regulations' (Stiglitz, 1999, p. 19) rather than only (often nominal) change of ownership. Ironically, 'while privatization was supposed to "tame" political intrusion in market processes, privatization provided an additional instrument by which special interests, and political powers, could maintain their power' (ibid., p. 20).

Critics of the 'shock therapy' transition also emphasize the overshooting of price liberalization, macroeconomic stabilization, and trade openness. They argue that price liberalization was too abrupt: the sudden change in relative prices made many SOEs uncompetitive virtually overnight, without giving them a chance to adjust, reform, and restructure (Popov, 2007). A more staggered price adjustment suited to the capacity of the economy to shift resources from old, uncompetitive industries, to new, competitive ones would have been better (Popov 2007; Kolodko, 2000; Kolodko and Nuti, 1997). They claim that it was preferable to keep people employed, even in (temporarily) uncompetitive SOEs, than to close them down, increase unemployment, and deepen the recession. Likewise, opening of domestic markets to trade without providing even a temporary protection had a similarly deleterious impact. As a result, many SOEs went bankrupt (something that many 'shock therapists' did not mind, but saw it as the welcome reflection of 'creative destruction'), pushing countries deeper into the economic doldrums and aggravating social costs. 'Gradualists' also blamed overly restrictive monetary, exchange rate, and fiscal policy, including discriminatory taxation of SOEs, for deepening the recession (Kolodko, 2000).

In addition, 'gradualists' underscored the failure of 'shock therapists' to modernize SOEs, which represented 30–70 per cent of GDP in the region at the beginning of transition (Kolodko, 2000; Roland and Verdier, 1999). They argue that for ideological rather than economic reasons SOEs were left behind to die rather than be helped to restructure, commercialize, and become ready for privatization. The same incentives that were given in the privatization process to private funds that managed SOEs could have been directly extended to SOEs to help them perform better (Stiglitz, 1999). SOEs should not have been 'punished' for being old, dirty, and 'communist', but helped to move on, restructure, and recover.

The proponents of gradual reforms also argue that 'shock therapy' neglected the important role of the state in guiding the transition by building infrastructure, investing in human capital, and reforming the business environment (Kolodko 2000; Berend 2009; Pinto, 2014). Ideological fervour for downsizing the state and 'killing the Leviathan' left the transition directionless. Neglect of industrial policy was the case in point: Balcerowicz and others believed that the best industrial policy was not to have any industrial policy (Berend, 2009). Successful examples of industrial policies in Asia were ignored (Lin, 2009). Blind belief in the market prevailed.

Lastly, 'gradualists' claim that 'shock therapists' were, in a sweet historical irony, 'market Bolsheviks'. This is because like Bolsheviks they used the same radical and ruthless methods to transform the economy, but this time in the opposite direction: from communism to capitalism rather than vice versa. As Stiglitz puts it (1999, p. 22), many radical reformers seemed to believe that 'only a blitzkrieg approach during the "window of opportunity" provided by the "fog of transition" would get the changes made before the population had a chance to organize (. . .) It is almost as if (. . .) the Bolsheviks had the wrong textbooks instead of the whole wrong approach'.

5.1.1. *What can we say After a Quarter Century? Who was Right?*

In retrospect, the picture seems to be much more nuanced than both sides of the debate would have us believe. In practice, the difference in actual policies would have been much smaller than that implied by the fierce rhetoric of both sides. Some reforms needed the 'shock', while others should have been more gradual. As Kolodko (2000, p. 269), one of the chief 'gradualists', acknowledges: 'the gap between the words of the "neoliberals" and the "leftists" is like the Grand Canyon, the gap between their deeds is like a little ditch'.

To answer the 'shock therapy' versus 'gradualism' question in more detail and weigh up the pros and cons, it is useful to look at the example of Poland, the blueprint for post-communist radical reforms.

5.2. 'Shock Therapy' in Poland after 1989

Leszek Balcerowicz was a Deputy Prime Minister and Minister of Finance in Poland's first democratic government elected in August 1989. With the help of Jeffrey Sachs and David Lipton, two American economists, and financing from the IMF and the World Bank, he designed and led a programme of reforms during 1989–1991, which later became synonymous with the 'shock therapy' approach to transition (Sachs, 1993). The 'Balcerowicz Plan', as it came to be called, was based on ten key legislative changes, which were enacted over 11 days in December 1989. The Plan came into force on 1 January 1990.

The short-term goal of the Plan was to restore macroeconomic stability; the long-term goal was to 'catch up with the West' (Balcerowicz, 2014, Kindle 633). The Plan focused on three main directions. First, it liberalized all prices (except the most socially sensitive prices such as those for heat, electricity, and gas, which were raised only gradually) that had hitherto been controlled by the state rather than the market. Liberalization of prices aimed to eliminate misallocation, clear markets in line supply and demand, and eliminate shortages. It was also designed to achieve a critical mass of change towards building a high-functioning market economy (Balcerowicz, 1995).

Second, the programme aimed to restore macroeconomic stability, restrain galloping hyperinflation, which exceeded 250 per cent in 1989 (and 585 per cent in 1990), and stabilize the budget. Under the Plan, the Polish currency (zloty) was devalued and fixed to the dollar. Central bank financing of budget deficit was prohibited. Discussions were initiated on restructuring of the defaulted foreign debt. Interest rates were increased to dampen inflation. Corporate taxation was extended to all state-owned firms and indexed to inflation. Budget constraints on SOEs were hardened, including through a tax on excessive wage growth. The end effect of these measures was a dramatic tightening of fiscal and monetary policies.

Third, the Balcerowicz Plan introduced market-oriented reforms aimed at opening up the economy to trade and competition, allowing bankruptcy of SOEs, and commercializing banks. Domestic trade monopolies were dismantled, privatization of small establishments (shops, small industry etc.) was initiated; subsidies to production were eliminated. Foreign trade monopolies were removed and replaced by customs tariffs. Registration of private companies was streamlined. Polish zloty was made convertible for current account transactions in export and import. An anti-monopoly agency was set up. The Balcerowicz Plan also included a reform of public administration and—at a later stage—introduction of basic institutions of a capitalist economy such as a stock exchange.

The reforms were implemented at an unprecedented speed. They all came into force in a Big Bang fashion on 1 January 1990, barely four months after establishment of the first post-communist government. Balcerowicz believed that Poland had no choice but to reform at a fast pace. He wanted Poland to break out of the deep economic crisis, reduce permanent shortages of even the most basic products, and build credibility among creditors to restructure the country's large foreign debt.

The reform programme was among the most radical economic reform programmes ever implemented in peace-time in global history. The radicalism was guided by Balcerowicz's conviction that 'only a radical strategy could succeed (. . .) because Poland in 1989 was in largely uncharted waters' (Balcerowicz, 2014, Kindle 680). There was no time for gradualism. 'A risky strategy'—as Balcerowicz put it—'was preferable to a hopeless one' (Balcerowicz, 2014, Kindle 680). There were also political reasons for radical reforms: the democratic euphoria opened the door for 'extraordinary politics, when it is easier than during normal times to push through difficult reforms' (Balcerowicz, 1995, pp. 202–31). Radical reforms were also needed for psychological reasons: to convince the population of the irreversibility of reforms and that 'there was no going back'. Everyone needed to know that communism was gone forever and adjust accordingly.

The reforms first focused on macro-stabilization and only then on institutions. Balcerowicz believed that because of the dire initial conditions 'the economic team had to devote much of its attention to problems [such as macroeconomic stability] other than institutional reforms' (Balcerowicz, 2014, Kindle 643). He was convinced that macro-stabilization and liberalization reforms had to be implemented before institutions not only because of the need to stabilize the economy, but also because they 'could bring much faster results than most of deeper institutional change' (ibid., Kindle 648). There was also little knowledge about institutional and social reforms among the key policy makers, including Balcerowicz himself, as well as among international institutions. This helped make macro-stabilization a priority and postpone institution-building for later.[7]

Looking back at the results of the 1989–1991 reform period from the 2014 perspective, Balcerowicz argues that 'the choice of a radical strategy was correct' (Balcerowicz, 2014, Kindle 752). He believes that it was not possible to 'find a single example of a non-radical strategy (delaying reform or stabilization, slowing the pace of macro-stabilization and liberalization policies, etc.) that in similar initial and external conditions would have produced superior outcomes' (ibid., Kindle 752–5). He rejects the criticism that 'institutions were neglected'. As proof, he cites 'massive organizational de-monopolization of the Polish economy, the substantial hardening of SOEs' budget constraints, the unification of the exchange rate, the introduction of convertibility of the Polish zloty, and the establishment of an independent central bank' (ibid., Kindle 755–64). He concludes that the 'shock therapy' reforms were the reason why Poland was the first postcommunist country to start growing again in 1992 and later become the continent's growth champion.

5.3. Criticism of 'Shock Therapy'

Critics of the Balcerowicz Plan disagree with this positive assessment. They argue that the Plan unnecessarily deepened the post-transition recession: the planned 3.1 per cent fall in GDP was supposed to last just one year, but in practice turned into an 18 per cent decline in GDP during 1990–1991; unemployment skyrocketed to levels not seen since the Global Crisis in the 1930s and real wages declined by 25 per cent, the largest fall ever in peace-time (GUS, 2014). The post-communist recession 'lasted two or three times longer than expected; the output collapse was more distressing than the most distressing scenario, and the recovery, when it ultimately came, was only sluggish' (Kolodko, 2000, p. 253).

They also claim that fiscal and monetary policies were too restrictive, devaluation of the exchange rate too excessive, and hardening of budget constraints on SOEs too abrupt (Kolodko and Nuti, 1997). Even the conservative IMF

[7] David Lipton, an IMF economist working in Poland in 1989, admitted that at the beginning of the transition the IMF 'had no experience in designing and executing the sweeping changes needed to convert economies from the communist system to capitalism' (IMF, 2014, p. 9). In fact, the whole Western community was unprepared for the post-communist transition: Kolodko (2000) makes an intriguing point about how the West was not ready for the collapse of communism: even in 1987, the Reagan administration thought that preparing an analysis on how to promote economic recovery after a thermonuclear war was more useful than preparing an analysis of what to do if communism collapsed.

admitted in 1992 that 'in some European countries [such as Poland] there were substantial budget and current account surpluses in the early stages of the reform programs, which might, ex post, suggest that macroeconomic policies could have been less restrictive' (IMF, 1992, p. 46).

The detractors of Polish 'shock therapy' also claim that the liberalization of foreign trade was too rapid and did not give enough time for Polish companies to become sufficiently competitive to withstand the onslaught on the Polish market of Western multinationals. Specifically, while trade has rightly been liberalized in terms of regulations and legal restrictions, customs tariffs should have been kept sufficiently high to keep the domestic markets temporarily protected (Kolodko, 2000; Bruno, 1992; Blejer and Skreb, 1997).

Kolodko (2000) and others also emphasize the dramatic social costs of the transition: unemployment skyrocketed from virtually zero (a centrally planned economy had no official unemployment; rather, there was overemployment) to more than 12 per cent in 1991 and 14 per cent in 1992. In some parts of the country, particularly those where large SOEs and state-owned farms collapsed, unemployment reached 30 per cent. Inequality, as measured by the Gini coefficient, increased at a fast rate, from less than 25 in 1989 to more than 30 in the late 1990s (GUS, 2014). Poverty went up from virtually zero to almost 4 per cent in 1996.[8] Social support was cut. This was in line with a philosophy, as Balcerowicz later put it, that 'expanding the social state is the result of bad and immoral politics. Its supporters and creators do not have the right to the moral high-ground against those who oppose it. In contrast, they deserve to be morally condemned' (Balcerowicz, 2006).

Lastly, the opponents of economic radicalism believe that Poland's post-communist transition was undermined by slow institution-building. This deepened the post-transition recession, undermined the efficiency of reforms, and stymied the pace of the post-recession recovery. They argue that institution-building, public administration reform, and strengthening of the capacity of the government should have been the key priority of reforms, on par with liberalization of markets and macroeconomic stability (Kolodko and Nuti, 1997; Kowalik, 2012; Kolodko, 2009). Kolodko (2000, p. 45) summarizes the view of many by saying that

> there should be no doubt about the inadequacy of the concept of "shock therapy". The Polish success has been achieved *not because of it, but in spite of it,* and the reasoning behind shock therapy and interventions based upon the concept must take much of the blame for the great slump [italics added].

---

[8] Poverty defined as the share of population with incomes below the $3.1 threshold (in 2010 international dollars PPP). See the World Bank's poverty database for details.

5.4. 'Shock Therapy' or 'Shock Failure'?

What are the conclusions from the debate today? Given the many possibilities, trade-offs, and choices, there can be no clear-cut answer to what would have been the optimal policy. This is especially so given that transition involved dramatic economic and political changes, which had no precedent before.

My bottom line is that Polish 'shock therapy' was on the whole an important success, but the post-transition recession could have been shallower, recovery faster, and the social cost lower. That said, if there was no Balcerowicz, other (reasonable) policy makers would likely have followed a broadly similar strategy. This is largely because Poland's dire economic conditions required a radical response and there was not much wiggle room to experiment with different policies. In the end then, the difference in impact between the 'shock therapists' and 'gradualists' would have been noticeable but not dramatic.

Given what was at stake—a historically unprecedented shift from communism to capitalism, or as Lech Wałęsa put, turning a fish soup back into an aquarium—it is difficult to see how the transition could not in one way or another be 'radical'. The aim of the Polish transition was not to 'reform' the old system, as has been the case, for instance, in China or Vietnam, but to replace it with a totally new one. Radicalism was the price to be paid to move to the new system.

It is now also largely clear that the post-communist recession was inevitable. This is because of the accumulated distortions and the need to move labour force from the uncompetitive heavy industry, which had absorbed most investment during communism, to modern manufacturing and services. In this respect, Poland (and CEE) was different from China, which at the beginning of its gradual transition was an overwhelmingly agricultural economy (with more than 70 per cent of total workforce employed in agriculture) and did not need to deal with SOEs restructuring.[9] This compares with only a quarter of agricultural employment in Poland in 1990 and more than two-thirds of total labour force employed in various types of (largely uncompetitive) SOEs.

There is strong empirical evidence that countries that have moved faster with reforms such as Poland outperformed countries that have been more gradualist such as Slovenia, Romania, Bulgaria, or—among post-Soviet countries—Ukraine or Moldova.[10] Figure 5.3 shows that indeed countries that implemented reforms at a fast speed subsequently resumed growth earlier than

---

[9] In China, industrial SOEs employed only 8 per cent of the workforce in 1989 (Sachs, 1994).
[10] IMF (2014); Berg *et al.* (1999); De Melo, Denizer, and Gelb (1996); EBRD (2001); Fischer and Sahay (2000); Havrylyshyn and Wolf (2001); World Bank (2002a).

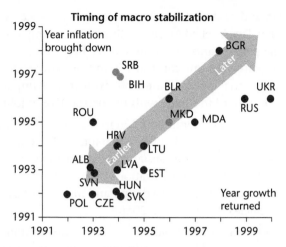

Figure 5.3. Speed of reforms and timing of economic recovery.
Source: IMF (2014).

others. Fischer and Sahay (2000, p. 1) conclude, based on empirical analysis and survey of other studies, that among post-communist countries 'the faster the speed of reforms, the quicker the recovery and the higher the growth'.

Even the detractors of 'shock therapy' admit that speed was essential in liberalizing prices and stabilizing transition economies. As noted by Kolodko (2000, p. 41): 'The more the economy has been controlled and the greater the financial instability at the start, the more reasonable it is to take advantage of the radical approach toward liberalization and stabilization'. Similarly, Stiglitz (1999, p. 22) admits that he has 'no great quarrel with "shock therapy" as a measure to quickly reset expectations, say, in an anti-inflation program'. Many other gradualist economists take the same approach, suggesting that there is almost a consensus that there was a need to liberalize and stabilize the Polish economy before it could be reformed further.

Furthermore, it is not clear that there would have been better ways of reforming Polish SOEs and conducing industrial policy, although the unequal treatment of SOEs, verging on discrimination, unnecessarily deepened the recession.[11] This is for a number of reasons:

- industrial policy à la Japan, Korea, or China would have been difficult to achieve in a robust democracy, with a kaleidoscope of changing governments (since 1989, there were 17 different governments in power, from

---

[11] Unlike the private sector, under the Balcerowicz Plan Polish SOEs in 1990–1991 became subject to a minimum asset tax and an excessive wage tax levied on the difference between the nominal wage growth in SOEs and a wage benchmark indexed to CPI. The idea for both taxes was to prevent SOEs from excessive growth in wages driven by anticipation of new state bailouts.

the right, left, and centre). This is especially so as the successful industrial policy of Asian Tigers relied on promoting private companies, not SOEs. In China, the performance of Chinese SOEs has been rather mixed and there are limits to what one can learn from this experience. In addition, Asian-style industrial policy, based on explicit and implicit subsidies, would have been hard to square with the perspective of joining the EU.

- it is doubtful that public administration in the early 1990s had sufficient capacity to conduct industrial policy and reform SOEs, especially without being captured by private interests (as was the case in Russia and Ukraine). Even today, the public administration, despite dramatically increased capacity, continues to struggle to design and implement even much less challenging policies (World Bank, 2016).

- the fate of SOEs in East Germany, which despite substantial subsidies from Western Germany have mostly gone bankrupt, suggests that the potential for SOEs restructuring was limited. The fact that communist Poland had a much less competitive industry than East Germany implies that it would have been difficult for Poland to expect a better result.[12]

- it is doubtful whether a gradual approach to reforms would have imposed the same hard budget constraints on the SOEs and provide sufficient pressure to restructure. SOEs could have behaved like frogs in a pot of water on a stove: without external pressure, SOEs would likely delay restructuring until they would have gone bankrupt. Alternatively, they would become strong vested interests, which would oppose their own restructuring. The fate of the Polish mining industry, which despite receiving more than $40 billion of subsidies since 1989, has not fully restructured and continues to make losses even today, suggests that with more time to organize other SOE-intensive industries could have behaved like miners too.

In any case, SOEs in Poland actually did better than elsewhere. As argued by Pinto (2014, p. 59), 'large SOEs were in the forefront of Poland's economic turnaround even before they were privatized'. He argues that the Polish SOEs did relatively well because of

uncompromising hard budgets, with credible signals from the Ministry of Finance that an enterprise had to make it on its own or go bust, competition from imports, which compressed profit margins and forced efficiency, and SOE directors' desire

---

[12] Although the SOEs' competitiveness in Eastern Germany was undermined by high unit labour costs, following the decision in 1990 to equalize wages and pensions in Eastern Germany with those in Western Germany. That said, even without high wages, Eastern German industry was far from competitive in international markets (Maier, 2012).

to signal their managerial abilities in conjunction with their expectation that privatization, albeit delayed, was inevitable.[13]

He adds that SOEs were helped by Poland avoiding an excessive real exchange rate appreciation, especially after introduction of a crawling peg in 1991 and a parallel nominal devaluation. There was also relatively little 'destruction': there were hardly any SOE bankruptcies in 1990 (Pinto, 2014). Finally, during 1989–1991, as a result of the fast restructuring of SOEs, Poland experienced an unprecedented transfer of labour from SOEs to the private sector: employment in SOEs fell by more than three million, or more than 20 per cent of total employment in the economy, taking down the share of employment in the public sector from about three-quarters to about half of the total (Pinto, Belka, and Krajewski, 1993).

On the whole, faced with credible threats to their existence, 'tough love' from the state owner—as a CEO of one of large SOEs put it in the early 1990s: 'I had no choice but to survive'[14]—and tightened lending policies of the banks,[15] Polish SOEs adapted to the capitalist markets quite well. It also helped that the management of SOEs had the right incentives to restructure their companies: they could benefit from a follow-up privatization by cashing in stocks, which were to be allocated for free as part of the privatization process, and keep the managerial position if their performance justified it (Pinto, 2014).

In retrospect then, it is not clear how much better Polish SOEs could have performed even under optimal conditions. No other transition economy seems to have done better. Even in the optimal scenario, with the right dose of hard budget constraints and robust support for SOE restructuring, given the track-record of other countries in the region, the impact on GDP would likely not have been substantial (probably not more than 1–2 per cent of GDP). This is all the more so as—while the elites were engaged in seemingly endless debates about the pros and cons of various SOE policies—the growth of the private sector overwhelmed the SOE sector by an order of magnitude. What ultimately decided the success of failure of transition was not the restructuring of SOEs, whose share in the economy was fast declining anyway, but the pace of growth of the private sector. This was the case for Poland, in which the size

---

[13] https://www.brookings.edu/blog/future-development/2015/01/23/taking-stock-of-transition-enduring-lessons-25-years-later/, accessed 12 June 2017.

[14] The hard budget constraints on SOEs were additionally strengthened by a wholesale replacement of top officials in tax administration with new cadres to sever communist era relationships and reduce corruption (Balcerowicz, 2014).

[15] Pinto (2014) highlights the crucial importance of commercialization of the nine largest state-owned banks in late 1991, which helped harden budget constraints on SOEs by cutting lending to loss-making enterprises. In a follow-up firm level survey, SOEs reported that banks ceased to be 'cashiers' and turned into 'partners'.

of the private sector increased from about a quarter of GDP in 1989 to almost two-thirds of GDP in 1995.

As regards the 'shock' delivered by the 'shock therapy', in reality it seems that there has been less than presumed. In particular, the initial fall in GDP and real wages, while undoubtedly deep, was likely lower than reported by the national statistics. This is because after 50 years of communism, statistical offices were not able to properly account for the exuberant growth of the micro- and small-scale private sector after 1989. In addition, much of the post-transition decline in production resulted from elimination of products that no one wanted to buy anymore, excessive stocks, and energy waste. The decline was also deepened by the removal of subsidized prices for oil and gas charged by Russia and their alignment to global market prices (Aslund, 2001). Furthermore, during communism, statistical offices used different methodologies from those in the West: they were based on the net material product rather than GDP and excluded the service sector (which was considered to be 'useless'). Adjusting for the new methodology, Czyżewski, Orłowski, and Zieńkowski (1996) argue that the real fall in GDP in Poland during 1990–1991 was closer to 7 per cent rather than 18 per cent reported by the official statistics. Finally, the transition brought a dramatic change in incentives for enterprises to report their performance: they quickly moved from over-reporting to meet and exceed the production targets under communism to under-reporting to reduce and evade taxes under capitalism (Campos and Coricelli, 2002).

Similarly, real wages in 1990 collapsed by about one-quarter, but they partly responded to high wage growth in 1988–1989. Relative to 1987, real wages in 1990 were only 7.7 per cent lower (Gomulka, 2016).[16] Similarly, Berg and Sachs (1992) argue that real consumption in Poland in 1990 fell by only about 4 per cent, when adjusted for liberalization of markets and prices, which helped remove shortages, increase consumer choice, eliminate petty corruption, and liquidate lines.[17]

In the same vein, the social cost of transition, while dramatic, has been partly mitigated by a growing welfare state. While real wages decreased in 1990 by a quarter, thanks to social transfers the real gross household incomes decreased by 15 per cent in 1990, but grew by almost 6 per cent in 1991 (GUS, 2014). In addition, deep price and trade liberalization, which at first sight

[16] All the official numbers ignore a large shadow economy, which was estimated to account for some 15 per cent of GDP in Poland in 1994 (Kaufmann, 1997a). Many official salaries were supplemented by additional cash payments, as well as earnings from small trade and entrepreneurship.
[17] I can confirm it from my personal experience: on 2 January 1990, as a fifteen-year-old I was amazed to be confronted for the first time ever with a choice of more than one cheese in my neighbourhood store. See also IMF (2014).

should have undermined the poor, was actually neutral for inequality as it helped lower prices for most basic products that the poor consumed (Milanovic and Ersado, 2012).

Moreover, pension system and disability allowances became *de facto* instruments of social policy as many Poles retired early or took advantage of lax criteria for disability. Between 1990 and 1995, the number of Poles receiving disability payments increased by half a million and the number of pensioners increased by 1.5 million (GUS, 2014).[18] As a result, public pension expenditure in Poland increased from 13.4 per cent in 1993 to 14.4 per cent in 1996. Poland was one of the few post-communist countries where pension expenditures increased; in many other post-communist countries, pension expenditures decreased, sometimes dramatically (in Bulgaria, for instance, pension expenditures decreased from 14.1 per cent to 9.5 per cent of GDP; IMF, 1998). In 1993, almost one-third of Polish adults were on retirement pension or disability pension, in comparison with only 18 per cent in the United States (Sachs, 1994). In the end, adjusting for higher public expenditures on pensions and disability payments (although this type of ad hoc 'social policy' was detrimental to labour supply and fiscal balance), the actual social support was much higher than commonly assumed. Indeed, OECD data show that public social spending in Poland during the early years of transition was higher than the OECD average and higher than among regional peers such as Hungary or the Czech Republic. It was also dramatically higher than in East Asia: South Korea, for instance, was spending less than 3 per cent of GDP on social policy during 1990–1995, a fraction of Poland's 22 per cent.[19] Rutkowski (1998, p. 3) concludes that 'contrary to expectations, the welfare state has increased rather than diminished during the economic transition'.

Economic policies during transition were also largely circumscribed by the expectations of Western creditors, international financial institutions, and capital markets. Poland had no choice but to follow Western advice to receive financial support from the IMF, restructure foreign debt owed to Western governments and banks, and claim its future membership in the European Union. Any policy maker, not only Balcerowicz, would have faced similar constraints. An alternative economic policy, such as adopted by Slovakia or Ukraine in the 1990s, would have undermined Poland's push to join the West, regardless of its own merits (which would be doubtful in any case). Poland had

---

[18] Balcerowicz (2014) admits not paying enough attention to the pension and social reforms and to 'missing' the implications of the decisions of Poland's Labor Ministry to allow early retirement and disability payments. In the end, and somewhat ironically, social policy was more welfarist not because but despite the aims of the chief economic policy maker.

[19] https://data.oecd.org/socialexp/social-spending.htm, accessed on 20 June 2017.

to play by the Western rules. It could correct certain policies, but could not change the main direction.

We now know that the speed of institution-building was one of the key drivers of successful transition, as discussed in more detail in Chapter 6. 'Gradualists' are right to emphasize the role of institutions, both formal and informal institutions, in explaining divergent development trajectories of transition economies. They are also right to argue that the post-transition recession was largely driven by the collapse of old institutions and the disorganization that followed, while the economic recovery was driven by the speed of building new institutions (Blanchard, 1997).

That said, there is no universal yardstick of how quickly to build institutions. For example, it is far from obvious if the reforms of the judiciary would be more effective if they took two months or two years. Some changes need to take time for their own benefit. Much also depends on the specifics and context of each country. Legislation can be changed quickly, but it will not ensure improved efficiency without changes in human capital, social norms, and 'ways of doing things', which ultimately decide whether institutional reforms produce results. While it is better to start building institutions as quickly as possible, it will still take many years. Furthermore, while institution-building seems to have been neglected at the beginning of transition, partly because the Western advisors came from developed countries where market institutions were taken for granted, many have quickly caught on. For instance, soon after the start of the transition in Poland, in its financing programme the IMF introduced conditions on the development of institutions and provided substantial technical assistance to build them (Fischer and Sahay, 2004).

In the end, the whole assessment of the 'shock therapy' versus 'gradualism' ultimately comes down to the question of whether gradual reforms would have been possible without political reversals. Could Poland have reformed gradually, while keeping anti-reform forces, vested interests, and populism at bay? One way to answer this question is to assess the trade-off between, on the one hand, the additional fall in GDP because of the radicalism of the 'shock therapy' (assuming that a gradualist approach would indeed have been better) and, on the other hand, the benefit of preventing the return of communism. Assuming that a gradual approach to transition would increase the probability of political reversals from, say, 20 per cent to 40 per cent, and the potential political reversals would reduce long-term income by less than 10 per cent relative to the actual performance, radical reforms would be unjustified. But if we assumed that the risks of political reversals under a gradual scenario were at 80 per cent and the negative impact on potential GDP would rise to 50 per cent (not far from the case of Ukraine or Moldova), then the 'shock therapy' would be more than justified.

Of course, there is no objective way of measuring the probabilities and the counterfactual impacts of the political reversals. Each policy maker in the 1990s had his/her own estimates, based on personal moral priors, experience, and biases. 'Shock therapists' believed that the risks of political reversals were extremely high and therefore they felt justified to move quickly on reforms. Their approach was akin to buying car insurance: in return for a premium (deeper economic recession), they wanted to eliminate the risks of costly damages or total destruction of the car (return of communism). 'Gradualists' in turn seem to have thought that the risks of political reversals were much lower. This was the case for Poland, where the post-communist party turned out to be equally reformist (and in some ways, even more reformist) than Solidarity parties. But it was not the case in other transition countries, when the return of post-communist parties slowed reforms.

The actual experience of transition suggests that 'shock therapists' were broadly justified: slow pace of reforms often produced policy slowdowns or reversals. This was the case for Bulgaria and Romania in the 1990s and most countries in the former Soviet Union throughout the transition, with the exception of the Baltic States. It was better to go fast, even if there were to be an additional cost, than go slow. In a democratic context, the Chinese option was not available (Box 5.1).

Finally, the debate on the early transition is framed by social disenchantment with the 'shock therapy' and high social aspirations. As noted by Sachs (1994, p. 271), the sobriquet of 'shock therapy' seemed to imply that 'one jolt of economic reform would reinvigorate the "patient" and allow the society to return to normal life'. Many Poles seemed to believe that just removing the shackles of communism would almost instantaneously help them achieve Western European standards of living. They were also not ready for the long grind of convergence that would take decades. They wanted the results 'now'. Sachs is right when he asserts that 'no economic reform, however brilliant, could bridge an economic gap that had grown over decades [or rather centuries, as I argue in this book], and indeed that had already been significant between Eastern and Western Europe before World War II' (ibid, p. 271). Not even the most brilliant government could have ever met these expectations. After long centuries of backwardness, it was simply impossible for Poles to become as rich as the Germans within just one generation, as this would require that Poland's GDP grew at truly exorbitant Chinese-like rates. But this is what many Poles seem to have been expecting (without necessarily wanting to be like China in everything except the growth rates).

The disenchantment has also been driven by a culture shock and the need for people to learn to live with uncertainty again. Berend (2009, p. 199) explains that people in CEE

Box 5.1. DOES CHINA PROVE THAT GRADUALIST POLICIES IN CEE COULD HAVE WORKED?

When 'gradualists' argue in favour of a more gradual approach to transition, they often cite the successful examples of countries such as China or Vietnam where gradualism has worked well (Stiglitz, 1999). However, these countries share little with Poland and other democratic post-communist countries. First, China and Vietnam are not, at least explicitly, moving to capitalism; they are still reforming socialism. Second, they are not exactly democracies. Third, they do not aspire to join the West; rather, especially China, they want to join the global order on their own terms.

Most important though, one-party states such as China have an ability to control social disenchantment, mitigate the power of vested interests (with the exception of the communist party itself), and reduce the risks of political reversals. The Chinese state is sufficiently strong to exercise such control.[20] As a result, China could allow itself to go slow on reforms and keep the risks of political reversals in check. But this is not the case in democratic countries: by definition, a democratic society allows for social discontent to be reflected in the political process. As a result, gradualist policies do not seem to work well. There is hardly any example of a democratic country that would go gradual and become successful in transition. Slovenia, often portrayed as the blueprint example of benefits of gradual reforms (see, for instance, Berend, 2009), has grown much slower than countries with more radical reforms. Since 1989, Slovenian GDP increased by less than half, while Poland's more than doubled.

---

grew accustomed to living in security and not taking risks. [Under communism], they earned little, but could make a living ... retire with a modest but guaranteed pension ... Since most people suffered from the same lack of opportunity, it was easier to tolerate ... The secure social situation offered by state socialism had become internalized by the people.

Similarly, Slavenika Drakulic, a Croatian writer, wrote that under the newly installed capitalism

instead of fulfilment of the promise of an instant welfare society, everyone has to work hard, and only a few will get rich. And it does not guarantee you a job or security, or medical care of a pension. The idea of social justice, even if it means no more than poverty for everyone, is still felt strongly here, if not politically then morally.   (Drakulic, 1997, p. 50)

Leder (2013) looks at the Polish case and concludes that a large part of social disenchantment, especially among blue collar workers, has been driven by the loss of 'symbolic capital' and social prestige that the proletariat benefitted

---

[20] On a personal note, I am always amazed by the honesty of taxi drivers in China: every time I take a cab from the airport, I am driven directly to the right spot and pay by the meter. Aside from a cultural explanation, there must be strong incentives for drivers not to cheat, including possibly because of the high price of punishment. This is not the case in most other developing countries, where cab theft is rampant. Want to know the country's state capacity? Take a cab ride.

from during communism. After 1989, it all changed. What used to be a source of pride under communism, became a source of shame under capitalism. The young quickly adapted, but older citizens stayed behind and became disillusioned, dismayed, and depressed.

5.5. After the 'Shock Therapy': Policy Corrections and Further Reforms

Poland's performance during transition cannot obviously be judged only on the impact of initial policies in 1989–1991. One needs to take a much longer perspective on the reform process that has taken place throughout the whole quarter of a century. The fundamental reforms initiated in 1989 were followed by measures, which corrected the excesses and abuses of the 'shock therapy', further strengthened markets, and built the missing institutions. The long-term reform process allowed Poland to accede to the EU in 2004 and then benefit from the EU accession to become a high-income country by 2009.

The post-Balcerowicz reforms can be divided into three main waves:

1. 'Kolodko Plan' or the 'Strategy for Poland' implemented during 1994–1997;
2. Pre-EU accession reforms 1999–2003;
3. Dealing with the global crisis, 2008–2014.

'Strategy for Poland' or the 'Kolodko Plan' was developed and implemented by Grzegorz W. Kolodko, Poland's Deputy Premier and Minister of Finance in the coalition government of the post-communist party (SLD) and the peasant party (PSL). The overarching objective of 'Strategy for Poland' was to reduce social costs of reforms, enhance social equity, and accelerate institution-building to support faster growth and prepare Poland for future accession to the European Union (Kolodko, 1994). In line with the 'Strategy', the government strengthened the wage negotiating process between employers and employees, started a pension reform, increased investment in human capital, and improved governance of state assets. It also increased domestic savings, introduced systemic brakes on fiscal policy, and promoted exports. It also took measures to reform and strengthen the capacity of public administration. Finally, it granted full independence to the central bank (Kolodko, 1994).

The 'Strategy' had a critical role in amplifying the positive effects of Balcerowicz Plan, while mitigating the social costs and completing the foundations for long-term development. Accession to the OECD in 1996, a rich-countries club, was a crowning moment. During the implementation of the 'Strategy', Poland achieved the highest growth rates in the whole post-1989 period, exceeding 6 per cent per year between 1994 and 1997.

The 'Strategy for Poland' was followed by another wave of reforms in the run-up to the EU accession in 2004. In 1999, the post-Solidarity government, with Leszek Balcerowicz again leading the economic agenda, introduced a new set of reforms. It included a new pension system, which transformed the old pay-as-you-go-system into a three pillar, defined contribution system. As a result, incentives for labour supply improved and long-term fiscal liabilities declined. It also introduced an important educational reform, which extended the length of compulsory education and aligned the tertiary educational system with the EU Bologna framework. Finally, it implemented ground-breaking local administration reform, which decentralized decision-making, enhanced fiscal authority, and strengthened governance of 16 newly created regions (down from 49 regions before).

Later, between 2001 and 2004, another post-communist government returned to power. In line with its EU accession commitments, the government introduced a swathe of administrative, institutional, and regulatory reforms (discussed in more detail in Chapter 6). It also negotiated the final accession agreement with the EU, including a large package of EU financing, the amount of which in the period 2004–2008 alone exceeded today's value of the post-Second World War Marshall Plan (Piatkowski, 2013).

Finally, during 2008–2014, a liberal government led by Donald Tusk, the future President of the European Council (2014–2019), strengthened fiscal rules, increased the retirement age to 67, and enhanced the macro-financial framework.[21] Most of all, however, it presided over the global crisis, which Poland has survived with flying colours. In 2009, Poland was the only country in the EU to avoid a recession. Overall, between 2008 and 2016, Poland's GDP increased by more than 30 per cent, while GDP of many countries in the EU has barely exceeded its pre-crisis level.

Poland's success with dealing with the global crisis owed much to aggressive Keynesian fiscal policies, appropriate response of monetary policy, and weakening of the Polish zloty, which boosted exports. In addition, economic growth has been supported by a surge in EU inflows. It has also received a boost from a healthy banking sector, which did not need a single zloty of public support. The domestically owned banks played a particularly positive role as they continued to provide credit even when foreign-owned banks retrenched (Piatkowski, 2015a). Poland's relatively large domestic economy limited the country's exposure to falling international trade. Finally, low level of public and private debt was also helpful (World Bank, 2017a).

---

[21] The increase in the retirement age was revoked by the new Law and Justice government in 2017: the retirement age was lowered to sixty years for women and sixty-five years for men.

Overall, during the whole twenty-five-year period, seventeen governments of all political convictions have consistently implemented reforms, which have eliminated the last vestiges of the old communist system, completed the building of institutions critical for the proper functioning of competitive markets, and ensured that most of the society benefited from growth.

5.6. What Made Poland More Successful Than its Post-Communist Peers?

As documented in Chapter 4, Poland experienced the smallest decline in post-transition output, was the first post-communist country to start growing again after the initial recession, and has grown the most in Europe since 1989. There is no single silver bullet that can explain this remarkable performance. But a number of factors made Poland different from other countries in the region and beyond.

5.6.1. Large Private Sector at the Beginning of Transition

On the eve of transition in 1989, Poland had the largest private sector among all communist countries. The share of the private sector amounted to about a quarter of Polish GDP and almost half of total employment, albeit mostly in low-value added agriculture. In Hungary, the private sector represented 20 per cent of GDP and employment. But there was hardly any private sector elsewhere: in Czechoslovakia, for instance, the private sector represented only about 10 per cent of GDP and 16 per cent of employment (Figure 5.4). Poland's large private sector mattered because it helped cushion the 1990–1991 recession by replacing the ailing SOEs and meeting the large pent-up consumer demand. It also provided a springboard for the dramatic growth that ensued, with the size of the private sector increasing to 60 per cent of GDP in 1995. Other countries in the region caught up with Poland only then.[22]

The large size of the private sector was largely a legacy of the 'Polish road to socialism', pursuant to which in 1956 the Polish communist party stopped farm collectivization, allowed private farmers to keep about 80 per cent of the total land, and tolerated a relatively large private market in trade and services. More private citizens than elsewhere in the communist camp were also involved in international private trade (or, to be more precise, international smuggling). Many of today's fortunes owe their humble beginnings to the

---

[22] The large size of the private sector in the Czech Republic in 1995 was the result of the mass privatization implemented in the early 1990s. In reality though, many of the companies were privatized only formally, with no clear private owner.

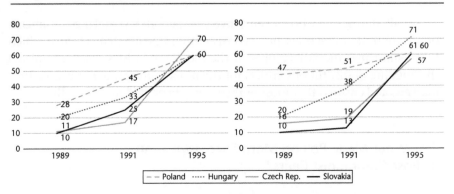

Figure 5.4. Private sector share in GDP and employment, 1989–1995.

Note: Estimates for Hungary in 1991, sorted by the size of employment in 1991.

Source: Author's own based on EBRD (1999, 2003) and Borish and Noel (1996).

crazy times in the late 1980s. Finally, the large private sector was also the result of the larger-than-elsewhere shortages in products and services, which it helped fill.

5.6.2. A *Legacy of Pro-Market Reforms Before 1989*

Unlike most other communist states, with the exception of Hungary, Poland undertook a plethora of pro-market reforms during the 1980s. Their objective was to move from a 'planned market-type socialism' to a 'market-type planned economy', where central planning was to be used only to improve the functioning of the market system (Kolodko, 2000; Bąk, 2009). As documented in Chapter 6, communist Poland reformed monetary and foreign exchange policy, liberalized the private sector, and freed more than half of all prices.

As a result of these reforms, by 1989 Poland had the most liberalized market in the communist system, except for Hungary. As the OECD (1992, p. 12) noted, on the eve of the transition communist Poland was 'very far from the typical idea of a centrally planned economy'. The reforms helped support the remarkable growth of the private sector growth, ease SOE restructuring, and get a head start on other transition economies.[23] There is empirical evidence that pro-market reforms implemented under communism had an important role in explaining the success of the subsequent transition.[24]

[23] An early start in corporate self-management helped Polish SOEs to restructure much faster than in other communist economies after 1989 (Kolodko, 2000; Pinto, 2014; Pinto, Belka, and Krajewski, 1993).

[24] Blanchard (1997); Gomulka (2016); Kolodko (2000); Blanchard (1997); Csaba (2007).

5.6.3. *Rapid Market Liberalization During 1989–1991*

Poland's reforms have been among the most radical in post-communist countries, as discussed earlier in this chapter. Only Czechoslovakia's reforms in 1990 and later those of the Baltic States, after they regained independence in 1991, can compare with the reforms implemented in Poland in terms of their radicalism (Aslund and Djankov, 2014).

On the whole, the rapid opening of markets, liberalization of prices, and dismantling of monopolies gave a big boost to growth and helped Poland start the economic recovery earlier than its regional peers. The reforms helped stimulate entrepreneurship by offering huge untapped consumer markets. Almost overnight, the reforms eliminated shortages of products, which were more prevalent in Poland than in other countries behind the Iron Curtain (Poland was one of only a few communist countries in which many basic products such as meat, butter, and chocolate were rationed through coupons). SOEs also restructured at a fast pace. Finally, the reforms opened up Poland to increasing inflows of FDI, which brought the much needed new investment, technology, management practices, access to international markets, and business know-how.

5.6.4. *Healthy Banks and Strong Financial Sector Supervision*

Poland was one of only three post-communist countries, next to Estonia and Romania, which avoided a banking crisis (Laeven and Valencia, 2012).[25] This helped prevent large fiscal losses and supported growth by allowing banks to provide credit to the burgeoning private sector. Others were not that lucky: the Czech Republic, for instance, experienced a large banking crisis during 1996–2000, which cost it 6.8 per cent of GDP; Hungary experienced two crises—during 1991–1996 and then again in 2008—which resulted in cumulative fiscal losses of about 12.7 per cent of GDP and contributed to much slower economic growth.

Poland's governments took a number of measures to keep the banking sector stable, profitable, and healthy, building on the reforms already introduced in 1988. Among the most critical measures, in 1993 Poland introduced a revolutionary Act on Bank and Corporate Restructuring, which helped banks to successfully deal with the mountain of non-performing loans (NPLs) inherited from the 1980s and the first years of the 'shock therapy'. The Act allowed banks to exchange debt for equity in companies, which presented credible restructuring programmes, or write off the rest of NPLs and clean their

---

[25] Defined as a crisis with a fiscal cost exceeding 5 per cent of GDP.

books. As a result, banks quickly got rid of most NPLs, strengthened their capital ratios, and re-started lending.

Furthermore, Poland gradually opened the banking sector to foreign investment. What was unique relative to other post-communist countries is that foreign banks could obtain a banking license only if they had partnered with a Polish bank, bought part of its equity, and shared its know-how (the large size of the Polish market gave the authorities a larger negotiating leverage over foreign banks than, say, in Latvia or Estonia). This helped improve the local banks' governance, enhance risk management, and upgrade the quality and breadth of banking products and services.

In addition, Poland created robust financial supervision, which over the years built a strong reputation for its competence, professionalism, and even-handed treatment. As a result, unlike in many other countries in the region, banks did not cease to fear the regulator.[26] The Polish supervisor has also been acting pro-actively: in 2006, for instance, it introduced a number of regulations ('recommendations'), which forced banks to slow lending at the peak of the pre-crisis boom. Together with a focus on a utility banking model, this helped the banking sector survive the global crisis in 2009 unscathed (Piatkowski, 2011a).[27]

Finally, unlike among peer countries, Poland did not sell all of the banks to foreign capital: about one-third of the whole banking sector's assets remained domestically owned (especially by the state-controlled market leader, PKO BP bank).[28] Domestic ownership came in handy during the 2009 crisis, when the Polish banks were the only ones not to cut lending. It helped save Poland from a recession (Piatkowski, 2012).

As a result of all these measures, the Polish banking sector achieved a 'sweet spot' in development: according to the IMF, which assessed the relationship between financial development and growth, Poland's banking sector is just big enough to provide sufficient credit to the economy, but not too big to endanger the financial sector's stability and economic growth (Figure 5.5).

[26] To give a poignant example of the strength of the supervisor's reputation: in 2009, at the bottom of the global financial crisis, the supervisor—Polish Financial Sector Authority—sent letters to CEOs of all banks with a request not to pay out dividends to help sustain the sector's capital position. Amazingly, even though the letters were not legally binding, all banks complied with what amounted to a polite request, including banks owned by global megabanks.

[27] I had an interesting personal experience with it: in May 2008, I joined PKO BP, the largest bank in Poland, as its Chief Economist. On the first day of my work, I walked into the bank's treasury department and asked about the bank's proprietary trading and positions. To my astonishment, all traders rolled their eyes: they explained that they never took any positions for longer than a couple of hours and their work fully focused on servicing client orders. How different from what was then happening on Wall Street, I thought, where the bulk of trading revenues came from market speculation rather than from clients.

[28] Following the sale in 2016 of PEKAO SA, the second largest bank in the market, by the Italian Unicredit to Polish insurance company PZU, the share of domestically owned-assets in the market increased to 45 per cent.

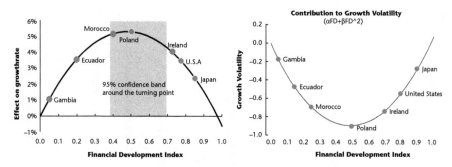

Figure 5.5. Optimal size of the financial sector versus growth.

Note: Financial Development index is based on indicators of financial depth, access, and efficiency for 176 countries.

Source: IMF (2015).

In addition to a robust banking sector, Poland also developed strong capital markets. The Warsaw Stock Exchange (WSE), set up in April 1991, has become the largest market in Central and Eastern Europe, eclipsing in size the Vienna Stock Exchange. In 2016, the total value of more than 800 domestic companies listed on the WSE amounted to around 30 per cent of GDP.[29] WSE also operated an innovative trading platform for small and medium enterprises, called NewConnect, which helped provide equity financing to growing businesses. In 2016, more than 100 SMEs were listed on NewConnect, creating one of the largest SME equity markets in Europe.

5.6.5. *Large Domestic Market*

Size is the most visible difference between Poland and its regional peers. Poland is by far the largest economy in the region, with GDP of more than $500 billion or almost 40 per cent of the total GDP of the eleven new EU member states from CEE.

Despite unprecedented growth in openness since 1989, when the share of exports in GDP doubled from around 25 per cent of GDP in 1990 to about 50 per cent in 2015, a higher share than in Germany or South Korea, Poland is still much less dependent on foreign trade than the regional peers (Figure 5.6). This has helped Poland insulate itself from external trade shocks such as those that happened during the global financial crisis in 2009, and grow on the basis of domestic demand (World Bank, 2017a; IMF 2014). Poland's exports are also more diversified than among regional and global peers: not a single item has

---

[29] https://data.worldbank.org/indicator/CM.MKT.LCAP.GD.ZS?locations=PL, accessed 15 September 2017.

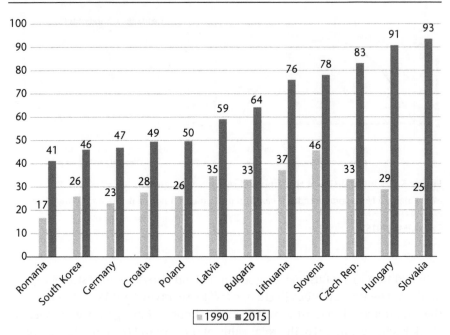

Figure 5.6. Export openness of Poland and its peers, per cent of exports in GDP, 1990 and 2015.

Note: 1990 or the earliest available.

Source: Author's own based on the World Bank's WDI.

more than a 6 per cent share in total exports, reducing exposure to sectoral shocks.[30] In contrast, Slovakia's exports, for instance, are dominated by cars and car accessories.

5.6.6. Solid and Pragmatic Policy Making

It is widely accepted among international observers and institutions that Poland's governments conducted broadly pragmatic, responsible, and effective economic policy during the whole post-transition period (IMF, 2014; World Bank, 2017a; EBRD, 2013). All seventeen consecutive governments since 1989 maintained macroeconomic stability, built institutions, and supported private sector development.

A comparison of economic performance of Poland and Hungary is a good illustration of the importance of policies. In 1989, Hungary started as the leader of the post-communist transition, largely thanks to an impressive list of pro-market reforms under communism, which liberalized prices and markets

---

[30] http://atlas.media.mit.edu/en/profile/country/pol/#Exports, accessed 5 June 2017.

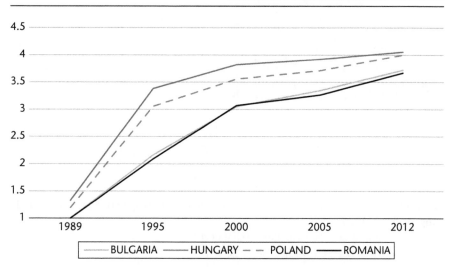

Figure 5.7. Index of structural reform indicators, 1989–2012.

Note: Average of six structural indicators: large-scale privatization, small-scale privatization, governance and enterprise restructuring, price liberalization, trade and forex system and competition policy.

Source: Author's own based on the EBRD dataset.

before everyone else (Bokros, 2014). It built institutions at the same pace as Poland and much faster than Bulgaria or Romania (Figure 5.7). And it attracted around half of total FDI in the region until 1995 (Berend, 2009).

Yet, despite the auspicious beginning, during the subsequent 20 years, Hungary grossly underperformed Poland and most regional peers in terms of growth. Hungary's GDP per capita grew at an average rate of only 1.2 per cent during 1990–2016, while Poland's grew at 3.1 per cent. As a result, by 2011 Poland had become richer than Hungary in terms of GDP per capita (PPP) for the first time in centuries (Figure 5.8). By 2020, the gap in incomes is projected to increase even further.

What can explain this divergence in performance between the two countries? While there are many reasons for the divergent performance, there are a few of them that stand out.

First, in 1989 both Poland and Hungary faced a large foreign debt bequeathed by the communist governments. However, only Poland managed to restructure debt; Hungary refused to do so, hoping that good behaviour would lower the cost of debt and sustain the country's reputation (Aslund, 2001). Poland's debt was cut by half, decreasing the foreign debt burden from 89 per cent of GDP in 1990 to 33 per cent in 1996 (Van Wijnbergen and Budina, 2001). Hungary continued to service the full debt. As a result, Hungary was permanently saddled with high public debt, exceeding 80 per cent of GDP in 1995 and still amounting to more than 70 per cent of GDP in

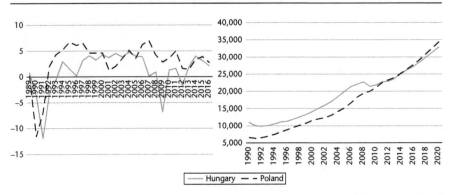

Figure 5.8. GDP growth (left chart) and changes in GDP per capita (PPP) in Poland and Hungary, 1989–2020.

Note: Projections until 2020 based on IMF WEO April 2017.

Source: Author's own based on WDI and IMF WEO 2017.

2016, more than twenty years later. At the same time, Poland kept public debt below 55 per cent of GDP, with foreign debt's share at around only one-third of the total. Lower debt burden helped rebuild confidence of foreign investors in the early 1990s, when it mattered the most, and kickstarted the transition. Hungary's bet that its good behaviour would be sufficiently rewarded by international investors seemed to have backfired.[31]

Second, Hungary adopted a series of ill-designed fiscal policies in the 2000s, which have undermined the growth rate. The new policies included drastic raises of public sector wages (salaries of civil servants were raised by 50 per cent), increasing monopolization of markets, and expansion of government expenditure to more than 50 per cent of GDP, the highest ratio in the region (Bokros, 2014). At the same time, Poland was going in the opposite direction, keeping the size of the government under control at around 40 per cent of GDP, deregulating the economy and improving the business environment. As to the latter, between 2005 and 2016, Poland became the fastest improving economy in the World Bank's Doing Business ranking, moving from seventy-sixth position in 2009 to twenty-fourth position in 2016. Hungary was stuck at forty-first position.

Lastly, both countries adopted different approaches to the global crisis in 2009. The Polish government reacted to the crisis by aggressively increasing the public budget deficit from 3.6 per cent in 2008 to 7.3 per cent in 2009 and 7.5 per cent in 2010 to replace the declining private sector demand and support growth. It also loosened monetary policy (interest rates were cut to

---

[31] Poland and Bulgaria were the only post-communist countries to achieve debt restructuring. Bulgaria signed a debt-restructuring agreement with the London Club in 1994 (Aerdt and Houben, 1995).

the historical low of 1.5 per cent) and provided ample liquidity to the banking sector. Hungary was much more cautious: because of high burden of public debt, which in 2008 amounted to 71.5 per cent of GDP, it could not fully use fiscal policy to stimulate the economy. Its fiscal expansion was meagre, with the deficit increasing from 3.6 per cent in 2008 to only 4.6 per cent and 4.5 per cent in 2009 and 2010, respectively. Monetary policy also had to be tighter. Consequently, Poland become the only country in the EU to avoid a recession in 2009, while Hungary experienced a 6.8 per cent fall in GDP.[32]

Aside from the specific policies, which helped Poland grow faster than others, day-to-day pragmatism and bi-partisan cooperation also mattered. Despite loud and often contradictory rhetoric, governments from both sides of the aisle often continued good economic policies of their predecessors and cooperated on the key reforms. There could hardly be a better example of pragmatism in policy making than the example of the two giants of the Polish transition—Leszek Balcerowicz and Grzegorz W. Kolodko—who despite deep-seated ideological differences and little personal affinity implicitly cooperated with each other during the critical years of the Polish transition.[33]

The successful debt restructuring is a case in point. Negotiations on debt restructuring were initiated by Leszek Balcerowicz in 1989. In 1991, the Paris Club, consisting of fourteen Western lenders, agreed to cut Poland's official debt by half (some countries, such as the USA, agreed to cut the debt by even more) to support Poland's transition.[34] However, the debt relief was to be delivered in two steps—a 30 per cent reduction in 1991 and a 20 per cent reduction in 1994—subject to Poland's adherence to the reform programme supported by the IMF. Grzegorz W. Kolodko, deputy premier in the new, post-communist government, which took over power in 1993, ensured that Poland complied with all the conditions and received the second portion of debt relief. In 1994, Kolodko also successfully completed debt restructuring with the so-called London Club of foreign creditor banks and cut private debt by half too.

Similarly pragmatic was the approach towards the ambitious pension reform, which in the late 1990s introduced a modern, three pillar pension system. The original idea was proposed in Kolodko's 'Strategy for Poland', but the legislation was enacted only during Balcerowicz's reign in the new

---

[32] Of course, other factors mattered too: the size of the market, the response of the private sector, the situation in the banking sector, and so on.

[33] Balcerowicz and Kolodko both managed an extraordinary feat: despite living in Warsaw and mingling within the same small world of policy makers and economists, they succeeded in not meeting each other in person since the early 2000s. They also managed to hardly ever mention each other's names in their numerous books and publications on the transition.

[34] Poland received 'special treatment' in debt negotiations because of its 'political uniqueness' and its lead in helping dismantle communism (Greenhouse, 1991).

post-Solidarity government. Finally, in 1996 during his term as the deputy premier and minister of finance, Kolodko supported Balcerowicz's idea to introduce a clause into the new Constitution that put a ceiling of 60 per cent of GDP on public debt. The new Constitution proposed by the post-communist party was enacted thanks to the crucial support of Balcerowicz's opposition party. The rest of the opposition, mainly other post-Solidarity parties, was against the new Constitution.

5.6.7. Lower GDP at the Beginning of Transition

According to the conditional convergence hypothesis, poorer countries should grow faster because of higher returns to scarce capital, larger scope for productivity-enhancing structural changes (such as the shift of employment from agriculture to industry and services), and imports of technology from abroad (Barro, 1991). Poland's GDP at the beginning of transition was lower than among most regional peers, but during the subsequent 25 years it grew faster than predicted by conditional convergence (Figure 5.9).

Lower initial GDP can thus 'explain' only a part of faster growth after 1989. 'Explain' in quotes because conditional convergence is far from automatic: as the name suggests, it is 'conditional' on the development of institutions, appropriate policies to support structural reforms, and changes in the external environment. This is not easy, as evidenced by the fact that over a long period of time most poor countries in the world do not converge on developed countries. It shows that there is no unconditional convergence, that is being

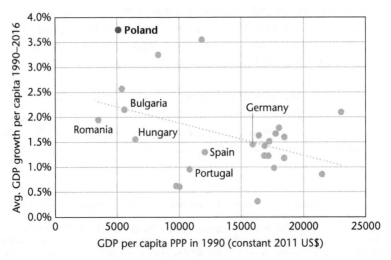

Figure 5.9. GDP per capita in 1990 PPP versus average GDP per capita growth 1990–2016. *Source*: Author's own based on IMF WEO April 2017.

poor by itself does not guarantee growth. In that sense, Poland used all the potential for growth and more. It was not the case for other countries in the region such as Hungary which have grown slower than predicted by the conditional convergence hypothesis.

5.6.8. *Increase in the Volume and Quality of Education*

Poland experienced a dramatic educational boom after 1989, which was much larger than anywhere else in the region. Thanks to a liberal law on education adopted in the early 1990s, which allowed for setting up of private universities, increased wage premium to high skills, and large interest of parents in securing university education for their kids,[35] the percentage of Polish youth enrolled in tertiary education increased from around 10 per cent in 1990 to more than 50 per cent at the end of the 1990s. Between 2000 and 2014, Poland registered the highest increase in tertiary education rates among OECD countries, next to South Korea (Figure 5.10). As a result, the percentage of the working population with university education tripled from 10.2 per cent in 1992 to 32.4 in 2014 (Figure 5.11). The annual number of university graduates increased from 56,000 in 1990 to 485,000 in 2012 and the number

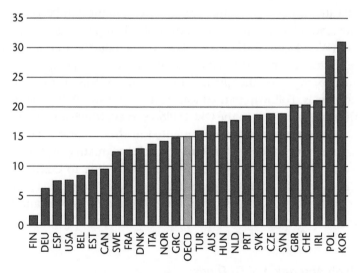

Figure 5.10. Change in tertiary education attainment rates, 2000–2014, percentage points.
Source: OECD (2016a).

---

[35] In 2015, more than 80 per cent of adult Poles wanted their children to have university education (Czapinski *et al.*, 2015).

191

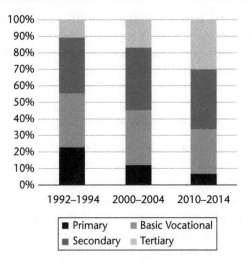

Figure 5.11. The educational structure of Polish workers, 1992–2014.
Source: Lewandowski and Baran (2016).

of students skyrocketed from 400,000 in 1990 to almost 1.7 million in 2012 (GUS, 2014).

The educational boom supported a rapid increase in the number of high-skilled occupations, which was higher than in the rest of Europe and among peer global economies (World Bank, 2017a). It was key to fast productivity growth, improved structure of production, and enhanced sophistication of exports.

Poland also improved the quality of education, at least at the primary and secondary levels. Following an educational reform in 1999, Poland became one of the star performers in the OECD PISA survey, which assesses functional literacy of fifteen-year-olds. As documented in the Chapter 4, Poland's high school pupils have much better results in science, maths, and reading than suggested by the country's level of income. According to OECD PISA 2015 (OECD, 2016b), Poland's fifteen-year-olds have better functional literacy than all other post-communist states with the exception of Estonia and Slovenia. They are also better educated than average Americans.

5.6.9. High Absorption of EU Funds

Since its accession in 2004, Poland has been the largest recipient of EU funds. It received more than $150 billion of EU funds by 2016 to build infrastructure, support human capital, and enhance innovation. Against initial expectations (World Bank, 2006, cited in World Bank 2017a), Poland's public administration at the central and regional level proved to be quite effective in absorbing

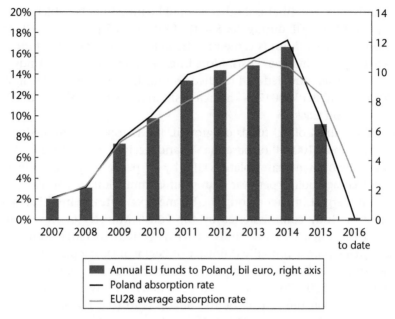

Figure 5.12. Absorption rate of EU funds, 2007–2016.
Source: IMF (2017b).

EU funds: since at least 2007, it had a higher absorption rate than the EU-28 average (Figure 5.12).

EU funds have been key to upgrading Poland's abysmal infrastructure, roads, railways, and broadband networks, which has lagged behind the West and its regional peers. Thanks to EU financing, Poland has now built a functional highway network for the first time ever.[36] The length of highway and express roads has increased more than sixfold since 2000 from less than 500 kilometres in 2000 to 3,300 kilometres in 2017.[37] By 2030, the nationwide highway network will be fully complete, closing the infrastructural gap—because of the low starting base—by more than in countries which always had much better infrastructure such as the Czech Republic, Slovakia, or Hungary.

[36] As I argued in Piatkowski (2013, p. 24), 'Poland never had a good road infrastructure': Osęka (2011) argues that in 1939 in Poland only 7 per cent of all roads were modern, paved with asphalt or concrete, and suitable for automobile use, out of the total of 340,000 kilometres. This compares with 100 per cent in Denmark, 90 per cent in France, 70 per cent in Germany, and more than half in Czechoslovakia. In addition, all good roads in Poland were only single-lane, not two-lane highways. There was not a single modern road connecting any two major cities. The average travel speed was about only 40 km per hour'.

[37] https://pl.m.wikipedia.org/wiki/Autostrady_i_drogi_ekspresowe_w_Polsce#/media/Plik%3APL-Motorways-pl.svg, accessed 22 July 2017. See also an animated map of improvements in the highway infrastructure in Poland between 1932 and 2015: https://upload.wikimedia.org/wikipedia/commons/a/af/Historia_budowy_autostrad_i_dr%C3%B3g_ekspresowych.gif, accessed 22 July 2017.

EU funds have also financed other key public investments, which boomed to 4.6 per cent of GDP during 2005–2014 from the 3.5 per cent of GDP pre-accession average. EU funds came in extremely handy especially during the 2009–2010 global financial crisis. More intense absorption of EU funds—the inflows more than doubled and reached around 1.5 per cent of GDP in 2010 and 2011 (World Bank, 2017a)—helped cushion the external shocks and keep the economy on track.

As to the impact of EU funds on growth, the European Commission estimated that almost 100 billion euro that Poland received during the EU's 2007–2013 budget would increase Poland's GDP by 4.1 per cent by 2022 or by close to 0.5 percentage points per year (European Commission, 2014). This would be the third largest impact among the EU member states, behind Latvia and Lithuania. A study commissioned by the Polish Ministry of Development estimated the impact of EU funds on GDP growth to range from 0.4 to 0.7 percentage points annually (Ministry of Regional Development, 2013).

Other studies estimated the impact to be as large as 1.1 percentage points per year during 2005–2011 (Varga and Veld, 2009). A forward looking report by Erste (2014) on the impact of 105 billion euro that Poland will receive during the new EU budget 2014–2020 suggests a similarly sized impact of about 0.5 percentage points of additional GDP growth per year until 2020. This would be slightly lower than in Romania and Hungary (0.7 percentage points per year), equal to Slovakia, but higher than in the Czech Republic (0.3 percentage points).

5.7. Benefits of Delayed Privatization

Transition by definition was about shifting from a state-owned economy to a privately owned economy. Privatization was thus key. State ownership predominated in all communist economies and the stock of companies to be privatized was unprecedented. Given that private capital was scarce in post-communist Europe and that there was a need to privatize quickly, countries had to come up with new ways to privatize.

In Poland, there was an overwhelming urge to privatize the large companies as quickly as possible. Leszek Balcerowicz and many other Polish policy makers identified with Vaclav Klaus (2014, Kindle 1682), who opined that 'transformation has no meaning without early, rapid, and widespread privatization. Privatization must be carried out without waiting for the much-needed restructuring of firms or the emergence of domestic capital'.

Poland started the preparations for privatization early and implemented small-scale privatization of stores, artisan businesses, and small service outfits quickly. But privatization of large SOEs hit a snag: the original bill

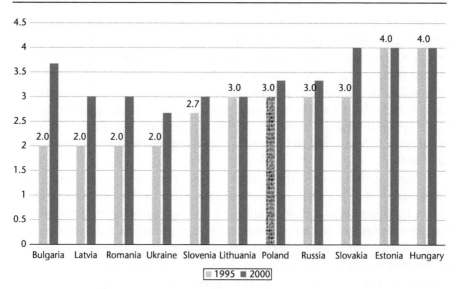

Figure 5.13. EBRD Index of Large Scale Privatization, 1995 and 2000.

Note: Scores from 1 (no privatization) to 4 (all privatized).

Source: Author's own based on EBRD data.

on large-scale privatization was passed by the government in February 1990, but owing to strong political opposition (coming from within the Solidarity coalition rather than from the post-communist party), the process of bulk large-scale privatization was delayed until 1996. By 1995, only 13 per cent of large industrial companies were privatized (Berend, 2009, p. 60). According to the EBRD's index of progress in large-scale privatization, Poland was far from being a leader among the transition economies in 1995 and even in 2000 (Figure 5.13).

Ironically, it was the very delay in the large-scale privatization that seems to have helped ensure that Poland's privatization did not produce oligarchs as in Russia, did not engender wide public disenchantment as in Bulgaria or Romania, and did not end up having to be repeated as in the Czech Republic. This is because of four main factors.

First, delayed privatization helped Poland learn from the failure of mass voucher privatization in the Czech Republic and Russia and adjust the mass privatization programme accordingly. Poland decreased the number of participating companies from the originally planned more than 2,000 to 514, equivalent to about 10 per cent of book value of all SOEs or around $3 billion (in 1995 prices). By comparison, the Czech mass privatization was at least three times larger: it included companies valued at about 30 per cent of GDP, or about $7.5 billion at the time (Kolodko, 2000). Poland also strengthened corporate governance and monitoring of fifteen private funds that were responsible for managing and restructuring the privatized SOEs.[38] Each of the funds was listed on the Warsaw Stock Exchange and had to provide regular and audited updates of their performance. Importantly, private management funds were created in consortia with Western management companies, which ensured transfer of know-how, skills, networks, and capital. Finally, private management funds had a strong incentive to perform well to enhance the value of 15 per cent of shares, which they received in each of the managed companies (Borish and Noel, 1996).

Second, the delay in privatization gave Poland enough time to strengthen institutions—the rule of law, capital markets, free media, and so forth—to ensure transparency and close monitoring and to avoid asset stripping, which happened in many other transition economies, especially in the Czech Republic and Russia. Third, the value of enterprises to be privatized was much easier to ascertain in the mid-1990s than in the early days of transition, where there was hardly any market for assets. This helped privatize companies at prices closer to market values and ease concerns about the country's 'family silver' being sold for 'nothing'.

Finally, delayed mass privatization helped introduce other, more transparent privatization methods, including sale through the stock exchange. This method proved popular with the large part of population (which could buy shares from the state in each company at preferential prices), helped build mass shareholding, and strengthened governance and oversight by outsourcing it to domestic and foreign stock market investors. As a side benefit, IPOs of SOEs helped the Warsaw Stock Exchange become the largest, the most transparent, and the most sophisticated stock market in the region.

In the end, delayed privatization worked well and showed that 'haste makes waste'.

Slower privatization in any case did not stop the sale of large enterprises, mostly to foreign investors, on a case-by-case basis. For instance, in the first large privatization in February 1992, Poland sold 80 per cent of shares in the country's largest pulp and paper company to International Paper, an American multinational, for $120 million. This successful privatization, which helped safeguard employment, improve productivity, and boost exports, became a blueprint for further privatizations with foreign investors.

---

[38] *The Economist* (1998, p. 50) commented thus on the Czech mass privatization: 'Mr Klaus has only himself to blame... His hasty mass privatization program, which made ordinary Czechs the formal owners of most enterprises, but gave control to state-owned banks with no interest in improving them, created a crisis that culminated in a humiliating devaluation of the currency in May last year. Now unemployment and inflation are rising and real incomes are falling; the economy grew by just 1 per cent in 1997 and will at best barely make 2 per cent this year'. See also Richter (2010).

It also mattered that the company's staff received 15 per cent of the company's shares for free, which it then sold at a large profit to the new owner.[39] There is strong empirical evidence across all transition economies that privatization produced the best results when companies were sold to foreign investors rather than to insiders, managers, and staff (Djankov and Murrell, 2002).

Delayed privatization also did not stop SOEs from reforming: as discussed earlier, faced with hard budget constraints and the chance to receive 15 per cent of the company's shares for free during privatization, many SOEs successfully went through internally driven restructuring (Pinto, Belka, and Krajewski, 1993). The restructuring of SOEs was additionally supported by acceleration of the so-called 'corporatization' or transformation of SOEs into state-owned joint-stock companies governed by the commercial code, which improved governance and reduced legal uncertainty (Kolodko, 2000). SOE restructuring was also supported by relatively high managerial skills, a legacy of early reforms in the 1980s and high quality of management education (Koźmiński, 1993).

It also turned out that the speed and the methods of privatization mattered much less than expected. The link between privatization and economic growth has been less robust than assumed (Bennett, Estrin and Urga, 2007). Poland's example suggests that privatization did not need to be rushed and that building institutions first was more important. IMF (2014, p. 22), agreed that privatization in transition economic could enhance efficiency only when 'supporting legal and regulatory institutions were in place. Clear property rights, hard budget constraints, and adequate competition seem to have been necessary conditions to ensure a growth dividend'. In other words, privatization was not key to successful transition: it was a competitive economic environment, strong rule of law, robust governance, and good management skills, no matter what type of ownership, that proved to be the most important.

Finally, Poland also showed that privatization could be handled with few casualties and low negative effects. It proved wrong those such as Vaclav Klaus (2014, Kindle 1663–5), who argued that '[privatization in the Czech Republic] had casualties and imposed socially negative side effects. But these effects were the price to be paid for transformation and privatization—or to put it differently, for communism'. It has also proven Balcerowicz (2014, Kindle 789–91) wrong, who remains convinced that 'the performance of the Polish economy would have been even better if the SOE privatization had been faster, which would have required the early introduction of some scheme of mass privatization'. It has also proven the Western advisors wrong.[40] However, in the end

---

[39] http://kwidzynopedia.pl/index.php?title=International_Paper-Kwidzyn.

[40] David Lipton and Jeffrey Sachs, key advisors to Poland in 1990, argued that 'Poland must begin a rapid process of privatization of state firms, not only to assure efficient resource use in the future, but to prevent the collapse of the stabilization itself in the medium term' (Lipton and Sachs, 1990, p. 127). To their credit though (ibid., p. 295), they doubted that 'privatization will produce

privatization turned out to be much less important than envisaged, as it was overwhelmed by the dramatic growth of the private sector. Poland privatized the economy much faster than it privatized SOEs (Dabrowski, Gomulka and Rostowski, 2001).

Overall, among all the factors above which made Poland different from its peers, which were the most important? It is virtually impossible to answer this question given the complex interactions among all the factors, from the speed of initial reforms through quality of education, to the benefits of starting from a low income base. Depending on the initial assumptions, each cross-country regression could produce different results. While there is empirical evidence that early reforms helped Poland's growth, it is much harder to prove the impact of other policies or approaches to policy making. After all, it is hard to quantify the impact of pragmatism. The bottom line is that many factors mattered and supported one another, because—as Kolodko (2011, p. 26) put it—'things happen the way they happen because many things happen at the same time'. Poland got most of its policies right and reaped dividends from it.

5.8. Could Poland Have Grown Faster?

In principle, Poland could have grown even faster than it did. This is because the Polish governments made a number of mistakes. One of the biggest mistakes was the overly strict monetary policy of the National Bank of Poland in 2000–2001, led since January 2001 by Leszek Balcerowicz, that almost plunged the country into a recession for the first time since 1991. In 2000, nominal interest rates were increased to 19 per cent, despite inflation of only 8.5 per cent and a current account deficit of 6 per cent, whose financing was assumed to be at risk. The impact of this self-engineered crisis was felt for a number of years: GDP growth collapsed from 4 per cent in 2000 to only 1.0 per cent in 2001 and 1.4 per cent in 2002. Unemployment skyrocketed to almost 20 per cent. Growth got back to the pre-crisis speed only in 2004. The other policy mistakes included an overly restrictive monetary and fiscal policy in 1990–1991, slow implementation of a number of important institutional reforms in the early 1990s, and a few mistakes in structural policies, including slow restructuring of farming and coal mining.

How much faster could Poland have grown if it got all the policies exactly right? It is obviously difficult to measure the counterfactual. It is not clear how deep the initial post-transition recession would have been under an

immediate, large increases in productivity and managerial efficiency. The real gains from private ownership will take years to manifest themselves'.

optimal scenario. There are no such assessments in the literature. A less restrictive fiscal and monetary policy during 1990–1991—assuming the usual fiscal multipliers—could have likely saved a few per cent of GDP over the two years of recession. Restructuring of SOEs would need to take time and its potentially positive effects would not show up until later. In the short term, the impact of optimal SOE restructuring on GDP would likely not be substantial. Likewise, institution-building would also take time and its effect would be visible only with a lag. Lack of monetary policy overshooting in 2000–2001 could have produced larger gains, as the economy could be growing close to the 4 per cent trend rather than the actual 1 per cent. Faster structural reforms also could have added a few extra percentage points of GDP growth over the period.

What would be the overall impact? We can assume that thanks to a better policy at the very beginning of the transition—Balcerowicz Plan crossed with Kolodko Plan—GDP would decline by only half of the actual decline, that is by 5.7 per cent in 1990 and 3.5 per cent in 1991 instead of 11.5 per cent and 7 per cent growth, respectively. We can also assume, and call it a 'sky is the limit scenario', that owing to even better policy making throughout the remaining twenty-five-year period, Poland would always grow at least as fast as the average for all other CEE transition economies (and sometimes faster, when Poland's actual growth was higher than the regional average). As Poland grew slower than the regional average during 2001–2007, the growth rate is thus revised up to equal the regional average. Figure 5.14 illustrates the results of such a hypothetical scenario.

Under these 'sky is the limit' assumptions, Poland's level of GDP in 2015 would amount to 273 per cent of GDP from 1989 instead of the actual 217 per cent. This would translate into the level of GDP per capita PPP in 2015 of almost $33,500, only slightly below the level of income in Spain and about $7,000 more than in the actual scenario (Figure 5.15). However, the 'sky is the limit' scenario might not actually be optimal because it aligns Poland's growth rates up during 2001–2007 with the regional average, when other countries in the region grew fast because of rapidly increasing debt. It all ended badly for them, as every single country aside from Poland ended up with a deep recession in 2009. A better scenario for Poland would be then to assume that during 2001–2007 it grew not close to 6 per cent per year as the regional average, but at 4 per cent a year, in line with its potential growth rate. Under such 'less pain in 1990–1991 and 4 per cent growth in 2001–2007' scenario, Poland's GDP per capita in 2015 would amount to around $29,200. This would only be about 10 per cent more than in the actual scenario. Hence, in contrast to Kolodko (2009), who argues that Poland's transition achieved only two-thirds of its potential, this hypothetical scenario suggests that Poland accomplished between three-quarters and nine-tenths of what was possible.

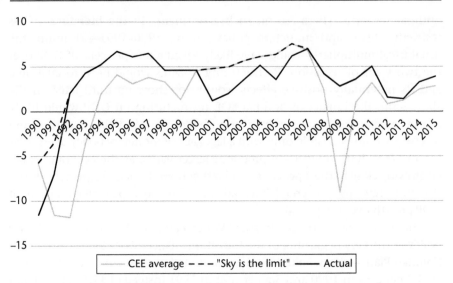

Figure 5.14. Actual and optimal policy GDP growth scenario in Poland, 1990–2015.
Note: Unweighted average for eleven new EU member states from CEE.
Source: Author's own based on EBRD and IMF data.

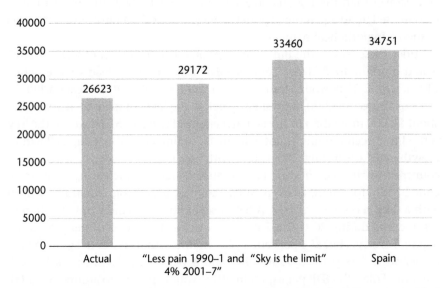

Figure 5.15. Poland's alternative growth scenarios, 1989–2015, GDP per capita in 2015 US$ PPP.
Source: Author's own based on IMF WEO April 2017.

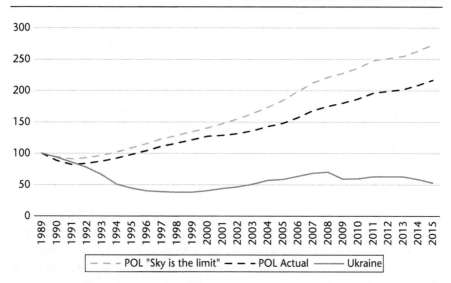

Figure 5.16. Poland versus Ukraine, actual and alternative growth scenarios, 1989–2015, GDP in 1989=100.

Source: Author's own based on IMF WEO April 2017.

This is especially so as both the 'sky is the limit' and the more reasonable '4 per cent growth' scenario should be juxtaposed against the worst case scenario of Poland failing to reform and grow. If Poland reformed as slowly as the neighbouring Ukraine, Poland's income today could be somewhere around $8,000 instead of almost $27,000 in 2016. Lives of at least another generation—my generation—would have been blighted. Such performance would have taken Poland back to its long-term black developmental hole, well known for the previous 500 years, from which it would be difficult to escape. It is important to remember that hardly anyone would be surprised with this outcome: Poland has underperformed for hundreds of years and another twenty-five years of subpar performance would not raise anyone's eyebrows.

Putting on the scales the actual economic transition—which eventually and unexpectedly helped Poland become the European and global growth champion for the first time ever—and the prospect of becoming another Ukraine, the judgement is obvious. Even in the best case scenario, Poland's growth would have been only slightly higher. But under the worst case scenario, it would have been incomparably worse (Figure 5.16).

5.9. Conclusions and Lessons Learned

There is no single explanation for Poland's success since 1989. And there should not be, because growth is multi-faceted and there is no single silver bullet. It seems though that Poland was more successful than its regional peers because of a number of key pro-market reforms already implemented under communism, deep reforms in 1989, and a rapidly rising quality of human capital. The large size of the domestic market, broadly transparent privatization, and a healthy banking sector also mattered. Above all though, Poland did better than others because of its consistent, growth-oriented, and pragmatic policy making. The initial 'shock therapy', although in practice it was much less shocking and much more gradual than the rhetoric would imply, put Poland on a growth path. Subsequent governments corrected the excesses of the 'shock therapy' and moved to build institutions, support reforms of state-owned enterprises, and lower the social costs.

Relative to its global peers, emerging markets such as Brazil, Mexico, and Turkey as well as much more developed countries such as South Korea, Poland's success was driven by a string of critical reforms undertaken on the path to the European Union accession. Without the EU, Poland would have never reformed as much. Poland benefited from the opening of markets for trade, capital, and people following the EU accession in 2004. Combined with high productivity and low labour costs, this helped Poland join the global value chains, especially those intermediated by Germany, and become a European manufacturing hub. Inflows of gigantic EU funds, amounting to a multiple of what Western Europe received under the post-Second World War Marshal Plan, played a key role in improving infrastructure and enhancing productivity. EU funds for Poland were what natural resources were for other countries: a manna from heaven.

Could Poland have grown faster? Yes, it could have (is there any country that could not?). Under a 'sky is the limit' scenario, assuming a less deep post-transition recession and a leading position in economic growth rate throughout the whole post-transition period, Poland's level of GDP in 2015 would be close to that of Spain. However, under a more realistic scenario, with Poland growing closer to its potential growth rate and without accumulating macroeconomic vulnerabilities, GDP per capita in 2015 would have been about 10 per cent higher than in the actual scenario. This is not a big difference, suggesting that Poland's performance during transition, despite all its flaws and social costs, was almost 'as good as it gets'.

What is more important is that Poland's performance could also have been much worse. It is easy to forget that back in 1989 hardly anyone expected Poland to succeed. For sure no one imagined that it would become the most successful economy in Europe. No one also predicted that twenty-five years later Poland's level of income would catch up with the West, even if only with its poorest members, Portugal and Greece. Many things could have easily gone wrong and derailed the transition. Instead of becoming the leader of transition, Poland could have failed again and ended up not much better than where Ukraine is today. Based on the dismal historical track-record, it would have been much easier to explain Poland's failure than its success.

What are the lessons learned for policy makers in other countries? There are a number of important lessons. First, it is important to move quickly on macroeconomic and structural reforms when an opportunity arises. In doing so, however, it is crucial to involve every stakeholder in the public debate to help them 'own' reforms. As Balcerowicz (2014, Kindle 601–3) notes, 'the political groups and leaders not represented at the Round Table talks [in Poland] turned out to be the most populist critics of the economic program launched in early 1990'. It is also important to look for partners in supporting reforms. Enemies of the vested interest can become the policy makers' best friends. In addition, it is key to link less popular reforms with more popular reforms in one large reform package. This prevents cherry picking, helps build a larger coalition of support, and helps face the vested interests, the opposition of which is the same regardless of the size of the reform (Laar, 2014; Kolodko, 2002). Second, it is crucial to de-monopolize the economy, strengthen the rule of law, and build institutions before privatizing. Poland's transition showed that there is no good reason for hastening for privatization before building institutions: what could look like a short-term success—getting rid of state property—is likely to turn into a long-term failure: private monopolies, state capture, and a disillusioned population who turns populist. Privatizing too early is like giving a car to an eighteen-year-old student rather than a twenty-five-year-old young father with kids: a small difference in age, but a huge difference in the potential impact. Finally, privatization should not become a 'fetish': it should be only a means to an end, not an end in itself.

Third, active social policy is needed to mitigate the costs of reforms and keep inequality in check. By definition, all reforms create losers. They may be much fewer than the winners, but their losses are much more concentrated and therefore visible, putting a shadow on much larger benefits for everyone else. Growing inequality undermines growth and commitment to further reforms and increases risks of political reversals. The solution is to help the losers get back on track and adopt active income policy to ensure that rising prosperity is shared by everyone.

Finally, the institutional and regulatory framework for policy making is key. On the path to the EU accession Poland adopted the whole body of EU laws, rules, and regulations, the so-called *acquis communautaire*. But it also designed its own additional rules to further enhance the stability of policy making. It was one of the first countries in Europe and in the world to introduce a public debt threshold of 60 per cent of GDP into the Constitution. It supplemented it with additional public finance rules on the debt levels and on the growth in public expenditure. It was also one of the first transition economies to give full independence to the central bank and introduce a monetary policy council to collectively decide on the interest rates. At the same time, banking supervision has been proactive in introducing rules of behaviour, which helped create and sustain a 'utility banking' model. On the whole, the strong regulatory and institutional framework helped Poland to lower the volatility of growth below the regional and global peers and thus support faster convergence.

Going forward though, the key question is *why* Poland chose to adopt good rather than bad policies? What was different this time from the long past? This is what we turn to next.

6

Fundamental Sources of Poland's Growth

The Role of Institutions

> Europe invented a 'convergence machine', taking in poor countries and helping them become high income economies.
>
> Indermit Gill

> In establishing the rule of law, the first five centuries are always the hardest.
>
> Gordon Brown

> Commerce and manufactures can seldom flourish long (. . .) [if] people do not feel themselves secure in the possession of their property.
>
> Adam Smith

If the good policies documented in Chapter 5 drove good economic perform-ance, then what drove good policies? What was the role of institutions in Polish economic success? And what drove good institutions?

In Chapter 5, I discussed the proximate sources—policies, factors, and endowments—of Poland's economic rise after 1989. In this chapter I focus on the fundamental causes of Poland's performance, namely the adoption of Western institutions. I start by documenting how the prospect of the EU accession drove the institution-building. I show what institutions Poland adopted and how they were key to the country's economic performance. I argue that Poland—next to Hungary, the Czech Republic, and the Baltic States—was among the fastest adopters of Western institutions, which helped it grow more rapidly than other transition economies.

I then go on to focus on the fundamental question of why Poland *wanted* to adopt good institutions from the West rather than look for a 'third way'. I argue that the positive legacy of communism was the key reason for why Poland built democracy and an open, inclusive economy for the first time in its history. It is because communism eradicated all pre-modern, feudal social structures and eliminated oligarchic elites, which prevented Poland from building growth-promoting institutions throughout its history. Communism created a society with unprecedentedly low wealth and income inequalities. In line with the predictions of the institutional development framework proposed in this book, such egalitarian distribution of economic resources helped ensure that in 1989 all economic, political, and social players had a keen interest in building institutions, which would give everyone an equal chance to succeed and prevent emergence of an oligarchic system. Unlike in the past when *szlachta* monopolized economic and political power, this time no social class was strong enough to impose their own choice of institutions. The prospect of joining the EU provided the critical anchor for the new political, social, and economic deal.

There were also additional factors, which helped Poland build good institutions: a historically unprecedented social and political consensus to 'return to Europe', high-quality, Westernized, and growth-oriented elites, and emergence of a strong middle class. Finally, Western European readiness to embrace CEE and help it develop was also critical. All these unique factors worked together to allow Poland to adopt Western growth-promoting political and economic institutions for the first time ever. I conclude by offering insights for other countries.

6.1. Which Institutions Drove Poland's Transition?

As noted in Chapter 5, Poland was one of the leaders of institution-building among transition economies. It started to build market institutions even before the transition. It first joined the IMF and the World Bank in 1986, as only the third communist country to do so (Romania joined in 1972, Hungary joined the IMF in 1982) and signed up to all the accompanying obligations. In the same year it also introduced a ground-breaking anti-monopoly law. Soon after, the government reformed the governance of SOEs to strengthen market-based incentives, lessen importance of directive-type planning, give managers larger incentives to perform, and improve management education based on Western practices (Koźmiński, 2008a, 2008b, 2014; Bielecki and Koźmiński, 2003). In 1987–1989, Poland introduced a two-tier banking system, with the central bank spinning off its regional branches and transforming into commercial banks. The reform freed monetary policy from its reliance on centrally planned targets and allowed the central bank to behave like a standard central bank rather than a mere distributor of cash.

During 1988 and 1989, Poland also allowed registration of private firms and opened markets to inflows of FDI. And it freed prices: at the beginning of 1989, half of all prices were already liberalized, as opposed to close to zero in Romania. In early 1989, the last communist government also partly liberalized the foreign exchange market to align the official exchange rate with the black market one (Bąk, 2009). Finally, unlike other states in the Soviet camp, throughout the whole communist period Poland continued to use the 1934 commercial and bankruptcy law.[1] Courts, while not independent from the communist party, were nonetheless broadly trusted to adjudicate civil, labour, and commercial cases.

The 1989 transition gave a big boost to institution-building. The 'Balcerowicz Plan' liberalized prices, dismantled monopolies, and introduced equal treatment of all property rights, eliminating former privileges of state-owned enterprises. It also opened up the markets to new players and established an Anti-Monopoly Agency to promote competition and fight monopolies. Capital markets were also developed: in 1991 Poland was the first post-communist country to establish a Securities and Exchange Commission and set up a stock exchange. In parallel, the government reformed the commercial law to align it with the requirements of capitalist markets and gave full independence to the courts.

Further institutional reforms followed, especially in the run-up to the EU accession in 2004. Institutional reforms continued after the accession: most recently Poland introduced a ground-breaking macro-prudential framework and a new bank resolution framework. It also fundamentally reformed the bankruptcy and corporate restructuring law (Table 6.1).

As a result of this rapid institutional building, by 2016, Poland had built a broad range of institutions in all areas that matter for political and economic development, from 'voice and accountability', 'government effectiveness' through 'regulatory quality' to the 'rule of law' and 'control of corruption'. Poland's level of institutional development has become much more advanced than the average quality of institutions among its global upper-middle-income peers and only slightly behind the most developed countries (Figure 6.1).

Progress in the strength of rule of law, the fundamental economic institution, has been particularly robust. Between 1996 and 2015, Poland's improved its percentile score on the rule of law from 66 to 76, one of the fastest improvements among its global peers. Only South Korea was equally impressive, as it improved its score from 69 in 1996 to 81 in 2015. Some

---

[1] The 1934 commercial and bankruptcy laws were amended on multiple occasions after 1945, but remained binding until they were replaced by entirely new pieces of legislation in 2001 and 2003, respectively.

Table 6.1. Poland's major institutional reforms, 1988–2016

Year	Institutional reform
1988	New banking law; establishment of nine new commercial banks, former branches of the National Bank of Poland
1989	Co-operation agreement between European Community and Poland: gradual removal of tariffs and non-tariff barriers to trade; new law on free media
1990	Balcerowicz Plan: price liberalization; dismantling of trade monopolies, currency convertibility, beginning of privatization, equal treatment of all property rights, establishment of competition watchdog
1991	EC Association Agreement: removal of some restrictions on labour and capital movement, gradual introduction of free trade, promise of EU membership
1991	Founding of the Warsaw Stock Exchange; establishment of Securities and Exchange Commission; new Foreign Investment Law aligned with EU legislation
1994	Establishment of collective wage bargaining within Tripartite Commission
1995	Accession to WTO
1996	Accession to OECD
1997	Adoption of a new Constitution; new law on the National Bank of Poland: introduction of a Monetary Policy Council and strengthening of the Bank's independence
1998	New law on professionalization of public administration; new anti-corruption law
1999	Education, health, and pension system reforms. Local administration reform: establishment of sixteen new regions, decentralization of tasks and fiscal authority
2001	Establishment of new regulatory agencies, including Energy Regulatory Authority, Office of Telecommunication Regulation
2004	Accession to the European Union: freedom of movement of capital, goods, labour (with time-bound restrictions in some countries), and services
2006	Establishment of Polish Financial Services Authority, a financial sector mega-regulator
2007	Establishment of National Research & Development Centre for R&D financing and commercialization
2013	Deregulation of 250 professions
2015	New macro-prudential framework, new bankruptcy and corporate restructuring law
2016	New bank resolution framework, aligned with EU directives

Source: Author's own based on World Bank (2017a), Duval *et al.* (2016); MICREF reform database for Poland.

countries such as Russia or Ukraine have hardly progressed. Others, such as Thailand, have regressed over the period (Figure 6.2). Scores for other elements of the institutional framework—regulatory quality, government effectiveness, or voice and accountability—tell the same story.

The overall progress in building institutions has translated into a decline in corruption, which is a useful proxy for the overall quality of the institutional framework. According to the Transparency International's Corruption Perceptions Index 2016, Poland was in twenty-ninth place out of 175 countries worldwide and had much lower corruption than suggested by its level of

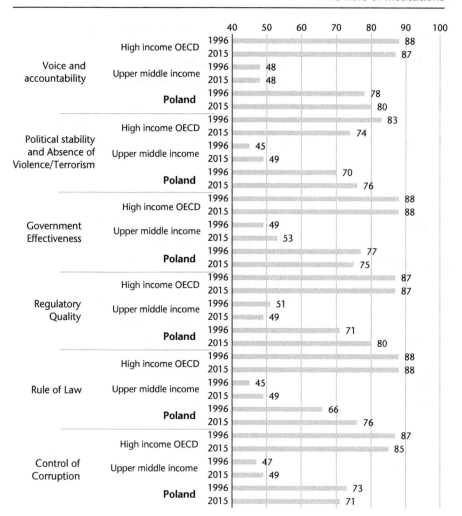

Figure 6.1. Changes in Poland's institutions versus upper-middle-income and high-income peers, 1996–2015.

Source: Author's own based on http://info.worldbank.org/governance/wgi/index.aspx#reports.

income (Figure 6.3). Poland is now less corrupt than the much richer Spain, Italy, or South Korea, and less corrupt than its regional peers, the Czech Republic, Hungary, and Slovakia. Poland was also one of the fastest improvers in fighting corruption, moving up in the ranking at a fast pace since 1996.[2]

---

[2] See the historical series at: https://www.transparency.org/permissions.

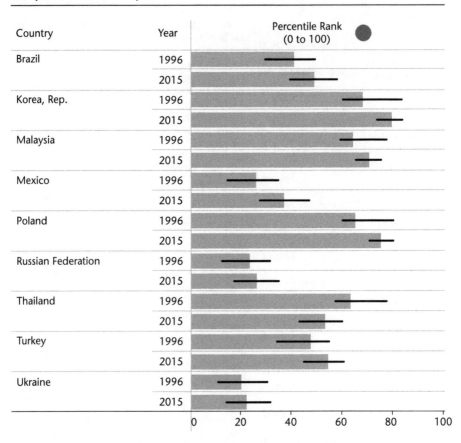

Figure 6.2. Changes in the strength of the rule of law, selected countries, 1996–2015. *Source*: Kaufmann, Kraay, and Mastruzzi (2010).

6.2. Poland's Institutional Quality in the Long-Term Perspective

As a result of the institutional progress after 1989, Poland has built by far the best institutions in its whole history. While there are no long-term indicators of institutional quality going back into the distant past (the World Bank's Governance Indicators, for instance, go back to 1996 only), it is possible to use the tax revenue to GDP ratio as a proxy for the quality of institutions and state capacity.[3]

According to this indicator, Poland had been a European laggard in institutional development throughout all of its history. It had by far the lowest tax

---

[3] For the connection between tax revenue and state capacity, see Hendrix (2010), Lieberman (2002), and Dincecco and Katz (2016). Dincecco and Katz also found a strong link between fiscal centralization and long-term economic growth until the First World War.

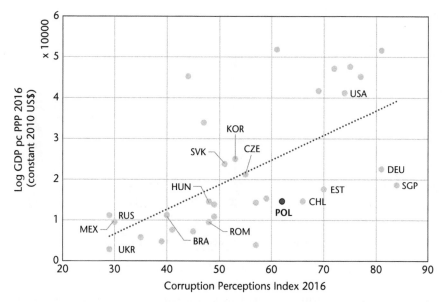

Figure 6.3. Perceptions of corruption versus GDP per capita, 2016.

Note: The Corruption Perceptions Index shows data on a scale of 0–100 where 0 equals the highest level of perceived corruption and 100 equals the lowest level of perceived corruption.

Source: Author's own based on Transparency International and the IMF.

revenue in Europe between 1500 and 1789. The situation did not improve much after Poland regained independence in 1918: in 1936, Poland's state tax revenue per capita was at only about 12 per cent of the tax revenue in the UK. The tax intake improved during communism, but other inefficient institutions ensured that the system collapsed later. It is only in the last twenty-five years that the institutional structure of Poland (and the rest of CEE) has become largely aligned with most developed countries in the world. In 2015, Poland's tax revenue to GDP was actually higher than in the UK (Figure 6.4).[4]

Another way to look at the long-term quality of institutions is to use expert assessment of the level of development of a number of key institutions such as the rule of law or the intensity of market competition. Table 6.2 shows my take on the quality of Poland's institutions since 1500AD, where full circle stands for 'good', half-full stands for 'average', and empty circle stands for 'bad'.

As discussed in Chapter 2, since 1500AD until the country's collapse in 1795, Poland's institutions, never strong to begin with, have become extremely

---

[4] Of course, the usual caveats apply in terms of different social models, efficiency of public spending, etc. But tax revenues are the only proxy for institutions, which can be measured across centuries.

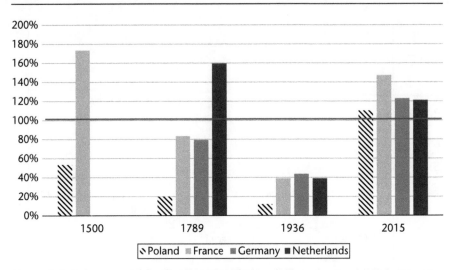

Figure 6.4. State tax revenue during 1500–2015 as a proxy for the quality of institutions, Poland, France, Germany, and the Netherlands, United Kingdom=100.

Note: Karaman and Pamuk (2013) for 1500–1789 (annual revenue per capita/daily urban wage, fifty-year averages), GUS (2014), and IMF WEO (general government revenue as per cent of GDP) for 2015.

Source: Author's own based on sources in the Note.

Table 6.2. Quality of institutions in Poland from 1500AD to present

Institutions	Poland 1500–1795	Partitions 1795–1918	Interwar 1918–1939	Communism 1945–1989	Transition 1989–now
Rule of law	◒	◒	◒	◒	●
Competition	○	◒	◒	○	●
Social mobility	○	◒	◒	●	●
Contestable political system	◒	◒	◒	○	●
Free press	○	◒	◒	○	●
Property rights	◒	●	●	◒	●
Efficient state	○	◒	◒	◒	◒

Source: Author's own.

weak: there was no free competition, no social mobility, no free press, and—for all practical purposes—no public administration, as reflected in *inter alia* low state tax revenue. The political system was contestable only in a sense that kings did not have absolute power and were subject to election by the gentry. Only the latter could participate in the political process. Other social classes such as merchants or peasants were excluded. *Szlachta* and its elite, the aristocracy, were also the only ones to enjoy the rule of law and property rights, although the enforcement was lacking. The vast majority of the society, the serf peasants, had hardly any rights.

The quality of institutions improved during Poland's occupation by the three neighbouring powers, Russia, Prussia, and Austria between 1795 and 1918. They introduced the rule of law, enhanced the security of property rights, and improved social mobility by eliminating serfdom. They also introduced modern public administration. Prussia (later Germany) had the most efficient state; the Russian and the Austro-Hungarian Empires were less efficient (hence the half-empty circle in Table 6.2).

During the interwar period, the newly independent Poland built on the institutional progress achieved before the First World War. However, the efficiency of the state relative to the regional and European peers did not improve, largely owing to low tax revenue and class-based society, which blocked the less-privileged from taking good jobs. Because of the difficult access to education, finance and markets, social mobility was low. Rule of law was strong, but only for those who could afford it.

During communism, free press, competitive markets, and a contestable political system disappeared. The rule of law and property rights were partly preserved (for agricultural land and real estate, if not for the nationalized manufacturing). Public administration played the key role in the economy, but became gradually overwhelmed by the challenges inherent in managing a planned economy. The biggest achievement of communism was the unprecedented social mobility, which lifted millions of poor peasants and blue collar workers out of grinding poverty and gave them a chance to advance socially and economically.

It was only after 1989 that Poland could report an almost clean green sheet for the first time in the country's history. Across all indicators, it has improved its institutions to the level only slightly lower than in Western Europe and other developed countries. Poland developed a strong rule of law, robust competition, and secure property rights. It also enjoyed robust democracy and free press. Social mobility was higher than in developed countries, as argued in Chapter 5. Only the efficiency of the state left room for improvement as it continued to struggle to improve as fast as the private sector.

6.3. The Impact of Institutions on Growth in Poland

Empirical literature details how Poland's rapid institutional building helped spur growth during the transition. Beck and Laeven (2006) analyse how institutional development affected the growth rate of GDP per capita between 1992 and 2004 for twenty-four transition economies, including Poland. They found that the quality of institutions can explain a large part of cross-country differences in performance, controlling for initial conditions, macroeconomic policies, and the speed of reforms. Specifically, they showed that 'one standard deviation in Institutional Development (0.62) can explain a growth difference of 1.6 percentage points per year' (p. 20). In other words, over twelve years since the beginning of transition, countries with better institutions such as Poland could increase their GDP per capita by more than 20 per cent relative to countries with slower institutional reforms.

Back and Leaven (ibid.) also found that the speed of institution-building mattered: countries that reformed institutions earlier, such as Poland, Hungary, or the Czech Republic, experienced faster growth after 1989. Indeed, by 1995, these three countries were the most advanced in introducing market-oriented institutions (Figure 6.5). Other EU candidate countries were initially slower in the institutional take-up, but they largely caught up with the leaders around the time of the EU accession in 2004 and—in the case of Romania and

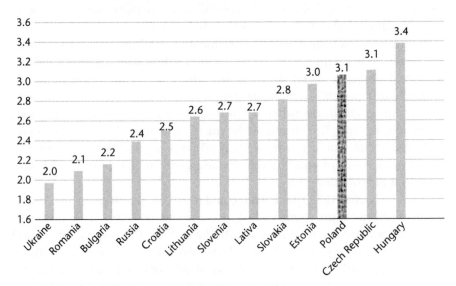

Figure 6.5. EBRD Index of Institutional Reform in 1995.

Note: Index is based on an average of scores for enterprise restructuring, large-scale and small-scale privatization, liberalization of markets and trade, competition policy, financial sector and infrastructural sector reforms. Range from 1 to 4.5.

Source: Author's own based on EBRD, various Transition Reports.

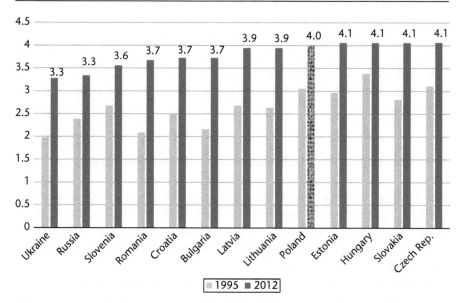

Figure 6.6. EBRD Index of Institutional Reform, 1995 and 2012.

Note: Index is based on an average of scores for enterprise restructuring, large-scale and small-scale privatization, liberalization of markets and trade, competition policy, financial sector and infrastructural sector reforms. Range from 1 to 4.5.

Source: Author's own based on EBRD, various Transition Reports.

Bulgaria—in 2007. However, Russia and many other post-Soviet states have been building institutions at a much slower pace (Figure 6.6).

Many other studies corroborated the importance of institutions for economic performance during the post-communist transition. Grogan and Moers (2001) and Havrylyshyn and Van Rooden (2003) showed a positive relationship between institutions and growth. Murrell (2003) emphasized the importance of formal institutions in development. Blanchard and Kremer (1997) highlighted the crucial impact of the rule of law. Roland (2000), Kolodko (2000), and Campos and Coricelli (2002) provided additional evidence of the positive role of institutions in driving prosperity.

There are also several studies that focus on the specific channels through which institutions affected growth in transition. Luengnaruemitchai and Schadler (2007) found that the EU accession and the institution-building that it engendered helped decrease borrowing costs in the private markets below what would be expected given the level of the countries' 'fundamentals'. This 'EU halo effect' had a positive impact on the cost of capital, investment, and economic growth in the EU countries. Bevan *et al.* (2004) found that development of legal institutions had a positive effect on FDI inflows to transition countries in Europe. Murrell (1996) argued that Poland's anti-monopoly office played an important role in promoting a competitive level playing field. Nunberg (1999) showed how the introduction of a Commissioner for Civil Rights Protection and reforms of the Administrative Court helped strengthen the rule of law in Poland. Finally, Pistor (2001) documented how Poland's independent capital markets supervision authority implemented robust regulations and built a strong stock market, while the Czech Republic did not.

6.4. The Role of the EU Accession in Institution-Building

The prospect of the accession to the EU was the key driver of institution-building in Poland and other new EU member states in CEE. Poles craved Western prosperity, stability, humanity, and dignity. They knew that joining the EU was key to making their dream come true. And they were ready to do everything to make it happen.

But adopting the Western institutions was far from easy. The EU accession turned out to be a long, arduous, and difficult process, which took almost fifteen years from start to finish. The process commenced in 1989, when Poland signed an agreement on trade and economic cooperation with the European Communities (later renamed the 'European Union'), and ended on 1 May 2004, when Poland and nine other countries in CEE joined the EU (Bulgaria and Romania joined in 2007 and Croatia in 2013). Table 6.3 shows the key dates in the EU accession calendar.

In many ways, the EU accession process could be likened to an old-fashioned story of courtship: Western Europe played a skittish 'hard to get' bride, which was never fully convinced about the marriage (even after it happened), while CEE was like an overly eager, poor, but ambitious groom, with a large dose of raging hormones, who could not wait to consummate the marriage (and once it did, the reform process slowed).

The EU accession was predicated on meeting several key political and economic criteria. They were agreed by EU leaders at a summit in Copenhagen in 1993 and were thus known as 'the Copenhagen Criteria'. In the European Commission's own words, the EU membership required that:

> a candidate country has achieved stability of institutions guaranteeing democracy, the rule of law, human rights, respect for and protection of minorities, the existence of a functioning market economy as well as the capacity to cope with competitive pressure and market forces within the Union. Membership presupposes the candidate's ability to take on the obligations of membership including adherence to the aims of political, economic and monetary union ... The associate countries in CEE that so desire shall become members of the European Union as soon as an associate country is able to assume the obligations of membership by satisfying the economic and political conditions required. (Berend, 2009, p. 88).

Table 6.3. Key events during Poland's EU accession process

Date and place	Event
19 September 1989, Warsaw	Poland signs the agreement on trade and economic cooperation with the European Communities
25 May 1990, Brussels	Poland submits an official application for the opening of negotiations for association agreement with the European Communities
16 December 1991, Brussels	Poland signs the Europe Agreement, thus becoming a country associated with the European Communities
20 October 1992, Warsaw	The President of the Republic of Poland ratifies the Europe Agreement, which comes into force in February 1994
21–22 June 1993, Copenhagen	The European Council officially states that EU enlargement is also the EU's goal, conditional on the candidate countries fulfilling certain political and economic criteria, known as the Copenhagen criteria
8 April 1994, Athens	Poland hands the formal application for accession to the EU to the representative of the Greek Presidency
28 January/22 May 1997, Warsaw	The Council of Ministers/Parliament adopt the National Strategy for Integration, a document that systematizes the tasks to be completed in the period preceding EU membership
12–13 December 1997, Luxembourg	The European Council officially invites ten countries, including Poland, to initiate formal EU membership negotiations
31 March 1998, Brussels	Initiation of EU accession negotiations
12–13 December 2002, Copenhagen	The European Council approves the result of accession negotiations with ten candidate countries for EU membership, including Poland
16 April 2003, Athens	The Accession Treaty is formally signed by representatives of twenty-five countries—fifteen EU member states and ten candidate countries
7–8 June 2003	In a nationwide referendum, 77.45% of Poles vote for Poland's accession to the EU
1 May 2004	Poland becomes a member state of the EU

Source: Belka (2014).

In a nutshell, the CEE groom had to be democratic, law-abiding, tolerant, market-oriented, and able to successfully compete with others to be allowed to kiss the Western bride. But the Western bride did not stop there: she soon realized that the adherence to formal requirements alone was not sufficient to ensure that both the letter and the spirit of the EU laws were followed. Smoke and mirrors would not be enough this time.

Hence, in 1995, the membership criteria were extended to include new requirements. The candidate countries had to prove that they not only adopted the EU legislation, but also that they could efficiently implement it. All candidate countries were made to reform their public administration, adopt a system of professional, de-politicized civil service, and align administrative structures with those in other EU member states. They also had to enhance the capacity of public administration and prove that it could act fully in line with the European principles and ensure proper implementation of EU regulations. Thus, Poland adopted a new law on civil service in 1998, which explicitly stated that its objective is to ensure 'professional, conscientious, bipartisan and politically neutral implementation of the state objectives' by public administration.[5] All other candidate countries followed suit.

The EU accession also required the prospective member states to incorporate into their national legislations *acquis communautaire*, a summa of European laws developed since the founding of the EU. The *acquis* encompassed thirty-one chapters and almost 100,000 pages of text, covering areas from democracy to the rule of law, transport to employment, and from immigration to the environment (Berend, 2009). The wholesale adoption of these rules required far-reaching changes in legislation, sometimes even in constitutions.

Finally, the formal EU membership requirements were supplemented by a meticulous monitoring process. When Poland formally applied for EU membership in 1994, the European Commission (EC) sent a 200-page questionnaire for Poland to take stock of its progress in aligning with the EU regulations. Polish answers to the questionnaire amounted to 2,600 pages, although Bulgaria later broke the record with 5,000 pages (Berend, 2009). From 1998, the EC started to monitor the implementation of the *acquis*, public administration reforms, and overall alignment with the key European political and economic criteria. The results of the review were presented in detailed annual reports, which assessed each aspect of the accession process for each of the candidate countries. The EC's assessment reports worked as a reform scorecard, which encouraged EU candidate countries to compete on who would make the most progress on the way to the EU.

Each monitoring report had a detailed list of recommendations. They covered an unprecedentedly wide range of political, economic, social, and environmental issues (Berend, 2009). As Bokova (2000, p. 67) reports: 'The pre-accession strategy directly affects virtually all aspects of life in an applicant country—in its industry, agriculture, commercial and financial sectors, consumer practices, the environment, standardization, education and foreign policy. It involves profound changes which sometimes touch the very fabric of society'. The EU's 'recommendations' were taken seriously: laws and policies in candidate countries were duly changed in response to them (Baun, 2000).[6] The Western bride played the courtship game to the maximum.

But that was not the end: the candidate countries not only had to fully adopt EU-inspired rules and regulations, but also accompany them by changes

---

[5] Law on Civil Service, 18 December 1998. Full text: https://dsc.kprm.gov.pl/sites/default/files/ustawa_z_dnia_18_grudnia_1998_r._o_sluzbie_cywilnej.pdf, accessed 12 May 2017.

[6] For example, EU recommendations included a request to repeal a 2001 Hungarian law on special rights for Hungarian minorities abroad (the law was duly revoked in 2003), put limits on the amount of public subsidies to the Polish shipyard industry (the shipyards soon went bankrupt), and close down nuclear plants in Lithuania and Bulgaria (Berend, 2009, p. 92).

in secondary legislation, implementation methodologies, and ways of doing things. In Latvia, for instance,

> serious changes [were] needed in the legal methodology, which civil servants and judges use in applying norms of rights... Latvia must undergo a serious and conscientiously promoted 'legal revolution' as part of a broad intellectual and educational 'revolution'. Only then will it have a chance... of becoming a modern, law-based country. (Levits, 1998, p. 195)

By the time of the EU accession in 2004, Poland and other EU candidate countries 'downloaded' 50,000 new laws and regulations and thousands of new norms of behaviour and ways of doing things modelled on the West (Berend, 2009).

6.5. The Impact of the EU on Income Convergence

The EU has played an unprecedented role in transforming countries from being poor to being rich. Since 1960, there have been only twenty-four countries worldwide, which according to the World Bank definition (GNI per capita of at least $12,476) have become high income.[7] An unprecedented two-thirds of them are countries which became developed thanks to EU membership (Table 6.4). The first group of countries includes Portugal, Spain, Greece, and Ireland, which joined the EU in the early 1980s and within the following two decades became high income. The second wave of countries included Poland, the Czech Republic, Slovakia, Slovenia, Hungary, and the three Baltic States, which all became high income a few years after acceding to the EU in 2004. Bulgaria and Romania are slated to become high income in the near future.

Campos, Coricelli, and Moretti (2014) estimated the overall value of EU membership. They asked what would have been the GDP of a specific transition country if it had not acceded to the EU and not adopted Western institutions. They found that without the EU, GDP per capita in CEE would have been, on average, about 12 per cent lower than otherwise. Given other negative spillover effects on politics, culture, and social consensus, which the authors did not calculate, the negative impact would likely have been much larger. Poland and other CEE countries would never succeed if they were left outside the EU. Poland would at best be like Belarus, and at worst like Ukraine.

Aside from the EU, there is no other institution, country, or organization in the world that helps their members become rich so quickly. The USA is a good

[7] Not counting countries with oil. Full list of high-income countries: https://datahelpdesk.worldbank.org/knowledgebase/articles/906519#High_income.

Table 6.4. How the EU makes countries rich: countries that have become high income since 1960

Non-European Union	European Union
1. Chile	1. Croatia
2. Israel	2. Cyprus
3. Puerto Rico	3. Czech Republic
4. South Korea	4. Estonia
5. Singapore	5. Greece
6. Taiwan	6. Hungary
7. Trinidad and Tobago	7. Ireland
8. Uruguay	8. Latvia
	9. Lithuania
	10. Poland
	11. Portugal
	12. Slovakia
	13. Slovenia
	14. Spain
	15. Bulgaria*
	16. Romania*

Note: Excludes rich OECD countries, small island states and oil-rich countries.
* Romania and Bulgaria are projected to become high income in the near future.

Source: Author's own based on data from the World Bank.

example: despite being the global pre-eminent economic power, their southern neighbours have not made it rich yet. Only the EU has achieved this.

6.6. Drivers of Good Political and Economic Institutions

A literature review suggests that there were several drivers of post-transition institution-building. Roland (2014) shows that the strength of the rule of law, government effectiveness, and control of corruption in transition economies was positively affected by the strength of democracy and EU membership. Natural resource rents, ruggedness, landlockedness, and a country's length of history mattered much less or not at all (Treisman 2014a, 2014b, 2012). EBRD (2013) and Roland and Verdier (2003) found that the EU accession had a key role in promoting institution-building. Lastly, Beck and Laeven (2006) showed that availability of natural resources and entrenchment of communist elites driven by how long the country lived under communism affected institution-building during transition. They argued that the more abundant the natural resources and the longer the period of communism among transition economies, the weaker the quality of institutions.

But none of these studies explain *why* Poland wanted to join the EU and build good institutions in the process. But this is the fundamental question. If we know that good institutions produce good policies and good economic performance, why would any country in the world not want to have them?

Poland wanted to adopt good institutions and succeed economically because of a few unique factors that happened at the same time for the first time. I take them in turn.

6.6.1. *Positive Legacy of Communism*

Communism provided the key conditions for emergence of an inclusive society post 1989, which helped Poland absorb good, Western institutions. As mentioned in Chapter 3, communism (and the Second World War) demolished the old, feudal, extractive structures that prevented Poland from building growth-promoting institutions throughout its history and replaced these structures with a broad-based, socially mobile, egalitarian, and well-educated society. None of these conditions had existed before. In addition, communism helped distribute economic resources with unprecedented equality.

The decline in inequality was supported by a huge shift in employment from agriculture to industry: during 1950–1970, almost 5 million peasants, or close to 20 per cent of the country's total population, moved to cities and became employed in industry. Poland experienced the largest social transformation in Central and Eastern Europe and one of the largest social transformations in the world, in proportion to total population (Berend, 2009).

Communism also helped educate the society. Poland shifted from the prewar apartheid-like educational system, which was reserved largely for the rich, to an egalitarian, comprehensive, and all-encompassing educational system, which offered free, uniform, and public education to everyone, while offering special privileges to the disadvantaged groups, peasants, and proletariat.

Lastly, the combined effect of unprecedented social mobility, egalitarianism, and easy access to education engineered by communism affected transition in the most direct way: the sons and daughters of the communist social advancement in the 1950s later became the fathers and mothers of Poland's post-1989 growth miracle. Leszek Balcerowicz, the key architect of Poland's transition, was born in 1947 into a poor peasant worker family in Lipno, a small village around Torun. His father was a butcher's apprentice, who oversaw a small state poultry farm. His mother finished school at the age of 13 (Balcerowicz and Stremecka, 2014). Thanks to communism, Balcerowicz's life chances were much different. He received free education, which led him to become an economics professor and a future key post-1989 reformer. Similarly, Grzegorz W. Kolodko, the other hero of post-communist transition, was born into a family in provincial Tczew that was far from being well-to-do. He worked his way up to become a professor at the Warsaw School of Economics and Poland's deputy prime minister and minister of finance. Other key protagonists of the Polish economic (as well as political, social, and cultural) transition have similar biographies.

Table 6.5. Forbes List 2016: top ten richest Poles

	Name	Wealth in 2015 (in $US million)	Wealth in 1989 (in $US million)
1	Sebastian and Dominika Kulczyk*	4,000	1
2	Zygmunt Solorz-Zak	2,500	0
3	Michal Solowow	2,300	0
4	Dariusz Milek	890	0
5	Jerzy Starak	725	1
6	Leszek Czarnecki	535	0
7	Furman family	400	0
8	Jaroslaw Pawluk	400	0
9	Antoni Ptak	375	0
10	Solange and Krzysztof Olszewski	350	0

*: Sebastian and Dominika Kulczyk inherited their wealth from the late Jan Kulczyk, who according to his own estimates was worth about 1 million dollars in 1989; author's own estimates for other businessmen's wealth in 1989.

Source: Author's own based on Forbes 2016 List of 100 Richest Poles.

Except for just one minister of finance, Jan Rostowski, who was born into a well-heeled Polish family in London, all other twenty-five ministers since 1989 largely owed their professional success to communist social advancement. They would have never had the same chance to grow if they were born before 1939.

Communist egalitarianism also helped create a brand-new business class. In 2016, the richest top ten Poles were all 'self-made' men who hardly had any money at the beginning of transition, but had good education, energy, and entrepreneurial spirit instead (Table 6.5). The same 'rags to riches' stories are shared by virtually every other member of the country's list of the richest 100 businessmen (Cienski, 2014). Never in the history of Poland have so many new fortunes arisen from nothing in such a short time.

The bottom line is that thanks to the shock of communism, Poland moved from the extractive society equilibrium from before 1939, based on a narrow distribution of economic resources, to an inclusive society after 1989, based on an egalitarian distribution of assets. This shift, as predicted by the institutional development framework proposed in Chapter 1, helped ensure that the whole society for the first time in the country's history had an overwhelming interest in building inclusive institutions. There was no single social class or oligarchic elite, such as *szlachta* in the past, which would be powerful enough to impose their own choice of institutions. All social classes—intelligentsia, proletariat, peasants, political dissidents, and even communist party members—agreed that democracy and open markets would be the optimal arrangements for all. The spectre of EU membership provided the anchor around which the whole society coalesced and adopted the Western political and economic institutions in the process for the first time ever.

6.6.2. Social Consensus to Return to Europe

The second reason why Poland wanted to adopt Western institutions was a historically unprecedented social and political consensus to 'return to Europe' and become 'European' again.[8] There were several reasons for such a strong consensus.

One of the reasons was that Poland was by far the most open society in the communist camp. Thus, unlike Romanians, Czechs, and many others around the region, Poles could see the differences in the quality of life between Poland and the West first hand and draw the obvious conclusions. Poland had opened its border to travel to Western Europe after 1956, when it ditched Stalinism and decided on its own, Polish road to communism. In 1954, when Poland was still closed (and as many other communist countries remained until much later), only 52 Poles could travel to the West (Stola, 2010). But the post-Stalinist 'thaw' after 1956 gradually opened the country up: by the end of the 1970s, almost 700,000 Poles travelled to the West per year and 200,000 Poles worked abroad on temporary contracts.

In the 1980s, the contact with the West intensified further. In 1981, just before the introduction of the martial law in December of that year, more than 1.2 million Poles travelled to Western Europe, which was more than the combined number of Poles who travelled abroad between 1949 and 1969 (Stola, 2010). In the late 1980s, about 600,000 Poles had a seasonal job in the West.

Contacts with the West pervaded the whole society, from communists to dissidents. Aleksander Kwasniewski, the youngest minister in the communist government in the 1980s, and the future President of Poland between 1995 and 2005, is a good example of a Westernized 'communist': during his studies in the 1970s, he held student jobs in the USA (moving rental cars across the country) and in Sweden (picking up strawberries). He was not unique: many of his communist party colleagues did the same. On the other side of the political aisle, the Solidarity dissidents were equally well travelled: Tadeusz Mazowiecki, the first democratic prime minister of Poland, visited the West often during most of his pre-1989 career. In 1987, he spent the whole year lecturing around Europe, visiting Belgium, France, Germany, Italy, and Austria (Wolek, 1997). Bronislaw Geremek, another Solidarity dissident and intellectual, who was the leader of one of the main post-Solidarity political parties in the 1990s and then Poland's minister of foreign affairs in the late 1990s, completed postgraduate studies in France in 1956–1958, lectured at Sorbonne from 1960 to 1965, and published numerous books in ten languages on medieval Western Europe.[9]

---

[8] Back in the early 1990s, when Poles were travelling to the West, they were saying that they were going to 'Europe'. They do not say it anymore. But Ukrainians, Russians, and many others east of Poland still do.

[9] https://en.wikipedia.org/wiki/Bronis%C5%82aw_Geremek, accessed 20 June 2017.

Such significant openness of a communist country was totally unprecedented. All other communist countries, with the possible exception of Hungary, were almost totally closed, not unlike North Korea today. Among Eastern German academics, for example, it was considered more attractive to be included on the list of people, who could travel abroad than earning 'habilitation' (a second PhD needed to become a professor), even if being on the list did not guarantee that foreign travel would indeed be possible (Niederhut, 2006). A higher level of political repression also mattered: as Stola (2016, p. 170) put it, Poland was different from its communist peers because of 'the relatively low level of fear'.

In addition, Poland's openness was supported by a large diaspora, mostly located in the West, which was larger than among any other country in the Soviet Bloc (Stola, 2010). The diaspora increased by an additional 2 million people or more than 5 per cent of the population during communism. Millions of Poles living abroad helped keep the nation wedded to the West by sending remittances, financing non-communist media and culture, and keeping the society informed through private visits and correspondence.

Finally, Poland's unprecedented openness was also reflected in the experience of millions of Poles, who were engaged in petty, 'suitcase trade' in the region to—as Stola nicely described it—'exploit large disparities in prices and the availability of various consumer goods in the countries of CEE as well as inconsistencies in their currencies' exchange rates' (Stola, 2010, p. 476). It is estimated that there were between 1 and 2 million of such trade trips by the late 1970s. Because of a higher level of repression and closed borders (as well as less evident shortages of goods than in Poland), the number of such traders in other countries behind the Iron Curtain was much lower. Poles were the Phoenicians of the Soviet Camp.

The second reason for the strong social consensus in 1989 to 'return to Europe' was that Poland was the only communist country in which the Catholic Church played an important social role and was a transmitter of Western values. More than 90 per cent of Poles, including communist party members, considered themselves to be Catholic. The fact that the Pope, John Paul II (1979–2005), was Polish gave the Church additional salience. In no other communist country would it be imaginable to welcome the Pope for a visit. But the Polish Pope visited Poland three times before 1989. His visits attracted million-strong crowds, who eagerly listened to his thinly veiled messages calling for freedom. There is a strong consensus among historians that the Polish Catholic Church played an indispensable role in the collapse of communism (Blusiewicz, 2016).

Furthermore, it also mattered that the civil society was stronger in Poland than in other countries in the region, which helped create the post-1989 social consensus in favour of the EU. The strength of the civil society was reflected *inter alia* in the potency of the Solidarity movement, the first independent labour union behind the Iron Curtain. At its height in 1981, Solidarity numbered 10 million people or a mind-boggling one-third of the total working age population (Smolar, 2009). At the same time, in the Czech Republic Vaclav Havel's Charter 77 dissident movement counted at best a few thousand sympathizers (Hitchcock, 2003). There were hardly any significant dissident movements in other communist countries. In particular, there were only few dissidents in East Germany: Eastern (and Western Germans) were surprised when the Berlin Wall fell. And for a good reason: they had little to do with it.

In addition, the social consensus for joining Europe was for the first time ever shared by the whole population. Prior to 1939, only a thin sliver of Polish intelligentsia aspired to the Western values. The majority of the society, peasants, who represented more than two-thirds of the population, and blue-collar worker, were too poor, too uneducated, and too removed from social and political participation to be part of any social consensus. 'Returning to Europe' would sound absurd to them. In contrast, in 1989, the whole population, now much richer, educated, informed, and involved, was united in the quest to become European again.

Finally, some deeper, more ingrained cultural factors also played an important role. Poland and most of CEE has been part of the Judeo-Christian and Western cultural sphere from the very beginning of its history. Their citizens wanted to reclaim it as quickly as possible. In contrast, people in Eastern Orthodox and Muslim countries did not share the same cultural background. As a result, the former built democracy quickly, the latter much slower or not at all (I develop this point further in Chapter 7).[10] Poles also built their national identity around the historical narrative of the country's heroism (for instance, almost 150,000 deaths during the ill-fated Warsaw Uprising in 1944 are feted by many today as an emblem of a national heroism rather than of national disaster), its appreciation of a fight for 'our freedom and yours', and rejection of authority.[11] All these factors helped to revolt against communism and seek freedom in Europe.[12]

---

[10] Djankov (2016) explores this point in more detail. For more on the ongoing debate on the importance of religion in explaining economic performance, see for instance, McCleary and Barro (2006), who argue that religion matters, and Noland (2005), who holds the opposite view.

[11] As Wikipedia explains: 'For our freedom and yours (Za naszą i waszą wolność) is one of the unofficial mottos of Poland. It is commonly associated with the times when Polish soldiers, exiled from the partitioned Poland, fought in various independence movements all over the world'. https://en.wikipedia.org/wiki/For_our_freedom_and_yours, accessed 14 May, 2017.

[12] Although it is difficult to quantify or document, Poles arguably also felt more humiliated by communism than elsewhere in the Soviet camp and thus wanted to join the West even more. This was because, on the one hand, of the economic failure of the Polish communist republic, which—with the exception of Romania—delivered less prosperity than any other country in the Soviet Camp (see Chapter 3). On the other hand, it was driven by Poles' megalomaniac perception of the country's political, economic, and cultural strength in the past, especially during the

6.6.3. *Strong, Westernized and Growth-Oriented Elites*

The third reason Poland wanted to adopt good institutions was because it was governed by elites that were more open, independent, and Westernized than anywhere else in the region. These elites first helped bring down communism and then efficiently take over power after the transition. This was not the case for many other communist states—such as Bulgaria, Romania, or Ukraine— where alternative elites hardly existed and (transformed) communists remained in power.

While there is no obvious standard of how to measure the strength of elites or the degree of their Westernization, one can nonetheless try by looking at several proxies. First, Polish elites were more Westernized than elsewhere. Polish elites—artists, writers, scientists, and economists—were communicating, travelling, and working with the Western world much more than elites in any other communist country (Berend, 2009). Polish economists are the case in point: almost every single minister of finance since 1989 has spent considerable time in the West before 1989, studying, researching, lecturing, and earning degrees. Visits to the West helped them learn modern economics, establish Western networks, and—above all—internalize Western values, which guided them during the transition.

This was not the case in other countries in the post-Soviet camp, especially in the critical period at the beginning of the transition: in Bulgaria, for instance, the key economic policy makers until 2000 had no Western experience whatsoever (see Table 6.6). It did not help that they did not speak English either. Lack of Western experience was also largely the case in Romania as well as in all post-Soviet Union countries. Only the Czech Republic and Hungary could compare, if not fully, with Poland.

Such strong Western orientation of the Polish elites was historically unique. Throughout most of the country's history, the ruling elites were ambivalent about Western values. The ruling elites preferred to keep equal balance between the West and the East. As Marshall Józef Piłsudski, Poland's independence hero and the country's autocrat leader until his death in 1935, eloquently put it:

> in foreign policy, our field of action is in the East, where we can be strong. It is pointless for Poland to get too involved in Western foreign relations, because there's nothing else waiting for us there than kissing the West's ass . . . and getting shit upon.[13]

country's sixteenth century 'Golden Age' (as explained in Chapter 2), and the feeling that they deserved 'better'.

[13] http://jpilsudski.org/artykuly-historyczne-pilsudski/cytaty-jozefa-pilsudskiegom, accessed 2 July, 2017.

Table 6.6. Western experience of Polish and Bulgarian ministers of finance, 1989–2000

Poland's ministers of finance 1989–2000	Western connection	Bulgaria's ministers of finance 1989–2000	Western connection
Leszek Balcerowicz (12 Sep 1989–5 Dec 1991)	Fulbright Fellow at Columbia University (1972), USA; MBA from St. John's University in New York, 1974, visiting fellow at the University of Sussex (1985), the Marburg University (1988)	Ivan Kostov (20 Dec 1990–30 Dec 1992)	n.a.
Karol Lutkowski (23 Dec 1991–26 Feb 1992)	Professor of international finance at Warsaw School of Economics, multiple research trips abroad in the 1970s and the 1980s	Stoyan Aleksandrov (30 Dec 1992–17 Oct 1994)	n.a.
Andrzej Olechowski (26 Feb 1992–5 Jun 1992)	Economist at The World Bank, Washington, D.C. (1985–87); Economic Affairs Officer, UNCTAD, Geneva (1982–84)	Christina Vucheva (17 Oct 1994–25 Jan 1995)	n.a.
Jerzy Osiatyński (11 Jul 1992–26 Oct 1993)	Post-graduate studies in the UK in the 1970s	Dimitar Kostov (15 Jan 1995–12 Feb 1997)	n.a.
Marek Borowski (26 Oct 1993–8 Feb 1994)	n.a. (prohibited by the communist party from leaving the country after 1968)	Svetoslav Gavriyski (12 Feb 1997–21 May 1997)	n.a.
Grzegorz W. Kołodko (28 Apr 1994–4 Feb 1997)	Senior Fulbright Fellow at University of Illinois in Urbana-Champaign (1985–1986), Research Fellow at UNU/WIDER in Helsinki in 1988 and 1989	Muravey Radev (21 May 1997–24 Jul 2001)	n.a.
Marek Belka	Fulbright Fellow at Columbia University (1978–1979), scholarships in the 1980s at University of Chicago and London School of Economics		
Leszek Balcerowicz (31 Oct 1997–8 Jun 2000)	As above		

Source: Author's own based on various sources.

Needless to say, communist elites in Poland after 1945 were not Western-oriented either, at least until the 1970s and the 1980s.

Polish economic as well as political, social, and cultural elites before 1989 were also more independent than elsewhere in the region. The large autonomy, intellectual freedom, and social prestige of Polish universities was the main reason for the relative independence of the elites. This was largely not the case in other communist countries, where universities were often just another extension of the communist party (Connelly, 2000).

At the time of a complete monopoly of Marxist-Leninist propaganda around the region, Jacek Kochanowicz, a leading Polish economic historian, spoke for many, when he recalled the atmosphere of open intellectual discourse during his studies at the Warsaw University in the 1960s:

> In our course of political economy of capitalism we read Marx's Capital, but discussed it like any other text. But we also read Keynes (...) and the famous Paul Samuelson's Economics. The course of political economy of socialism was taught by Włodzimierz Brus, a leading revisionist. (Kochanowicz, 2014)

Similarly, Leszek Balcerowicz (2014, Kindle 558) reminisced about his studies in the 1970s and the 1980s:

> I graduated from the foreign trade faculty of the Warsaw School of Economics, probably the most open economic faculty in the socialist countries. In the textbooks and lectures on international economics, we were warned against the perils of import substitution and taught the virtues of an open economy. I strongly internalized these beliefs.

The Polish elites' intellectual openness, independence, and Western connections helped create Solidarity and contributed to destroying communism in 1989. This also helped to establish democracy: Bruszt et al. (2012) found that countries with strong dissident movements and civil society became democratic in 1989, while other countries adopted presidential regimes that quickly became non-democratic.

Educated, Westernized, and high-quality elites took the lead on all sides of the political spectrum. To take economists as an example, Leszek Balcerowicz led economic policy in the consecutive governments of liberal, Christian democratic, and conservative parties that emerged from the Solidarity camp, while Grzegorz W. Kolodko oversaw economic policy in the governments of the reformed post-communist party. Both were in charge of economic policy for 8 of out 10 years in the 1990s and then several additional years in the 2000s.

Probably the biggest difference between Poland and the rest of the Soviet Camp was that a significant number of Polish communists wanted the country to be democratic, successful, and European almost as much as the Solidarity elites. It was the Polish communists who together with Solidarity were responsible for taking down communism. It was them who came up with the idea of sharing power with the opposition following the Round Table talks in early 1989 and them who organized the first semi-democratic elections behind the Iron Curtain later in the same year. It was also them, who—most surprisingly—made Balcerowicz's 'shock therapy' happen: they controlled two-thirds of seats in the 1989–1991 parliament, which enacted all Balcerowicz' revolutionary reforms. Finally, it was the former communists who supported a bill on large-scale privatization in 1993, prevailing over 'no' votes of many former Solidarity dissidents.

Why did communists cooperate? They cooperated because they believed that the new Solidarity elites would keep the system open and let the old elites safeguard their privileged position. They were right about the former (Box 6.1), but largely wrong about the latter (Box 6.2).

Finally, the overall quality of the elites mattered. If we agree that the quality of education, Westernization, and intellectual openness are good proxies for the quality of elites, then Poland never had better elites before. This applies for both Solidarity and post-communist elites.

As to the post-communist elites, a good proxy for their quality was the ability of the communist party to re-invent itself and return to the political mainstream. As argued by Grzymala-Busse (2002), only in Hungary and Poland did the communist parties manage to transform themselves and win the popular vote soon after 1989: the Polish post-communist party returned to power in 1993 with more than 30 per cent of the popular support, while the Hungarian post-communist party won elections in 1994 with 33 per cent of support. In contrast, the Czech and Slovak parties have not transformed and never governed again.[14]

Grzymala-Busse (2002, p. 8) argues that the quality of the party elites explained the difference in the electoral performance. The elites of all the four post-communist parties were quite different in terms of skills, ideas, and ability to appeal to a large electorate. The elites of the Czech post-communist party were the worst: they had 'little experience with reform, or societal negotiation'. They stuck to old views and failed in democracy. The Slovak post-communist party also floundered. Both parties played no positive role in the transition, which happened not because of them but despite them. In Bulgaria and Romania, the communist parties hardly changed, but because of a lack of alternative elites they were nonetheless able to cling to power after 1989.

---

[14] The Polish post-communist party went on to win elections again in 2001, with more than 40 per cent of popular support.

Box 6.1. WHY DID POLISH COMMUNISTS AGREE TO RELEASE POWER?

In 1989, the original plan of the communist party was to co-opt Solidarity into an effort to reform the economy—which in the 1980s the communists realized they could not do on their own—in exchange for semi-democratic elections. However, to everyone's surprise, in the June 1989 elections Solidarity won all the available one-third of seats in Sejm, the lower chamber of Parliament, and ninety-nine out of 100 seats in the newly resurrected Senate. It became clear that the communist party had no social mandate to continue to be in power. The Polish communists acquiesced and let Solidarity create the first democratic government. Other countries followed soon after and communism was dead.

But why did communists agree to release power? How did they know that the new elites would not 'go after' them once the change in the system was completed? What made them trust that the new elites would not renege on their promise to keep the system open?

There were a couple of reasons. Communists believed that the new, non-communist elites wanted to keep the country open and democratic because they wanted to be considered Western and European, which was a deep source of their cultural identity. The new elites also needed to 'behave' to win Western support to restructure the crushing foreign debt. Without the West's benevolence, Poland would quickly go bankrupt. Polish communists also released power because they lost their 'religion': in the 1980s, the party elites became convinced that the communist system was doomed and it could not be saved.[15] It helped that, despite various privileges, even the top communists sometimes suffered deprivations which were not that much different from those faced by the rest of the society. During the 'lost decade' of the 1980s, the collapse of living standards did not spare anyone.[16]

Fourth, the party elites let go because they were just as attracted by the allure of the West as the rest of the society. This can explain why after 1989 the post-communist party became pro-Western, pro-liberal, and pro-democratic.[17] It was the post-communist party that led Poland to the OECD in 1996 and spearheaded the

---

[15] Aleksander Kwasniewski, a former key communist apparatchik, just after his election to become the President of Poland said that 'From an ideological point of view, I was never a Communist. In Poland I have seen very few Communists, especially since 1970s. I met a lot of technocrats, opportunists, reformers, liberals [but not Communists]' (Higley *et al.*, 1996, p. 139). Similarly, Kolodko (2000, p. 16) argues that while in other communist countries the elites still seemed to believe in the long-term future of communism, the Polish communist elites were already convinced that 'real socialism was doomed' and were getting ready 'for a safe landing for the outgoing system and a smooth takeoff for the market regime, though this was never admitted publicly'.

[16] Adam Michnik, one of the famous Solidarity activists, dubbed this collapse in the living standards as the 'Doctrine of the Radiators'. He explained it in his speech at the University of Michigan in the early 1990s: 'Three years ago all of the heaters (radiators) stopped working', said Michnik. Shivering in his apartment he thought that at least the Party officials were warm in their dachas. Then he met the wife of the former Polish premier at a friend's wedding. She was shivering. 'Why are you cold?' he asked. She said 'My husband is sitting at home wearing the fur hat given to him by Kosygin [Soviet high official]'. The country's heaters were on a 'permanent strike'. Reported in Michigan Alumnus, Jan–Feb 1990, pp. 11–12, Cited in Lipton and Sachs, 1990, p. 76.

[17] A former Reuters journalist recounts how in 1993 he met Aleksander Kwaśniewski, a young star of the communist party in the 1980s, then a leader of the transformed communist party after 1989, and the future President of Poland during 1995–2005, as he was exiting the parliament

enactment of a new, democratic Constitution in the same year. It was the post-communists, who reduced corporate income tax from 40 per cent to 19 per cent in the mid-1990s and reduced personal income tax. It was also the post-communist party, which staunchly supported accession to the EU and NATO. Finally, it was the post-communist party which, somewhat bizarrely, tried to introduce a flat tax on personal incomes in 2003. As argued by Grzymala-Busse (2010), the Polish post-communist party's political views were firmly in the centre of the political scene.

Finally, Polish communists decided to let go of power because of the existence of a credible commitment mechanism: the EU and—to a lesser extent—the US played a critical role as implicit third-party enforcers of the 'deal' between communists and Solidarity to create inclusive institutions. As argued by Acemoglu, Johnson, and Robinson (2005), the lack of a credible commitment mechanism is the main reason why countries are stuck with extractive institutions: in the absence of a third-party enforcer, the ruling elites cannot be sure that when they share or relinquish power, the new elites will keep their side of the bargain and will compensate the old elites for the lost rents. They also cannot be sure that new elites will keep the political and economic system open so that economic and political losses to the old elites will be limited. Thus, the old elites rarely let go.

It is only the elites of the Polish and Hungarian post-communist parties that succeeded in the new, democratic environment. As Grzymala-Busse puts it (2002, p. 9), 'In Poland (and in Hungary), skilled new elites both broke with the past and centralized the parties. These new elites had extensive experience in earlier policy reform, negotiation, and responding to popular concerns'. They were also able to convince the electorates of their competence in economic management (almost 80 per cent of electorates in the early 1990s thought that the economy was the key challenge (Kitschelt, 1995; Kitschelt et al., 1999)). It helped that the Polish communist party programme was largely pro-market (Grzymala-Busse, 2002).[18] Even the communist party's political adversaries such as Leszek Balcerowicz or members of parliament from Solidarity 'acknowledged that the [post-communist] party was extremely professional and competent' and had 'immensely-skilled elites' (Grzymala-Busse, 2002, p. 22). Kolodko (2000, p. 49) summarizes it nicely when he says that in Poland during 1994–1997 'there were more professors in the

following a crucial vote on a new privatization law. Asked about why the post-communist party decided to vote in favour of privatization, Kwasniewski quipped: 'We did this so that Reuters could write that Polish ex-communists are pro-reform'. The-tongue-in-cheek remark was actually an admission. Polish ex-communists remained sceptical of privatization but craved credibility 'as a Western-style leftist mainstream that can be trusted to keep Poland on the reform path' (Jasser, 2017, p. 10). Not much changed later: in 2004, on the day of Poland's accession to the EU, Aleksander Kwasniewski said that 'We have passed the test of being Europeans'. Indeed. http://news.bbc.co.uk/2/hi/europe/3675507.stm, accessed 14 April 2017.

[18] In 1997, Leszek Balcerowicz admitted that 'SLD's [the post-communist party] economic policies and goals expressed by Marek Belka, the new Finance Minister, are virtually indistinguishable from those of UW [Unia Wolnosci, one of the leading Solidarity parties]', Financial Times (1997), quoted in Kolodko and Nuti (1997), p. 24.

Box 6.2. POLAND'S TRANSITION DID NOT MUCH BENEFIT THE COMMUNIST *NOMENKLATURA*

There is much debate as to what extent former communists could safeguard their privileged social position and join the new, post-1989 elites. While a relatively large part of the Polish society believes that many former members of communist *nomenklatura* (top level communists) could find themselves cushy economic and social positions after 1989, according to Berend (2009, p. 24), only 9 per cent of the Polish former communist top party members held higher political offices after 1990 (3 per cent in the Czech Republic and 6 per cent in Hungary). The vast majority of the old communist elites became 'déclassé'. Less than 6 per cent of the communist elite turned into entrepreneurs and only 1–2 per cent of them became top managers in business (Eyal, Szelenyi, and Townsley, 1998, p. 199). However, the situation was different in Russia, where the old communist elites did better: in 1993, 10 per cent of top managers in Russia were former communist apparatchiks. Berend (2009, p. 244) concludes that in countries such as Poland 'the transformation did not lead to the reproduction of the old power structure, and capitalism was built (. . .) "on the ruins" of [socialism]'. Szelenyi, Treisman, and Lipinski (1995) and many others paint a similar picture.[19] EBRD (2016a) shows that the impact of having a parent in the communist party on today's equality of opportunity in Poland is negligible.

The situation was somewhat different with the economic elites in Poland: 31 per cent of former managers of SOEs remained company managers in 1993. Yet, while most of them belonged to the communist party before 1989, because they had to, they were nonetheless often just managers rather than party apparatchiks. Their skills proved useful in the new capitalist system, as reflected in the successful restructuring of Polish SOEs in the early 1990s (Pinto, 2014). In any case, very few if any at all of the former top communist-time managers became wealthy during the transition: there are hardly any of them on Poland's Forbes list today (which does not mean that there were no specific cases of *nomenklatura*-driven asset stripping and privatizations that attracted well-justified social ire).

Adoption of lustration laws in the 1990s in Poland and most of Central Europe, which restricted the participation of former communist elites and secret police members and collaborators in public administration, also helped keep *nomenklatura* under wraps. However, Bulgaria, ex-Yugoslavia, and the former Soviet Union (except Georgia) never introduced such laws. Thus, as argued by Djankov (2016, p. 27) 'Three of the parties in the Bulgarian parliament are led by former members of the communist-era secret police. In Russia and Serbia, members of the former secret police dominate political life, and even—in the case of President Vladimir Putin, a former KGB colonel—run the country'.

[post-communist] government than there had been generals in the martial law governments of the 1980s'.

High quality of political elites also enhanced the political competition. The Polish post-communist party was considered a credible alternative to the government in power, which kept the ruling party on their toes. This reduced rent-seeking and helped build formal institutions to embed the open-access

---

[19] See also Slomczynski and Shabad (1996), Mach (2000), and Goryszewski (2014).

system. The Czech Republic and Slovakia were different: weaker opposition to the ruling governments allowed the ruling government to get away with less transparency, weaker oversight, and weaker formal institutions (Grzymala-Busse, 2010). It also allowed them to go slow on promoting free media: Poland was the first country in the region to open the media market to wide competition. The Czech Republic and Slovakia, not to mention Romania and Bulgaria, which for a long time were run by post-communists, were tangibly slower (Giorgi, 1995; Bastian, 1996). More robust political competition also helped constrain growth in bureaucracy: civil service employment grew faster post 1989 in the Czech Republic and Slovakia than in Poland and Hungary (Grzymala-Busse, 2010). Finally, robust political competition can also help explain why today Poland's level of corruption is much lower than in the Czech Republic and Slovakia as well as all other Central European countries (only Baltic States are doing better). It seems that competition is good not only in economic, but also in political markets.[20]

6.6.4. *Openness of Western Europe*

The fourth reason why Poland adopted good institutions was Western European readiness to embrace CEE and help it succeed. After centuries of conquest, beggar-thy-neighbour policies, and sometimes open animosity, Western Europe has become an unequivocal force of good.

Western Europe opened to Poland and CEE for three main reasons. First, it was out of a sense of moral obligation for having 'failed' CEE after the war and for allowing it to languish behind the Iron Curtain. The Germans, in particular, driven by a special sense of moral responsibility, became the key promoters of the 'return to Europe' and the EU enlargement. As Chancellor Helmut Kohl put it in the early 1990s, Europe cannot 'disappoint the trust that these countries have put in us' (Baun, 2000, 10, cited in Berend, 2009, p. 84). Similarly, Jacques Delors, the French President of the European Commission during 1985–1995, was quoted saying that

> The Twelve [EU12] cannot control history but they are now in a position to influence it once again. They did not want Europe to be cut in two at Yalta and made hostage in the Cold War. They did not, nor do they, close the door to other European countries...[The EU has to help] the countries of CEE to modernize their economies.   (Delors, 1998, pp. 59, 66, as cited by Berend, 2009, p. 84)

In 2001, Gunter Vergheugen, the EC Enlargement Commissioner, talked about enlargement to the East as 'both an historic opportunity and an

---

[20] There is empirical evidence from other countries that political competition reduces rent-seeking, see, for instance, Rose-Ackerman (1999).

obligation for the European Union' (European Commission, 2001, p. 2). Many other Western policy makers shared the same sentiments.

Moreover, enlargement to CEE was part of a vision shared by the Western European elites of uniting Europe, creating the 'United States of Europe' and securing peace on the most war-ravaged continent on Earth. The vision, first evidenced by Winston Churchill, then Jean Monet and Robert Schuman, was shared by many key European policy makers. In 1992, Helmut Kohl, the German Chancellor, said that

> In Maastricht we have laid the foundation for completion of the European Union. The Treaty on European Union marks a new, decisive step in the process of European integration that in a few years will lead to the creation of what the founding fathers of modern Europe dreamt of after the last war: a United States of Europe. (quoted in Reding, 2012, p. 6)

Likewise, Jacques Santer, Prime Minister of Luxembourg and the future President of the European Commission between 1995 and 1999, said on 8 November 1988 that 'We Christian Democrats in the European People's Party want the European Community to become a United States of Europe' (ibid., p. 6).

Lastly, openness towards CEE was driven by economic interests. Western companies were excited about the prospects of expanding their business into new, largely virgin markets with more than 100 million consumers. They also looked forward to enhancing their competitiveness by accessing a large pool of cheap and well educated labour (Berend, 2009). What China and Mexico was for the USA, CEE needed to become for Western Europe. They also counted on enhancing the economies of scale within the European market. Western European business would much agree with the European Commission (2001, p. 5), which in 2001 argued that 'The addition of more than 100 million people [in CEE], in rapidly growing economies, to the EU's market of 370 million will boost economic growth and create jobs in both old and new member states'. In 2004, on the day of the EU enlargement to the East, German Chancellor Gerhard Schroeder concluded that 'Enlargement will not make us poorer, but richer in the future'.[21] He was right indeed (Box 6.3).

6.6.5. Emergence of a New Middle Class

Finally, adoption of good institutions was driven by the emergence of a new middle class and a business elite. As explained in Chapter 2, Poland never had a middle class of its own that would enjoy full political rights. Until 1939, the policy of *szlachta* and the political elites has been to outsource business to immigrants (Germans, Jews, Armenians, and others) to ensure that a Polish merchant class would not emerge and become a potential competitor to

---

[21] http://news.bbc.co.uk/2/hi/europe/3675507.stm, accessed 28 May 2017.

Box 6.3. HOW EASTERN ENLARGEMENT HELPED WESTERN EUROPE

Opening to CEE helped Western Europe enhance competitiveness and avoid annihilation by globalization. The EU enlargement helped Western Europe in at least five ways.

First, it helped increase Western European competitiveness by expanding supply chains into low-cost CEE. Second, it helped keep wage growth in Western Europe low: faced with the threat of shifting production to the new EU member states, labour in Western Europe had no choice but to acquiesce to the employers' demands and keep wage growth in check.[22] Indeed, Western European countries most exposed to Eastern competition had the slowest wage growth: in Germany, median real wages had largely stagnated since the early 1990s (see Chapter 4).[23] Third, EU enlargement helped increase the size of EU markets and enhance economies of scale for EU companies.[24] Fourth, enlargement also helped Western Europe directly by increasing exports and creating hundreds of thousands of additional jobs. Since 1989, Western European exports to the new EU member states have more than quadrupled. In addition, per the estimates of Poland's Ministry of Economic Development, for each euro of EU funds invested in Poland, EU-15 countries collected 46 cents back on average in terms of faster growth. The German economy, the biggest beneficiary of the EU enlargement, collected 85 eurocents on each euro spent in Poland (Bienias, 2011). Since the EU accession in 2004, Poland has become Germany's eighth largest export market, with almost $60 billion of exports in 2015, larger than exports to Russia.[25] Finally, embedding CEE helped lower security and military risks (at least until Russia's annexation of Crimea in 2014 and the war in Ukraine) and saved tens of billions of dollars a year on military spending.

Given the size of Western European GDP—amounting to around 16 trillion euro in 2016—all the various benefits of EU enlargement are likely to amount to tens of billions of euro of additional GDP per year. It is estimated that in the case of Germany alone, the EU enlargement has increased its GDP growth by 0.5 percentage points or 15 additional billion euro per year.[26] The size of the EU financial assistance to the new EU member states, which amounts to only 0.3 per cent of the EU GDP per year, pales in comparison (European Commission, 2009). Overall, the EU enlargement has been a great win-win for all: it helped poor CEE become rich and Western Europe remain rich.

---

power. Immigrants and non-ethnic Poles, even though they had *de jure* political rights as Polish citizens, were *de facto* removed from the political process.

---

[22] Of course, there were also other factors driving slow wage growth, including technology, globalization, and changes in policy. For more details, see, for instance, Milanovic (2016a).

[23] Berend (2009, p. 100) recounts how workers in Siemens and Bosch factories in Germany agreed to work five additional hours per week with no additional compensation to ensure that the jobs were not moved to CEE.

[24] Although the benefits of EU enlargement were not distributed evenly: it helped the strong countries such as Germany to become even more competitive, but it made the weak such as Greece, Italy, or Portugal even weaker by re-directing FDI and taking over market shares in the EU. Gill and Raiser (2012) argue that the difference in the size of companies was one of the key differences between northern and southern Europe: it was easier for larger companies in the north to benefit from the EU enlargement by outsourcing production than for SME-predominated economies in the south.

[25] http://globaledge.msu.edu/countries/germany/tradestats, accessed 15 June 2017.

[26] https://www.bundesregierung.de/Content/EN/StatischeSeiten/Schwerpunkte/Europa/2005-11-08-europa-vorteile-der-erweiterung_en.html, accessed 15 June 2017.

Year 1989 brought a historical break. The post-transition entrepreneurial and educational boom spawned a middle class for the first time ever in the country's history. More than 3.5 million new businesses were set up after 1989, of which—thanks to the communist social advancement and egalitarianism—two-thirds were established by entrepreneurs from blue-collar and farming families (Berend, 2009, p. 245).

Additional millions came from a new class of business professionals, who were hired to work in companies owned by foreign investors. This was an entirely new class of people. They were younger, better educated, and more Westernized than the average. And it was not by coincidence: foreign investors actively discriminated in favour of young Poles, who were not tainted by the old system and could be trained from scratch to adapt to the Western corporate culture.[27] As a result, within a few years from 1989, a totally new middle class emerged, which had a collective interest to support institutions that would safeguard their property, keep the markets open, and sustain a level playing field. It joined the political process with gusto and consistently voted for parties that supported the middle-class interests (Jackson, Klich, and Poznanska, 2005).

Good institutions were also supported by a new business elite. They were all 'self-made' men, who started in 1989 from scratch (see Table 6.6). The new millionaires had the same incentive as the middle class to support democracy and the rule of law (if not exactly always the open markets). Strong market competition, robust free media, independent courts, and transparent privatization ensured that none of the new rich became oligarchs.[28] According to EBRD (2016a, p. 20), in 2015 the wealth of Polish billionaires represented only about 2 per cent of GDP, while it amounted to 25 per cent of GDP in Russia, 13 per cent in Germany and Mexico, and almost 15 per cent of GDP in the USA.[29]

6.6.6. Other Factors

Life is too complicated to be explained by a neat list of factors. There are many other factors that have affected the extent and speed of Poland's

---

[27] My own example is illuminating: I got my first full-time job in Citibank Poland at the age of 21, barely after the second year of undergraduate studies. Practically all my colleagues were younger than 30. Anyone older than that looked suspicious or must have been a foreigner. This was not a coincidence: Citibank, and many other foreign multinationals, focused on hiring young Poles, who spoke English, learned modern economics, and were ready to be moulded in Western ways. Foreign firms invested heavily in the new cadre: in 1997, I, for instance, was dispatched for an almost two-month-long mini-MBA training organized by Citibank in Istanbul, Turkey. Many of my peers experienced the same.

[28] Unlike in other countries in the region, throughout the whole transition period Polish businessmen were shunted by political parties for fear of being seen too close to business. And vice versa, there have been only a few examples of rich businessmen entering politics, none of them ultimately successful.

[29] The data cover only wealth above one billion US$, so is skewed against smaller countries.

adoption of Western institutions. One of them was a vibrant political competition and fast turnover of political parties in the government, as parties in power had incentives to put institutions in place, which would safeguard their legacy for longer (Grzymala-Busse 2010). It also helped that—unlike, for instance, in Russia—Poland had no natural resources and thus no rents for oligarchs to take over and then use to undermine institutions. Moreover, Balcerowicz's de-monopolization of the economy during the 'shock therapy' eliminated an important source of economic rents and state capture. Russia, Ukraine, and many other countries in the region were not so lucky. Furthermore, Polish ethnic homogeneity made it easier to create social consensus to join Europe and cooperate to support democracy and strong economic institutions. Pre-war ethnic fractionalization, where minorities represented about one-third of the society, proved not to be helpful. This is still the case in many other countries around the world (Alesina and La Ferrara, 2005; Alesina, Baqir, and Easterly, 1999). Finally, Poland also wanted to follow Western rules to be admitted to NATO, which it considered to be the key guarantee of its security against Russia. It succeeded in doing so in 1997.

6.7. Conclusions

I have argued in this chapter that the prospect of the EU accession drove Poland's institution-building after 1989. Poland wanted to accede to the EU because Poles knew from the very beginning of the transition where they were going: they wanted to 'return to Europe' and feel European again. They also dreamed of Western prosperity, stability, humanity, and dignity. They knew that joining the EU was key to make their dream come true. And they were ready to do everything to make it happen.

Thus, after 1989 Poland fully adopted Western institutions for the first time ever. It 'downloaded' centuries-worth of Western Europe's institutional heritage—democracy, secure property rights, independent monetary policy, robust competition, free press, and so on—which made Western Europe what it is today: the most humane, civilized, prosperous, and democratic continent on Earth.[30] Poland and other transition economies imported institutions that it took the West centuries to create with an unprecedented speed: never before in the history of mankind have some many countries imported so many new

---

[30] Or, as the World Bank report (Gill and Raiser, 2012) put it, a continent with 'arguably the highest quality of life in human history'.

institutions, values, rules, and ways of doing things in such a short time as CEE did between 1994 and 2004.

The adoption of Western institutions and accession to the EU worked well for the new EU member states: Poland, the Czech Republic, Hungary, Slovakia, Latvia, Lithuania, Estonia, Slovenia, Croatia, and soon Bulgaria and Romania represent almost half of only twenty-four countries that have become high income since 1960. Together with the earlier EU entrants—Greece, Portugal, Spain, and Ireland—the EU is responsible for two-thirds of countries on the list. Outside of the EU, only Japan, Korea, Taiwan, Singapore, and Israel (among large and non-oil economies) became developed without the EU.

The EU also helped prove that Asian-style authoritarianism is not necessary for economic success: democracy can be equally or even more successful. CEE has become high income without needing to imprison political dissidents, thwart labour code, and restrict human rights and basic freedoms, as has been the case for many Asian countries during much of their catching-up period. For this and many other reasons, including the role of the EU in keeping Europe peaceful, the EU deserves to be considered the biggest institutional achievement in the history of mankind. It is thus in the European and global interest to keep the EU strong and for other countries in the world to be able to replicate it.

Why did Poland want to import Western institutions? The positive legacy of communism was critically important for the success of Polish transition. This is because communism helped eliminate old, anti-growth elites, ensure broad distribution of income and wealth, and provide universal access to education. For the first time in Poland's history no one had a monopoly on power and all segments of the society had an equal interest in adopting democracy, opening markets, and creating a level-playing field. Poland moved away from extractive institutions, which blighted its development for centuries, and moved to inclusive institutions, which drove its economic success. Eagerness to adopt Western institutions was also driven by the strong social consensus to re-join Europe, Westernized elites, openness of Western Europe, and the emergence of a new middle class. None of these factors existed before. This unique combination of factors helped Poland discard centuries of backwardness in one go and shift from being poor to being high income within one generation.

What does it all mean for other countries? For those that are in Europe, the choice is easy: do everything to enter the EU as fast as you can. But of course, it is easier said than done, otherwise all post-Soviet countries as well as the Balkans and Turkey would have already been EU members or would be on their way to the EU. Yet, hardly anyone is. Even Moldova and Ukraine, one of the most pro-Western countries in the East, will likely not enter the EU for long decades to come, if ever.

The main reason is that while most of these countries seem to have built a modicum of a middle class, they nonetheless are missing several critical ingredients that Poland and other new EU members possessed. These include a broad social consensus to 'return to Europe', strong and Westernized elites, and openness of the West to embrace new entrants. Above all, however, some post-communist countries seem to have missed what could be most important factor for their development: a chance to create an inclusive society. Unprecedented egalitarianism created by communism, which underpinned the adoption of democracy and markets in countries like Poland, seem to have been largely lost among post-USRR countries during the early 1990s. Lack of strong alternative elites, low quality of post-communist elites, weak national identity, botched privatization, and a non-Western culture seem to have all combined to create an oligarchic, extractive society. Given how hard it is to shift from extractive to inclusive institutions—and no one wants another murderous Stalin to 'help' with the process—the long-term growth prospects for many post-Soviet countries may not be promising.

What about countries outside Europe that cannot join the EU? They cannot be EU members, but they can import Western institutions and adapt them to their needs. The few successful countries outside Europe that caught up with the West after 1945 did so largely because they imported Western institutions in some way or another. Japan adopted German civil code during Meiji Restoration and American-type constitution in 1945; China, Korea, and many other Asian countries introduced Western legal systems during the twentieth century; Singapore and Hong Kong did not need to change anything as they already relied on the British legal and institutional system (Fukuyama, 2017; Parente and Prescott, 2005). All Asian countries developed thanks to the Western liberal order, which opened up the global markets to trade and let Asian countries become rich. No one outside the West has ever developed anything better, not Russia, China, or Japan. Among high-income countries today (with the exception of oil-rich countries), there is no country that would not be Western or Westernized in some way.

But the key question is what would make poor countries around the world adopt such good institutions? The trouble again is that most countries seem to be caught in an extractive equilibrium, where the elites want to keep the system as is rather than build new inclusive institutions that would undermine their power. As I argue in this book, short of a large external shock, which would fundamentally change the distribution of economic resources, it is difficult to imagine what would break the harmful *status quo*. The extractive societies may still grow economically, as they do now, but might never become high income.

Still, the extractive elites may sometime decide to adopt formal Western institutions, to please the donors, for instance. But if changing the formal institutions were sufficient, all extractive countries would just adopt the same Western institutions, become rich and 'live happily ever after'. However, formal adoption of institutions without changes in the underlying sources of economic and political power does not work: the extractive elites will ensure that the new institutions become only facades hiding the old, ugly system. *Plus ça change, plus c'est la même chose.*

Finally, the institutions might not work properly because they are not supported by the right set of values, norms, and behaviours. Institutions do not work on their own: they are only as strong as the culture that underpins them. This is the reason why Western institutions worked well in Poland and the neighbouring countries, but failed to work in Russia, Ukraine, or Belarus and many other transition and non-transition economies. In short, culture matters. This is what I turn to next.

7

The Role of Culture, Ideas, and Leadership

The price system is not, and perhaps in some basic sense cannot be, universal. To the extent that it is incomplete, it must be supplemented by an implicit or explicit social contract.

Kenneth Arrow

[Culture] is the collective programming of the mind which distinguishes the members of one group or category of people from another.

Geert Hofstede

Character, in the long run, is the decisive factor in the life of an individual and of nations alike.

Theodore Roosevelt

What was the role of culture in the Polish economic success? Did Poland grow despite or because of its culture? What were the roles of individuals, ideas, and ideologies?

In this chapter I highlight the critical contribution of culture to the functioning of political and economic institutions in transition economies. People's beliefs, stereotypes, mindsets, and unwritten ways of doing things ultimately decide whether institutions are efficient or not. I then focus on the interaction of culture, institutions, and growth in Poland and try to explain the puzzle of why Poland's seemingly conservative culture, which in many respects seems to be at odds with Western European culture, especially as regards religion, has not prevented the country from becoming Europe's growth champion. I argue that it was the case because of strong elites that internalized Western values, an implicit *quid pro quo* between the new elites and the more conservative parts of the society to install European institutions and promote Western values in exchange for the promise of economic prosperity, and the generally non-fundamentalist nature of religion in Poland. I also discuss the key roles of individuals, ideas, and luck in Poland's post-transition performance.

7.1. Impact of Culture on Institutions and Growth in Transition Economies

As argued in Chapter 1, the way the institutions perform and the way they affect the economy crucially depends on the existing social norms, beliefs, and ways of doing things (World Bank, 2015a). North (1994, p. 364) argued that

> economies that adopt the formal rules of another economy will have different performance (...) because of different informal norms and enforcement. The implication is that transferring the formal political and economic rules of success-ful Western economies to third-world and Eastern European economies is not a sufficient condition for good economic performance.

Similarly, Kaushik Basu (2015, p. 157), former chief economist of the World Bank, asserts that

> economic development depends critically on the presence of appropriate social norms, mindsets and institutions. These social and psychological conditions are often fundamental in the sense that if they are not in place, standard economic policies are likely to have little traction (...) in rich and industrialized countries, the "right" norms are in place; and since much of economic theory has been developed in industrialized countries, there has been a tendency to relegate social norms to the background... This is why many conventional policy prescriptions given to developing countries (...) had little positive impact and often actually backfired.

He also points out (ibid., pp. X–XI) that 'all economies are embedded in a mesh of intricate norms, collective beliefs, and behavioral habits. These can make or break an economy'. Robert Putnam, an eminent sociologist, con-cludes that 'social context and history profoundly condition the effectiveness of institutions' (Putnam, 1993, p. 182).

What then is the impact of culture on growth in transition economies?

There is a growing literature on the role of culture in development, which I discussed in Chapter 1, but few of the studies focus on Poland and transi-tion economies. Among the few, the work of Gorodnichenko and Roland (2010, 2011a, 2011b, 2013) is particularly interesting. In the first three papers, Gorodnichenko and Roland analyse three different cultural data sets from Hofstede (2011), Schwartz (1994), and the World Value Survey, the largest survey of cultural values around the world. Their bottom line based on the extensive analysis and review of the data is that countries with individualistic cultures, that is cultures in which 'it is believed that individuals are supposed to take care of themselves as opposed to being strongly integrated and loyal to a cohesive group' (ibid. 2011a, p. 2), perform better economically than countries with a collectivist culture. They explain (Gorodnichenko and Roland 2011b, p. 1) that individualism matters for growth because 'individualist culture attaches social status rewards to personal achievements and thus, provides not only monetary incentives for innovation but also social status rewards, leading to higher rates of innovation and economic growth'. In turn, growth in collectivist cultures is lower likely because these cultures praise social harmony and conformity, which are at odds with innovation, entrepreneurship, and 'creative destruction'.

The impact on individualism on growth is significant: one standard deviation change in individualism (moving from the level of individualism in Venezuela to Greece or from Brazil to Luxemburg) can translate into a 60–87 per cent increase in the level of GDP (ibid., 2011b, p. 2). Gorodnichenko and Roland (2001b) also found, based on the analysis of data from the World Value Survey, that trust and tolerance are also important for growth, but not as much as individualism.[1] Other cultural factors such as power distance, masculinity, and uncertainty avoidance, as defined by Hofstede (2001), or hard work and thrift, pro-market attitudes, and egalitarianism, as defined in the World Value Survey, do not seem to matter.

Against this background, Gorodnichenko and Roland (2011b) include also transition economies in their analysis and find that Poland and other post-communist countries (Hungary, the Czech Republic, Estonia, and Slovakia) are high on Hofstede's index of individualism. Bulgaria and Romania are more collectivist. Polish culture is more individualistic than the culture of Spain, Austria, or Israel. Poland is on the regression line relative to the log GDP per capita, suggesting that Polish culture is where it 'should be' relative to its level of development (Figure 7.1).

In their follow-up paper, Gorodnichenko and Roland (2013) used the same framework to analyse the impact of culture on institutions in transition economies. They found that transition countries with a more individualist culture, such as those in CEE, established democracy earlier than countries with a collectivist culture, such as China or Vietnam. Roland (2014) argues that institution-building in transition economies was strongly influenced by the level of the civil society development and preference for authoritarianism versus democracy. He posits that both factors are deeply rooted in the countries' slow-moving cultural traditions. He concludes that CEE seems to be better positioned to sustain democracy and good economic institutions than transition economies further east.

---

[1] World Values Survey and its European counterpart, the European Values Survey, are the longest running and most exhaustive surveys of culture around the world available since 1981. The most recent surveys covered more than 90 countries. The database developed by Inglehart *et al* (2000) with the results of these surveys is the staple of research on the role of culture in development.

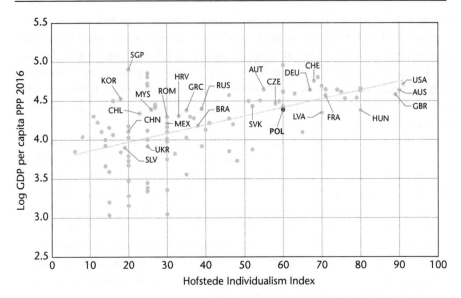

Figure 7.1. Correlation between individualism and GDP per capita in 2016.

Source: Author's own based on Gorodnichenko and Roland (2011b) and Hofstede (2011).

Raiser (1997) makes a similar point. He emphasizes the importance of social capital, trust, and morality for growth. He argues that all three can by promoted by good political institutions and strong economic performance. He contends that the choice of institutions and the efficiency of their functioning in transition economies is 'conditioned to a substantial extent by the inheritance of a given set of informal institutions that shape people's expectations' (ibid., p. 27). These informal institutions, or culture, are subject to long-term trends, which are not easy to change.

Raiser *et al.* (2001) focus on the specific importance of social capital, defined as trust and civic participation, on growth in transition economies. They find that social capital in transition economies is much lower than in Western Europe, but nonetheless it had little impact on economic performance. But trust in public institutions is positively correlated with growth. This is so despite the low starting base, as all post-communist countries suffer from a general distrust of public administration driven by the legacy of imperialism, colonialism, and communism. They argue that social trust and economic development are in a positive feedback loop: the more trust there is, the more likely it is to support economic development, which in turn supports more trust and so on.

Others, however, did not find much positive evidence of any type of social capital. This is likely because of the overall low levels of trust in post-communist countries. Paldam and Svendsen (2001) argue, for instance, that in many transition economies social capital can have a negative impact on growth, if it is in the form of networks of former communists and special service agents. Djankov (2014) makes this point forcefully for Bulgaria.

Frye (2001) focuses on the importance of ingrained social beliefs in explaining the strength of the rule of law. He compares Poland with Russia and finds that in the 1990s almost two-thirds of Warsaw small-store owners had no qualms about suing the local government if their property rights were undermined. In Moscow, only one-quarter did. The difference in revealed preferences of Poles and Russians indirectly suggests a large difference in social capital and cultural norms.

7.1.1. Religion

Djankov (2016) focuses on the role of religion in development in transition economies. He asserts that religion has a big impact on political and economic institutions among transition economies. Countries that are Catholic or Protestant are doing much better than Eastern Orthodox and Muslim countries on economic freedom, the quality of business environment, political rights, and democracy (Figure 7.2).

Djankov argues that the religious divide goes back all the way to the fifth century, when the Roman Empire split into two parts. This led to the eventual schism between the Roman Catholic and Eastern Orthodox Church in 1054. A quick look at the map of religious Europe in 1054 shows that the religious divide from almost 1,000 years ago looks very much like the income divide today: Catholic Europe is much more developed than Eastern Orthodox Europe as well as Muslim Europe in the Balkans and parts of Turkey (Figure 7.3). Catholic countries in Central and Eastern Europe—Poland, the Czech Republic, Slovakia, Slovenia, and Hungary—have also been much more successful during the transition than Eastern Orthodox countries.[2]

7.1.2. Legacy of Empires

Djankov (2016) also emphasizes the importance of the historical background of transition economies, that is whether they earlier belonged to the Austro-Hungarian, Russian, or the Ottoman Empire. He shows that countries such as the Czech Republic, Slovakia, Hungary, and parts of Poland that belonged

---

[2] It was not just in terms of income that the long-term cultural legacies mattered: since 1989, Poland, the Czech Republic, Slovakia, Hungary, and Slovenia have also experienced 'probably the most rapid decrease in coronary heart disease ever observed', while Eastern Orthodox Europe lagged behind (Zatonski, Campos, and Willett 2008, p. 4, cited in Djankov 2016).

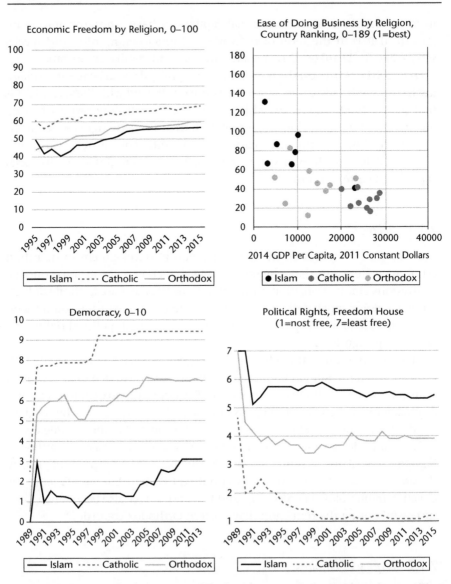

Figure 7.2. Impact of religion on political and economic institutions in transition economies.

Note: The Catholic group represents nine countries in Central Europe and the Baltics; the Orthodox group represents eleven countries in CEE and the Caucasus; and the Muslim group represents nine countries in parts of the former Yugoslavia, the Caucasus, and all Central Asia. The Index of Economic Freedom and democracy ranges from 0 to 10, the higher the better. The Doing Business ranks countries from 1 to 189, with #1 being the most business-friendly environment. The Political Rights index ranges from 7 to 1, with lower scores representing more rights.

Source: Djankov (2016).

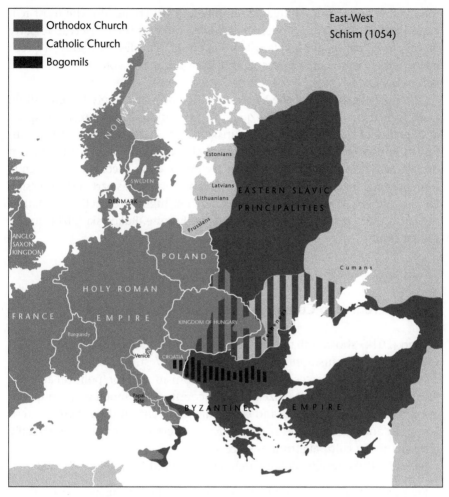

Figure 7.3. Religious divide of Europe in 1054AD.
Source: Brujić (2005).

to the Austro-Hungarian Empire are much more democratic and much more pro-market than countries that were part of the Ottoman and Russian Empire.

As various parts of today's Poland belonged to three Empires during 1795–1918—Prussian, Russian, and Austro-Hungarian—this makes for interesting research on the persistence of cultural norms. Grosfeld and Zhuravskaya (2015) show that almost 100 years after the end of the partitions, there were still visible cultural differences among the different parts of Poland that were governed by the three empires. For instance, in the 2007 parliamentary elections, the Eastern and South-Eastern parts of Poland that formerly belonged to

the Russian and Austro-Hungarian empire and which are also the most religious parts of the country, overwhelmingly voted for the conservative party
of Law and Justice, led by Jarosław Kaczyński. The less religious Western
lands, which were part of Prussia and later Germany, voted for the liberal
parties instead.

Other papers show that the historical differences also apply to generalized
trust, voter turnout, and even the quality of education, which affects the speed
and quality of development. Wysokinska (2011, 2016) argues that the continued impact on institutions and culture shaped by the imperial legacy can
explain why, controlling for all other factors, average incomes and revenue
from personal income taxes in Western Poland, which was part of the Prussian
Empire, are 10–20 per cent and 12–25 per cent higher, respectively, than in
the lands that once belonged to the Russian Empire. Bukowski (2014) found
similar results.

7.2. Differences in Culture Between CEE and the West

Roland (2014) showed that there continues to be a substantial difference in
values between transition economies and the West. He built an index of
cultural preferences for 'economic interventionism' and for 'political authoritarianism' and found that citizens of CEE countries are much more in favour
of political authoritarianism and economic intervention than their Western
European and American peers (Figure 7.4).[3] There has also been remarkably
little change in cultural attitudes since 1990.

Based on these results, Roland argues (Roland 2014, Kindle 5645) that

> the rapid institutional change that led Central and Eastern European transition
> economies to become new member states of the European Union has hidden the
> fact that values in those countries remain more authoritarian and nationalistic
> than in Western Europe and the United States.

He then rather presciently concludes, given the win of the conservative Law
and Justice party in the 2015 elections in Poland and its ensuing illiberal
policies, that 'one can thus predict tension for quite some time between values
and beliefs in these countries and the EU institutions that were adopted'.

---

[3] Although the difference between Eastern and Western Europe is much smaller than that
between China and Western Europe, for instance.

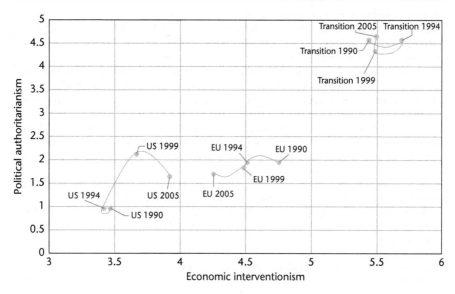

Figure 7.4. Cultural differences between Eastern and Western Europe and the USA, 1990–2005.

Note: Transition economies include Belarus, Bulgaria, the Czech Republic, Estonia, Latvia, Poland, Romania, Russia, Slovakia, and Slovenia. Range from 1 to 10.

Source: Author's own based on Roland (2014).

7.3. Culture and Economic Performance in Poland

Poland is 'exhibit one' of the tension between culture and institutions. This is because its culture, largely based on conservative attitudes, high religiosity, and strong survival values, is a statistical outlier in Europe.

Inglehart and Welzel (2005) argue that most variation in human cultural values can be explained by positioning individual values along two broad dimensions: traditional versus secular-rational values and survival versus self-expression values (see detailed definitions in Box 7.1). Based on this framework and data from the World Value Survey, they produce an Inglehart–Welzel Cultural Map, which covers most countries in the world.

The resulting Cultural Map (Figure 7.5) shows that in 2015 Poland was located on the border between Latin American and African-Islamic countries, that is Polish culture was not much different from that of Argentina, South Africa, Brazil, and Chile. It was distant from any other European country. It was also far from all developed countries, which largely congregated in the right and northern corner of the map. Quite shockingly, the earlier editions of the map, based on the results of the consecutive World Value Surveys since

---

Box 7.1. DEFINITIONS OF TRADITIONAL VERSUS SECULAR-RATIONAL VALUES AND SURVIVAL VERSUS SELF-EXPRESSION VALUES

Traditional values emphasize the importance of religion, parent-child ties, deference to authority, and traditional family values. People who embrace these values also reject divorce, abortion, euthanasia, and suicide. These societies have high levels of national pride and a nationalistic outlook.

Secular-rational values have the opposite preferences to the traditional values. These societies place less emphasis on religion, traditional family values, and authority. Divorce, abortion, euthanasia, and suicide are seen as relatively acceptable. (Suicide is not necessarily more common.)

Survival values place emphasis on economic and physical security. These are linked with a relatively ethnocentric outlook and low levels of trust and tolerance.

Self-expression values give high priority to environmental protection, growing tolerance of foreigners, gays, and lesbians, and gender equality, and rising demands for participation in decision-making in economic and political life.

Source: http://www.worldvaluessurvey.org/WVSContents.jsp.

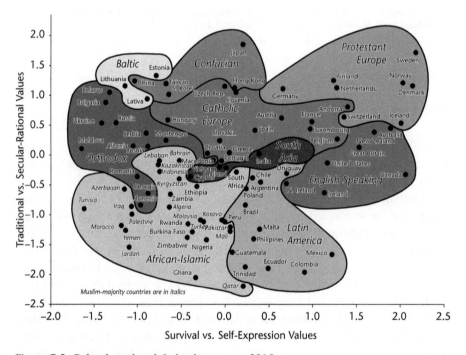

Figure 7.5. Poland on the global culture map, 2015.

Note: Upward shift reflects a move from traditional values to secular-rational and from survival values to self–expression values.

Source: World Values Survey. Cultural Map, http://www.worldvaluessurvey.org/WVSContents.jsp.

1990, placed Poland among countries in 'South Asia' and close to countries with 'African-Islamic' culture.[4]

Other studies, based on different definitions of culture, confirm the same findings: even though Poland has outperformed all its CEE neighbours in economic development since 1989, it was a statistical outlier in cultural values. Since 1989, Poland was the slowest in moving away from the authoritarian, hierarchical organizational structures prevalent during the Soviet era toward flatter, more democratic, individualistic, and autonomous structures, which traditionally are closely correlated with economic development and prosperity (Inglehart, 2008; Mączyński and Wyspianski, 2011, Klingemann, Fuchs, and Zielonka, 2006).

Kochanowicz and Marody (2003, p. 362) attempt to describe the main elements of the Polish economic culture. They argue, based on a review of several other studies as well as their own research, that the Polish economic culture is based on eight elements: 'familialism, aversion to large, moral "solidarity", anarchic collectivism, ambiguous entrepreneurship, time myopia, consumptionism and ambiguous attitudes towards wealth'. They review each of the eight dimensions of their definition of the Polish economic culture in detail. They assert, for instance, that Poles trust only small groups of people, their close family and friends, which works well in small enterprises, but undermines efficient teamwork in larger organizations when the teams involve strangers. They also emphasize that Poles distrust large institutions and have limited 'civilizational competences' (Sztompka, 1993). They underline Poles' ambiguous approach to wealth: they crave it, but are suspicious of people who have it. Even entrepreneurship is considered a mixed bag, as it can define both the positive entrepreneurial spirit but also a tendency to be 'entrepreneurial' in cutting corners, disregarding rules, and free-riding the system. The conclusion from reading the paper is that Polish economic culture seems to have many more downsides than upsides, which should undermine economic performance.

How can one then explain the puzzle that Poland became a European growth champion despite a culture that seems much at odds with developed peers? There are several possible explanations. First, the cultural map may not show the cultural values that matter for development. The strong correlation between the specific type of culture and economic development visible in the cultural map might be spurious, that is the bunching of countries in the same areas of the map may be driven by common factors other than those reflected in the adopted framework.

---

[4] For earlier editions of the map, see http://www.worldvaluessurvey.org/WVSContents.jsp. There is also an entertaining video.

For instance, individualism, as argued by Gorodnichenko and Roland (2011a, 2011b) and as discussed earlier in this chapter, could possibly explain most of the variance on the map. It could also partly elucidate Poland's success, although the country is no more individualistic than the Czech Republic and Slovakia, and less individualistic than Hungary (see Figure 7.5). Alternatively, the cultural map may have an inherent design flaw: it might have been designed to show results that 'make sense', that is the variables were chosen to show that rich countries tend to cluster with one another. Finally, it might be that the causality is going the other way: rich countries adopt certain cultural traits only after they have become rich rather than the other way around.

A second possible explanation for why Poland succeeded despite having the 'wrong' culture is simply that the survey data might not be reliable: it is a well-known methodological problem that people with different cultures may respond differently to the same questions. Also, survey results may be misleading to the extent that the questions focus only on, for instance, outward religiosity rather than the set of values they underlie it (see Box 7.2). Moreover, the quality of the survey might not be sufficient: it would be extremely difficult to explain, for instance, why in the European Values Survey the 'percentage of people that have a great deal or quite a lot of confidence in the justice system' in Poland declined from more than half in 1990, at the height of the post-communist turmoil, to only about 40 per cent in 2008 in the already well-established democratic country.[5] Finally, the data may be misleading because they may ignore the fundamental difference between the cultural values of the young and the old, post-Soviet generation, as discussed more below.

The third explanation may be that the successful transition is likely to have happened because of the Westernized elites, which used the lure of Western prosperity and the strong social consensus to 'return to Europe' to 'hijack' the conservative part of the society and introduce European institutions and Westernize the country. The new institutions and imported cultural values in turn helped to strengthen Westernization and create a positive feedback loop. The young, Westernized generation taking over many of the positions on the commanding heights of the country's political and business life supported this trend.

Fourth, the disciplining effect of Western institutions on the Polish culture may also have mattered, as this changed incentives, proposed new models of behaviour, and constricted the scope for old types of behaviour. For instance, the European Union's limits on subsidies to enterprises forced Polish

---

[5] http://www.europeanvaluesstudy.eu/page/longitudinal-file-1981-2008.html, accessed 16 May 2017.

Box 7.2. POLISH SUCCESS: DESPITE OR BECAUSE OF RELIGION?

Is religion bad for growth? It depends. The economic literature is equivocal (Barro and McCleary, 2003; La Porta *et al.* 1997; Guiso, Sapienza, and Zingales, 2003). For every Max Weber (1905/2002), who emphasized the benefits of the Protestant ethic, there is a Douglass North (1990), who dismissed it. For every America, where religion plays an important role and every President feels obliged to exhort God to 'bless it', there is a Sweden where religion is almost non-existent, at least in the outward form.

In the case of Poland, high religiosity—almost 90 per cent of Poles consider themselves Catholic—and strong family values seem to be the main key differences between Poland and other countries in Europe. Inglehart (1990) identified these two values as two of the most resilient elements of a nation's traditional cultural make-up. Both can be explained by Poland's unique historical background, where religion and the Catholic Church were the main pillars of Polishness during Russian, German, and Austrian occupation between 1795 and 1918 (Catholic churches, for instance, were often the only places were Poles could freely speak Polish). The incentive to survive was also the same reason for developing strong family values and keeping others outside the network of trust. Polish culture evolved to help the nation survive not to thrive.

But what is important in the Polish context is that Polish Catholicism has little to do with religious fundamentalism: most Poles engage in traditional religious ceremonies, which have by now become part of the national culture, but their moral choices have little to do with the teachings of the Church. To give a revealing example, Poles have a liberal, Western European-like approach to premarital sex, with most Poles having no objections to it (Jung, 2016). In this respect, and in many others too, Poles are more liberal than Americans and most other, non-Western European societies in the world. The bottom line is that formal religiosity in Poland has little to do with moral attitudes.

There are downsides to high religiosity, however: by promoting risk aversion and weakening the importance of rational thought it is believed to undermine technology absorption and innovation, which are critical ingredients of long-term growth. Religion also may make it more difficult to adopt democracy by delegitimizing secular governments. Many studies of Muslim countries give much ammunition to these claims (Kuran, 2004; Guiso, Sapienza, and Zingales, 2003; Rubin, 2017). High religiosity can also help support conservative political parties, which tend to be less pro-growth than liberal parties.

In the case of Poland, however, the former is difficult to prove—Poland's level of innovation, while rather low, is not much different from that of its global peers. There is some evidence that the more religious people in Poland have a lower voter turnout (Grosfeld and Zhuravskaya, 2015), but this in itself does not reflect the strength of support for democracy. Finally, Polish conservative parties have so far been as pro-growth as the liberal parties.

But there are also upsides to high religiosity: The Polish Catholic Church and John Paul II played an unquestionably positive role in helping to demolish communism (Blusiewicz and Gayte, 2011). In addition, high formal religiosity arguably helped Poles sustain a high degree of national identity, shared values, and a strong social consensus. All these factors positively affect growth (Akerlof and Kranton, 2011). High religiosity is also a key ingredient of happiness: data from the World Values Survey suggest that people and nations that are more religious tend to be more satisfied with life than the average.

stakeholders to look for new solutions to restructure companies or accept bankruptcy, even in the case of the eponymous shipyards, which were the bedrock of the Solidarity movement. The EU's limits on the budget deficit have had a similarly disciplinary impact, even with the supposedly populist governments (which, paradoxically, have never so far breached the 3 per cent deficit threshold, while the liberal governments did). Finally, behaving like (Western) Europeans has become cool, especially among the newly emerged middle class and in large cities. As a European, certain things—paying bribes, cutting corners, distrusting others—one just does not do.

Finally, it may also be that the impact of culture depends on the level of development. It could be argued that Polish arguably 'weak' economic culture did not stymie post-1989 growth, because the growth was based on relatively simple growth reserves that did not require a more 'sophisticated' culture. However, as the country continues to develop, simple growth reserves will disappear and the complexity of economic development will increase, the importance of the 'right' culture—based on team work, high social trust, long-term planning, and so on—will gain in importance.

Which explanation is closest to the mark? There is some truth in all the explanations. But I find the last three explanations—'hijacking' of the nation's values by the new elites, the disciplining effect of the EU rules, and the impact of the level of development—to be the most convincing (although more research is needed to provide evidence of each of these factors).

The hypothesis of 'elite hijacking' seems to be particularly interesting. It could be argued that after 1989, Westernized elites took the lead in creating institutions and conducting policies based on Western and European values. The conservative part of the society was not able to counteract this because of its low social capital and inability to self-organize (as evidenced by the results of large social surveys conducted systematically every few years; see Czapiński, 2015), diffused understanding of their interests, and lack of effective political representation (at least until 2015 and briefly during 2005–2007, when the conservative political party of Law and Justice under the leadership of Jarosław Kaczyński, won elections and assumed power).[6] The overall Zeitgeist of 'returning to Europe' and the implicit *quid pro quo* with the whole society of 'sacrificing' old values for European economic prosperity must have also played a role.

---

[6] In 2015, the Law and Justice party won elections with only 37.5 per cent of the vote, but because of the electoral bonus system and unexpected (and ironic) failure of the post-communist coalition to clear the 8 per cent election threshold, the party was able to gain more than half of the seats in parliament and take full power. This was the first time since 1989 that one party had full control over the government; all previous governments had to create coalitions to be able to govern.

7.4. Evolution of Culture Since 1989

Despite the headline conservatism, the Polish culture is becoming more secular, liberal, and European. While the number of Poles who identify themselves as Catholic remained at close to 90 per cent, the number of Poles participating in Sunday mass decreased from 50 per cent in 1980 to 39 per cent in 2014.[7] Zimmerman (2014) confirms these results based on data from consecutive editions of the European Values Survey and World Values Survey.

Poles are also becoming more pro-market and pro-democracy: in 2016, 40 per cent of Poles supported market economy over a planned economy, up from 30 per cent in 2010. Almost 60 per cent also supported democracy, up from less than half a few years earlier (Figure 7.6).[8] In both categories, Poland was above the average for all transition economies, although still far from the average for Western Europe (represented by Germany and Italy).

The improvement in scores has been partly driven by generational change: Polish youth are much different from their parents and much more like their

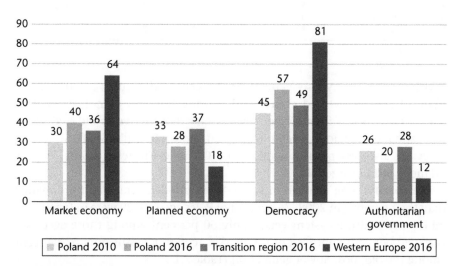

Figure 7.6. Attitudes towards market economy, planned economy, democracy, and authoritarianism in Poland, transition economies, and Western Europe, 2010 and 2016.

Note: Western Europe representing average for Germany and Italy.

Source: Author's own based on EBRD (2016b).

---

[7] http://wiadomosci.dziennik.pl/wydarzenia/artykuly/509696,kosciol-ujawnia-dane-prawie-40-procent-polakow-uczestniczy-w-niedzielnych-mszach-swietych.html, accessed 1 June 2017.

[8] The Life in Transition survey is the largest survey in transition economies. The last edition was between 2015 and 2016 (EBRD, 2016b) and comprised 34 countries, including Germany and Italy.

Table 7.1. Attitudes towards multiparty systems and a market economy in transition economies, 2009

No.	Country	18–29	30–49	50–64	65+	Oldest-youngest gap
Multiparty system						
1	Russia	65	60	46	27	−38
2	Bulgaria	56	61	51	37	−19
3	Czech Rep.	87	82	76	70	−17
4	Poland	76	76	65	60	−16
5	Lithuania	59	58	56	43	−16
6	Hungary	60	59	55	45	−15
7	Ukraine	34	39	22	20	−14
8	Slovakia	74	76	65	65	−9
9	East Germany	90	85	86	81	−9
Market economy						
1	Russia	63	56	39	27	−36
2	Bulgaria	66	60	49	32	−34
3	Slovakia	75	73	60	46	−29
4	Ukraine	48	43	24	20	−28
5	Poland	80	78	68	53	−27
6	Czech Rep.	83	87	76	63	−20
7	Hungary	51	47	48	36	−15
8	Lithuania	53	53	51	41	−12
9	East Germany	82	83	87	77	−5

Source: Pew Research Center (2009).

Western peers. The young generation is much more secular: in 2014, more than 40 per cent visited church only during holidays or not at all. This compares with less than 23 per cent among those 65 years old and older, who attended religious ceremonies much more often (GUS, 2015). Young Poles are also less prone to follow the Catholic Church's points of view (Mandes and Rogaczewska, 2013).

The Polish young generation is also more pro-democracy and pro-market than their parents: in 2008, 76 per cent of Poles aged 18–29 were in favour of a multiparty political system versus only 60 per cent among those aged 65+ years; 80 per cent approved of the market economy versus only 53 per cent among the old, post-Soviet generation (Table 7.1).

7.4.1. The Most Competitive Young Generation Ever

The major reason why the new generation is more secular, democratic, and liberal, is because it is much better educated than ever before: in terms of functional literacy, which assesses the ability to evaluate, understand, and use written texts, young Poles are much better educated than both the older generations and their OECD peers (Figure 7.7). Poland also reports the third largest difference among OECD countries, after Singapore and South Korea, between tertiary educational attainment of the young and the old: in 2015,

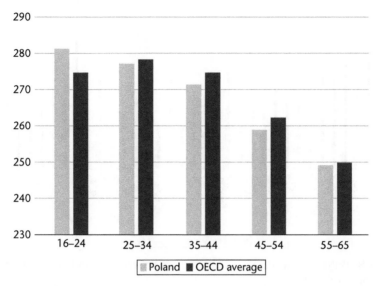

Figure 7.7. Adults' functional literacy in Poland and OECD countries, 2015, by age.
Source: Author's own based on OECD (2016b).

47 per cent of young Poles aged 25–34 had tertiary education as opposed to only 15 per cent among the 55–65-year-old generation, a 32 percentage point difference. The generational difference in educational attainment was only 1.4 per cent in Germany, 5 per cent in the USA, and 16 per cent in the OECD average (Figure 7.8).

The young Poles are at the core of a new Polish generation, which is the most educated, westernized, technologically savvy, and open-minded generation in the country's history. More young Poles now speak English than young French, Belgians, or Spaniards.[9] Anecdotal evidence also suggests that it is the most ethical generation, with the level of corruption much lower than among the older generation (giving bribes or 'presents' is simply not 'cool'). The new generation's values—reflected in attitudes towards the importance of hard work, intelligence and skills, and political connections in explaining success in life—are virtually the same as those of their Italian and German peers (Figure 7.9). Such cultural convergence between Poland and the West has never happened before.

7.4.2. Emergence of Middle Class and Bourgeois Values

Hard work, intelligence, and skills are the core values usually associated with the middle class. A robust and politically active middle class is the backbone of

---

[9] http://languageknowledge.eu/languages/english, accessed 20 June 2017.

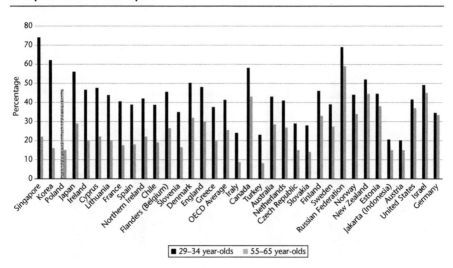

Figure 7.8. Difference in educational attainment between old and new generation in OECD countries, 2015.

Source: Author's own based on OECD (2016b).

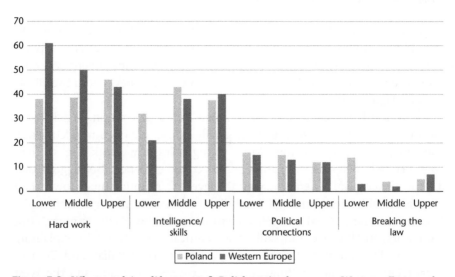

Figure 7.9. What explains life success? Polish attitudes versus Western Europe, by income level.

Note: Western Europe represents an average for Germany and Italy.

Source: Author's own based on EBRD (2016b).

democracy, open markets, and free competition. Middle class has the strongest incentives to support robust institutions, which will safeguard property rights, promote equality of opportunity, and ensure an efficient and noncorrupt public administration. The middle class is also the biggest enemy of oligarchs, state capture, and autocracy. There are no developed, non-oil-rich countries without a thriving middle class.

Aristotle was first to note the importance of the middle class: 'it is manifest that the best political community is formed by citizens of the middle class, and that those states are likely to be well-administered, in which the middle class is large' (Aristotle 306BC, quoted in Decornez, 1998). Landes (1998, pp. 217–18) points out that 'a relatively large middle class' is a key to the 'ideal growth and development society'. He also argues that a large middle class was the main reason for England's early industrialization. Adelman and Morris (1967) assert that middle classes played a key role in the development of Western Europe. The middle class also has a critical role in providing political stability and improving the quality of democracy and its institutions.[10]

There is empirical evidence that the existence of a middle class supports democracy and open markets. Easterly (2001) found that countries with a high share of income going to the middle class and high ethnic homogeneity, which he calls 'a middle-class consensus', had 'more income and growth, more human capital and infrastructure, better national economic policies, more democracy, less political instability, more "modern" sectoral structure and more urbanization' (ibid., 2001, p. 332). Gould and Hijzen (2016) link the strength of the middle class with the level of social trust, while Brown and Hunter (2004) document the interaction between the middle class and the quality of human capital. Mateju (1996, 2000) shows that in Poland, the Czech Republic, former East Germany, Hungary, and Slovakia, respondents who considered themselves middle class were more likely to vote for mainstream political parties. Loayza, Rigolini, and Llorente (2012) reveal how middle classes play an important role in supporting institutional reforms. Finally, EBRD (2013) shows that the existence of a middle class in transition economies strongly correlates with democracy. The bottom line is that a middle class creates a virtuous cycle in which middle class supports faster development, which contributes to a more robust middle class, which then promotes further growth.[11]

The Polish middle class emerged after 1989 for the first time in the country's history as the private sector flourished and created a new class of entrepreneurs, business professionals, and public administration officials.[12] It was

---

[10] Thurow (1984); Barro (1999); Fukuyama (2011); Lipset (1959); Alesina and Perotti (1996).

[11] See also OECD/World Bank (2016).

[12] Andrzej Walicki, Polish eminent economic historian, argues that (Walicki, 1991, p. 32) 'the republican and democratic tradition existed in Poland but it was not grounded in capitalist economy or an individualistic and liberal set of values. Poland was not transformed by the Protest work ethic, and its nation-building elite (first the nobility and later the intelligentsia) did not acquire "bourgeois" characteristics such as entrepreneurship and thrift'.

then joined by the traditional intelligentsia, including artists, lawyers, doctors, architects, and teachers. The new middle class has grown from a few hundred thousand at the beginning of the transition to at least 3 million today, almost 10 per cent of the population.[13] As it grew, it played an increasingly critical role in the transition, as it voted for parties which supported democracy, open markets, and 'the return to Europe' (Jackson, Klich, and Poznanska, 2005).

The new middle class also unequivocally adopted a Western, bourgeois set of values and ideology, something that had never happened before in Polish history (Ferge, 1997). A study of the Polish middle class in 2007 revealed that it indeed adopted bourgeois, Western, or even protestant values of moderation, saving, and avoidance of conspicuous consumption. The study concluded:

> In terms of their consumption and brand preferences, the Polish middle-class' lifestyle is not lavish. In many everyday situations, they behave in a similar way to the rest of the population. They prefer moderately priced branded products and only indulge in luxury products when they feel it is important.
>
> (Millward Brown, 2008)[14]

As argued by McCloskey (2016), middle class and bourgeois values are key to long-term economic development and political freedom. Poland's story backs it up.

7.5. The Role of Leadership

As discussed in Chapter 1, individuals and leaders matter. The history of the world would have been much different without Napoleon, Hitler, or Stalin. And so would the Polish transition: was it not for individuals such as Leszek Balcerowicz or Grzegorz W. Kolodko, the Polish miracle might not have happened.

---

[13] There are various definitions of 'middle class', focusing both on the type of jobs that middle class members have and the income that they earn. The most recent trend is to consider middle class as households with an income between 75 and 125 per cent of the median household income per capita. This, however, is a very mechanical way to measure middle class. In Poland, and in CEE, self-characterization of respondents matters more, regardless of income. For instance, a teacher is likely to consider himself and be considered middle class, even though his income may not necessarily be high. Based on both definitions, it is estimated that in 2013 Poland's middle class counted at least 3 million people. From: https://www.obserwatorfinansowy.pl/tematyka/makroekonomia/klasa-srednia-rosnie-w-polsce-w-sile/, accessed 20 June 2017.

[14] The report was based on a survey conducted between May and June 2007 of 680 randomly chosen Poles with a minimum monthly net income of PLN 5,000 (U.S. $2,300) for single-member households and PLN 7,000 (U.S. $3,222) per month for households with two or more members (Millward Brown, 2008).

Treisman (2014a) argues that Poland's success has much to do with the leadership of Leszek Balcerowicz in the early 1990s. His radical economic policy at the beginning of transition set Poland apart from others and helped put the Polish transition on the right path. Among almost 120 economic policy makers in transition countries since 1989, only Yegor Gaidar in Russia had a similar significance. Similar results would have likely been produced also for Grzegorz W. Kolodko, who took the lead over economic policy making between 1994 and 1997 and presided over the largest economic boom in Poland's transition history. Treisman (2014a, Kindle 5755) poetically compares these successful policy makers to 'explorers climbing mountain ranges that had never been mapped. They had to trust their intuition and improvise around obstacles, expecting to be swept away at any moment by avalanche'. Indeed.

Balcerowicz and Kolodko mattered not only because they conducted the right policies at the right time, but also because they set new, growth-promoting patterns of behaviour, which were then replicated by policy makers that followed. For example, they set a new standard of personal integrity: unlike in the case of some of their peers in CEE and the former Soviet Union, no one has ever questioned their personal integrity. More than twenty-five years after the beginning of transition, they now both live modest, middle class lives. No other minister of finance in Poland has been different.

In one important way, Polish economic leaders have even become global blueprints of moral behaviour. Unlike in America or to a lesser extent in Western Europe, neither Balcerowicz nor Kolodko have ever 'sold' themselves to business, but returned to academia after each of their spells in policy making. By doing so, they sent a strong signal to those that followed them in the government that accepting positions in business is just not what one should do, because it could create conflict of interests and ultimately undermine the integrity of public policies.[15] They set a pattern that has been largely followed by most other key policy makers since (Table 7.2).

The selection of individuals such as Balcerowicz or Kolodko to take the lead economic policy making roles also speaks volumes about the quality of the political class: in some countries, ministers of finance are chosen not for their skills in managing the country's budget, but for skill in mismanaging it. Since 1989, Poland has consistently chosen key economic policy makers, whose

---

[15] It is difficult not to be mesmerized by the American culture of the revolving doors between policy making and Wall Street or other big business and the apparent belief among the American elites that their policy making is not influenced by their later job prospects in the business sector. If you want to work for Goldman Sachs after you leave the government, is your behaviour while in the government not affected by it? Americans seem to believe so. There is possibly also a less visible aspect of such culture in the form of signals that it sends to people that stay behind in public administration, which could be summarized as 'if you are going to be nice to Wall Street, you are going to get your reward too'.

Table 7.2. No revolving door in Poland: occupations of Polish ministers of finance before and after being in office, 1989–2016

Occupation before	Tenure as minister of finance (1989–2016)	Occupation after
Academia	Leszek Balcerowicz (12 September 1989–5 December 1991)	Academia
Academia	Karol Lutkowski (23 December 1991–26 February 1992)	Academia
Policy making	Andrzej Olechowski (26 February 1992–5 June 1992)	Politics, consulting
Academia	Jerzy Osiatyński (11 July 1992–26 October 1993)	Academia
Academia	Marek Borowski (26 October 1993–8 February 1994)	Politics, academia
Academia	Grzegorz W. Kołodko (28 April 1994–4 February 1997)	Academia
Academia	Marek Belka (4 February 1997–17 October 1997)	Policy making, academia
Policy making, academia	Leszek Balcerowicz (31 October 1997–8 June 2000)	Policy making
Policy making	Jarosław Bauc (8 June 2000–28 August 2001)	Business
Policy making	Halina Wasilewska-Trenkner (28 August 2001–19 October 2001)	Policy making
Policy making, academia	Marek Belka (19 October 2001–6 July 2002)	Policy making, academia
Academia	Grzegorz W. Kołodko (6 July 2002–16 June 2003)	Academia
Academia, business	Andrzej Raczko (16 June 2003–21 July 2004)	Policy making
Academia, business	Mirosław Gronicki (21 July 2004–31 October 2005)	Consulting
Policy making, academia	Teresa Lubińska (31 October 2005–7 January 2006)	Academia
Academia	Zyta Gilowska (7 January 2006–24 June 2006)	Policy making
Business	Paweł Wojciechowski (24 June 2006–10 July 2006)	Policy making
Academia	Stanisław Kluza (14 July 2006–22 September 2006)	Academia, policy making
Academia	Zyta Gilowska (22 September 2006–16 November 2007)	Policy making
Academia	Jan Vincent-Rostowski (16 November 2007–27 November 2013)	Academia
Business	Mateusz Szczurek (27 November 2013–16 November 2015)	International institution
Academia/NGO	Paweł Szałamacha (16 November 2015–28 September 2016)	Policy making
Business	Mateusz Morawiecki (since 28 September 2016)	

Source: Author's own, based on various sources.

integrity has never been questioned. Incentives must have mattered: given the strong political competition, all governing parties had to choose professionals to prove their credibility in economic policy making. But a certain culture and a set of specific values must have also mattered.

Poland was also lucky: it chose its ministers of finance and other key policy makers based on their strong reputation as economists. But being a strong economist is only one of many factors that matter whether an economic policy maker is successful. Economic policy makers need to be not only superb professionals, but also managerial and political leaders at the same time. As Grzegorz W. Kolodko liked to quip: 'when you enter the Ministry of Finance, you stop being an economist and turn into a politician'. None of these qualities come easy; Balcerowicz (2014, pp. 954–6) is right when he argues that 'few people combine the intellectual, managerial, and political qualities necessary to be successful reformers. Whether such people take on leadership positions is largely a matter of chance'.[16]

7.6. Ideas and Ideology

The oft-repeated quote by John Maynard Keynes (1936, pp. 383–4) on the importance of ideas and how 'the world is ruled by little else' exemplifies the power of thought to change the world. The post-communist transition was not different.

It could be argued that Ronald Reagan and Margaret Thatcher were the father and mother of the post-communist transition. It was not in a sense that they helped communism to collapse—here the opinions differ—but in a sense that the economic policies that they popularized have become the economic orthodoxy of the 1980s and 1990s. This affected the transition by inspiring the leaders, guiding the international institutions and influencing the global markets.

The influence of neoliberal ideas has been particularly powerful in Poland, especially as it triumphed over the inherent distrust of *laissez faire* economics by the Solidarity labour union, which—as one of the eminent Polish historians put it—'was certainly not a movement in favor of capitalism' (Friszke, 2014, p. 975). Leszek Balcerowicz was one of the most zealous believers in the religion of neoliberalism. He explicitly mentioned how in the early 1980s he was 'struck by the naïveté of the "socialist side," represented by research of Oskar Lange and the reasonableness of the "antisocialist" camp, represented by Ludwig von Mises and Friedrich Hayek' (Balcerowicz, 2014, Kindle 570–2). It is therefore not surprising that later in 1989 he implemented policies, which were fully in line with the 'antisocialist' type of economic

---

[16] Georgia is another good example of the power of strong leaders. Mikheil Saakashvili, Georgia's President during 2003–2008, introduced revolutionary reforms, which changed the country beyond recognition. He opened up the markets, privatized SOEs in a broadly transparent way, revolutionized the business environment, and cut corruption. As a result, a country that has been dominated by Russia and then the Soviet Union for most of its history, has become a beacon of economic freedom, high-quality business environment, and low corruption among all transition economies (Djankov, 2016).

thinking. The Balcerowicz Plan ticked off all the dogmas of the 'Washington Consensus', the 'bible' of neoliberal ideology. Poland became the poster child of 'neoliberalism' as it adopted strict fiscal discipline, cut public subsidies, introduced tax reforms, liberalized financial markets, adopted a single exchange rate, liberalized trade, eliminated barriers to FDI, started privatization of state-owned enterprises, deregulated market entry, and secured property rights.[17]

Balcerowicz's close advisors and international institutions shared the same ideology. In their 1990 paper, Jeffrey Sachs and David Lipton, two American economists who helped put together the reform programme, called for policies that were at the core of the 'Washington Consensus', including tight fiscal and monetary policies, full liberalization of trade and prices and 'a rapid process of privatization of state firms' (Lipton and Sachs, 1990, p. 127). The IMF and the World Bank, who supported Poland's transition in the early 1990s, promoted the same ideas (Kolodko, 2000; Pinto, 2014).

The clearly positive side of the prevailing ideology of the 'Washington Consensus' was its focus on open markets, free trade and untrammelled competition. It did not need to be this way. One could easily imagine that in 1989, as during the interwar period, the world's prevailing ideology could have promoted closed borders, protectionism, and beggar-thy-neighbour policies. If this was the case, Poland's miracle would have not happened. The 'Washington Consensus', despite all its flaws, gave Poland an opportunity to fully benefit from the global open markets and lift itself up from underdevelopment and poverty.

7.6.1. Other Factors

Aside from culture, leaders and ideas, other factors all mattered for Poland's success, including geography and luck. Needless to say, Poland's location did not change much during the transition, but the pros and cons of being in the middle of Europe changed fundamentally. Poland's heretofore dismal geographic location—a flatland seemingly designed for large-scale manoeuvres of German and Russian armies—suddenly became an important economic asset. After 1989, probably for the first time ever, Poland's proximity to Germany became a boon rather than a bane, as it helped Poland attract FDI, join the global value chains, and become one of the European manufacturing hubs (Stöllinger, 2016). In addition, Germany's high level of income and its economic success in the last twenty years also helped give additional lift to Poland's growth. Treisman (2014a) showed that GDP per capita of

---

[17] For the original formulation of the 'Washington Consensus', see Williamson (1990).

post-communist countries grew faster if they bordered richer neighbours. Bordering Germany became a big plus. Finally, proximity to the West helped transfer ideas and tacit knowledge inherent in trade and investment. Treisman (2014a) also argued that transition economies' political and economic institutions tended to converge on their most immediate Western neighbours. Hence, the Baltic States have become a bit more like Scandinavia, the Czech Republic like Austria, and Poland a bit more like Germany (although the impact on the Polish sense of humour has not yet been analysed). As in life, it is good to have a rich, smart, and pleasant neighbour.

Poland was also lucky. Stalin's unexpected gift of changed borders—as part of the Yalta Agreement Poland was moved about 300–400 km to the West in 1945—helped lay the foundations for the post-1989 economic miracle by eliminating ethnic frictions, increasing urbanization, and physically bringing Poland closer to the Western core of the continent. It was also lucky with the choice of its transition leaders and its timing, with Poland's transition happening at just the right moment, when the West was ready to embrace CEE on benevolent terms. Finally, the transition happened during the most peaceful time in mankind's history, helping Poles concentrate minds on becoming rich rather than yet again defending their country.

7.7. Conclusions

In this chapter I showed, using Poland as an example, that culture has a profound impact on the success or failure of economic development. It affects how formal institutions translate into real life. People's beliefs, stereotypes, mindsets, and ways of doing things ultimately decide whether institutions are efficient or not.

But culture is not destiny. In 1989, looking at the Polish conservative, Catholic, peasant, and survival-type culture, which *prima facie* seems to have little to with Western ideals, it would have been easier to predict why it would do much worse than its more liberal and secular neighbours such as the Czech Republic or Hungary. And yet, it was Poland that became the biggest transition success.

This happened for several reasons. First, it seems that being Catholic and religious on its own does not need to undermine development. What mattered is that Polish Catholicism is far from being fundamentalist, as Poles distinguish between formal religiosity and day-to-day attitudes and decisions. In addition, Polish Catholicism does not necessarily intrude into economic life. Getting rich and prosperous is not frowned upon anymore. To the contrary, the Church often takes part in the economic bonanza. Second, it also helped that Polish elites were the most Westernized in the country's history.

They internalized Western values, which helped keep transition on the right course. Third, Polish success seems to have had much to do with the Westernized elites, hailing both with Solidarity and the post-communist camp, which leveraged the promised nirvana of Western European prosperity and membership in the EU to 'hijack' the more conservative parts of the society, introduce new values, and install European institutions. The implicit *quid pro quo* worked well at least until the EU accession, preventing the more conservative parts of the society from undermining the economic, social and political progress. Finally, the emergence of a new middle class and bourgeois values for the first time in the country's history played a critical role, as it helped to sustain democracy, promote open markets, and support liberal governments. As the Polish middle class expands in line with the growing prosperity, its positive role in Poland's development will continue.

Poland's recent history also shows that individuals matter. Without economic policy leaders such as Balcerowicz, Kolodko, or Belka, Poland's transition would have been much less successful or not successful at all. They promoted the right policies at the right time. But they also set new standards of behaviour among policy makers and exemplified the importance of personal integrity, professionalism, and managerial and political skills. They have become the role models, who eschewed the lure of easy (but often corrupt) money in business and shallow appreciation in public life. Their followers continued on their path.

Ideas and ideologies had a big impact on transition too. The 'Washington Consensus' captured the minds of economic elites in transition economies. There was supposed to be no alternative. The 'Washington Consensus' policies failed in many transition countries, undermining their growth prospects. But it worked better for Poland, as it helped it use its competitive muscles and flourish in the global markets. That said, the fact that many neoliberal policies were adjusted in the mid-1990s during the implementation of the 'Strategy for Poland' saved Poland from an excessive dose of neoliberalism and set the country on the right path before it was too late.

Geography also mattered. Poland's position in the middle of Europe between Russia and Germany has become an important asset. Being Germany's neighbour in particular helped attract more FDI, expand trade, and absorb Western ideas. Finally, Poland was also lucky. It was lucky with the quality of elites it inherited from communism, the choice of key policy makers during transition, and with timing as it put an end to destroyed communism at the right time, when Western Europe was ready to embrace Poland and when the global markets were open as never before. But, as the saying goes, good fortune favours the bold, the brave, and the prepared. The Poles were.

But will Poland's success continue? This is what I turn to next.

8

Will Poland's Success Continue?

Projections, Scenarios, and Risks

The future is not what it used to be.

Yogi Berra

A man only becomes wise when he begins to calculate the approximate depth of his ignorance.

Gian Carlo Menotti

If everything seems under control, you are not going fast enough.

Mario Andretti

Will Poland continue to grow and fully catch up with the West for the first time ever? What are the likely scenarios? What could go wrong?

In this chapter I discuss the growth prospects of Poland. I analyze long-term projections produced by international institutions and the private sector. I discuss a number of upside and downside risks to the projections. I argue that Poland should continue to grow and converge with the West at least until 2030 and achieve around 80 per cent of the Western European level of income. This would be the highest relative level of income and quality of life in Poland's history. The country's true Golden Age would flourish. After 2030, however, convergence is likely to slow and later might even reverse, unless the reforms proposed in Chapter 9 are implemented.

I then discuss how much economists understand what makes countries grow. I assert that we economists know much less than we think we know. I also briefly review various challenges that economists face in moving from economic theory to economic practice, from behavioural biases to conflicts of interests.

I conclude by looking at the pros and cons of international economic rankings. I argue that they play an important role by 'naming and shaming' countries into reforms, but that their economic usefulness and explanatory power is often grossly overappreciated.

8.1. Poland's Growth Prospects

All long-term growth projections suggest that Poland should grow at a solid rate and continue to converge with the West, at least until 2030. This is also in line with the projections of the European Commission's Ageing Report (European Commission, 2015), which is the most comprehensive source of long-term growth projections for all EU member states. The projections are based on detailed prognoses of changes in the labour force, employment rates, educational attainment, and labour productivity until 2060. The most recent Ageing Report 2015 projects that until 2023 Poland should be the fastest growing economy in the EU and grow at almost 2.8 per cent per year on a per capita basis. During 2020–2060, the growth rates are projected to gradually decline, mostly because of the ongoing demographic decline (Poland's population is projected to fall from 38.6 million in 2016 to 32 million in 2060 and age significantly at the same time), from 2.8 per cent in 2025 to only 1 per cent after 2050 (Figures 8.1 and 8.2). OECD (2012) has similar projections, while PWC (2017) is slightly more optimistic, projecting higher GDP per capita growth rates for longer.

According to the European Commission, Poland will continue to converge with Western Europe until 2045, reach about 80 per cent of the euro zone level of income in 2030 and peak at 85 per cent in 2045. This implies that Poland's Golden Age, which started around 2015 when Poland's GDP per capita PPP exceeded the highest levels of income relative to Western Europe since

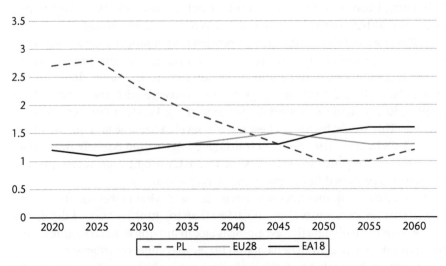

Figure 8.1. Projected potential GDP growth per capita in Poland, EU-28, and the euro zone, 2020–2060.

Source: Author's own based on the European Commission (2015).

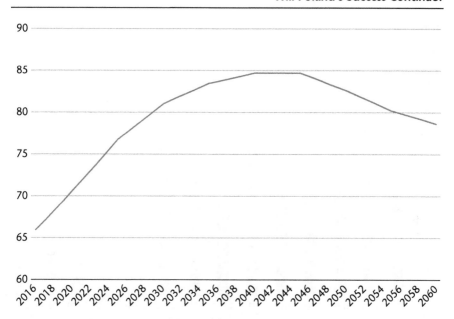

Figure 8.2. Poland's projected GDP per capita relative to the euro zone, 2020–2060, PPP, euro zone=100.

Source: Author's own based on the European Commission (2015).

1400AD would continue for at least another 30 years (Figure 8.3).[1] The quality of life and the level of well-being would be even closer to Western Europe than implied by income alone. However, after 2045 Poland's income would stagnate and the catching up would stop.

8.1.1. How Realistic are the Long-Term Growth Scenarios?

We will never know until we get there, of course. The track record of economists and their economic models in predicting the future is far from perfect, to put it mildly, as hardly any economist predicted the last 2008 global crisis. This applies to the International Monetary Fund, the preeminent global economic institution, millions of economists and economic experts, and all Nobel Prize Winners. Some of the latter, such as Robert Lucas, even argued that crises cannot happen anymore.[2] Financial markets were no better: the

---

[1] The most recent data from Bukowski *et al.* (2017) show that Poland achieved the highest income relative to the West in 1910, when it reached 56 per cent. However, the data reflect GDP per capita of the Polish territories under the occupation of the Prussian, Russian, and Austro-Hungarian Empires, when an important portion of GDP accrued to foreign elites rather than to the Polish society. Hence, the average income of a Pole was lower than suggested by the headline number.

[2] In 2003, Robert Lucas (2003, p. 1), a Nobel Laureate in Economics, argued in his lecture to the American Economic Association that 'macroeconomics in this original sense has succeeded: Its central problem of depression prevention has been solved, for all practical purposes, and has in fact been solved for many decades'.

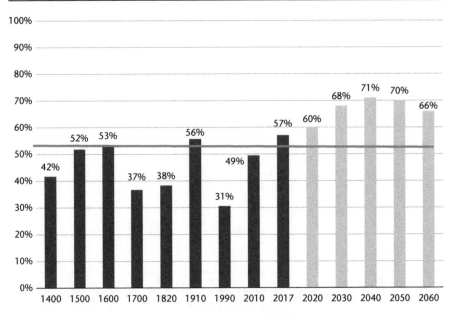

Figure 8.3. Projected GDP per capita in Poland until 2060, euro zone=100.

Note: Projections are based on 1990 $GK prices to ensure consistency with historical data. Eurostat PPS data show higher relative income levels for Poland at 66 per cent of the euro zone level in 2016 as in Figure 8.2. The projections do not consider the hard-to-predict, but nonetheless likely increase in PPP prices, which would accelerate the convergence process further.

Source: Author's own based on Malinowski and van Zanden (2015); Bolt and van Zanden (2014); Bukowski *et al.* (2017); own projections for 2011–2060 based on European Commission (2015).

well-paid economic 'talent' on Wall Street and in London's City was happily investing in Greek assets at a price only negligibly higher than those of Germany until the Greek crisis struck. Overall, there were only a few people, including such economists as Nouriel Roubini or investors depicted in the 'Big short' movie, who predicted the crisis.

Even if some economists appear to get their predictions right every time (the winning formula is to present a lot of projections, then ignore those that did not pan out and highlight those that did),[3] it is not clear whether economists' projections are any better than those based on the wisdom of crowds, random projections, or trends. After having reviewed projections of thousands of political scientists and economists, Tetlock (2005) concluded that the value of the experts' projections was not much different from the average for the

---

[3] It is also good to include some crazy statistical outliers: if you get it wrong, there are plenty of good reasons to explain it, but if you get it right, you can become an instant guru. It is also important to learn to speak in the Delphic way: when in 2008 I became the Chief Economist of PKO BP, the largest bank in Poland, I quickly learned to say things like: 'I believe that the next year's growth will be around 3 per cent, but I cannot exclude that it could be much lower'. If said right, it can cover almost 100 per cent of probabilities. Most experts on TV do the same.

whole population. In an interesting twist, he also showed that TV pundits had lower scores on predictive power than the society's average. In a similar vein, Freedman (2010) and Schulz (2011) provide entertaining accounts of how often experts get their predictions wrong and explain why we nonetheless continue to listen to them.[4] Finally, it is surprising how rarely we ask about the track record of previous projections to assess the credibility of the adopted models. It was only recently that the IMF and other institutions started to evaluate the accuracy of their past projections. Such an approach is, however, still far from universal.

The bottom line is that projections are, well, just projections, and much can go wrong. If this was not the case, all countries would already be rich, as practically all projections invariably assume that countries will grow in the future (unless they are already in a deep crisis and being optimistic would look a bit too naive). The solution is to always treat projections with a pinch of salt and accompany them with upside and downside scenarios. This is what I do next.

8.2. Upside Risks to the Growth Scenarios

There are several reasons to predict that Poland's future performance could actually be better than as shown in the long-term projections. First, in the past, Poland performed better than predicted by the economic growth models. The European Commission's earlier Ageing Report 2012 projected that during 2010–2020 Poland's GDP per capita would grow at an average rate of 2.5 per cent per year. In reality, during 2010–2017 it has grown at 3.2 per cent per year, 0.7 percentage points higher than the projection. This difference suggests that there may exist a 'Polish growth dividend', an unexplained part of the model, which has been calibrated for the whole EU rather than Poland only, that may not sufficiently account for all Poland's strengths.

The 'Polish growth dividend' may be driven by a number of factors. In particular, the economic models are likely to underestimate the importance of strong institutions, built on the way to EU accession. The models also likely underestimate the value of EU membership, which imposes on Poland an institutional, political, and cultural straitjacket. Such a straitjacket—as I argued previously (Piatkowski, 2013, p. 21)—plays a critical role in supporting

---

[4] Many economists are aware that predicting the future is a fool's game. The usual quip among them is that if you project a number in the future, you should never give a date; if you give a date, you should never give a number. But the pressure of the public and the mass media forces economists to predict 'something'. I am not immune from that pressure either. As I already committed the sin of giving both a number and the data (i.e. that Poland's GDP per capita will be close to 80 per cent of that of the euro zone by 2030), the only thing left for me is to come up with upside and downside scenarios.

development as it 'limits the scope for growth-damaging populist economic policies, which—as abundantly shown in many other countries in the past—are ultimately the biggest danger to long-term growth'. The last decade showed that even politically populist governments such as those of Poland's Kaczyński or Hungary's Orban have continued to follow EU rules on the economy. Brazil, Mexico, Malaysia, and many other countries comparable with Poland do not have the same straitjacket. They are therefore inherently much less stable than CEE.

Furthermore, the models may underestimate the high quality of human capital (especially at the secondary level, where Poland is doing better than many Western European countries), much improved infrastructure (which will pay growth dividends for long decades), good business environment (Poland has the best business climate among all countries in Central Europe), and a better-than-expected quality of management (partly because of more developed and higher quality management education, including at places such as Kozminski University, the highest ranked business school in Central and Eastern Europe). Finally, the models do not consider the strength of Polish entrepreneurial spirit, materialistic ambitions of the society (which pushes Poles to work harder than in other countries), and a strong work ethos. As Albert Einstein said, not everything that counts can be counted, and not everything that can be counted counts.

Second, the EC projection is likely to be too pessimistic about the pace of Poland's demographic decline, the key driver of the projected slowdown in growth in the future. The projection assumes that Poland's fertility rate will oscillate between 1.4 and 1.6 until 2050, way below the 2.1 replacement rate. Yet, this projection (already upgraded relative to the 2012 Ageing Report) does not reflect the expected increase in fertility because of the introduction of a generous child cash transfer in 2016. According to the government's projections, the new programme should help increase the fertility rate from 1.3 in 2014 to 1.6 soon after 2020, about 30 years earlier than the EC's projection.

More important though, the EC projection assumes that despite rising incomes Poland will hardly attract any immigrants. Specifically, it projects that Poland will have a zero-net balance of migration until at least 2035 and only negligible positive inflows afterwards. This is unrealistic. Contrary to the model's projections, in 2017 there was already more than a million Ukrainians working in Poland.[5] Their number is likely to increase further as labour shortages increase. In addition, rising incomes should attract not only Ukrainians, but also other immigrants, much in line with the experience of

---

[5] http://www.polityka.pl/tygodnikpolityka/spoleczenstwo/1664626,1,milion-ukraincow-w-polsce-kim-sa-gdzie-pracuja.read, accessed 15 June 2017.

Western European countries. If Poland followed the same pattern of immigration flows as the West, by 2050 at least 5 per cent of the population would be foreign-born, versus zero today (Piatkowski, 2013). Finally, rising incomes could attract home more than 2.4 million Poles who emigrated to the West after 2004 as well as some part of the 20 million strong Polish diaspora living abroad (Ministry of Foreign Affairs, 2013).

Third, growth models do not account for the fundamental difference in Poland between the old generation and the new, European generation. The 50+ generation is much different from the new generation because it had learned skills to survive under communism, while the new generation has acquired skills needed to thrive under capitalism. The difference in the cultural, social, and economic profile of the two generations is therefore much larger than in the West. As argued in Chapter 7, Poland now has the most competitive young generation ever. The new generation is more travelled, cosmopolitan, urban, open-minded, and European than ever before. It is also more polyglot, more hard working, and more materially motivated.[6] And it is much better educated than the older generation and many of the Western peers. The positive impact on the Polish economy of the most competitive generation ever will be felt throughout the better part of the century. Crunching numbers in growth models without adjusting for this fundamental generational difference—the old and the new generation are almost different species—is like comparing old and new computers: the same name, but a totally different performance.

Fourth, Poland has already escaped the 'middle-income trap', which might have stopped its convergence. The concept, developed by Gill and Kharas (2007), is based on the finding that many countries stop converging with high-income countries when they reach a middle-income status. This has been the case for Brazil, Mexico, Thailand, and many other countries that lost their economic oomph as their simple growth reserves, mainly based on cheap labour, dissipated. While there are many doubts as to whether the trap actually exists—for me and many others, the 'middle-income trap' is a sexy media concept, but a shaky economic one[7]—Eichengreen, Park, and Shin (2013) nonetheless estimate that the upper ceiling of the 'middle-income trap' is somewhere around $15,000–16,000 of income per capita PPP. Relative to this threshold, all new EU member states in CEE have already escaped the 'trap' as their incomes are above the upper ceiling. For example, in

---

[6] The Economist (2013c) argues that 'the first thing Polish immigrants brought to Britain (...) was an admirable work ethic'. This was hardly ever the case before (Piatkowski, 2013).

[7] If the 'middle-income trap' really existed, more and more countries would converge around the same middle-income level. But this has not been the case. See, for instance, The Economist (2013b).

2017 Poland's GDP per capita PPP of $28,300 was 75 per cent more than the upper ceiling.

Finally, Poland could experience positive growth surprises fueled by unexpected events, Talebian 'black swans' (Taleb, 2006). By definition, we do not know what these could be. But the impact of such 'black swans' could be substantial. For instance, up until a few years ago, no one predicted that shale gas and oil could so dramatically and so quickly change the American and the global energy markets. Something similar could happen in Poland if, for instance, the recently discovered large deposits of shale gas prove to be commercially viable at some point (the gas is there, but a new technology is needed to get it out cheaply). This would ensure Poland's energy independence, improve the fiscal situation, and support growth. Faster-than-projected growth in the EU, especially in neighbouring Germany, could be another 'black swan'. The 'sclerotic' Europe could get its groove back and grow much faster than before. Alternatively, it could grow at the same pace as in the past, but grow faster in relative terms as the US and China increasingly butt heads in their historical fight for global hegemony (including anything from trade wars to real wars).[8] Finally, Poland could also benefit from being one of the least susceptible countries to the potential negative effects of climate change (World Bank, 2013a).

Overall, and assuming no changes in economic policies, in the upside scenario Poland could grow at a pace of at least 3 per cent a year on a per capita basis. This would allow it to reach 85 per cent of the euro zone level of income in 2030 and fully catch up with the West around 2040. Implementation of a new economic growth model, as discussed in Chapter 9, could accelerate the convergence further.

8.3. Downside Risks

What could go wrong? Plenty of things, of course. Demographic decline could prove to be much faster than projected, if the fertility rate does not increase and Polish general public decides to block immigration. Poland's age structure would change from what looked like a 'fat lady' in 2004, with plenty of young

---

[8] As I argued in Piatkowski (2011), contrary to the usual complaining about the rise of Asia, Europe may actually benefit from the fact that after 500 long years the epicentre of global conflicts will now permanently move from Europe to the Pacific Ocean. The growing and not necessarily always peaceful rivalry between China and the USA will leave Europe more secure, peaceful, and prosperous (and able to withstand the antics of Russia). Europe may benefit from finally being 'the quiet corner' of the world. As the Polish proverb goes: 'Where the two fight, the third benefits'.

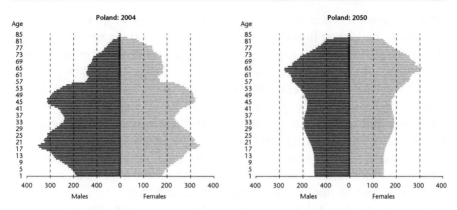

Figure 8.4. Poland: age structure in 2004 and projections for 2050.
Source: Carone *et al.* (2006).

and middle-aged people and relatively few pensioners, to something resembling a 'kebab', with plenty of pensioners and few youngsters (Figure 8.4). An ageing population would undermine competitiveness, weaken public finances, and undercut demand. The negative effect could be compounded by the growing importance of older voters, who may vote in favour of distributional policies benefiting pensioners to the detriment of younger generations.

Given that the EU accession is long done and there is seemingly nothing else that could replace its role as a reform anchor (hopes that the euro accession could provide the new reform anchor were dashed by the euro zone crisis), Poland's institutions and policies could gradually deteriorate and slow growth. The weakening of institutions during the Law and Justice government, which took over power in 2015, is the case in question. While we do not know what specific impact the institutional weakening, especially of the rule of law, could have on growth and how long it would last, in the worst case scenario the lack of the rule of law could undermine business confidence, stymie investment, and ultimately stop Poland's economy in its tracks. It does not look to be the case today (I am writing this in early 2017), but it is not impossible.

In addition, the projected decline of inflows of EU funds when the current 2014–2020 EU budget perspective expires, could have a more deleterious impact than projected by the growth models today. Since the accession, EU funds have been responsible for around 0.5 percentage points of GDP growth per year (Ministry of Regional Development, 2013). But the unaccounted for spillover effects of the EU-funded investment could be much larger. Unless the EU funds are replaced by higher domestic investment, the potential growth rate will decline.

There is also a risk that Poland's innovation could never take off. Despite a siginificant increase in innovation funding over the last decade, generously supported by the EU, R&D spending (at only 1 per cent of GDP in 2016) and innovation outputs have improved only slightly (Kapil et al., 2013; World Bank, 2016a). Poland is not far from the bottom of the European Innovation Union Scoreboard, being euphemistically called a 'moderate innovator'. As TFP growth will likely be responsible for more than two-thirds of GDP growth in the future, reinvigorating innovation will be critical. If because of continued reluctance of the private sector to invest in innovation and slow reform of the public innovation support system, innovation will not kick in, Poland's productivity growth might stagnate faster than predicted.

Lastly, the single most powerful risk to Poland's Golden Age would be a disintegration of the European Union. Short of war, it is hard to imagine what could endanger Poland's growth prospects more than the end of the EU. The EU has been the driver, the foundation, and the chaperone of the Polish success. The EU's possible (although still very unlikely) collapse would push Poland back into the European economic periphery and the security grey zone, from which it would struggle to escape. Access to markets, capital, and trade would be lost. Cost of capital would increase. FDI would decline. Geopolitical security would deteriorate. Devoid of EU-imposed institutional constraints, populist forces could take over the government and start to look for a political and institutional 'Third Way', which has never worked well for Poland before.

Altogether, in the downside scenario Poland's growth rate could decline to below 2 per cent per year by 2030 or—in the worst case scenario of the collapse of the EU—stop growing altogether. The Polish Golden Age would stall.

Which risks predominate? On balance, looking at both the upside and downside risks to the baseline projections, the upsides seem to be slightly more probable than the downsides, at least until 2030. The 'Polish growth dividend' still has some life left in it. After 2030, however, downside risks will gradually increase, especially as the effects of demographic decline start to fully kick in, EU funding disappears, and improvements in the innovation capacity disappoint. Table 8.1 shows how the three scenarios—the baseline scenario based on the projections of the European Commission and the upside and downside scenarios described here—would translate into GDP per capita growth rates between now and 2060 relative to the euro zone-18.

The three growth scenarios imply three difference development paths. Under the upside growth scenario, Poland fully catches up with the euro zone around 2040 and then continues to grow until it reaches about 110 per cent of the euro zone income in 2060 (Figure 8.5). Under the baseline scenario, it will reach about 85 per cent of the euro zone income around 2040 and then

Table 8.1. Growth scenarios for Poland 2020–2060 and euro zone-18, 2020–2060, average projected five-year GDP per capita growth rates

	2025	2030	2035	2040	2045	2050	2055	2060
Upside scenario	3.5	3	3	2.5	2	2	2	2
Baseline	2.8	2.3	1.9	1.6	1.3	1	1	1.2
Downside scenario	2.5	2	1.5	1.5	1	1	1	1
EA18	1.1	1.2	1.3	1.3	1.3	1.5	1.6	1.6

Source: Author's own projections. Baseline scenario for Poland and projections for EA18 based on European Commission (2015).

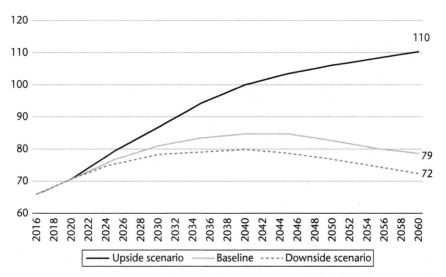

Figure 8.5. Three growth scenarios for Poland, euro zone level of income=100, 2020–2060.

Note: IMF growth projections until 2020. Author's own projections for 2020–2060 for the upside and downside scenario. Baseline scenario based on European Commission (2015).

Sources: Author's own.

gradually decline to below 80 per cent in 2060. Under the downside scenario, Poland's level of income barely touches 80 per cent of Western Europe in 2040 and then declines back to around 73 per cent in 2060.

In each of the scenarios, however, Poland reaches levels of relative income never achieved before in its history. In terms of absolute incomes, even under the baseline scenario an average Pole is projected to earn about $60,000 per year on a PPP basis in 2060, more than double the income today (Figure 8.6). Under the upside scenario, the income would exceed $80,000. In the downside scenario, the income should reach $55,000. The conclusion is that unless there is a war or Poland gets its policies decidedly wrong, even in the downside

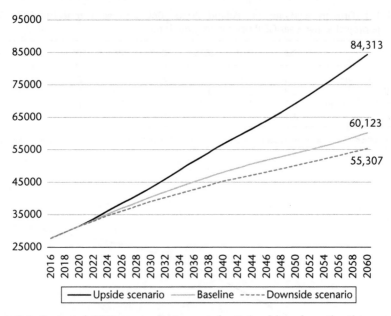

Figure 8.6. Projected GDP per capita income for Poland based on the three growth scenarios, 2020–2060, in USD PPP.

Note: IMF growth projections until 2020. Baseline scenario based on European Commission (2015).

Sources: Author's own.

scenario, the next generations of Poles will enjoy much higher quality of life than their parents did.

8.4. Economic Literature and the Drivers of Economic Growth

What actually happens in the future will fundamentally depend on the type of policies that Poland adopts. However, to understand what such policies should look like, we need to first understand what we economists know and do not know about drivers of growth.

Economists know a lot about conditions, which are necessary for economic growth. It is difficult not to appreciate the importance of macroeconomic stability, security of property rights, high quality of education, open trade, or a well-developed infrastructure. However, even if these conditions are met, growth will not necessarily happen. Many other conditions need to be in place for growth to occur.

The bottom line is that economists know a lot about the basic growth fundamentals, but much less about the specific set of conditions, contexts, and circumstances needed for countries to develop. Hence, the best answer to any question on what drives development is 'it depends'.

Indeed, the 2008 World Bank's Growth Commission, headed by Michael Spence, Nobel Laureate in economics, concluded its long search for optimal developmental models with a statement that 'no generic formula' exists for policies to support growth as 'each country has specific characteristics and historical experiences that must be reflected in its growth strategy' (World Bank, 2008, p. 2). The Commission also argued that 'it is hard to know how the economy will respond to a policy, and the right answer in the present moment may not apply in the future' (ibid., p. 29). Similarly, Olivier Blanchard, Joseph Stiglitz, and Paul Krugman, key authors of the Barcelona Development Agenda (2004), concluded that 'there is no single set of policies that can be guaranteed to ignite sustained growth' and that 'effective institutional innovations are highly dependent on a country's history, culture and other specific circumstances'.[9]

Empirical literature has so far failed to conclusively identify the list of factors that explain differences in growth performance among countries over time (Hausmann, Pritchett, and Rodrik 2005). But it has not been for the lack of trying: economists have so far found 145 variables which could drive growth (Cohen and Easterly, 2009). There is also no shortage of media-friendly advice on the 'real' drivers of growth, from economists and otherwise (Scharma, 2016). If data are 'tortured' enough, everything seems to matter.[10] Only luck is somehow missing from the list, albeit many would agree that it is an important driver of success.[11] Economists, like other human beings, seem not to believe in randomness.[12]

Cohen and Easterly (2009) show that there is no consistency in the pace of countries' economic growth rates over a long time and hence no certainty as to the existence of perpetual growth drivers. As in the well-known fallacy of a 'hot hand' in basketball, fast growing countries most often fail to repeat the good performance and reverse to a lower pace of growth. The World Bank (2005) shows that—much against initial expectations—countries that implemented comprehensive economic reforms in the 1980s and 1990s have grown at a slower pace than countries that reformed less.

---

[9] This section is based on Piatkowski (2014).

[10] The running joke at the IMF, when I worked there during 2004–2008, was that we needed to torture the data until it would confess.

[11] Frank (2017) has a good account of the importance of luck in our lives, how we tend to ignore it and rationalize failure or success ex post.

[12] Humans are hard wired to find 'reasons' and 'explanations' for perfectly random events. The same with economists, who find no trouble explaining differences in countries' performance even if the reasons are random. Like everyone else, they are fooled by randomness (Taleb 2005). Haidt (2012) explains why it makes evolutionary sense for humans to see patterns in random events.

Even the most accomplished economists have trouble putting a finger on the sources of growth and the policies needed to achieve it. Robert Solow, the dean of the growth theory, once noted that 'in real life it is very hard to move the permanent growth rate; and when it happens the source can be a bit mysterious even after the fact.' (Solow, 2007, p. 5). Arnold C. Harberger (2003, p. 215) summarized his long-term research about sources of growth by saying that 'there aren't too many policies that we can say with certainty deeply and positively affect growth'. In a similar vein, Paul Ormerod (1994, p. 34) asserted that 'the ability of orthodox economics to understand the workings of the economy at the overall level is manifestly weak (some would say it was entirely non-existent)'. Joseph Stiglitz, the economic star and a Nobel prize winner, likes to emphasize that economic theory and literature would find it much easier to explain the failure of China's unorthodox economic policies rather than its economic success (Stiglitz, 2002). Easterly (2008, p. 129) sums up the ongoing debate and says that there is no 'universal factor X that works everywhere to reliably raise growth'.

There are also other reasons for why economists struggle to recommend the appropriate economic policies to drive development. First, this is because of the inherent uncertainty of social behaviour: predicting how certain policies might ultimately pan out is akin to predicting the weather. Unstable social behaviour (luckily so, we are not robots, yet) is compounded by economic and political 'black swans' (Taleb, 2006). The 2008 global financial crisis exemplified the changing economic environment well when macroeconomic textbooks had to be discarded to deal with the new crisis. What seemed totally impossible before—money printing, capital controls, foreign exchange interventions, state ownership, or negative interest rates—suddenly became possible and even *de rigueur*.

Second, economists are also not good at getting their policy recommendations right because they are influenced by social norms, values, fads, and cognitive biases. Kahneman (2012) rolls out the whole list of human biases, which economists are not immune from, that make short shrift of their ability to seek an objective truth, including a confirmation bias, a framing effect, and herd behaviour.[13]

Third, economists are subject to pressures to publish (for academics), find supporting evidence for certain ideas (in government or in international financial institutions), or to eschew sensitive topics (such as the importance of culture). They also love storytelling and its inherent simplifications and

---

[13] Economists also are not above prosaic, but impactful calculation mistakes. The applies to the famous claim of Reinhart and Rogoff (2009) that GDP growth slows down after public debt exceeds 90 per cent of GDP. This finding contributed to the euro zone's policies on fiscal austerity, which undermined euro zone growth and the post-crisis recovery. It later turned out that the authors made a mistake in Excel-based calculations and that no growth-inhibiting debt threshold existed.

exaggerations such as that 'lower taxes pay for themselves' or that 'minimum wages kill jobs' (Sedlacek, 2011; Schiller, 2017). They also delight in following the same intellectual fads, having a sense of 'belonging' (Akerlof and Kranton, 2011), and sharing advice while having 'no skin in the game' (Taleb, 2012).

Finally, economists also, of course, react to incentives: it pays to be pro-Wall Street, pro-business, and pro-low taxes rather than pro-trade union, pro-people, and pro-higher taxes. The former will help you get a cushy bank job, a well-funded research chair, and a coveted spot on business TV. The latter will confine you to the dark corners of unionism, alternative youtube channels, and street protests. If you are a young, aspiring student of economics who wants to succeed in life, what do you choose?[14] The conclusion is not that economists do not know what drives growth. They do. It is mostly thanks to the ongoing progress in economics that the global economy has continued to grow, increase global living standards, and lift billions from poverty. Over the last few decades, economists have helped create trillions of dollars of additional value (Litan, 2014). They more than paid for themselves. That said, we should not overestimate what economists know: overall we know much less about what drives growth than many people think. And much less than we believe ourselves to know.

8.5. The Importance of Rankings

International economic rankings can be a useful instrument for identifying drivers of growth. They can also promote the corresponding economic reforms by 'naming and shaming' governments into action. The World Bank's Doing Business ranking or the World Economic Forum's Global Competitiveness Rankings have created billions of dollars of additional GDP over the last decade thanks to various reforms that the shamed governments felt obliged to perform. I know this first hand from my own experience (Box 8.1). But the veracity, credibility, and importance of rankings should not be overestimated. There is much less science to them than many, especially in the mass media, seem to believe.

Let's take the example of arguably the most famous Global Competitiveness Ranking published every year by the World Economic Forum. The name of the ranking suggests that countries that are at the top of the ranking are more

---

[14] Research on income and wealth inequality shows how such incentives may work in practice: while American economists dominate virtually all research areas in economics, economists from Europe such as Branko Milanovic, Thomas Piketty, Emmanuel Saez, or Gabriel Zucman, are the undisputed leaders of the global debate on inequality (Semuels, 2016). As to the conflict of interests, please see the Oscar-winning movie 'The Inside Job' and Zingales (2013).

Box 8.1. HOW POLAND BECAME THE GLOBAL CHAMPION IN DOING BUSINESS REFORMS

When I joined the World Bank office in Warsaw in late 2009, Poland was languishing in seventy-sixth place in the World Bank's 2009 Doing Business ranking, which assessed 189 countries on the ease of doing business. The Polish government, similar to many other governments in the world then and now, was dismissive of the ranking, arguing that it was biased, outdated, and based on unreliable methodology and data. I set out to change it.

I started to persuade the government that the ranking mattered. But progress was slow. In Doing Business 2010 and 2011, Poland moved up in the ranking, but only by a notch. The breakthrough came in 2011 when I organized the first ever visit of the Washington DC-based Doing Business team to Poland. We met with the Polish government, experts, and private sector respondents to the Bank questionnaire. It turned out that the business environment was in fact much better than reflected in the ranking. Because of the mission and subsequent update of the data, Poland moved up to sixty-second place in the Doing Business 2012 ranking. I used this success to stir up interest in the ranking within the Polish government and prove that the government's reform efforts could indeed impact the score. I sought out and allied with Jarosław Bełdowski, an influential advisor to the Minister of Justice. We asked the government to collect source data for each of the Doing Business indicators, updated the list of respondents, and involved all relevant public authorities in the process.

In the next Doing Business 2013 ranking, Poland became the fastest reformer in the world and moved up to a fifty-fifth place in the ranking. This success prompted Poland's Prime Minister, Donald Tusk, to join the big public launch of the ranking (this was apparently the first time Poland's Prime Minister joined a World Bank event). The Prime Minister's interest in Doing Business sent a powerful signal to all ministries to treat the ranking seriously and undertake reforms that would help Poland move up in the ranking even further. Over the next few years, I worked with the government on several projects to enhance the business environment, including business registration, contract enforcement, construction permit process, and corporate insolvency (World Bank, 2013b, 2013c).

Thanks to the reforms, Poland kept on moving up in the ranking. And prime ministers kept on coming to the ranking's launches. When I left the Warsaw World Bank office in 2015, Poland was in twenty fourth position in the Doing Business 2017 ranking (Figure 8.8), outscoring France and the Netherlands. Over the period 2009–2017, Poland became the fastest reforming economy among the EU and OECD countries. The reforms have considerably improved the business environment and created tens of billions of dollars of additional GDP.

competitive and should therefore grow faster. And vice versa, countries that are at the bottom are uncompetitive and should not grow fast (or at all). Yet, the actual data show the exact opposite: over the period 2004–2016, countries that had a lower place in the 2004 ranking, subsequently grew much faster than countries with higher rankings (Figure 8.7).

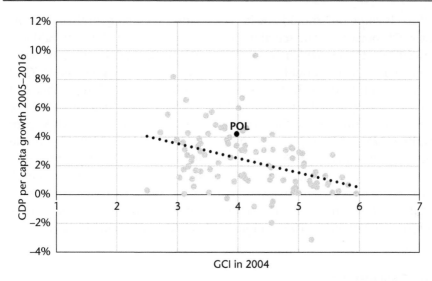

Figure 8.7. Global Competitiveness Report 2004 and GDP growth per capita 2005–2016.

Note: Values of GCI (Global Competitiveness Index) range from 1 to 7.

Source: Author's own based on WDI and GCR.

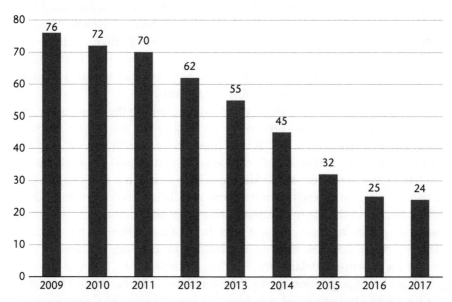

Figure 8.8. Poland's position in the World Bank's Doing Business ranking, 2009–2017.

Note: Results based on consecutive Doing Business rankings. Year 2009 applies to the Doing Business 2009 ranking, which was published in late 2008 based on data from July 2007 to June 2008. Similarly, the 2017 ranking is based on data collected between July 2015 and June 2016. There were also changes in the methodology of the ranking, but these did not affect the overall trend.

Source: Author's own based on the sources in the Note.

What is going on? Should one lower a countries' ranking for them to grow faster? Of course not. The actual results are much in line with the conditional convergence theory, which suggests that poor countries should grow faster while rich countries should go slower. 'Competitiveness' as defined by GCR has not much to do with it. One interpretation of the ranking is that rich countries are 'competitive' because they are rich (and therefore have the supportive institutions, infrastructure, innovation, and so on), while poor countries are poor because they are poor. The other, less tautological and more sensible interpretation is that the ranking should not be expected to predict future growth rates and should not be considered an 'economic Bible'; rather, it is merely a useful snapshot of the important factors of growth, which should better inform the public debate about the needed reforms based on a comparison with peers. This is a lot, yet much less than many expect.

8.6. Conclusions

In this chapter I discussed the growth prospects of Poland going forward. I analyzed several long-term projections and argued that in every scenario Poland should continue to grow and converge on the West at least until 2030. The convergence will be driven by Poland's high level of competitiveness based on a combination of high quality of human capital, high productivity, and low labour costs. A conducive business climate, improved infrastructure, and the best young generation that Poland has ever had will also support growth. The country's true Golden Age will flourish.

That said, there are a few upside and downside risks to the projections. On the upside, Poland should continue to converge with the West because it created an inclusive society. If this is maintained—and inclusive societies are persistent, as explained in earlier chapters—Poland should grow, slower or faster, but grow nonetheless. In addition, Poland's growth is likely to be more sustainable than in emerging markets and middle-income countries. This is mainly thanks to the EU institutional straitjacket that minimizes the risk of disastrous policy reversals. Poland's political, social, ethnic, and religious stability, which most less developed countries are missing, will also be useful. On the downside, Poland and—per proxy the rest of CEE—will need to grapple with fast population ageing, falling inflows of EU funds, and low level of innovation. The biggest risk will, however, involve a potential deterioration in institutions and policies and—in the worst-case scenario—disintegration of the EU, which would push Poland and CEE into the continent's dark periphery.

Which scenario will win out will much depend on the policies adopted. These policies must be based on a good understanding of drivers of growth in CEE. I argued in this chapter that economics cannot provide answers that apply to all countries. Aside from some basic economic truths about the importance of macroeconomic stability, open trade, human capital, and so on, all other policy recommendations must be embedded in the specific context, circumstances, and situation of each country. One size does not fit all.

I also showed that economists are often blind to their blindness, especially when their employment depends on it. They are exposed to biases, wrong incentives, and sometimes even conflicts of interests. This does not mean that what economists produce is not credible. Not at all. It only means that we need to be humble about what we know and cautious about how to interpret the complicated world around us. Finally, I discussed international economic rankings. They are amazing global public goods, which enhance our knowledge and prompt countries into reforms. But their importance and their meaning is often exaggerated. No single ranking will show all that matters.

What will matter for Poland and CEE then in the future? What must happen for the upside growth projections to come true? This is what I discuss in Chapter 9.

9

The New Growth Model for Central and Eastern Europe

'The Warsaw Consensus'

People can perfectly well explain what they could not predict the day before.

Amos Tversky

Everybody has a plan until they get punched in the mouth.

Mike Tyson

You do not measure the health of a society by GNP but by the condition of the worst off.

Zygmunt Baumann

What can Poland and CEE do to fully catch up with the West for the first time ever? Do they need a new growth model? What should it look like and why?

In this chapter, I argue that Poland needs to continue to reform to catch up with the West. While the current growth model has worked well—after all, Poland has become the European and global growth champion—past success does not guarantee future success. I argue that Poland and the rest of the region needs to re-adjust its growth model to sustain a high growth rate and to successfully compete with the high-achieving emerging markets.

I then introduce the concept of the 'Warsaw Consensus', a set of ten policy prescriptions that should guide further convergence of Poland and CEE with the West. The 'Warsaw Consensus' upgrades, corrects, and enhances the 'Washington Consensus', and embeds it in the specific context of the region. It deals with the key challenges to the region's growth such as low domestic savings, population ageing, and low level of innovation, and offers practical solutions on how to deal with them.

I conclude by arguing that the implementation of the 'Warsaw Consensus' should be based on a new policy approach of experimenting, evaluating, and pragmaticizing (being pragmatic), and be assessed against its impact on economic growth, well-being, and happiness. Countries should also make sure that they minimize the risks of crises and become anti-fragile.

9.1. Does Poland Need a new Growth Model?

The current growth model for Poland and CEE has worked quite well, as all countries in CEE are going through the best period in their histories, their Golden Age. All over the region, the level of income (and quality of life) relative to the West has never been higher (Figure 9.1). The Czech Republic, the leader of the region for the last few centuries, has never been richer: even at its last peak in 1937, its level of income was less than two-thirds of the average for Western Europe; in 2016, it was more than 80 per cent. Except for Bulgaria and Romania, all new EU member states from CEE are now considered 'high-income' (Bulgaria and Romania should move to the new income category in the near future).

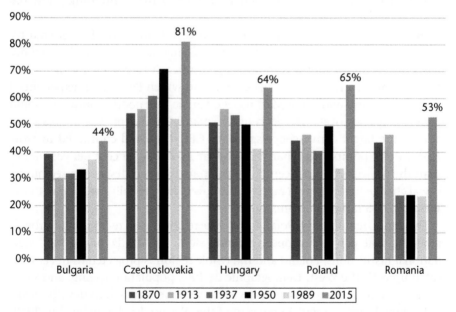

Figure 9.1. GDP per capita in CEE versus Western Europe, Western Europe=100, 1870–2015.

Note: Data for 1870–1989 from Bolt and van Zanden (2014); data for 2015 from Eurostat, based on a different set of prices (euro zone-18=100).

Source: Author's own based sources in the Note.

In a number of ways, the Polish and CEE growth model has proven to be superior even to the Asian 'tiger' model. This is because the CEE economic success has been achieved without resorting to capital controls, undervalued exchange rates, protectionism of domestic markets, subsidies to industries, and a close relationship between the government officials and business. CEE, largely thanks to the EU membership, has caught up with the West in a beautiful style.

So, as Ronald Reagan liked to say, 'if it ain't broke, why change it?' In the same way that high financial returns in the past do not guarantee high returns in the future, there is no guarantee that Poland's and the region's fast growth over the last twenty-five years will continue. There are only a few countries in the world that have managed to maintain high growth rates for a long time. Most successful countries at some point stop growing quickly and their growth rates reverse to the mean (Pritchett and Summers, 2014).

Indeed, the pace of convergence of Poland and—to a larger extent—CEE with the West is declining. During 1995–2005, Poland was converging with Germany at an annual rate of 3.1 percentage points per year. However, during 2005–2015, the convergence rate fell to 2.4 percentage points. It is projected to decline further to 1.5 percentage points by 2022 (Figure 9.2). The European Commission (2015) assumes that Poland's convergence rate will decline to around 1 percentage point around 2025 and to the frighteningly low 0.6 percentage points after 2030.

Such a decline in the convergence rate is not unheard of: as a country becomes richer, the growth rate naturally declines as the country's economy moves closer to the global technological frontier. It is difficult for rich countries to grow at a rate above 4 per cent a year, which Poland has experienced since 1995. Barro and Sala-i-Martin (1992) argue that poorer countries should converge at a rate of about 2 per cent on a per capita basis per year. This should also be the target convergence speed for CEE. If Poland continued to grow 2 percentage points faster than the West, at about 3.5 per cent per year rather than the projected 2.8 per cent, over the next two decades such a seemingly trivial change in the growth rate would allow Poland to fully catch up with the West by 2035 rather than after 2040.

The other reason why Poland and the region must re-adjust its growth model is that per the European Commission, the OECD, and other international institutions, Poland and the whole region is projected to never fully catch up with the West. Demographic decline, population ageing, and slowing growth in productivity are projected to stop the region in its development. Poland might reach about 85 per cent of the Western level of income in 2040, but then slowly decline to below 80 per cent by 2060. The happy end of full convergence with the West might not happen.

Finally, the global crisis in 2008–2009 showed that CEE (except for Poland) is vulnerable to shocks. Despite a much lower level of income, CEE's GDP

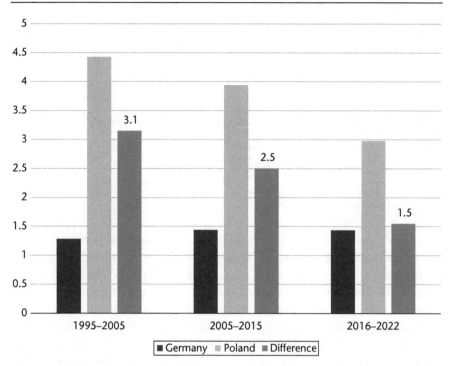

Figure 9.2. Poland's speed of convergence with Germany: GDP growth rate during 1995–2022.

Note: Projections for 2017–2022.

Source: Author's own based on IMF World Economic Outlook database, April 2017.

declined during 2009 as much as that of Western Europe. The Baltic States have gone through the equivalent of an economic heart attack: Latvia, for instance, lost almost 20 per cent of GDP during 2009–2011. Such crises should not be allowed to happen again.

9.2. The 'Warsaw Consensus'

To continue to converge with the West, Poland and CEE ought to re-adjust its growth model.[1] I propose a new growth model, which I will call the 'Warsaw Consensus'.[2] It is based on economic growth theory, diagnosis of the most binding constraints to growth in the region, and lessons from the 2008–2009

---

[1] Many others share this view. See, for instance, Gil and Raiser (2012); Darvas (2015); Atoyan (2010); Aslund and Djankov (2016); Kolodko (2000); Kolodko and Tomkiewicz (2011); Lin (2009).

[2] Tanzi (2006) was first to use the term the 'Warsaw Consensus', but he used it in the context of fiscal policy only.

Table 9.1. The 'Warsaw Consensus' versus the 'Washington Consensus'

'Warsaw Consensus'	'Washington Consensus'
1. Strengthen institutions	1. Maintain fiscal discipline
2. Increase domestic savings	2. Eliminate subsidies, fund education, health, infrastructure
3. Promote education and innovation	3. Broaden tax base, moderate marginal tax rates
4. Boost employment rate	4. Keep real interest rates positive
5. Open up to immigration	5. Maintain competitive exchange rate
6. Keep exchange rate competitive	6. Liberalize trade
7. Sustain strong financial supervision	7. Liberalize FDI
8. Urbanize	8. Privatize SOEs
9. Keep growth inclusive	9. Deregulate the economy
10. Focus on well-being	10. Safeguard property rights

Source: Author's own based on Piatkowski (2014).

global crisis, and is embedded in the political, social, and economic context of the region (Piatkowski, 2014).[3] It builds on the best features of the current growth model—open borders to capital, trade, and people, macroeconomic stability, and European social values—but combines them with the best characteristics of other developmental models, such as those in Asia, which emphasize high savings, controlled real exchange rate appreciation, and export-led growth.

The 'Warsaw Consensus' is a reformed version of the (in)famous 'Washington Consensus', which many merit (or blame) for what happened in the global economy and in CEE since 1989. The 'Warsaw Consensus' emphasizes the critical role of institutions, the key missing element of the 'Washington Consensus', high domestic savings, strong financial sector supervision, and urbanization. It also focuses on the need to ensure that growth is inclusive and that it enhances well-being. But it stays close to the basic economic fundamentals that the 'Washington Consensus' also shares: the need to keep the exchange rate competitive, promote education, and keep markets open to competition. The 'Warsaw Consensus' policy prescriptions are largely in line with the views of the majority of economists in the region and beyond.

Table 9.1 lists the ten policy prescriptions of the 'Warsaw Consensus' next to the prescriptions of its older Washingtonian brother. In the section that follows, I discuss each of the elements of the 'Warsaw Consensus', using Poland as a proxy for the rest of CEE.[4]

9.2.1. *Strengthen Institutions*

As this book argues, inclusive institutions have been key to Poland's and CEE's success in growing out of poverty and becoming high income during the life of

---

[3] See, for instance, Barro and Sala-i-Martin (2003) for a useful review of theoretical foundations of economic growth models, on which the 'Warsaw Consensus' is built.

[4] This part of the book expands on my previous research in Piatkowski (2014).

just one generation. Without Western institutions, Poland would have never become the European growth champion. It would have failed again, as it had many times previously. Going forward, Poland should thus continue to strengthen its institutions, by sustaining open and competitive markets, enhancing the rule of law, and promoting Western values, social norms, and culture.

Open and competitive markets did not exist in Poland before 1989, as argued in earlier chapters. This kept Poland backward and underdeveloped. This changed after 1989, when Poland finally leveraged the benefits of open markets and competition in terms of increased productivity, improved consumer choice, and enhanced equality of opportunity. Open markets must be sustained at all costs. They cannot fall victim to vested interests, corruption, and institutional sclerosis (Olson, 1982).

Poland must continue to keep the economy open to everyone who wants to do business, regardless of where they come from and who their parents are. It requires low barriers to business entry (as few licences, permits, and registration procedures as possible), a fast insolvency process for those who do not make it, and a robust competition watchdog. As to the watchdog, competition authorities in the region ought to be strengthened further and become as independent and powerful as a central bank. They should have a free hand and a sufficient institutional capacity to go after all businesses that undermine competition, regardless of the strength of their political, economic, and social networks. It is in the interest of business to ensure that there is a level playing field for everyone. Finally, Poland should remove all privileges assigned to specific groups (aside from the poor, handicapped, and other vulnerable groups of people). Privileges were Poland's curse in the past and they should not be allowed to re-appear.

Aside from the domestic reform agenda, Poland and CEE should also be the leading force promoting competition in the EU. There are plenty of areas in which the EU is hobbled by lack of competition. This especially concerns the services, which—despite their ever-growing importance in the EU economy—continue to be stymied by a myriad of domestic and EU-wide formal and informal restrictions. These should all be lifted. There is a clear agenda for what must be done (Bruegel, 2017; Aslund and Djankov, 2016). The benefits would be immense, for CEE and—above all—for the whole EU. Bruegel (2017) estimates that lifting barriers to trade in services would increase the EU's long-term GDP by a whopping 14 per cent. The World Bank (2016b) projects a lower impact of about 5 per cent, but then emphasizes additional benefits, including better jobs, enhanced innovation, and higher consumer surplus.

There is also a lot of scope to improve the rule of law, the key long-term foundation of economic development.[5] Poland's courts continue to be slow,

---

[5] For instance, Nguyen and Jaramillo (2014) argue that firms' willingness to innovate in countries such as Poland rises in line with improvement in institutions such as the rule of law.

costly, and inefficient. As the economy matures and becomes ever more sophisticated, contract enforcement must be upgraded. Businesses should not need to wait almost 700 days to resolve their commercial dispute in a Warsaw court, as they do now.[6] The solutions include full introduction of e-government into courts, de-bureaucratization that should allow judges to judge rather than have to deal with the red tape, and reduction in the inflow of cases, also through expanded access to arbitrage and mediation (World Bank, 2013b).

The best illustration of how frustratingly inefficient the Polish justice system can be is the Amber Gold Ponzi-type scandal: since 2012, it has taken Polish courts more than five years to start prosecuting two Amber Gold fraudsters, who embezzled some 100 million dollars.[7] The court case is still ongoing. In comparison, the US courts took only a few months to put Bernard Maddoff in jail for 150 years for embezzling billions of dollars. Trust in the justice system and the rule of law will continue to be hobbled unless Poland becomes more like (although not necessarily exactly like) the US in terms of enforcement of justice and court efficiency.

Poland must keep its key legal institutions strong, especially the Constitutional Court, which was fatally weakened by the Law and Justice government upon its takeover of power in late 2015. A fully independent, robust, and bipartisan Constitutional Court is critical for Poland because it had not had a strong rule of law before. Weakening of the Court is a throwback to the old, harmful status quo, in which only the strong were winning, regardless of who was right and who was wrong. Any politician with Kaczyński's, the leader of the Law and Justice Party, contempt for the rule of law, institutions, and a system of checks-and-balances should never be allowed to rule Poland again.

Finally, Poland should be the leader in the rapid adoption of all new EU legislation and institutions—while maintaining flexibility in designing the specific arrangements—as well as spearheading its own initiatives to deepen EU institutional integration. A strong EU, ideally in the form of the United States of Europe at some point in the future, is in Poland's and the region's long-term interest. Ever closer union for Europe translates into an ever-better life for CEE.

Formal institutions cannot function well if they are not embedded in a conducive culture. One cannot write everything into the Constitution or the law. There will always be scope for interpreting what the law means. The refusal of the Law and Justice government in 2016 to publish the decision of the Constitutional Court (a formal requirement to make the decision legally

---

[6] http://www.doingbusiness.org/data/exploreeconomies/poland, accessed 1 July 2017.
[7] As of May 2017, the Amber Gold-related court proceedings were still ongoing, almost five years after the beginning of the scandal (the two plaintiffs have spent most of the time in jail, however, awaiting the trial and the verdict). For more on the Amber Gold case, see http://www.economist.com/blogs/easternapproaches/2012/08/polands-shadow-banking-scandal; for more on the Madoff case, see http://www.nytimes.com/2009/06/30/business/30madoff.html.

binding)—although the reading of the Constitution makes it obvious that the government has no right to question the decision of the Court and should publish it immediately—shows that bad intentions can undermine even the best law. Continued import of Western values, social norms, and culture is required to ensure that the rule of law and all other institutions are adhered to not only in theory, but also in practice.

How can one promote such cultural change? The good news is that it is already happening as the new generation is more Western, democratic, and law-abiding than the old one and in time it will fully replace it. However, this process can be further strengthened by opening Poland to the world even more (it would be useful to further expand Erasmus, probably the most effective public EU programme ever, and guarantee that every student can study abroad, if he or she wishes), keeping the politicians responsible for behaving in line with the European norms, and introducing behavioural nudges to promote the preferred types of behaviour (through, for instance, 'soap operas' that emphasize the importance of the rule of law). The World Bank (2015a) and Toborowicz (2017) provide useful examples of how such behavioural nudging could function.[8]

9.2.2. Increase Domestic Savings

Poland does not save enough to support high investment. The country's saving and investment rate has oscillated below 20 per cent of GDP in the last two decades, much below the average for the regional peers and the Asian Tigers, which for decades maintained investment exceeding 30 per cent of GDP per year (Figure 9.3). The decline in inflows of EU funds after 2020, which so far have financed investment worth about 2 per cent of GDP per year, will additionally undermine investment. Finally, if domestic savings do not increase, Poland will struggle to deal with labour shortages and the resulting fast growth in real wages. Companies must invest in new capital to substitute for labour, but require higher savings to finance it.

Low domestic savings also enhance Poland's exposure to volatile foreign portfolio investments. When times are good, such inflows support the growth rates, but when times are bad—as many crises have shown before in Asia, Latin America, or in the Baltic States during 2009–2010—'hot' foreign capital can leave overnight, including through the foreign-owned banking sector, and turn a bad situation into a full-blown crisis. Even if one could import

---

[8] Of course, the promotion of Western values does not seek to undermine what makes Poles Polish: all the beautiful elements of the Polish culture—heroism, entrepreneurial spirit, and adoration of freedom—are here to stay. Rather, it seeks to strengthen the elements that have not yet developed sufficiently.

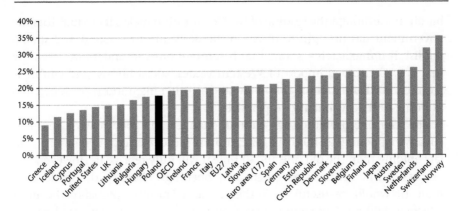

Figure 9.3. Saving rates in Poland and regional and global peers, 2000–2011.
Source: Eurostat.

stable portfolio investment, the resulting net foreign liabilities cannot grow forever.

Finally, low domestic savings prevent Poland from building up its assets abroad and benefitting from growth in emerging and developing economies. With the ongoing population ageing and declining pace of growth, high-return investment in poor countries must help pay for future pensions. For now, Poles pay pensions to foreigners who own capital invested into Poland. There is nothing wrong with this at this stage for development, but at some point the direction of inflows should reverse.

If Poland could save more and invest around 25 per cent of GDP every year, it would be able to sustain GDP per capita growth at around 3.5 per cent until 2030, above the 2.8 per cent growth in the baseline scenario (World Bank, 2014).[9] If domestic savings were supplemented with imported savings, ideally in the form of FDI, domestic investment could reach close to 30 per cent of GDP. Poland would then finally reach the investment ratios of the successful catch-up countries in Asia (World Bank, 2008).

How can domestic saving be increased? There are several good ideas for increasing private saving (which are the sum of household and corporate saving) and public saving. Household saving (I assume that corporate saving should be fully spent on investment, albeit this has not always been the case, World Bank, 2014) should increase automatically as the income and human capital levels increase: richer and more educated citizens, once they have met all their basic needs, tend to save more. But such an increase would not be sufficient to fill the gap in saving. More needs to be done.

---

[9] In the scenario of a lower TFP growth rate of 1.5 per cent per year, the national saving would need to increase to the impossible 35 per cent of GDP (World Bank, 2014).

First, there is scope to further increase employment rates (discussed later in more detail). The more people will be working, the more will earn salaries, and the more of them will have a chance to save. Second, it is important to promote higher saving through mandatory and voluntary saving pension schemes. Defined contribution systems, such as those implemented by Poland in the late 1990s (although much has changed since then) and in several other countries in the region, will be key for generating saving.[10] However, the mandatory saving mechanism should be complemented by voluntary saving programmes. These could include automatic pension enrolment plans for employees, 'Save More Tomorrow' programmes, which have proven their worth in the USA (Thaler and Benartzi, 2007) and cheap asset management services. Finally, well-targeted fiscal incentives, especially to nudge the less well-off into saving, are also needed. Altogether, the objective of these measures should be to significantly increase private voluntary saving beyond the current low levels: in 2016, the value of total assets of all voluntary retirement accounts in Poland amounted to less than 1 per cent of GDP (KNF, 2017).

There is also a need to increase public saving, or rather—given the perennial budget deficits—to decrease public dis-saving. To achieve this, fiscal policy must be based on robust fiscal rules that would keep structural deficits at a level consistent with a stable public debt, strong debt limits (Poland's constitutional 60 per cent of GDP debt limit adopted in 1997 could be a source of inspiration for others), and efficient oversight institutions, including fiscal councils. However, given the rising costs related to population ageing, such formal constraints might not be sufficient. Therefore, increases in taxes might be inevitable.[11] As taxes in CEE are below those of rich countries— Poland collects tax revenue of only 33 per cent of GDP, below the 35 per cent EU average, and way below countries such as France with tax intake exceeding 40 per cent of GDP—there is scope for selective increases in taxes. These could include a progressive tax on wealth, higher taxes on environment and on high-end consumption, and elimination of growth-distorting tax expenditures.

---

[10] During 2008–2016, Poland reduced the role of the privately managed and cash-funded private pillar of the defined contribution system. Hungary has liquidated this pillar altogether. The same may happen to Poland too. Without going into the details of the complicated discussion of the pros and cons of privately managed pension systems, including the associated costs, financial returns, and impact on public debt, mandatory saving mechanisms in one form or another are indispensable to enhancing private savings and paying for future pensions.

[11] In Poland, public spending on health and long-term care is projected to increase from around 5 per cent of GDP in 2013 to 7.2 per cent in 2060 in the optimistic scenario and a whopping 11.6 per cent of GDP in the pessimistic scenario. Spending on minimum pensions (for those who have not earned enough to obtain the minimum pension) will produce an additional 1–1.5 per cent of GDP of spending (World Bank, 2014).

There is also room for generating additional tax revenue by harmonizing tax policy in the EU. Tax harmonization could include adoption of a common corporate income tax base and a minimum CIT tax rate of at least 15 per cent. Such harmonization would help stem the harmful race-to-the-bottom in corporate taxation (Piatkowski and Jarmuzek, 2008), which benefits multi-nationals and immiserates countries. As Christine Lagarde (2014), the head of the IMF rightly noted, a 'race to the bottom leaves everyone at the bottom'. Countries should compete on what matters for development—the quality of institutions, human capital, infrastructure—not on taxes.

Finally, it would also be critical to eliminate tax havens (including some in the EU), which are a moral and economic scourge, and ensure that multi-nationals pay a fair share of taxes in the country in which the profit is generated. It should never be possible again for multinationals to avoid paying any taxes in Europe whatsoever. CEE should support the efforts of the European Commission to introduce a common, consolidated corporate tax based in the EU. If these efforts fail again, the EU should impose a minimum effective corporate tax rate on all multinationals.

9.2.3. *Promote Education and Innovation*

There is broad consensus behind this plain vanilla recommendation. It is unlikely that anyone would be against further improving the quality of education in Poland and CEE, which is high—above what would be expected based on the level of income—but still behind the best performing countries. This is particularly the case for university education, in which CEE lags behind other parts of the world, including some much less developed countries. According to the so-called Shanghai ranking (or, more formally, the Academic Ranking of World Universities) Poland has only two universities—Warsaw University and Jagiellonian University—among the global top 500 universities. Other countries in the region are no better.[12]

High quality of human capital is crucial to sustaining CEE's comparative advantage, especially in high-productivity manufacturing. As rightly argued by Rodrik (2013), manufacturing is special because—unlike agriculture or services—it can increase productivity and employment at the same time. The longer CEE holds on to manufacturing, the better.

But in the end, the region will also start to de-industrialize, as happened in the richer countries previously. It will de-industrialize because manufacturing will move to other, cheaper countries, the changing structure of demand towards services will weaken demand for manufactured products, and because

---

[12] http://www.shanghairanking.com/ARWU2016.html.

the continued fast progress in productivity will lower employment.[13] CEE will then have to gradually move to create jobs in high-end services such as finance, logistics, BPOs, entertainment, and others. High volume and quality of human capital will be key to making this switch.

To upgrade the quality of education, universities must change. It will be necessary to introduce professional management of universities (executive directors should replace rectors chosen from among the faculty), increase funding, and open the universities to the world by allowing more foreign students and faculty.

There is also big scope for larger investment into early age education. There is overwhelming evidence that early education enhances children's life-long skills, builds emotional intelligence, and reduces inequality of outcomes (Hansen, 2016). Governments should ensure that 100 per cent of kids are able to attend crèches and kindergartens. This will be a high-return investment into the quality of the future labour force, equality of chances, and well-being.

Innovation is equally critical to development as education, and similarly non-controversial. Who would not want to be more innovative? However, being innovative is easier said than done. To sustain a high pace of productivity growth, Poland—and per proxy other CEE countries—must gradually move from imitating to innovating, from quantity to quality, and from potato chips to microchips (Van Ark and Piatkowski, 2004; Piatkowski and Kapil, 2015; World Bank, 2011; Jorgenson, 2009). Otherwise, productivity growth will stagnate and convergence will first slow and then stop altogether.

Given the still large gap in productivity—Poland's productivity per hour amounts to only about half of that in Germany[14]—there is much scope for further imitation through technology absorption. But as Poland continues to shorten the distance to the global technology frontier, it will also need to increasingly innovate on its own and generate products and services new to the world. However, building this capacity will not be easy and this will take time. Poland (and the region) has never been technologically advanced and technological invention has not ever been part of the region's DNA. Building the capacity to innovate and invest in R&D will also support technology absorption (the former is a critical ingredient of the latter, as argued by Kapil *et al.*, 2013).

So far, despite occupying a low position in various innovation rankings and low spending on R&D (total expenditure on R&D in 2016 in Poland

---

[13] To illustrate the power of technological progress, in the 1980s, it took 10 labour hours to produce one ton of steel. Today, it takes only 0.4 hours (Cohen, 2017).

[14] http://stats.oecd.org/Index.aspx?DataSetCode=PDB_LV, accessed 15 May 2017.

amounted to only 1 per cent of GDP), Poland's labour productivity—the best reflection of the economy's inherent innovativeness—has been growing at a respectable clip. But there is no guarantee that this low-innovation growth model will continue to produce such good results. The bumblebee may stop flying.[15]

A fundamentally modernized public support system for innovation will be needed to help put Poland on an innovative path. More than 10 billion euro of EU funds available in the EU 2014–2020 budget must be invested more productively than before. A modernized public support system will also be key to support private sector innovation when the inflows of EU funds decline after 2020 and the country's budget will become the main source of financing.

Piatkowski and Kapil (2015) offer five key recommendations for innovation policy in Poland and CEE. They call for a full focus on outputs rather than inputs, putting business in the driver's seat of innovation policy, ensuring high-quality of implementation, opening to the world, and investing in top-notch institutional capacity. It will be crucial for the public sector to become fully professional, competent, and non-bureaucratic; old-fashioned institutions cannot drive new fashions.

The public sector should also be a role model and adopt cutting-edge technologies on its own. Without this, it will not be a credible partner for the private sector (World Bank, 2016a). Finally, the public sector should not be afraid to dream big and finance seemingly crazy ideas. Without the public sector's high risk appetite, there would be no Internet, no computers, and no i-Phones (Mazzucato, 2015). There is no reason to stop being bold (Piatkowski, 2015b).

Public sector support for innovation should also underpin a modern-type industrial policy. As emphasized by Rodrik (2008), smart industrial policy must be embedded in the country-specific circumstances, offer carrots-and-sticks, and be accountable. Innovation-based industrial policy in particular must be based on a bottom-up approach, which puts business in the driver's seat of innovation and adjusts public support instruments to the specific and changing needs of enterprises. The concept of 'smart specialization' developed and implemented in the EU, which promotes innovation-based industrial policy based on the identification of comparative advantages and endogenous strengths, provides a useful framework for government action. 'Smart specialization' is meant to help both the public and the private sectors to figure out what the country excels at producing. The implementation of this framework

---

[15] There is an anecdotal story that according to physicists, bumblebees are too heavy to fly and should never be able to get airborne. While this story may actually not be true, it still makes for a relevant analogy.

in Poland showed that innovation-based industrial policy, when well designed, implemented, and monitored, can work well (World Bank, 2016a).

However, innovation is not all about the public sector. The private sector must also step in. A modernized public support system cannot force the private sector to innovate. The latter must do the hard work on its own. The private sector must snap out from its innovative lethargy, hitherto fuelled by a combination of high human capital, low labour costs, cheap currency, and low taxes. These 'growth steroids' will not last forever. Given the population decline, labour costs are likely to rise at a fast rate, taxes might need to increase, and zloty will not be cheap forever. Polish entrepreneurs must discard the 'growth steroids' and focus on improving management skills, building R&D capacity, reaching out to science, and opening up to the world (World Bank, 2016a).

9.2.4. Boost Employment Rates

There will be no prosperity without work. Poland will never catch up with the West if all Poles do not contribute. The more will be employed, the larger the chance for continued convergence and ultimate success in becoming as prosperous as the West. However, today only about two-thirds of Poles of working age are employed versus three-quarters in the neighbouring Czech Republic, and almost four-fifths in the leading countries of Western Europe such as Sweden or Germany. In Iceland, Europe's leader, a remarkable 86.5 per cent of people aged 20–64 are employed.[16]

Such a low employment rate, despite recent improvements, means that with only two-thirds of working compatriots, Poles would all need to become Supermen to successfully compete in the long-run (when the current cost advantage disappears) against countries in which many more citizens pull the country forward. Fewer working people translates into lower GDP, reduced tax revenue, and higher fiscal burden when the state needs to support those not in employment. Lifting the employment rate of older workers alone to the level prevalent in Germany would increase Polish long-term GDP by 6 per cent (Arnhold et al., 2011).[17] Together with higher employment of women and the young, the benefits could amount to close to 10 per cent of GDP.

---

[16] http://ec.europa.eu/eurostat/web/products-datasets/-/t2020_10&lang=en, accessed 10 June 2017.

[17] The employment rate of Polish women is at 60 per cent, while it exceeds 70 per cent in Western Europe. Similarly, the employment rate for Poles aged 55–64 amounts to only around 40 per cent, below the 50 per cent EU average (Arnhold et al., 2011).

The key to raising the employment rate to at least 75 per cent is to increase effective retirement ages, enhance skills, and allow more flexible and part-time working arrangements for women, the young, and the old.[18] Of course, increasing the retirement age will be unpopular as people do not want to 'work until their death'. Poland's reversal of the earlier pension reform—it first increased the retirement age to 67 for both sexes, but then in 2017 lowered it back to 60 and 65, for women and men, respectively—shows how politically difficult it is to lengthen working lives. But given the ongoing increase in life expectancy—Polish women will soon live in retirement as long as in work—raising the effective retirement age is inevitable.

But the key focus should be on 'effective' retirement age rather than 'statutory' retirement. The solution is to design pension systems so that they provide strong incentives to stay in the labour force regardless of the statutory retirement age or whether there is one at all. One way to achieve this would be to transform pension systems from the old pay-as-you go systems to defined contribution systems. The latter automatically provide incentives for working longer: the more one accumulates during his working life, the more there is to spend during retirement. While Poland and many other countries in CEE have already introduced such systems, there is still some scope for making the transition complete.

It will also be important to make it easier for older people to work. This could include a shorter work week (a mandatory Friday off, for instance), shorter work hours during the day, and a 'senior sabbatical', an opportunity to take some time off from work (to take care of their health, family, travel the world) and have a guarantee of returning to the same job. The government could also help by promoting technologies that make it easier for older people to stay employed. These could involve specially designed call centres, online teaching or advice-sharing, or other, yet-to-be-invented ways of productively using the accumulated potential of soon-to-be hundreds of millions of ageing baby boomers, in Poland and around the world. Instead of spending scarce public R&D funding on the bells and whistles to the umpteenth version of an i-Phone or another blood-soaked computer game, public funding could be re-directed accordingly.

It would also be useful to promote changes in cultural norms: being employed at an old age should become a badge of honour and a sign of individual vitality and usefulness to society. This could be done in a variety of ways, including role-modelling by policy makers, celebrities, and actors in movies. Productive ageing will also be supported by technological progress: as robotization intensifies, fewer and fewer jobs will require psychical exertion,

---

[18] For such ideas, see, for instance, Chawla, Betcherman and Banerji (2007).

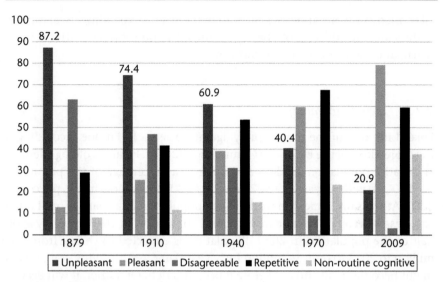

Figure 9.4. Percentages of unpleasant, disagreeable, repetitive, and cognitive jobs, 1870–2009, in per cent of US workers.

Source: Author's own based on Gordon (2016).

as has been the case throughout the last 150 years as technological progress eliminated gruesome, dirty, and often simply stupid work. In the USA, for example, the share of unpleasant jobs decreased from 87.2 per cent in 1870 to only 20.9 in 2009 (Figure 9.4).

Continued progress in medicine will also improve health. Thus, there will be fewer reasons for hypochondriac grumblings and more reasons for active ageing. If one lives longer, one should have to work longer too.

Higher employment rates and longer employment should not mean worse employment, however. Technological progress may make jobs less stable, less secure, and more precarious, but this does not mean that we are incapable of taking control of the progress, the same way we have done it before. Less secure jobs will require more support from the state in the form of job insurance, subsidies for low wages, and guaranteed publicly financed jobs. Changes in labour laws with also be necessary to balance technological progress with labour rights. People cannot be left to face the technology giants alone: they need help, protection, and security.

Finally, governments must complete the existing social safety net to ensure that no one is left behind. A basic income guarantee (BIG) would be the key instrument to achieve this. This already exists in a partial form—Poland, for instance, now pays cash subsidies to all families with at least two children (and to poor families with one child) and guarantees minimum pensions for the old—but this will need to be gradually strengthened in line with the growing

GDP, increasing precariousness of employment, and expanding fiscal capacity of the state. Introduction of a basic guaranteed income is not a matter of if, but when, and the process should start now.[19]

9.2.5. *Open up to Immigration*

Poland has one of the most rapidly ageing societies in Europe. According to the projections of the European Commission (2015), Poland's old-age dependency ratio (population aged 65 and more as a percentage of the population aged 20–64) will increase from 22 per cent in 2013 to a shocking 66 per cent in 2060. At the same time, the working-age population as a share of total population is projected to decline from around 70 per cent in 2013 to barely about half of the population in 2060. Population is expected to shrink from 38.5 million in 2013 to only 34 million forty years later. As the saying goes, Poland might become small and old before it becomes rich. Or, rather, it will become small, old, and never rich. One can hardly grow when half of the society is old and retired.

There are several solutions to dealing with the demographic decline. One is to continue to support pro-family policies and increase the fertility rate from the current dismal 1.4 to somewhere closer to the 2.1 replacement rate. There a number of well-established ways of doing this, including by providing universal access to childcare, increasing labour market flexibility for mothers, supplementing parents' incomes, and introducing fiscal and non-fiscal benefits for large families of three or more. But no matter what Poland does, it is near to impossible to expect that it would ever again achieve the replacement rate. Cultural norms, social perceptions of alternative costs of having children, and uncertainty in the labour markets have changed too much to allow this to happen. Even the much richer Germany, which spends hundreds of billions of euro per year on pro-family policies in one form or another, has a similarly low fertility rate of only 1.4 (European Commission, 2015). Clearly, money is not the (only) issue. Culture is.

Hence, to stem the demographic decline and to support the convergence, it is critical for Poland to open up to immigration. According to the European Commission (2012), by 2020 Poland will already require 1.3 million immigrants or 3.3 per cent of population to maintain the size of the working age population (20–64). Millions more will be needed later.

The good news is that, despite the dismal projections, reality has intervened and the gap in the size of the labour force seems to have been largely closed by

---

[19] For an excellent summary of the ongoing debate on BIG, please refer to Sandbu (2017) and his other texts.

the arrival of more than a million Ukrainians.[20] It is imperative that they are incentivized to stay and bring more compatriots with them. But it is not clear how many more Ukrainian immigrants will be forthcoming, especially as Ukraine is going through its own demographic decline. To keep immigration going, the solution would be to open up to immigrants from other, culturally similar countries in the East, countries such as Vietnam, which has already established a vibrant community in Poland, and from the European South.[21] Specific incentives could include a transparent and user-friendly immigration policy offering a clear path to citizenship, longer automatic resident permits for university graduates, and language training and financial support for those newly arrived. Poland could also expand repatriation programmes to millions of Polish diaspora. It will also be important to start competing in the global war for talent. Given that between now and 2100, global population is projected to increase by another 4 billion, mostly in poor countries, there will be a lot of new geniuses born around the world to choose from (United Nations DESA, 2015). Poland and CEE ought to start actively courting talented individuals to come, work, and stay. Finally, Poland could be innovative and introduce, for instance, special support programmes for international marriages.[22]

The ultimate objective of the immigration policy could be to increase Poland's population to 50 million by 2050. This is a long shot, but it is not impossible. The example of Spain, which in the early 1990s had the same population as Poland, but now—mostly thanks to immigration—has almost 47 million citizens, could serve as a useful example. Immigration would help increase fiscal revenues to pay for the ageing population, enhance innovation, and sustain high competitiveness by keeping wage growth in line with changes in productivity.

However, to make immigration happen and to lower the inevitable social costs of integration, Poland will need to redefine the definition of what it means to be Polish: it will now need to include not only those who were born in the country, but also all others who want to be Polish and who identify with the new country. At the same time, immigration should not be uncontrolled, as this could undermine the social, political and cultural consensus, erode institutions, and weaken national identity (Borjas, 2015). Each country has its absorption limit, which should be observed. Finally, immigrants will also need to work hard to assimilate into the new society and leave behind much of the

---

[20] http://www.polska2041.pl/spoleczenstwo/news-milion-trzysta-ukraincow-pracuje-w-polsce, nId,2340288, and NBP (2016).

[21] Poland has a history of successfully assimilating Greek immigration in the 1950s. (Sturis, 2017).

[22] My marriage to my beloved American wife, who later became Polish, could serve as a useful blueprint for such marriages. Details on request.

culture, beliefs, and institutions, which led them to emigrate from their home countries in the first place.

9.2.6. *Keep Exchange Rate Competitive*

Exports help pull poor countries from poverty and make them rich. This has been the case for all the Asian Tigers such as Japan, Taiwan, South Korea, or Singapore, where exports were the key driver of development. CEE should do the same.

However, it is difficult to expand exports without a competitive exchange rate. Overly expensive currency not only undermines exports, but also weakens a country's attractiveness to FDI and promotes re-allocation of resources from export-oriented sectors toward less productive non-tradable sectors. It is better to have cheaper currency, within reason, than an overly expensive one (Williamson, 2008; Eichengreen, 2008b; Rodrik, 2007).

How can the exchange rate be kept competitive when it is floating? One way is to pragmatically manage the nominal exchange rate, whenever possible. While central banks in the region have all adopted inflation targeting (or the euro), which made the interest rate the main instrument of monetary policy, excessive appreciation of domestic currency should be avoided by using verbal, market, and interest rate interventions. This is especially the case when the exchange rate deviates from the fundamentals. Policy makers should not let theory stand in the way of common sense.

The main solution to keeping the real exchange rate competitive, however, is to ensure that wage growth does not exceed growth in labour productivity. This requires flexible labour markets, openness to immigration, and active fiscal policies. The euro zone crisis that started in 2009 has shown that wage growth that is incompatible with changes in productivity undermines countries' competitiveness and leads to crises. The case of Greece, which since 2009 has lost more than one-quarter of its GDP, should serve as a salutary warning.

Control of real wage growth will be particularly important when the three largest economies—Poland, the Czech Republic, and Hungary—decide to adopt the euro. Although it is not likely to happen anytime soon—the euro zone needs to get its house in order and the benefits of giving up monetary independence need to become more obvious—when they do finally adopt the euro, they should make sure that they adopt it at a competitive exchange rate.

Finally, prudent fiscal policy must also play a role. Excessive spending leads to excessive currency appreciation. Therefore, fiscal policy must be kept under control. This has not been the case in countries in Southern Europe in the run up to the euro zone crisis, where high budget deficits contributed to excessive increase in wages and harmful real exchange appreciation.[23] CEE should not replicate this.

9.2.7. Sustain Strong Financial Supervision

Banks are like fire: indispensable to daily life, but deadly when it erupts and burns down the house. Abundant economic literature suggests that there is a well-established link between the development of banks and economic development. At the same time, however, there is also an understanding that the banking sectors tend to explode in crises from time to time and take down their host countries with them. Time and again this has proven to be true. Since the 1990s, banking crises have undermined growth in dozens of countries, from Sweden in the early 1990s, transition economies in the mid-1990s, Turkey in the early 2000s, to, of course, the USA and Europe during the 2008–2009 global crisis.

The key policy conclusion from that tumultuous period is that banks are way too dangerous not to be strictly supervised, even at the cost of slightly slower growth. There is no point of playing with fire. The solution is to support the strengthening of the European-wide supervisory control over the large foreign banks, which hold the dominant share in the region's banking sector, putting limits on foreign currency borrowing, and introducing bank resolution legislation to liquidate banks swiftly, when needed. In addition, CEE needs to build strong macro-prudential frameworks, which will react when credit growth gets out of hand. Poland's framework could serve as an example.

It will also be useful to diversify ownership of the banking sector: it is too risky to rely on funding from foreign banks only. The 2009 global crisis showed that foreign-owned banks in CEE were cutting credit lifelines regardless of the countries' specific economic situation, adding fuel to the crisis. Domestically owned banks expanded credit instead. In Poland, increased lending by the PKO BP bank, which stepped in to pick up the slack left by the panicking foreign-owned banks, has done much to help the country become the only economy in Europe to avoid a recession (Piatkowski, 2015a). The target could be for the locally owned banks to represent from about one-third to about one-half of the total banking sector's assets.

Finally, the authorities should make sure that banks do not speculate, US-style, but sustain conservative, utility-like business models. Utility banking—moving savings from savers to investors—is how banks contribute to social welfare. Many other bank products often end up being just a ruse to privatize

---

[23] The euro zone crisis was later made worse by lack of debt restructuring and excessive austerity, see Sandbu (2015).

profits and socialize losses. In particular, financial innovation in recent decades has often concentrated on various stratagems to game the markets and dupe the supervisors. As Paul Volcker (2009) memorably put it, in the last 30 years the most socially useful financial innovation was an ATM.

9.2.8. *Urbanize*

Countries must urbanize to become rich. There is a strong positive correlation between urbanization and development: rich countries are much more urbanized (World Bank, 2015b). As Michael Spence, the Nobel Prize Winner in Economics, noted: 'We know of no countries that either achieved high incomes or rapid growth without substantial urbanization' (Spence, Annez, and Buckley, 2009, p. X). Acemoglu, Johnson, and Robinson (2005) also show that urbanization and development go together and are remarkably persistent: countries that were well urbanized in 1500AD are much richer today than those that were not. While causality can go both ways—urbanization causes growth and growth causes urbanization—there is strong evidence that cities do drive economic growth: during 2005–2012, 72 per cent of the top 500 cities around the world grew faster than their country's economies (World Bank, 2015b).

Cities are also centres of technological, cultural, social, and civilizational progress. Smart and entrepreneurial people congregate in cities, which— through interaction with others—make these people even smarter and more entrepreneurial, which in turn attracts new smart and entrepreneurial people, and so on. Cities thus become centres of what Florida (2002) calls the 'creative class', which drives mankind's progress. Cities also make our lives 'greener, healthier, and happier' as in the title of the bestselling book by Edward Glaeser, a Harvard urban economist (Glaeser, 2012). In a world where agriculture's role in economic growth is constantly declining (in rich countries agriculture represents less than 2 per cent of GDP; even in Poland, agriculture now contributes a paltry 3 per cent), and where technological progress is at a growing premium, cities will be the key drivers of development in the future (World Bank, 2015b).

Poland lags behind in urbanization, however. In 2015, only 61 per cent of Poles lived in cities versus the European average of 75 per cent. Poland was much less urbanized than its regional peers, the Czech Republic, Hungary, or Slovakia (Figure 9.5). And progress in urbanization has not been faster than elsewhere in the region (Figure 9.6). Poland's largest city—Warsaw—has only 1.8 million citizens, making it proportionally one of the smallest metropolises in relation to the size of the country's population in Europe (Budapest and Prague, for instance, have more than 1.8 and 1.2 million citizens each, but both countries have only about 10 million inhabitants, versus 38.5 million in

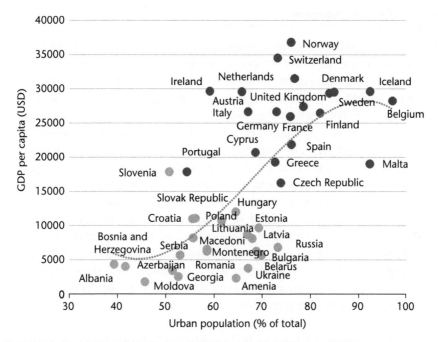

Figure 9.5. Level of urbanization and GDP per capita in Europe, 2015.

Source: https://www.bbvaresearch.com/wp-content/uploads/2016/12/European-urbanization-trends_.pdf.

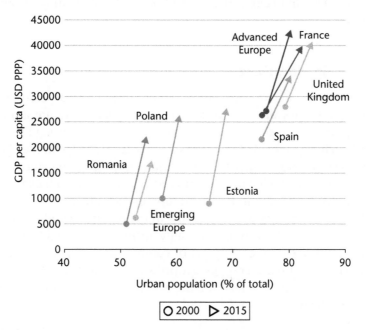

Figure 9.6. Change in the urbanization ratio and GDP per capita in Europe, 2000–2015.

Source: https://www.bbvaresearch.com/wp-content/uploads/2016/12/European-urbanization-trends_.pdf.

Poland). This matters because empirical evidence suggests that productivity increases with the size of cities (Spence, Annez, and Buckley, 2009).

How can urbanization be promoted? There are several solutions. First, countries should stop promoting the environmentally unfriendly and economically inefficient suburban sprawl and focus on increasing the density of existing cities instead. This could be achieved by, for instance, liberalizing and enhancing access to land in cities and promoting high, multi-story buildings. Both should help keep a lid on the real estate prices and attract the rural population, who otherwise could not afford to move to cities. Second, given the large spillover effects of city development, there is a strong case for central government's support for build-up of infrastructure in cities. Third, there is a good case for reducing subsidies given to rural areas, for instance—as in the case of Poland—in the form of separate pension and tax systems, which keep the population in economically inefficient rural jobs. Finally, there is the usual agenda of making cities attractive as a place to work, live, create, and have fun. This agenda is important regardless of the need to urbanize, but it supports it at the same time (Boni, 2009).

What would be the impact of higher urbanization on economic growth? It is hard to say and more empirical research is needed. But if Poland's urbanization ratio could reach the European average of 75 per cent of population, it would help to close an important part of the remaining income gap with the West.

9.2.9. Keep Growth Inclusive

Equality is like democracy: no country can become rich, prosperous, happy, and truly free at the same time without it. An abundant literature shows that promoting equality is key to supporting economic growth, lifting life expectancy, enhancing quality of life, and making people satisfied with life.[24] Equality also makes economic growth more stable and less vulnerable to social shocks. There is no trade-off between equality (within reasonable bounds) and growth: both go hand-in-hand and support each other.

CEE has done relatively well on equality in the past two decades. Following the post-communist transition, inequality increased—it would be hard to imagine anything else after 40 years of communism—but it still stayed at levels much lower than among global peers in Asia or Latin America. It is not different from the average for the whole of Europe, the most equal continent in the world.

---

[24] See, for instance, Piketty (2014); Milanovic (2016a); Pickett and Wilkinson (2011); Ostry, Berg, and Tsangarides (2014); Milanovic (2010) and Tomkiewicz (2017).

But there are risks that inequality might worsen going forward, in line with the global trends, and undermine the region's economic development and well-being. As argued by Piketty (2014), Milanovic (2016a), and others, within-country inequality in developed countries is likely to continue to rise because of high returns to capital, skills, and technology, which mostly benefit the top global 1 per cent and leave much of the rest behind. Capital has been winning against labour during recent decades, as reflected in the falling share of labour in GDP (IMF, 2017a). It is not clear what could stop this trend going forward short of a social revolution or a bloody war (Scheidel, 2017).

What can be done about this? It is not true as many economists maintain that inequality does not have much to do with policy. It obviously does. Inequality started to rise and incomes of the poor in rich countries started to stagnate in the 1980s, after Reagan and Thatcher came to power. If they could increase inequality, then we can decrease it back now.

The first set of solutions ought to help ensure the equality of opportunity and market incomes. Fixing inequality at its source is the best possible policy because—if done right—it could reduce the need for later public redistributive policies. The main pieces of reform agenda should include access to good education for everyone, from kindergarten until university (this would, for instance, necessitate larger public investment in early childhood education in rural areas and small towns), keeping markets open to all new entrants, preventing vested interests from blocking access to professions, providing good public health care, and sustaining an inclusive financial system.[25] In addition, given the substantial differences in wealth, which are much bigger than differences in incomes (in most countries Gini for wealth is about 0.7–0.9, more than twice as high as Gini for incomes), it would be useful to ensure that returns from capital are shared with the largest possible part of the society. This could be achieved by, among other things, providing incentives for accumulating savings in capital funds, with nominal limits on the contributions, expanding employee stock ownership plans, or introducing incentives for the less wealthy to own shares (Milanovic, 2017a, 2017b). Finally, it would make sense to give every 18-year-old in the EU an equal start in adult life with a capital endowment (of say, 20,000 euro or so). Such endowment could be financed by a European-wide tax administered by the European Commission and levied on the profits of multinationals operating in the EU. This would make economic sense because the multinationals benefit the most from the economies of scale in the EU single market, but pay less taxes

---

[25] During 2006–2015, Poland deregulated more than 200 professions to ease access for new entrants and lower prices. In the most notable example, easing access to legal professions—lawyers, attorneys, public notaries—created thousands of new jobs, increased consumer choice, and lowered prices. Lawyers' claims that opening of their profession would undermine public trust and quality of service proved unfounded.

for this privilege than SMEs.[26] Such a solution would not only help the young to kick-start their adult life, but would also help strengthen European cohesion (20,000 euro would be worth much more to a young Bulgarian than a young Luxembourgian), eliminate youth poverty, and strengthen European identity by giving each European a clear stake in the future of the EU.

However, market outcomes will never be equal: markets are created to promote efficiency, not equality. Even in Scandinavia, the inequality of market incomes is not much different from the US (Milanovic, 2016a). Hence, there will always be a role for the state to intervene to reduce inequality to more economically and socially justified levels. This will require the usual set of solutions, including more progressive taxes, earned income tax credits, and improved systems of vocational training. In addition, given the rise of automation and robotization—although the fears that they will replace humans soon are overblown—there will be an increasing need to gradually introduce a basic income guarantee (BIG). Finally, it will be important to provide guaranteed publicly financed jobs to every willing employee, as argued by Atkinson (2015). This would help increase the employment rate, reduce inequality, and enhance happiness.

The ultimate objective of all these policies should be to ensure that the incomes of the bottom half of the society should be rising faster than incomes of the rest of the society. In addition, the Gini coefficient ought to be kept close to 0.27–0.30, which—according to the IMF researchers—represents the optimal level of inequality (Robles and Grigoli, 2017; Paredes, Grigoli, and di Bella, 2016).

9.2.10. *Focus on Well-Being and Quality of Life Beyond GDP*

There is life beyond GDP. We all know it, but we often ignore it. While GDP growth is closely correlated with improved well-being and happiness, there are many other things that matter in life. Love, loyalty, altruism, meaning in life and many other uniquely human feelings do not have much to do with income, but are key drivers of happiness. Life would be unbearable if we counted and cared only about income. If economists had their way, people should not even have children, because they lower the household's GDP per capita.

---

[26] The new tax could be called a 'European Solidarity and Growth Contribution' and be paid as a percentage of annual gross profits of multinationals operating in the EU. It is estimated that the 2000 largest global firms generate about 3 trillion dollars of profits per year (Forbes, 2012). Assuming that about 1 trillion dollars of these profits come from the EU, and assuming a 10 per cent rate of the 'EU Contribution', it would provide 100 billion USD of annual tax revenue for the EU. This could finance 20,000 euro endowments for every young EU citizen as they reach 18. Additional revenue could also be sourced from ECB seignorage and a carbon tax.

Not every policy that may support economic growth will also support well-being and happiness. Cutting down a natural forest and selling the wood will boost GDP, but undermine the environment. Increasing labour market flexibility may also help growth, but the resulting job insecurity may depress the fertility rate and weaken demographic growth. Emaciated labour unions may help increase corporate profits, but increase income inequality and stymie well-being (Piatkowski, 2014).

What could be the solution? First, as what you measure is what you target, we need to move away from the excessive focus on GDP as the only measure of social and human development. Well-being and happiness (despite various measurement problems) should be tracked too. One idea would be to track Poland's development in line with the OECD's Better Life Index and monitor whether it is catching up with the West along all lagging dimensions. An additional option would be to follow the example of the Australian government and present the country's development along a larger set of social, economic, governance, and environmental indicators. This could include life expectancy, educational attainment, quality of natural environment, safety and security, availability of leisure time, public trust, or strength of social networks.[27] Governments should be held responsible for meeting the overall developmental targets, not just GDP.

The same applies to happiness: we increasingly know what makes people happy (and unhappy).[28] Layard (2003, 2005), Coyle (2015), and others are right when they call on governments to deal with the key sources of unhappiness: unemployment, mental sickness, solitude, lack of control, noise, and long commuting. These can often be dealt with at a low cost. What else can be done? Higher incomes will help, of course. And so will higher well-being. But this will never be enough as long as people's aspirations rise faster than improvements in reality. As in the economists' equation for happiness, happiness is reality divided by expectations. The higher the latter, the lower the happiness. Hence, there is need for a public debate about how to move away from the economy of excess and the accompanying rat race to the economy of moderation. It does not mean that we should all stop working and become hippies: it just means that we need to be aware that unless we change our mindsets, the growing incomes and improved lives will never make us fully

---

[27] http://www.abs.gov.au/ausstats/abs@.nsf/mf/1370.0, accessed on 15 May 2017.
[28] Although, ultimately, happiness may not be the sole end objective. If so, we could swallow Huxley's 'soma' every day and let our lives slide. What matters is also a sense of having a meaning in life, being good to others, and working on self-development, even if it does not always have to increase happiness. John Stuart Mill, a famous utilitarian philosopher, argued that the pursuit of happiness should not be the only principle to guide human lives. As he put it, it is better to be Socrates than a happy pig (Coyle, 2012).

satisfied and happy. Perhaps lack of complete satisfaction is what makes us successful and human. But couldn't we be successful and human in a slightly different way?

9.3. Implementation of the 'Warsaw Consensus'

Economic strategies are only as good as their implementation. Or as Mike Tyson put it, 'everybody has a plan until they get punched in the mouth'.[29] The same happens with many, often elaborate, governments' strategies: they are knocked down by reality.

What is needed is a new approach to implementing policies based on experimenting, evaluating, and pragmaticizing (being pragmatic), as depicted in Figure 9.7. First, governments should not be afraid of experimenting with new institutions, policies, and instruments. Such experimentation is critical to discovering what 'works' in the specific environment of each country (Rodrik, 2008, 2015; Cohen and Easterly, 2009). Second, they ought to rigorously evaluate policies to assess which have worked well and which have not. Good policies must be expanded, bad policies should be closed down. The latter is much more difficult than the former. But without eliminating the 'losers', there can be no good policy.

Third, governments must be pragmatic in implementing policies: they should eschew facile ideologies, fleeting fads, and intellectual fashions, and take decisions that fully consider the complex political, social, and economic environment of each country. What works in one country may not work in another country. Common sense needs to prevail.

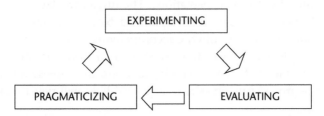

Figure 9.7. The implementation framework of the 'Warsaw Consensus'.
Source: Piatkowski (2014).

---

[29] http://articles.sun-sentinel.com/2012-11-09/sports/sfl-mike-tyson-explains-one-of-his-most-famous-quotes-20121109_1_mike-tyson-undisputed-truth-famous-quotes, accessed 20 May 2017.

The importance of pragmatism in the implementation of the Warsaw Consensus is much in line with the concept of 'new pragmatism' developed by Kolodko (2017).[30] He confronts two perspectives of modern capitalism—neoliberal capitalism and state capitalism—and argues that both have proven to provide wrong recipes for development. Like Rodrik (2015) and others, he calls for a new concept of economic policy based on an opportunistic, heterodox, and experimental approach to economic analysis and policy. He also underlines that under 'new pragmatism', economic policy must be guided by a balance among economic, social, and environmental sustainability. The same ideas apply to implementation of the 'Warsaw Consensus'.

Finally, being pragmatic also means that we must be humble about what we know. We know more and more about makes countries grow, but still not enough. Whenever we do not know what to do, we should not push new policies no matter what, but focus instead on minimizing risks and reducing vulnerability to shocks—or as Nasim Taleb (2012) puts it, become 'antifragile'—by closely monitoring public and private debts, keeping the financial sector in check, and maintaining the economy's flexibility. Reducing risks is key to long-term development: countries that have become rich have largely done so by avoiding economic depressions rather than by maintaining extraordinarily high growth rates. Economic history suggests that it is better to grow slower and avoid major risks than to shine brightly for a while, but then collapse into economic depressions, which take away all the previous growth (Piatkowski, 2009).

9.4. Impact of the 'Warsaw Consensus'

What would be the impact of the 'Warsaw Consensus' of economic and social development in CEE? Empirical evidence for the impacts of policies underlying each of the ten dimensions of the 'Warsaw Consensus' suggests that its implementation could increase Poland's and CEE's long-term GDP per capita growth rate by more than 1 percentage point a year. Boosting investment, the employment rate, and the pace of innovation could account for a major part of the projected improvement. But in the end, the actual impact of the 'Warsaw Consensus' will depend on the specific circumstances in the future, which are unknowable. What we can do instead is to show that if the 'Warsaw Consensus' helped add only 0.5 percentage points of extra growth per year—move the growth rate from, say, 2.5 per cent to 3.0 per cent—and remained at

[30] See also Kolodko (2014) and Bałtowski (2017).

that level for 50 years, around 2070 Poland's income per capita would amount to almost 138,000 dollars. With a slower 2.5 per cent rate, it would amount to 30,000 dollars less. In other words, the 'Warsaw Consensus' could increase incomes of Poles within the next 50 years (which, conveniently, is when I plan to die, after having helped to make it happen) by more than their whole income today.

9.5. Conclusions

Poland has done extremely well in the past twenty-five years. But its continued success in the future is far from guaranteed. The easy path to convergence based on low labour costs is coming to an end. Now starts the hard part, when Poland must compete on equal terms with the best.

To continue to grow, better insulate the region from future crises, and fully converge with the Western level of incomes, Poland and CEE should re-adjust its growth model. Further convergence should be guided by a new growth model based on the policy prescriptions of the 'Warsaw Consensus'. The re-adjusted growth model should keep what has worked well so far, but combine it with higher domestic savings, enhanced innovation, higher employment rates, and opening up to immigration.

The policy prescriptions that underlie the 'Warsaw Consensus' deal with the most binding growth constraints for the region. As the name suggests, the 'Consensus' reflects agreement among a large part of the community of economists in the region and beyond on what are the bindings constraints to growth. In addition, the 'Warsaw Consensus' focuses on well-being and happiness to ensure that by supporting GDP one does not forget that GDP is only a means to an end, not an end in itself. Higher incomes are needed to increase well-being and happiness, but other factors matter too.

Beyond the main policy directions, the 'Warsaw Consensus' also focuses on implementation. This is because many strategies look good on paper, but then fail to work in practice. The 'Warsaw Consensus' adopts a new approach to policy implementation based on experimenting, evaluating, and being pragmatic (pragmaticizing). Like generals during a war, policy makers should flexibly respond to the changing economic environment and adjust policies accordingly. Whenever policy makers are in doubt about what policies to adopt, it is best to minimize the risks and vulnerabilities and eliminate policies, which are clearly harmful (and there are plenty of those in each country). As in the Hippocratic oath taken by doctors, policy makers should 'do no harm' first.

Poland (and the region) now has the best opportunity ever in its 1000-year-old history to catch up with the West and become the economic (as well as political, cultural, and social) core of the European continent. It is positioned to do so like never before: it has never had a better educated workforce, stronger industry, more inclusive society, and more open borders. In addition, it has never been so deeply enmeshed with the West, largely thanks to its membership of the EU. Finally, there is nothing that we know of that should prevent CEE from becoming as rich as the West (although not necessarily as rich as Germany or Sweden, unless the deep-seated cultural values also change). Full implementation of the 'Warsaw Consensus' should help this happen within the life of one or two generations. But this opportunity might be lost if CEE does not re-adjust its growth model. The region has failed to catch up many times before. This time needs to be different.

10

Conclusions and the Way Forward

In this book I have described how, after centuries of underdevelopment and backwardness, Poland moved from being poor to high-income during the life of just one generation. In the process, it became a European and a global growth champion among countries at a similar level of development. Poles have never lived better.

How did it happen and what can the rest of the world learn from it? There are a number of important lessons learned from the Polish economic miracle.

The single most important lesson from the book is that it is extremely difficult to move from an extractive society, which keeps countries poor, to an inclusive society, which makes countries rich. Poland—and the rest of CEE—was backward for most of the last 1000 years because it developed an extractive society, in which the ruling aristocratic oligarchy and gentry monopolized political and economic power, created growth-inhibiting institutions, and nurtured a harmful culture that undermined development. It was not the fault of the country's geography, lack of natural resources, bad neighbours, or bad luck that kept Poland from growing, but its own harmful elites, which did everything to prevent the rest of the society from flourishing, even at the cost of economic stagnation and backwardness. For the extractive elites it was better to keep their share of the stagnant economic pie than benefit from economic growth. Opening economic opportunities to the rest of society and the potential political power that newly earned money could buy meant that the elites would risk losing their wealth and privileged status altogether. So, they never let it happen. Better a bird in hand, then two in the bush. So the thinking went.

The second important lesson is that throughout history moving from an extractive to inclusive society has required a period of intense violence, which was key to changing the distribution of economic resources and then to changing institutions. Most of the time, such violence took the form of external shocks such as foreign interventions, wars, or credible threats of both. Among slightly more than forty countries that the World Bank defines as high-income, the clear majority moved from being extractive to inclusive following external shocks. Without such shocks, the centripetal forces are too potent for the system to change on its own. Like a black hole, in which the force of gravity is too strong to let the light out, extractive societies are too well established to let development happen. It is thus no surprise that it is rare for countries to move to the inclusive equilibrium without external intervention or pressure. Only a few countries in history made it, including the UK, France, or the Netherlands. Still, each of these internal revolutions was accompanied by violence. This all makes intuitive sense, because the incumbent extractive elites have no reason to let go of their power. Someone else needs to take this power away from them by force.

Poland is an example of how the shock of the Second World War and externally imposed communism snapped it out of the centuries-long extractive society equilibrium. Despite its gargantuan economic failings, moral repugnance, and human cruelty, communism nonetheless eliminated the old elites and the feudal, pre-modern social structures, which kept the country backward, and created a new, classless, egalitarian, and inclusive society. In a paradoxically biblical twist, communism helped 'the last be the first' by giving education, employment, and social status to millions of peasants and poor blue-collar workers, the perennial 'underachievers' that never had a chance to pursue their own happiness before. Communism liberated CEE from its developmental trap and helped it flourish after 1989 for the first time ever. What Napoleon was to Western Europe, when he demolished old feudal structures during his invasions, communism was to Central and Eastern Europe.

Many underdeveloped countries in the world today are like Poland before 1939. They are ruled by extractive elites that have no incentive to change the status quo. It is not the lack of knowledge that explains why poor countries remain poor, but lack of willingness of the elites to make development happen. This helps explain why despite trillions of dollars of income from natural resources and foreign aid received by poor countries in the last 50 years, they remain underdeveloped.

What is the solution? There is no easy answer. External intervention in poor countries is clearly not a solution. External pressure can help, but might not be sufficient. The best we can hope for is that every so often there will be a country that will snap out of its extractive equilibrium because of a mixture of external and internal pressure. The pessimistic conclusion is that poor countries are here to stay. But we should not stop trying.

The third lesson from the book is that institutions matter. I described how bad institutions kept Poland and CEE from developing for most of their history. I also showed how institution-building was key to Poland's success after 1989. There is much empirical evidence that supports this finding. Institutions are important, albeit not just any institutions, but Western institutions. One can argue that the rule of law, property rights, open markets, free competition, democracy, and free media are not necessarily 'Western', but all these institutions have largely been a Western invention and were successfully implemented in the West before they were adopted by other countries.

Western institutions were the drivers of virtually all prominent cases of economic catching up in the last sixty years. This is plainly seen for two-thirds of countries that became high-income in the period, which are all from Europe. Countries such as Ireland, Spain, Portugal, Greece, and later Poland and CEE succeeded in becoming high-income because they 'downloaded' the full set of Western institutions. But the remaining one-third of high-achievers, countries such as Japan, South Korea, Singapore, or Chile, have also absorbed Western institutions, even if they adjusted them to the local circumstances. Western institutions may not be critical to growing—many countries, even extractive ones, can grow for some time—but they seem to be critical to becoming high-income.

The obvious solution is to fully import institutions from developed countries, while adjusting them to local circumstances. That said, the fourth lesson from the book is that unfortunately institutions are not likely to function well without supportive culture. Multiple examples show that simply importing Western institutions without changing culture is not likely to work. Most Latin American countries copied the US Constitution, yet the strength of their institutions and their level of income are not exactly American. Likewise, many post-Soviet countries adopted Western institutions, but this did little for their competitiveness as the relevant culture was missing. The fact that Russia can copy a Finnish anti-corruption law does not mean at all that its level of corruption will be Finnish. Poland's transition was successful because the imported Western institutions fell onto a largely fertile cultural ground.

Can culture be changed? Yes, it can, although it is never easy and it takes time. Poland is a good example of an ongoing change in culture. The cultural evolution has been supported by Westernized elites, which have internalized Western values and led cultural change by their own example. That no one has ever questioned the personal integrity of economic policy makers in Poland, the vast majority of whom have spent considerable time in the West, is a case in point. Cultural change has also been driven by exposure to the West through travel, work abroad, and FDI. This solution can be replicated by many other countries. Governments can also experiment with various nudges to align cultural values closer with the West, including through TV shows, educational programmes, and information campaigns. Finally, much will of course depend on whether the West—Western Europe and North America—continues to be the beacon of prosperity, solidarity, and equality for all.

The fifth lesson is the importance of a reform anchor, such as the EU. As the World Bank once put it, the EU is a convergence machine that takes in poor countries and makes them rich. This was the case with Southern Europe first—Spain, Portugal, and Greece—then with Ireland and finally with CEE. It is hard to overappreciate the importance of the EU for the economic achievements of CEE. Without the lure of the EU, CEE would not have adopted new institutions, changed culture, and behaved in a responsible way. It would also have had trouble becoming and then remaining democratic. The EU has also become an institutional straitjacket, which limits the scope of harmful political and economic populism. Kaczyński and Orban might be political populists, but they are not economic populists as they tread carefully to ensure that they do not breach EU regulations. Finally, the EU funding obviously also matters. Without it, Poland would have not built the best infrastructure in its history, with brand new highways, railways, universities, and R&D labs, which will support Poland's growth for decades to come. For all these reasons, the EU is the biggest institutional achievement in mankind's history and Poland and CEE has had the ultimate luck to be part of it.

Going forward, it is in the strategic interest of Poland and the rest of the region to continue to support the EU, make it deeper, more effective, and stronger. Weakening or disintegration of the EU would be the biggest single risk to the prosperous future of the country. The ultimate objective for Poland and all its fellow countries should be to create a United States of Europe, supported by citizens with both national and European identities. This is a long shot. But as Nelson Mandela put it, everything looks impossible until it is done. The idea of the EU was totally utopian a mere 60 years ago. Now, we can hardly imagine Europe without it. Let this miracle continue.

What are the lessons learned for others? Obviously, not everyone can become a member of the EU. But many countries and regions around the world can try to replicate it. In principle, there is no reason why Latin America, Africa, Asia, and other continents could not deepen and strengthen the existing institutional arrangements, Mercosur, ECOWAS, or ASEAN, and increasingly turn these into something that resembles the EU. If the Germans and the French or the Germans and Poles, with long histories of conflict and killing each other in the millions, can agree to open borders, share budgets, and decide on policies together, other countries around the world could do the same.

The sixth lesson is that, as argued by Kolodko (2011), things happen the way they happen when many things happen at the same time. Many stars had to align in the right positions for Poland to finally become prosperous. It had to have an egalitarian society, strong leaders, the EU anchor, and lots of luck. In retrospect, many may think that Poland's success was inevitable. But that is simply not true. Based on Poland's long-term dismal track record, it would have been easier to explain Poland's failure during the transition than its remarkable success. After all, who would expect a perennial economic 'alcoholic' to suddenly win the European and world championship in growth? This does not mean that countries cannot grow when only a few stars are well aligned. They can, as plainly shown by China and many others. If the extractive elites in poor countries reformed the business environment only, the boost to growth would be substantial. But such reforms would not be sufficient for these countries to become high-income. The richer you become, the more stars need to align to continue to grow. Virtually all high-income countries in the world today, except for oil-rich countries, are democratic, more egalitarian than elsewhere, have strong institutions, and boast of a growth-promoting culture. Almost 150 countries in the world that are not high-income can follow the same blueprint, albeit this is easier said than done.

The seventh lesson is that it is important to use the historical window of opportunity to go ahead with deep reforms. Communism used it to impose a new economic system on CEE. The new system was politically extractive, morally repulsive, and economically inefficient (which we know ex post, but did not know ex ante), but it did change the trajectory of development in Poland and the region. Communism was a response to the cruelties, moral repulsiveness, and economic inefficiency of capitalism, which kept most of the population in economic slavery, with no chance to develop. Poland's 'shock therapy' reforms in 1989 were paradoxically similarly Bolshevik in style. They were introduced almost overnight, with hardly any social debate, and were based on the assumption that the elites 'knew' better. In the same way the communist blitzkrieg bulldozed the old social and economic structures, the Balcerowicz Plan bulldozed the legacy of communism. It again changed Poland's development trajectory, this time in the opposite direction and with incomparably better results (also because the excesses of the 'shock therapy' were subsequently corrected). The lesson learned is that policy makers around the world should be alert and ready to leverage historical opportunities whenever they occur to put their countries on a new development trajectory. Such historical opportunities are rare. All the more reason to be ready to use them well.

The eighth lesson is that a strong and efficient state is critical to development. Poland from before 1795 was a dream state for libertarians and Tea Party supporters: it had no public administration, almost no taxes, and no collective responsibility. There was also hardly any rule of law, secure property rights, or open markets. In fact, the state hardly existed. The Polish ruling class, the gentry, had political representation, but without taxation. This did not end well: Poland disappeared from the map of Europe in 1795. When Russia, Austria, and Prussia partitioned Poland and imposed their institutions, the country started to develop. When Poland regained independence in 1918, the state capacity remained limited, partly because the ruling elites ensured that tax revenues remained low. Poland disappeared from the map again in 1939, partitioned by Hitler and Stalin. It was only after 1989 that Poland developed strong institutions and a strong state (even though there is still large scope for improvement). This underpinned the Polish economic turnaround.

The lesson learned is that a country is unlikely to become successful without building an efficient state. This does not mean that it must be big. It means that it must be strong in areas such as rule of law, property rights, open markets, equality of opportunity, environmental regulation, and consumer protection, where it matters and where no one else can take the responsibility. The economic accomplishment of the Asian Tigers and now China have also been underpinned by strong states. Less developed countries should take a cue and act accordingly.

The ninth lesson is that we need to keep the growth inclusive. Poland's economic history shows that the country could not become prosperous until it allowed all its citizens to pursue their own happiness, unburdened by class, wealth, and connections. All high-income countries today, with a few minor exceptions, have relatively low levels of inequality. This is not a coincidence. Inequality undermines economic growth, well-being, and happiness. It wastes human talent that cannot develop because of lack of chances and resources to get ahead. Society can never be successful when it is based on *who* you know rather than *who* you are and *what* you know.

The implication is that Poland and peer countries around the world must keep inequality low so as to prevent the return of elites that could monopolize the country in the same way the Polish gentry monopolized the country in the past. Public services, the ultimate social equalizer, must be improved. It is the role of the state to invest in public services to provide equal access to everyone, regardless of the circumstances they were born into. The *de facto* apartheid in access to public services must end. Finally, it is important to keep markets open, fight monopolies, maintain low barriers of entry to markets and professions, and ensure everyone's equal access to good quality education. In short, Poland and others need to sustain a system, which afforded an impecunious boy raised by a single mother in a small city in the middle of nowhere great life opportunities, including the chance to write this book.

The tenth lesson is that rising inequality is a danger to democracy. Because of high returns to capital, a society with unequal distribution of wealth and income will inevitably allow the elites to monopolize or manipulate politics at some point in the future and use this power to keep the status quo and bamboozle the poor. President Trump is a good example of how this can work. The elites will also promote an ideology—in many ways not much different from the Sarmatian ideology of the old Polish gentry—that they are somewhat genetically 'different' and 'better' than the rest. This should not to be allowed to happen. Poland and its peers should never be in the position of a chef in a presidential palace in Latin America, who—when asked whether the recent change of the president would force him to change the menu—responded that 'not at all. The guests will still be the same'.

The eleventh lesson is that we need to go beyond GDP. Do not misunderstand: promoting GDP growth continues to be important. Growing GDP is critical to improve people's lives, increase their well-being, and enhance overall satisfaction in life. Growing GDP is also needed to keep societies inclusive and egalitarian. There are hardly any new opportunities in an economically stagnant society. But GDP should not be the only target of economic policy. Countries should increasingly measure their performance not only through the prism of GDP, but also through the prism of the impact of growth on well-being such as health, level of inequality, or the quality of environment. Whenever there is a conflict between GDP and well-being, there needs to be a public debate about it. Measuring well-being well is key to getting such debates started. The same applies to people's subjective well-being or happiness.

It is also important to discuss how to deal with people's ever-rising aspirations. Obviously, this is not about poor countries' aspirations to become rich, but about aspirations of millions of people in developed countries, whose 'normal' needs have already been fully satisfied. How is meaning in life found in a world of affluence? Are there more valuable ways to fulfil our lives than buying yet another house, a third car, and new gadgets? How much is enough to have a good life, as Skidelsky and Skidelsky (2012) put it? And how do we grow without overgrowing? These are some of the fundamental questions that citizens of rich countries will need to increasingly ask themselves to keep their lives meaningful and save the planet in the meantime. And so will the Poles, as they continue to grow richer and catch up with the West.

The final lesson is that economics needs to become much more interdisciplinary to remain relevant. This book has described how difficult it is to explain Poland's success without going way beyond standard textbook economics. One must explore institutions, culture, the role of leaders, ideas and ideology, as well as the country's history to understand what makes countries tick and what is needed for them to develop. *Ceteris paribus*—all other things being equal—assumed in standard economics does not work in reality: other things are not equal, as they are constantly changing, driven by underlying political, social, technological, and historical forces. The dismal science ought to embrace it.

10.1. The Future

What does the future hold for Poland and CEE? It is always difficult to be an optimist. We are all hardwired to like to listen to bad news. Worrying kept us alive during millions of years of evolution. Good news is ignored; bad news makes the headlines. Cassandras know it and exploit it to their advantage. No one seems to mind that they are wrong, time and again. They continue to be listened to nonetheless.

And yet the truth is that Poland, the region, and the world have never been more prosperous, humane, safe, civilized, and happy than today. And progress will continue. Extreme poverty in the world is already the lowest on record and is destined to disappear during our lifetime. This has never happened before in mankind's history. Violence will continue to decrease. Terrorism and wars will not disappear—I am particularly worried about a possible big conflagration in the Pacific—but if we can believe the trend in the last 70 years, wars should be less frequent and less bloody. Our lives will continue to become longer. Japan has already stopped sending congratulatory letters to their 100-year-olds: they are too many of them. Other countries will experience the same. Progress in medicine will also make our lives healthier. We will eliminate or at least mitigate the impact of many diseases, perhaps even at some point beat cancer, although obesity—which already kills more people today than does poverty—will increase its toll.

Technological progress will continue at a fast pace as good ideas accumulate at an increasing rate and more and more people around the world receive sufficient education to contribute their own ideas. Robots will take some of people's jobs, especially those dirty, unpleasant, and dangerous jobs that no one will want to do anymore, but create new jobs too. A century ago agriculture employed more than two-thirds of people in most countries in the world, today it employs a few per cent in developed countries and yet unemployment is lower than before and incomes are more than ten times higher. The impact of robots will not be different. But we must ensure that the workforce of the future will be protected from instability and vicissitudes of labour markets and exploitation by the stronger. The world needs to move towards various versions of a basic guaranteed income. This will not make people lazy, but give them a modicum of stability and an opportunity to do what they are best at doing, to the benefit of everyone else.

Inequality, however, will not disappear, as returns on capital will continue to exceed the pace of growth. The economic and political power of the global 1 per cent will thus increase. But at some point in the future, those left behind will revolt and wipe away the elites, as has been the case throughout mankind's history. But social revolutions need not happen if countries find new ways and re-deploy old ways of fighting inequality. This would be in everyone's interest, including the elites. Better to lengthen the table than raise the wall.

Climate change is a real challenge that must be faced head-on. Better invest now and pre-empt a potential catastrophe, than be sorry later. But while we worry about the future of the world's environment, we should not become paranoid about running out of options and solutions. As Paul Romer (2008), now the World Bank's Chief Economist, rightly noted:

> Every generation has perceived the limits to growth that finite resources and undesirable side effects would pose if no new recipes or ideas were discovered. And every generation has underestimated the potential for finding new recipes and ideas. We consistently fail to grasp how many ideas remain to be discovered.

Naysayers were wrong before and will be wrong again in the future.

On the whole, new generations will have better lives than we do, as has been the case for almost every generation in the last 200 years (apart from the time of the two world wars). If we have achieved so much during the last 100 years, why would we not achieve the same or even more in the next 100 years? By 2070, median global income will likely be above $20,000 dollars PPP, more than the level of Bulgaria, Brazil, or Botswana today. Global average life expectancy will exceed 80 years. Everyone will benefit from technology that no one can even predict today. We will work many fewer hours—less than 1,500 hours a year, about as much as an average French or German works today. In developed countries, median incomes will come close to $100,000 (in today's prices) and life expectancy will be close to 100. The whole world will be a happier place.

Young Poles and other Central and Eastern Europeans will live much better than their parents did. Poland will continue to grow noticeably faster than Western Europe for quite some time, at least until 2030. The convergence will be driven by the unbeatable combination of its high quality of human capital, open borders, and high productivity combined with low labour costs. In addition, and above all, the convergence will be driven by the newly emerged inclusive society, supported by the nascent middle class that seems to have reached a tipping point in its size and influence. Inclusive societies seem to be a one-way street. Once you become inclusive, it is difficult to lose it. Many catastrophic things would need to happen for Poland and CEE to go back to the extractive society equilibrium, which blighted most of its history. Poland may grow once slower and once faster, but grow it will and Poland's Golden Age will continue.

However, after 2030 the pace of convergence is likely to decline and later could stop altogether as the negative effects of population ageing and slowing productivity growth accumulate. Nonetheless, Poland could still reach the level of income of Spain—Poland's most achievable target, judging by the countries' uncannily similar performance over the last five centuries—which in itself would be a historical achievement and a confirmation of Poland's Golden Age. However, Poland is not likely to reach the income levels of the core of Europe, Germany, France, or the Netherlands. This would require that Poland becomes, unlike ever before, a creator rather than an absorber of economic, social, political, and cultural ideas. It is not impossible, but it is not likely either unless Poles find strength to work together for long decades to start generating new, groundbreaking ideas that will inspire others. Catching up with countries like Germany would also require that Poland continues to change its institutions and culture and model them on the best examples from the world, especially in Western Europe. Lastly, Poland would also need to lead by example to show that a better, more prosperous, just, and dignified future is possible. Poland has made a great start. But it has only reached the end of the beginning.

References

Acemoglu, Daron. 2008. *Introduction to modern economic growth*. Princeton University Press.

Acemoglu, Daron and Simon Johnson. 2005. 'Unbundling institutions.' *Journal of Political Economy 113(5)*, 949–95.

Acemoglu, Daron and James A. Robinson. 2008. 'The Role of Institutions in Growth and Development', Commission on Growth and Development, Working Paper No. 10, Washington, DC.

Acemoglu, Daron and James Robinson. 2012. *Why Nations Fail: The Origins of Power, Prosperity, and Poverty*. The Crown Publishing Group. Kindle Edition.

Acemoglu, Daron and James A. Robinson. 2016. 'Paths to inclusive political institutions.' Economic history of warfare and state formation. Springer Singapore 3–50.

Acemoglu, Daron, Simon Johnson, and James A. Robinson. 2001. 'The Colonial Origins of Comparative Development: An Empirical Investigation', *American Economic Review 91(5)*, 1369–401.

Acemoglu, Daron, Simon Johnson, and James A. Robinson. 2002. 'Reversal of Fortune: Geography and Institutions in the Making of the Modern World Income Distribution,' *Quarterly Journal of Economics 117(4)*, 1231–94.

Acemoglu, Daron, Simon Johnson, and James Robinson. 2005. 'Institutions as the Fundamental Cause of Long-Run Growth.' In: Philippe Aghion and Steven Durlau (eds.) *Handbook of Economic Growth*, Volume 1A, ed. f, 385–472. Amsterdam and San Diego: Elsevier, North-Holland.

Acemoglu, Daron, Suresh Naida, Pascual Restrepo, and James A. Robinson. 2014. 'Democracy Does Cause Growth'. NBER Working Paper No. 20004. March.

Adelman, I. and C. T. Morris. 1967. *Society, Politics and Economic Development: A Quantitative Approach*. Baltimore: Johns Hopkins Press.

Aerdt, G. F. and J. Houben. 1995. 'Commercial Bank Debt Restructuring: The Experience of Bulgaria', IMF Staff Country Reports. April.

Allen, R. C. 2001. 'The Great Divergence in European Wages and Prices from the Middle Ages to the First World War', *Explorations in Economic History 38: 411–47*.

Aidt, Toke S. and Peter S. Jensen. 2014. 'Workers of the World, Unite! Franchise Extensions and the Threat of Revolution in Europe, 1820–1938.' *European Economic Review 72* (November): 52–75.

Akerlof, George A. and Rachel Kranton. 2011. *Identity Economics: How Our Identities Shape Our Work, Wages and Well-Being*. Princeton: Princeton University Press.

References

Akerlof, George A. and Robert J. Shiller. 2009. *Animal Spirits: How Human Psychology Drives the Economy and Why this Matters for Global Capitalism*, Princeton: Princeton University Press.

Albinowski, Maciej, Jan Hagemejer, Stefania Lovo, and Gonzalo Varela. 2016. 'The role of exchange rate and non-exchange rate related factors in Polish firms' export performance,' *World Bank Policy Research Working Paper Series 7899*, The World Bank.

Aldcroft, Derek. 2006. *Europe's Third World: The European Periphery in the Interwar Years*, Ashgate Publishing, Ltd.

Alesina, Alberto and Nicola Fuchs-Schundeln. 2007. 'Good-Bye Lenin (or Not?): The Effect of Communism on People's Preferences', *American Economic Review 97(4)*, 1507–28.

Alesina, Alberto and Paola Giuliano. 2015. 'Culture and Institutions', *Journal of Economic Literature 53(4)*, 898–944.

Alesina, Alberto and Eliana La Ferrara. 2005. 'Ethnic Diversity and Economic Performance', *Journal of Economic Literature 43(3)*, 762–800.

Alesina, Alberto and Perotti, R. 1996. 'Income distribution, political instability, and investment', *European Economic Review 40*, 1203–28.

Alesina, Alberto, Reza Baqir, and William Easterly. 1999. 'Public goods and ethnic divisions.' *The Quarterly Journal of Economics 114(4)*, 1243–84.

Alesina, Alberto, Paola Giuliano, and Nathan Nunn. 2013. 'On the Origins of Gender Roles: Women and the Plough'. *The Quarterly Journal of Economics 128(2)*.

Allen, Robert C. 2011. 'The great divergence in European wages and prices from the Middle Ages to the First World War.' *Explorations in economic history 38(4)*, 411–47.

Anthony, David W. 2007. *The Horse, the Wheel, and Language: How Bronze-Age Riders from the Eurasian Steppes Shaped the Modern World*. Princeton University Press.

Applebaum, Anne. 2012. *Iron curtain: the crushing of Eastern Europe 1944-56*. Penguin UK.

Arnhold, Nina, Kapil, Natasha, Goldberg, Itzhak, Piatkowski, Marcin, and Rutkowski, Jan. 2011. *Europe 2020 Poland: Fueling growth and competitiveness through employment, skills, and innovation*. Washington, DC: World Bank.

Ashraf, Quamrul H. and Oded Galor. 2017. 'The Macrogenoeconomics of Comparative Development'. *National Bureau of Economic Research No. w23199*.

Aslund, Anders. 2001. *Building Capitalism. The Transformation of the Former Soviet Bloc*, Cambridge University Press, Cambridge.

Aslund, Anders and Simeon Djankov, eds. 2014. *The Great Rebirth: Lessons from the victory of capitalism over communism*. Peterson Institute for International Economics.

Aslund, Anders and Simeon Djankov. 2016. *Europe's Growth Challenge*. Cambridge: Oxford University Press.

Aston, T. H. and Charles Philpin. 1985. *The Brenner Debate: Agrarian Class Structure and Economic Development in Early Modern Europe*. Cambridge: Cambridge University Press.

Atkinson, Anthony, B. 2015. *Inequality: What can be Done?* Harvard University Press.

Atoyan, R. 2010. 'Beyond the Crisis: Revisiting Emerging Europe's Growth Model,' *IMF Working Paper No. 10/92*, April.

Baines, Dudley, Neil Cummins, and Max-Stephan Schulze. 2010. 'Population and living standards, 1945–2005' in: Broadberry/O'Rourke (eds). *The Cambridge Economic History of Modern Europe: Volume 2, 1870 to the present.* Cambridge University Press.

Bairoch, Peter. 1982. International Industrialization Levels from 1750 to 1980. Journal of *European Economic History* 11: 269–333.

Bąk, Monika. 2009. 'Uwarunkowania transformacji gospodarczej w krajach Europy Środkowej iWschodniej', in: Grzegorz W. Kolodko and Jacek Tomkiewicz (eds) *20 lat transformacji. Osiągnięcia, problemy, perspektywy.* Warsaw: WAIP.

Balcerowicz, Leszek. 1995. *Socialism, Capitalism, Transformation.* Central European University Press.

Balcerowicz, Leszek. 2006. 'Gospodarka z kulą u nogi', *Puls Biznesu,* 29 March.

Balcerowicz, Leszek. 2010. Tekst wykladu w czasie Dni Uniwersytetu Ekonomicznego w Poznaniu, Ruch Prawniczy, Ekonomiczny i Socjologiczny 2, 2010, pp. 5–44.

Balcerowicz, Leszek. 2014. 'Stabilization and Reforms under Extraordinary and Normal Politics'. In Anders Aslund and Simeon Djankov (eds). *The Great Rebirth: Lessons from the Victory of Capitalism over Communism,* Peterson Institute for International Economics.

Balcerowicz, Leszek and Andrzej Rzońca (eds.). 2010. *Zagadki wzrostu gospodarczego. Siły napędowe i kryzysy—analiza porównawcza.* C.H. Beck.

Balcerowicz, Leszek and Stremecka, Marta. 2014. 'Trzeba sie bic. Opowiesc biograficzna'. Warsaw: Wydawnictwo Czerwone i Czarne.

Bałtowski, Maciej. 2017. 'Evolution of economics and the new pragmatism of Grzegorz W. Kolodko', *TIGER Working Paper Series,* No. 136, Kozminski University.

Barcelona Development Agenda. 2004. http://www.bcn.cat/forum2004/english/desenvolupament.htm

Barro, R. 1991. 'Economic growth in a cross section of countries', *Quarterly Journal of Economics* 106, 407–43.

Barro, R. 1996. 'Democracy and Growth', *Journal of Economic Growth* 1, 1–28.

Barro, R. J. 1999. 'Determinants of democracy', *Journal of Political Economy* 107, 158–83.

Barro, R. J. and Lee, J.-W. 2013. 'A new data set of educational attainment in the world, 1950–2010', *Journal of Development Economics* 104, 184–98.

Barro, R. J. and McCleary, R. M. 2003. Religion and economic growth across countries. *American Sociological Review* 68, 760–81.

Barro, Robert J. and Xavier Sala-i-Martin. 1992. 'Convergence'. *The Journal of Political Economy,* 100(2) (Apr., 1992), 223–51.

Barro, Robert J. and Xavier Sala-i-Martin. 2003. *Economic Growth,* 2nd Edition, McGraw-Hill.

Bastian, Jens (ed.). 1996. *The Political Economy of Transition in Central and Eastern Europe: The Light(s) at the End of the Tunnel.* Aldershot: Ashgate.

Basu, Kaushik. 2010. *Beyond the Invisible Hand. Groundwork for a New Economics.* Princeton University Press, 2010.

Basu, Kaushik. 2015. 'An Economist in the Real World; The Art of Policymaking in India', MIT Press.

Baten, J. and Szołtysek, M. 2014. 'A golden age before serfdom? The human capital of Central-Eastern and Eastern Europe in the 17th-19th centuries', MPIDR working PAPER WP2014–008.

Baun, Michael J. 2000. *A Wider Europe: The Process and Politics of European Enlargement*. Lanham: Rowman and Littlefield.

Beauvois, Daniel. 2014. 'Gdy Ukraina byla polska kolonia". Interview with Daniel Beauvois, *Newsweek Polska*, 26 May.

Beck, Thorsten and Luc Laeven. 2006. 'Institution Building and Growth In Transition Economies', *Journal of Economic Growth 11(2)*, 157–86.

Benavot, A. and P. Riddle. 1989. 'The Expansion of Primary Education, 1870–1940: Trends and Issues'. *Sociology of Education 61*, 191–210.

Bennett, John, Saul Estrin, and Giovanni Urga. 2007. 'Methods of privatization and economic growth in transition economies', *Economics of Transition, 15(4)*, 661–83.

Berend, Ivan. 1999. *Central and Eastern Europe, 1944–1993: Detour from the Periphery to the Periphery*. Cambridge University Press.

Berend, Ivan. 2009. *From the Soviet Bloc to the European Union: The Economic and Social Transformation of Central and Eastern Europe since 1973*. Cambridge University Press.

Berend, Ivan T. 2003. *History Derailed: Central and Eastern Europe in the Long Nineteenth Century*, University of California Press.

Berend, Ivan T. and G. Ránki. 1974. *Economic development in East Central Europe in the nineteenth and twentieth centuries*. New York: Columbia University Press.

Berend, Ivan and Gyorgy Ránki. 1990. *The European Periphery and Industrialization, 1780–1914*. Cambridge University Press, Cambridge.

Berg, Andrew and Jeffrey Sachs. 1992. 'Structural Adjustment and International Trade in Eastern Europe: The Case of Poland'. *Economic Policy* 14 (April), 117–55.

Berg, Andrew, Eduardo Borensztein, Ratna Sahay, and Jeromin Zettelmayer. 1999. 'The Evolution of Output in Transition Economies: Explaining the Differences', *IMF Working Paper No. 73*, Washington, DC.

Berglof, Erik, Lisa Bryunooghe, Herke Harmgart, Peter Sanfey, Helena Schweiger, and Jeronim Zettelmeyer. 2012. 'European Transition at Twenty: Assessing Progress in Countries and Sectors', in: Gerrard Roland (ed.) *Economies in Transition: The Long Run View*, Palgrave McMillan, UNU-WIDER Studies in Development Economic and Policy.

Bernanke, Ben and Harold James. 1991. 'The gold standard, deflation, and financial crisis in the Great Depression: An international comparison.' In: R. Glenn Hubbard (ed.) *Financial markets and financial crises*. University of Chicago Press 33–68.

Besley, Timothy and Torsten Persson. 2009. 'The Origins of State Capacity: Property Rights, Taxation, and Politics'. *The American Economic Review* 99, 1218–44.

Bevan, Alan, Saul Estrin, S., and Klaus Meyer. 2004. 'Foreign Investment Location and Institutional Development in Transition Economies'. *International Business Review 13*, 43–64.

Bienias, Stanislaw. 2011. 'Ex post evaluation of the National Development Plan', Poland's Ministry of Regional Development, PPT.

Bielecki, Witold and Andrzej K. Koźmiński. 2003. 'The Warsaw Melody of Business Education', *SYNERGY-A Quarterly Ukrainian Management Journal 5/2003*, 23–31.

Blanchard, Olivier. 1997. *The Economics of Post-Communist Transition*. Clarendon Press, Oxford.

Blanchard, Olivier. 2010. 'Institutions, markets, and Poland's economic performance'. Speech at the Kraków University of Economics, June 1.

Blanchard, Olivier and Michael Kremer. 1997. 'Disorganization'. *The Quarterly Journal of Economics 112(4)*, 1091–126.

Blejer, Mario and Martin Skreb (eds.). 1997. *Macroeconomic Stabilization in Transition Economies*. Cambridge University Press, 1997.

Blusiewicz, Tomasz. 2016. 'Ronald Reagan and the Solidarity Movement in Poland'. Paper prepared for Conference: Ronald Reagan and the Transformation of Global Politics in the 1980s. Unpublished.

Blusiewicz, Tomasz and Marie Gayte. 2011. 'The Vatican and the Reagan Administration: A Cold War Alliance?', *The Catholic Historical Review 97(4)*, 713–36.

Blyth, Mark. 2003. 'Structures Do Not Come with an Instruction Sheet: Interests, Ideas, and Progress in Political Science', *Perspectives on Politics 1(4)*, 695–706.

Bobrzynski, Michał. 1888. *Prawo propinacyi w dawnej Polsce*. Kraków: Jagiellonian University.

Bodewig, Christian and Lucas Gortazar. 2016. 'Education's hollow promise of social mobility in Europe'. Brooking Future Development Blog, December 7.

Bogucka, Maria and Henryk Samsonowicz. 1986. *Dzieje miast i mieszczaństwa w Polsce przedrozbiorowej*, Wrocław.

Boix, Carles. 2004. 'Spain: Development, Democracy and Equity', background paper for the World Bank World Development Report 2006 'Equity and Development', December 27.

Bok, Derek. 2010. *The Politics of Happiness. What Government Can Learn From New Research on Well-Being*. Princeton University Press.

Bokova, Irina. 2000. 'Integrating Southeastern Europe into the European Mainstream,' *South East Europe Review for Labour and Social Affairs* No. 3–4.

Bokros, Lajos. 2014. 'Regression: Reform Reversal in Hungary after a Promising Start', in: Aslund and Djankov (eds.) 2014.

Boldrin, Michele, David K. Levine, and Salvatore Modica. 2010. 'A Review of Acemoglu and Robinson's Why Nations Fail'. From: http://www.dklevine.com/general/aandrreview.pdf.

Bolt, Jutta and Jan Luiten van Zanden. 2014. 'The Maddison Project: collaborative research on historical national accounts', *The Economic History Review 67(3)*, 627–51.

Boni, Michal (ed.). 2009. 'Polska 2030. Wyzwania rozwojowe'. Warsa: Poland's Prime Minister Chancellery.

Borish, Michael and Michel Noel. 1996. 'Private Sector Development During Transition: The Visegrad Countries', *World Bank Discussion Paper No. 318*.

Borjas, J. George. 2015. 'Immigration and Globalization: A Review Essay'. *Journal of Economic Literature 53(4)*, 961–74.

Brainerd, Elizabeth. 2000. 'Women in transition: Changes in gender wage differentials in Eastern Europe and the former Soviet Union', *ILR Review 54.1*, 138–62.

Brenner, Robert. 1976. 'Agrarian Class Structure and Economic Development in Pre-Industrial Europe'. *Past & Present* No. 70, 30–75, Oxford University Press.

References

Broadberry, Stephen and Alexander Klein. 2011. 'When and why did eastern European economies begin to fail? Lessons from a Czechoslovak/UK productivity comparison, 1921–1991.' *Explorations in Economic History 48.1*, 37–52.

Broadberry, Stephen and Kevin O'Rourke (eds). 2010. *The Cambridge Economic History of Modern Europe. Volume 2, 1870 to the Present.* Cambridge University Press.

Brown, D.S. and Hunter, W. 2004. 'Democracy and human capital formation education spending in Latin America, 1980 to 1997'. *Comparative Political Studies 37*, 842–64.

Bruegel. 2017. 'Making the Best of the European Single Market', Policy Contribution Issue No. 3, Bruegel.

Brujić, Dragan. 2005. 'Vodič kroz svet Vizantije (Guide to the Byzantine World)'. Beograd. p. 51.

Bruno, Michael. 1992. 'Stabilization and Reform in Eastern Europe: A Preliminary Evaluation.' Unpublished paper, International Monetary Fund, March.

Bruszt, László, Nauro Campos, Jan Fidrmuc, and Gérard Roland. 2012. 'Civil Society, Institutional Change and the Politics of Reform: The Great Transition', in: Gerard Roland (ed.) *Economies in Transition: The Long-Run View.* London: Palgrave Macmillan.

Brzezinski, Richard and Mariusz Mielczarek. 2002. *The Sarmatians 600 BC–AD 450.* Oxford: Osprey Publishing.

Bueno de Mesquita, Bruce and Alastair Smith. 2014. *The Dictator's Handbook: Why Bad Behavior is Almost Always Good Politics.* Public Affairs.

Bukowski, Maciej, Piotr Koryś, Cecylia Leszczyńska, Maciej Tymiński, and Nikolaus Wolf. 2017. 'Wzrost gospodarczy ziem polskich w okresie I globalizacji (1870–1910)', *Ekonomista*, forthcoming.

Bukowski, Maciej and Aleksander Śniegocki. 2014. 'Ukryty rachunek za wegiel. Analiza wsparcia gospodarczego dla elektroenergetyki weglowej oraz gornictwa w Poslce', Warsaw Institute of Structural Economics (WISE), April.

Bukowski, Pawel. 2014. *Long-run persistence of the Empires. The impact of the Partition of Poland on education.* Mimeo, Central European University.

Bukowski, Pawel. 2016. 'How History Matters for Student Performance. Lessons from the Partitions of Poland', unpublished paper.

Bukowski, Pawel and Novokmet, Filip. 2017. 'Top incomes in Poland: from the 1890s until today', unpublished paper.

Campos, Nauro and Francisco Coricelli. 2002. 'Growth in Transition: What We Know, What We Don't, and What We Should'. *Journal of Economic Literature 40(3)*, 793–836.

Campos, Nauro, Francisco Coricelli, and Luigi Moretti. 2014. 'Economic Growth and Political Integration: Synthetic Counterfactuals Evidence from Europe', mimeo.

Cassidy, John. 1997. 'The Return of Karl Marx'. *The New Yorker.* October 20, p. 248

Castellano, Fernando Lopez, and Fernando Garcia-Quero. 2012. 'Institutional Approaches to Economic Development: The Current Status of the Debate.' *Journal of Economic Issues 46(4)*, 921–40.

Chalasinski, Jozef. 1938. 'Młode pokolenie chłopów: procesy i zagadnienia kształtowania się warstwy chłopskiej w Polsce, t. 1'. Spółdzielnia Wydawnicza 'Pomoc Oświatowa', Warszawa.

Chałasiński, Józef. 1946. *Społeczna genealogia inteligencji polskiej*, Spółdzielnia Wydawnicza 'Czytelnik', Warszawa 1946. Prace Polskiego Instytutu Socjologicznego, Seria: Studium Problemów Chłopskich i Robotniczych.

Chang, Ha-Joon. 2011a. 'Institutions and Economic Development: Theory, Policy and History.' *Journal of Institutional Economics 7(4)*, 473–98.

Chang, Ha-Joon. 2011b. 'Reply to the Comments on 'Institutions and Economic Development: Theory, Policy and History.' *Journal of Institutional Economics 7(4)*, 595–613.

Chase, Robert S. 1995. 'Women's labor force participation during and after communism: a study of the Czech Republic and Slovakia', *Economic Growth Center, Discussion Paper No. 768*, Yale University, November.

Chawla, Mukesh, Betcherman, Gordon, and Banerji, Arup. 2007. *From red to gray: the third transition of aging populations in Eastern Europe and the former Soviet Union.* Washington, DC: World Bank.

Chirot, Daniel. ed., 1991. *The origins of backwardness in Eastern Europe: Economics and politics from the Middle Ages until the early twentieth century.* Univ of California Press.

Chiu Yu Ko, Mark Koyama, and Tuan-Hwee Sng, 2014. 'Unified China and Divided Europe,' *MPRA Paper No. 60418*, posted 11. December.

Chmielewska, Iza. 2015. 'Transfery z tytułu pracy Polaków za granicą w świetle badań Narodowego Banku Polskiego', National Bank of Poland, Materiały i Studia nr 314.

Cienski, Jan. 2014. *From Comrades to Capitalists: How Poland's Entrepreneurs Built Europe's Most Competitive Economy.* Kurhaus Publishing.

Clark, Gregory. 2007. *A farewell to alms: A short economic history of the world.* Princeton University Press.

Cohen, Jessive and William Easterly. 2009. 'Introduction. Thinking Big versus Thinking Small', in: Jessica Cohen and William Easterly (eds.), *What Works in Development?: Thinking Big and Thinking Small*, Brookings Institution Press.

Cohen, Patricia. 2017. 'Steel industry, seeing a new dawn, is cheering for Trump', *New York Times*, May 11.

Collier, Paul. 2007. *The Bottom Billion: Why the Poorest Countries Are Failing and What Can Be Done about It.* Oxford, U.K.: Oxford University Press.

Collins, Susan Margaret, and Dani Rodrik. 1991. *Eastern Europe and the Soviet Union in the world economy.* Institute for international economics.

Comin, Diego and Marti Mestieri. 2014. 'If technology has arrived everywhere, why has income diverged?', mimeo, April.

Comin, Diego, William Easterly, and Erick Gong. 2010. 'Was the wealth of nations determined in 1000 BC?.' *American Economic Journal: Macroeconomics* 2.3, 65–97.

Connelly, John. 2000. *Captive University: the Sovietization of East German, Czech, and Polish Higher Education, 1945–1956.* The University of North Carolina Press.

Coyle, Diane. 2012. *The Economics of Enough: How to Run the Economy as if the Future Matters.* Princeton University Press.

Coyle, Diane. 2015. *GDP: A Brief but Affectionate History.* Princeton University Press.

Crafts, Nicholas. 2002. 'The Human Development Index, 1870–1999: Some Revised Estimates'. *European Review of Economic History 6*, 395–405.

References

Crafts, Nicholas and Gianni Tonioli. 2010. 'Aggregate growth, 1950-2000', in Broadberry/O'Rourke (eds.). *The Cambridge Economic History of Modern Europe: 2* Cambridge University Press.

Crampton, Richard. 1997. *Eastern Europe in the XX Century and After*, Routledge.

Csaba, Laszlo. 2007. *The New Political Economy of Emerging Europe*. Budapest: Akadémiai Kiadó.

Czapiński, Janusz. et al. 2015. 'Główne wyniki i wnioski. Diagnoza Społeczna 2015, Warunki i Jakość Życia Polaków – Raport'. *Contemporary Economics* 9/4, 16–24.

Czyżewski, Adam B., Witold M. Orłowski, and Leszek Zieńkowski. 1996. 'Country Study for Poland–A comparative study of causes of output decline in transition economies'. *Third Workshop on Output Decline in Eastern Europe. Prague. April*.

Dabrowski, Marek, Stanislaw Gomułka, and Jacek Rostowski. 2001. 'Whence reform? A critique of the Stiglitz perspective'. *Journal of Policy Reform 4(4)*.

David, Thomas. 2009. *Nationalisme économique et développement. L'industrialisation des pays de l'Europe de l'Est (1780-1939)*, Geneva.

David, Thomas. 2011. 'Why Finland and not Eastern Europe? Economic nationalism and industrialization during the interwar period.' The EBHA 15th Annual Conference Athens. Vol. 24.

Davies, Norman. 1998. *Europe. A History*. Harper Perennial.

Davies, Norman. 2001. *Heart of Europe: The past in Poland's present*. Oxford Paperbacks.

Davies, Norman. 2005. *God's Playground. A History of Poland*. Volume I and II. Columbia University Press; Revised edition.

Darvas, Zsolt. 2015. 'The Convergence Dream 25 years on', Bruegel, http://bruegel.org/2015/01/the-convergence-dream-25-years-on/.

De Melo, Martha, Eduardo Denizer, and Alan Gelb. 1996. 'From Plan to Market: Pattern of Transition', *World Bank Economic Review 15(1)*.

De Moor Tine, and Jan Luiten Van Zanden. 2010. 'Girl power: the European marriage pattern and labour markets in the North Sea region in the late medieval and early modern period.' *The Economic History Review 63.1*, 1–33.

De Pleijt A. M. and Van Zanden J. L. 2016. Accounting for the 'Little Divergence': What drove economic growth in pre-industrial Europe, 1300–1800?, *European Review of Economic History 20(4)*, 387–409.

Deaton, Angus. 2008. 'Income, Health and Well-Being around the World: Evidence from the Gallup World Poll.' *Journal of Economic Perspectives 22(2)*, 53–72.

Decornez, S. S. 1998. 'An Empirical Analysis of the American Middle Class (1968–1992)', PhD Dissertation, Vanderbilt University.

Delors, Jacques, [1989] 1998. 'Address by Mr. Jacques Delors, Bruges, 17 October 1989,' in Brent F. Nelsen and Alexander Stubb (eds.), *The European Union: Readings on the Theory and Practice of European Integration*, Boulder: Lynne Rienner.

Demidowicz, Tomasz. 2010. 'Reforma szlachectwa w Królestwie Polskim w latach 1836–1861', *Czasopismo Prawno-Historyczne*, Tom LXII—2010—Zeszyt 2.

Diamond, Jared. 1997. *Guns Germs and Steel: The Fate of Human Societies*. W.W. Norton & Co., New York.

Diamond, Jared. 2012. 'What makes countries rich or poor?' review of 'Why Nations Fail?', *The New York Review of Books*, June 7.

Dincecco, Mark and Gabriel Katz. 2016. 'State Capacity and Long-run Economic Performance.' *The Economic Journal 126(590)*: 189–218.

Dittmar, Jeremiah. 2011. 'Information Technology and Economic Change: The Impact of The Printing Press', *The Quarterly Journal of Economics 126(3)*: 1133–72.

Djankov, Simeon. 2014. Bulgaria: The Great Vacillations. In: Anders Aslund and Simeon Djankov (eds.). *The Great Rebirth: Lessons from the victory of capitalism over communism*. Peterson Institute for International Economics.

Djankov, Simeon. 2016. 'The Divergent Postcommunist Paths to Democracy and Economic Freedom', *Discussion Paper No. 78*. July.

Djankov, Simeon, José García Montalvo, and Marta Reynal-Querol. 2008. 'The Curse of Aid.' *Journal of Economic Growth 13(3)*, 169–94.

Djankov, Simeon and Peter Murrell. 2002. 'Enterprise Restructuring in Transition: A Qualitative Survey'. *Journal of Economic Literature 40(3)*, 739–93.

Dmowski, Roman. 1903. *Mysli nowoczesnego Polaka*. Wydawnictwo Zachodnie, Warszawa.

Domanski, Henryk. 1998. 'Transformations and social mobility', *Polish Sociological Review 124*, 313–31.

Domanski, Henryk. 2000. *On the Verge of Convergence: Social Stratification in Eastern Europe*. Central European University Press.

Drakulic, Slavenka. 1997. *Café Europa: Life After Communism*. W.W. Norton& Company.

Du Bois, W. E. B. 1903. *The Souls of Black Folk*. New York: A.C. McClurg & Company.

Dubnov, Samuel. 1918/2000. *History of the Jews in Russia and Poland. Volume 1*. The Jewish Publication Society of America.

Duval, Romain, Davide Furceri, Joao Jalles, and Huy Nguyen. 2016. 'A New Narrative Database of Product and Labor Market Reforms in Advanced Economies.' IMF Working Paper, International Monetary Fund, Washington, forthcoming.

Dwilewicz, Lukasz, Janusz Kalinski, Jacek Luszniewicz, and Dariusz Stola. 2010. 'Czy Polska rosla w sile i ludzie zyli dostatniej?', Pamięć i Sprawiedliwość, nr. 2.

Easterlin, Richard A. 1974. 'Does Economic Growth Improve the Human Lot? Some Empirical Evidence', *Nations and households in economic growth* 89, 89–125.

Easterly, William. 2001. 'The middle class consensus and economic development'. *Journal of Economic Growth 6*, 317–35.

Easterly, William. 2002. *The Elusive Quest for Growth: Economists' Adventures and Misadventures in the Tropics*. Cambridge: MIT Press.

Easterly, William. 2008. 'Commentary: The Indomitable in Pursuit of the Inexplicable: The World Development Reports' Failure to Comprehend Economic Growth Despite Determined Attempts, 1978–2008'. In: Y. Shahid (ed.) *Development Economics through the Decades: A Critical Look at Thirty Years of the World Development Report*, World Bank.

Easterly, William. 2013. *The Tyranny of Experts: Economists, Dictators, and the Forgotten Rights of the Poor*, Basic Books, New York.

Easterly, William and Ross Levine. 1997. 'Africa's growth tragedy: policies and ethnic divisions,' *The Quarterly Journal of Economics 112.4*, 1203–50.

Easterly, William and Ross Levine. 2003. 'Tropics, germs, and crops: how endowments influence economic development'. *Journal of Monetary Economics 50(1)*, 3–39.

EBRD. 1999. *Transition Report 1999. Ten Years of Transition*. European Bank for Reconstruction and Development.

EBRD. 2001. *Transition Report 2001*. European Bank for Reconstruction and Development.

EBRD. 2003. *Transition Report 2003. Integration and Regional Cooperation*. European Bank for Reconstruction and Development.

EBRD. 2013. *Transition Report 2013. Stuck in Transition*. London: European Bank for Reconstruction and Development.

EBRD. 2016a. *Transition Report 2016–17. Transition for all: Equal opportunities in an unequal world*. London: European Bank for Reconstruction and Development.

EBRD. 2016b. *Life in Transition survey*. London: European Bank for Reconstruction and Development.

Economist, The. 1998. 'Left turn?', June 11.

Economist, The. 2013a. 'The secret of their success', February 2.

Economist, The. 2013b. 'Middle-income claptrap', February 16.

Economist, The. 2013c. 'Another kind of health tourism', June 8.

Economist, The. 2016. 'Snip snap. Why more than half of newborn boys in America are circumcised', June 16.

Eichengreen, Barry. 1992. 'The origins and nature of the Great Slump revisited.' The *Economic History Review 45(2)*, 213–39.

Eichengreen, Barry. 2008a. *The European economy since 1945: coordinated capitalism and beyond*. Princeton University Press.

Eichengreen, Barry. 2008b. 'The Real Exchange Rate and Economic Growth'. *Commission on growth and development working paper; no. 4*. Washington, DC: World Bank.

Eichengreen, Barry and Kevin O'Rourke. 2010. 'What do the new data tell us?'. Vox column. March 8.

Eichengreen, Barry and Jeffrey Sachs. 1985. 'Exchange rates and economic recovery in the 1930s.', *The Journal of Economic History 45(4)*, 925–46.

Eichengreen, Barry and Mark Uzan. 1992. 'The Marshall Plan: Economic Effects and Implications for Eastern Europe and the Former USSR'. *Economic Policy 14*: 13–76.

Eichengreen, Barry, Donghyun Park, and Kwanho Shin. 2013. 'Growth Slowdowns Redux: New Evidence on the Middle-Income Trap', *NBER Working Paper No. 18673*, January.

Ericsson, Richard. 1991. 'The Classical Soviet-Type Economy: Nature of the System and Implications for Reform,', *Journal of Economic Perspectives 5(4)*, 11–28.

Erikson, Robert and John H. Goldthorpe. 1992. *The Constant Flux. A Study of Class Mobility in Industrial Societies*. Oxford: Clarendon Press.

Erste Bank. 2014. 'EU Cohesion Policy 2014-2020: Will EUR 167 billion of EU funds give CEE a boost?'. Erste Bank Press Release. March 11.

European Commission. 2001. 'Enlargement of the European Union: An historic opportunity. A general overview of the enlargement process and the pre-accession strategy of the European Union'. Brussels: The European Commission.

European Commission. 2009. 'Good to know about EU enlargement'. Brussels: the European Commission.

European Commission. 2014. 'Sixth report on economic, social and territorial cohesion'. July.

European Commission. 2015. 'The 2015 Ageing Report: Economic and budgetary projections for the 28 EU Member States (2013-2060)', European Economy 3. Brussels.

Eyal, Gil, Ivan Szelenyi, and Eleanor Townsley. 1998. *Making Capitalism Without Capitalists: Class Formation and Elite Struggles in Post-Communist Central Europe*, London: Verso.

Ferge, Zsuzsa. 1997. 'Is theWorld Falling Apart? A View from the East of Europe,' in Ivan T. Berend (ed.), *Long-Term Structural Changes in Transforming Central and Eastern Europe*, Munich: Sudosteuropa-Gesellschaft.

Ferguson, Niall. 2011. *Civilization. The West and the Rest*. Penguin.

Fernández, Raquel. 2010. 'Does Culture Matter?'. *NBER Working Paper No. 16277*. August.

Financial Times. 1997. 'UW is the Union for Freedom Party'; 27 March.

Fisher, Max. 2016. 'Where women work, and don't: A map of female labor force participation around the world'. *The Washington Post*, February 13.

Fischer, Stanley and Ratna Sahay. 2000. 'The Transition Economics Ten Years Later', *NBER Working Paper 7664*, April.

Fischer, Stanley and Ratna Sahay. 2004. *Transition economies: The role of institutions and initial conditions*. IMF. Preliminary Draft.

Florida, Richard. 2002. *The Rise of the Creative Class and How It's Transforming Work, Leisure, Community and Everyday Life*. Basic Books.

Flynn, James R. 1987. 'Massive IQ gains in 14 nations: What IQ tests really measure'. *Psychological Bulletin 101(2)*, 171–91.

Forbes. 2012. 'The World's Biggest Companies', by Scott deCarlo, April 18.

Frank, Robert H. 2017. *Success and Luck: Good Fortune and the Myth of Meritocracy*. Princeton University Press.

Freedman, David. 2010. *Wrong: Why experts keep failing us—and how to know when not to trust them*. Little, Brown and Company.

Frey, Bruno S. and Alois Stutzer. 2002. 'What Can Economists Learn from Happiness Research?' *Journal of Economic Literature 40*, 402–35.

Friedman, Benjamin. 2005. *The Moral Consequences of Economic Growth*. Knopf.

Friszke, Andrzej. 2014. *Rewolucja Solidarności 1980–1981*, Warszawa: Znak.

Frye, Timothy. 2001. 'Keeping Shop: The Value of the Rule of Law in Warsaw and Moscow,' in Peter Murrell ed., *Assessing the Value of Law in Transition Economies*, Ann Arbor: University of Michigan Press.

Fryer, Roland. 2010. 'An Empirical Analysis of 'Acting White'. *Journal of Public Economics 94(5–6)*, 380–96.

Fukuyama, Francis. 1995. *Trust: The social virtues and the creation of prosperity*. Free Press Paperbacks.

Fukuyama, Francis. 2011. *The origins of political order: from prehuman times to the French Revolution*. Macmillan.

Fukuyama, Francis. 2017. 'Transitions to the rule of law'. Box 3.4, p. 96–7, in: World Bank. *World Development Report. Governance and the Law*. Washington DC: World Bank.

Gaidar, Yegor. 2010. *Collapse of an Empire. Lessons for Modern Russia*. Brookings Institution Press, January.

Gill, Indermit, Homi Kharas, and Others. 2007. 'An East Asian Renaissance: Ideas for Economic Growth.' World Bank, Washington, DC.

Gill, Indermit and Martin Raiser. 2012. *Golden Growth. Restoring the Lustre of the European Economic Model.* Washington DC: The World Bank.

Gill, Indermit S. and Homi Kharas. 2015. 'The middle-income trap turns ten'. *World Bank Policy Research Working Paper*; no. WPS 7403. Washington, DC: World Bank Group.

Giorgi, Liana. 1995. *The Post-Socialist Media: What Power to the West?*. Averbury: Aldershot.

Gladwell, Malcolm. 2008. *Outliers. The Story of Success.* Little, Brown and Company.

Glaeser, Edward. 2012. *Triumph of the City: How Our Greatest Invention Makes Us Richer, Smarter, Greener, Healthier, and Happier.* Penguin Books.

Glaeser, Edward, Rafael la Porta, Florencio Lopez-de-Silanes, and Andrei Shleifer. 2004. 'Do Institutions Cause Growth?', *Journal of Economic Growth 9*, 271–303.

Góes, Carlos. 2015. 'Institutions and Growth: a GMM/IV Panel VAR Approach', *IMF Working Paper WP/15/174.*

Gomulka, Stanislaw. 2016. 'Poland's Economic and Social Transformation 1989–2013 and Contemporary Challenges', *Central Bank Review 16(1)*, 19–23, Central Bank of Turkey, March.

Gordon, Robert J. *The rise and fall of American growth: The US standard of living since the civil war.* Princeton University Press, 2016.

Gorodnichenko, Yuriy and Gerard Roland. 2010. 'Culture, Institutions and Long Run Growth.' *NBER Working Paper 16368*, Cambridge Massachusetts.

Gorodnichenko, Yuriy and Gerard Roland. 2011a. 'Which Dimensions of Culture Matter for Long Run Growth?', *American Economic Review Papers Proc 101*, 492–8.

Gorodnichenko, Yuriy and Gerard Roland. 2011b. 'Individualism, innovation, and long-run growth', Which Dimensions of Culture Matter for Long Run Growth?', *PNAS, 108, suppl. 4.*

Gorodnichenko, Yuriy and Gérard Roland. 2013. 'Culture, Institutions and Democratization'. University of California, Berkeley, Department of Economics, mimeo.

Goryszewski, Lukasz. 2014. Style konsumpcji polskiej klasy wyzszek. Kraków: NOMOS.

Gottfried, Robert S. 1983. *The Black Death. Natural and Human Disaster in Medieval Europe.* Free Press.

Gould, Eric D. and Alexander Hijzen. 2016. 'Growing Apart, Losing Trust? The Impact of Inequality on Social Capital'. *IMF Working Paper WP 16/176.*

Grafe, Regina. 2012. *Distant Tyranny: Markets, Power, and Backwardness in Spain, 1650–1800.* Princeton, NJ: Princeton University Press.

Greenhouse, Steven. 1991. 'Poland is granted large cut in debt', *New York Times*, March 16.

Greif, Avner. 1993. 'Contract enforceability and economic institutions in early trade: The Maghribi traders' coalition.' *American Economic Review 83(3)*, 525–48.

Greif, Avner. 1994. 'Cultural beliefs and the organization of society: A historical and theoretical reflection on collectivist and individualist societies.' *Journal of Political Economy 102.5*, 912–50.

Grogan, Louise and Luc Moers. 2001. 'Growth empirics with institutional measures for transition countries.' *Economic systems 25.4*, 323–44.

Grosfeld, Irena and Ekaterina Zhuravskaya. 2015. 'Cultural vs. Economic Legacies of Empires: Evidence from the Partition of Poland'. *Journal of Comparative Economics 43(1)*, 55–75.

Grzymala-Busse, Anna. 2002. 'The Programmatic Turnaround of Communist Successor Parties in East Central Europe, 1989–1998'. *Communist and Post-Communist Studies, 35(1)*, 51–66.

Grzymala-Busse, Anna. 2010. 'The Best Laid Plans: The Impact of Informal Rules', *Studies in Comparative International Development 45*, 311–33.

Guiso, Luigi, Paolo Sapienza, and Luigi Zingales. 2003. 'People's opium? Religion and economic activities'. *Journal of Monetary Economics 50(1)*, 225–82

Guiso, Luigi, Paolo Sapienza, and Luigi Zingales. 2006. 'Does Culture Affect Economic Outcomes?'. *Journal of Economic Perspectives 20(2)*, Spring.

Gulick, Sidney. 1903. *Evolution of the Japanese*. New York: Fleming H. Revell.

GUS. 1939. *Maly Rocznik Statystyczny Polski 1938*. Warszawa: Glowny Urzad Statystyczny.

GUS. 2014. 'Historia Polski w liczbach'. Warszawa: Glowny Urzad Statystyczny.

GUS. 2015. 'Zycie religijne w Polsce. Na podstawie badania spojnosci spolecznej'. Warszawa: Glowny Urzad Statystyczny.

GUS. 2016. 'Informacja o rozmiarach i kierunkach emigracji z Polski w latach 2004–2015', Warszawa: Glowny Urzad Statystyczny.

Haidt, Jonathan. 2012. *The Righteous Mind: Why Good People are Divided by Politics and Religion*. Vintage.

Harari, Yuval Noah. 2011. *Sapiens: A Brief History of Humankind*, Harper.

Harberger, Arnold C. 2003. 'Interview with Arnold Harberger: Sound Policies Can Free Up Natural Forces of Growth,' IMF Survey, International Monetary Fund, Washington, DC, July 14, 213–216.

Harris, Kevin. 2017. 'Was the Inca Empire a Socialist State? A Historical Discussion.' Eiu. edu. Accessed May 7, 2017. http://www.eiu.edu/historia/Harris.pdf.

Hansen, Keith. 2016. 'Early childhood development: a smart investment for life'. World Bank Blog, April 14.

Hausmann, Roberto, Lant Pritchett, and Dani Rodrik. 2005. 'Growth Accelerations', *Journal of Economic Growth 10(4)*, 303–29.

Havrylyshyn, Oleh and Ron Van Rooden. 2003. 'Institutions matter in transition, but so do policies.' *Comparative Economic Studies 45(1)*, 2–24.

Havrylyshyn, Oleh and Thomas Wolf. 2001. 'Growth in Transition Countries, 1990–1998: The Main Lessons', in O. Havrylyshyn and S. Nsouli (eds), *A Decade of Transition: Achievements and Challenges*, IMF.

Helliwell, John F., Richard Layard, and Jeffrey Sachs (eds.). 2017. *World Happiness Report 2017*, New York: Sustainable Development Solutions Network.

Hendrix, Cullen S. 2010. 'Measuring State Capacity: Theoretical and Empirical Implications for the Study of Civil Conflict.' *Journal of Peace Research 47(3)*, 273–85.

Herrnstein, Richard J. and Charles Murray. 1994. *The bell curve: The reshaping of American life by differences in intelligence*. New York: Free.

Herslow, Carl. 1946. *Moscow-Berlin-Warsaw*. Stockholm: Fritzes.

Higley, John, Jan Pakulski, and Judith S. Kullberg. 1996. 'The persistence of postcommunist elites.' *Journal of Democracy 7.2*, 133–47.

Hirschman, Alfred, O. 1992. *Rival views of market society and other recent essays*. Harvard University Press.

Hitchcock, William. 2003. *The Struggle for Europe: The Turbulent History of a Divided Continent, 1945 to the Present*. New York: Anchor Books. p. 302.

Hobbes, Thomas. 1651/2010. *Leviathan: Or the Matter, Forme, and Power of a Common-Wealth Ecclesiasticall and Civill*, ed. by Ian Shapiro, Yale University Press.

Hodgskin, Thomas. 1820. *Travels in the North of Germany*, vol. 1. Edinburgh, Archibald.

Hofstede, Geert. 2001. *Culture's consequences: Comparing values, behaviors, institutions, and organizations across nations*, (2nd ed.). Thousand Oaks, CA: Sage.

Hofstede, Geert. 2011. 'Dimensionalizing cultures: The Hofstede model in context.' *Online readings in psychology and culture 2.1*, 8.

Hutchings, Robert L. 1983. *Soviet-East European relations: consolidation and conflict, 1968–1980*. University of Wisconsin Press.

IMF. 1992. World Economic Outlook, October. Washington, DC: International Monetary Fund.

IMF. 1998. World Economic Outlook: Financial Crises, Causes, and Indicators, May. Washington, DC: International Monetary Fund.

IMF. 2014. '25 years of Transition'. International Monetary Fund.

IMF. 2015. 'Rethinking Financial Deepening: Stability and Growth in Emerging Markets', *IMF Staff Discussion Note SDN/15/08*, May.

IMF. 2017a. World Economic Outlook. Gaining Momentum? International Monetary Fund, April.

IMF. 2017b. 'Republic of Poland: Arrangement Under the Flexible Credit Line and Cancellation of the Current Arrangement', International Monetary Fund, January.

Inglehart, Ronald. 1990. *Culture Shift in Advanced Industrial Society*. Princeton University Press.

Inglehart, Ronald. 2008. 'Changing Values among Western Publics from 1970 to 2006'. *West European Politics 31(1–2)*, 130–46.

Inglehart, Ronald and Christian Welzel. 2005. *Modernization, Cultural Change, and Democracy: The Human Development Sequence*. Cambridge University Press.

Inglehart, Ronald, et al. 2000. "World Values Surveys and European Values Survey, 1981–1984, 1990–1993, and 1995–1997". ICPSR version. Ann Arbor, MI: Institute for Social Research [producer]. Ann Arbor, MI: Inter-university Consortium for Political and Social Research [distributor].

Jackson, John E., Jacek Klich, and Krystyna Poznanska. 2005. *The Political Economy of Poland's Transition: New Firms and Reform Governments*. Cambridge, U.K.: Cambridge University Press.

Janos, Andrew C. 2000. *East Central Europe in the Modern World. The Politics of the Borderlands from Pre- to Postcommunism*. Stanford University Press.

Jasser, Adam. 2017. 'Some lessons from privatization in Eastern Europe', mimeo.

Jerrim, John and Lindsey Macmillan. 2015. 'Income Inequality, Intergenerational Mobility, and the Great Gatsby Curve: Is Education the Key?', *Social Forces 94(2)*, 505–33, December.

Jones, Benjamin and Benjamin Olken. 2005. 'Do Leaders Matter? National Leadership and Growth Since World War II', *Quarterly Journal of Economics 120(3)*, 835–64.

Jones, Charles I. and Peter J. Klenow. 2016. 'Beyond GDP? Welfare across Countries and Time.' *American Economic Review 106(9)*, 2426–57.

Jones, Charles I. and Paul M. Romer. 2009. 'The New Kaldor Facts: Ideas, Institutions, Population, and Human Capital', *NBER Working Paper 15094*, June.

Jones, Garett. 2015. *Hive mind: How your nation's IQ matters so much more than your own*. Stanford University Press.

Jorgenson, Dale W., ed. 2009. *The Economics of Productivity*. Northampton MA: Edward Elgar Publishing.

Jorgenson, Dale W., and Daniel T. Slesnick. 2014. 'Measuring Social Welfare in the U.S. National Accounts.', in: Jorgenson, Landefeld, and Schreyer (eds.) *Measuring Economic Sustainability and Progress*, 43–88. Chicago: University of Chicago Press.

Jung, Jong Hyun. 2016. 'Cross-national Analysis of Religion and Attitudes toward Premarital Sex: Do Economic Contexts Matter?'. *Sociological Perspectives, 59(4)*, 798–817.

Kahneman, Daniel. 2012. *Thinking, Fast and Slow*. Farrar, Straus and Giroux.

Kahneman, Daniel and Angus Deaton. 2010. 'High Income Improves Evaluation of Life But Not Emotional Well-Being', *Proceedings of the National Academy of Sciences, 107(38)*, 16489–93.

Kapil, Natasha, Marcin Piatkowski, Ismail Radwan, and Juan Julio Gutierrez. 2013. 'Poland. Enterprise Innovation Support Review'. Washington: the World Bank.

Karaman, K. Kivanç and Şevket Pamuk. 2013. 'Different Paths to the Modern State in Europe: The Interaction between Warfare, Economic Structure and Political Regime', *American Political Science Review 107(3)*, 603–26.

Kaufmann D., A. Kraay and M. Mastruzzi. 2010. *The Worldwide Governance Indicators: Methodology and Analytical Issues*. Washington DC: The World Bank.

Kennedy, Paul. 1987. *The rise and fall of the great powers: economic change and military conflict from 1500 to 2000*. Random House.

Kennedy, Robert F. 1968. Remarks at the University of Kansas, March 18.

Keynes, John Maynard. 1936. *The General Theory of Employment, Interest and Money*. London: Palgrave Macmillan.

Kieniewicz, Stefan. 1969. *The Emancipation of the Polish Peasantry*. Chicago.

Kim, Wonik. 2007. 'Social Insurance Expansion and Political Regime Dynamics in Europe, 1880–1945.' *Social Science Quarterly 88(2)*, 494–514.

Kitschelt, Herbert. 1995. 'Formation of Party Cleavages in Post-Communist Democracies', *Party Politics 1(4)*, 447–72.

Kitschelt Herbert, Zdenka Mansfeldová, Radoslaw Markowski, and Gabor Tóka. 1999. *Post-communist party systems*. Cambridge: Cambridge University Press.

Klaus, Vaclav. 2014. 'Czechoslovakia and the Czech Republic: The Spirit and Main Contours of the Postcommunist Transformation:, in: Aslund, Anders and Simeon Djankov (eds) *The Great Rebirth: Lessons from the Victory of Capitalism over Communism*. Peterson Institute for International Economics.

Klees, Steven J. 2017. 'The False Promise of Cost-Benefit Analysis'. Project Syndicate, June 1.

Klingemann, Hans-Dieter, Dieter Fuchs, and Jan Zielonka. 2006. *Democracy and Political Culture in Eastern Europe*. London: Routledge.

Knack, Stephen and Philip Keefer. 1995. 'Institutions and Economic Performance: Cross-Country Tests Using Alternative Institutional Measures', *Economics and Politics* 7, 207–27.

Knack, Stephen and Philip Keefer. 1997. 'Does Social Capital have an Economic Payoff? A Cross-Country Investigation'. *Quarterly Journal of Economics 112(4)*, 1251–88.

KNF. 2017. 'Indywidualne konta emerytalne oraz indywidualne konta zabezpieczenia emerytalnego w 2016 roku'. Urzad Komisji Nadzoru Finansowego.

Kochanowicz, Jacek. 1991. 'Could a Polish Noble became an Entrepreneur? Mentality, Market and Capital' in: *Impresa, Industria, Commercio, Banca. Sec. XIII–XVIII*, Le Munier, p. 933–42.

Kochanowicz, Jacek. 2014. 'An Escape into History: A Personal Recollection', lecture presented as part of the series of EGO Lectures, Central European University, June 5.

Kochanowicz, Jacek and Mira Marody. 2003. 'Towards understanding the Polish economic culture.' *Polish Sociological Review 4*, 343–68.

Kolodko, Grzegorz W. 1994. *Strategia dla Polski*. Poltext.

Kolodko, Grzegorz W. 2000. *From Shock to Therapy: The Political Economy of Postsocialist Transformation*. Oxford and New York: Oxford University Press.

Kolodko, Grzegorz W. 2002. *Globalization and Catching-up in Transition Economies*, University of Rochester Press, Rochester, NY, USA, and Woodbridge, Suffolk, UK.

Kolodko, Grzegorz W. 2009. 'A Two-thirds Rate of Success', *UNU/WIDER Research Paper* No. 2009/14.

Kolodko, Grzegorz W. 2011. *Truth and Lies: Economics and Politics in a Volatile World*. New York: Columbia University Press.

Kolodko, Grzegorz W. 2014. 'The New Pragmatism, or economics and policy for the future', *Acta Oeconomica 64(2)*, 139–60.

Kolodko, Grzegorz W. 2017. 'New Pragmatism versus New Nationalism'. *TIGER Working Paper Series* No. 137, April 1.

Kolodko Grzegorz W. and D. Mario Nuti 1997. 'The Polish Alternative. Old Myths, Hard Facts and New Strategies in the Successful Transformation of the Polish Economy'. *Research for Action*, 33, The United Nations University World Institute for Development Economics Research, WIDER, Helsinki.

Kolodko, Grzegorz W. and Jacek Tomkiewicz (eds.). 2011. *20 years of Transformation: Achievements, Problems and Perspectives*. New York: Nova Science Publishers.

Komlos, John. 1985. 'Stature and Nutrition in the Habsburg Monarchy: The Standard of Living and Economic Development'. *American Historical Review 90*, 1149–61.

Konopczynski, Wladyslaw. 1948. *Chronologia sejmów polskich 1493–1793*. Kraków: Polska Akademia umiejętności.

Kornai, Janos. 1980. *Economics of Shortage*. North-Holland.

Kowalik, Tadeusz. 1994. 'The 'Big Bang' as a Political and Historical Phenomenon: A Case Study on Poland' in Ivan T. Berend (ed.), *Transition to a Market Economy at the End of the 20th Century*. Munich: SüdosteuropaGesellschaft.

Kowalik, Tadeusz. 2006. *Spory o ustrój społeczno-gospodarczy w Polsce, lata 1944–1948*, Warszawa.

Kowalik, Tadeusz. 2012. *From Solidarity to Sellout: The Restoration of Capitalism in Poland*. New York: Monthly Review Press.

Koźmiński, Andrzej K. 1993. *Catching Up? Case Studies of Organizational and Management Change in the Ex-Socialist Block*, SUNY Press, Albany.

Koźmiński, Andrzej K. 2008a. *Management in Transition*. Warsaw: Difin.

Koźmiński, Andrzej K. 2008b. 'Anatomy of systemic change: Polish management in transition', *Communist and Post-communist Studies* Nr. 41, 263–80.

Koźmiński, Andrzej K. 2014. 'Managerial contribution to growth in transition economies' in: Grzegorz W. Kolodko (ed.) *Management and Economic Policy for Development*, Nova Publishers, New York: 19–31.

Kremer, Michael. 1993. 'Population growth and technological change: One million BC to 1990', *The Quarterly Journal of Economics 108(3)*, 681–716.

Krugman, Paul. 1991. *Geography and Trade*. Cambridge, MA: MIT Press. p. 93, n. 3

Kumar, Manmohan S. and Jaejoon Woo. 2010. 'Public Debt and Growth', *IMF Working Paper* WP/10/174, Washington DC: International Monetary Fund.

Kula, Witold. 1962. *Teoria ekonomiczna ustroju feudalnego*. Panstwowe Wydawnictwo Naukowe.

Kuran, T. 2004. 'Why the Middle East is Economically Underdeveloped: Historical Mechanisms of Institutional Stagnation', *Journal of Economic Perspectives 18(3)*, 71–90.

Laar, Mart. 2014. 'Estonia: The Most Radical Reforms', in: Anders Aslund and Simeon Djankov (eds). *The Great Rebirth: Lessons from the Victory of Capitalism over Communism*, Peterson Institute for International Economics.

Laeven, Luc and Fabian Valencia. 2012. 'Systemic Banking Crises Database: An Update', *IMF Working Paper* No. 12/163, Washington DC: International Monetary Fund.

Lagarde, Christine. 2014. 'The Caribbean and the IMF—Building a Partnership for the Future', speech delivered at the University of the West Indies at Mona, Jamaica, June 27.

Landes, David. S. 1969. *The Unbound Prometheus: Technological Change and Industrial Development in Western Europe from 1750 to the Present*. Cambridge, New York: Press Syndicate of the University of Cambridge.

Landes, David S. 1998. *The Wealth and Poverty of Nations: Why Some are So Rich and Some So Poor*. W. W. Norton & Company, New York.

Landes, David. 2000. 'Culture makes almost all the difference' in: Lawrence E. Harrison and Samuel P. Huntigton (eds.) *Culture Matters. How Values Shape Human Progress*. Basic Books.

Lange, Oskar. 1936. 'On the economic theory of socialism: part one.' *The review of economic studies 4.1*, 53–71.

Lange, Oskar, Fred Manville Taylor, and Benjamin E. Lippincott. 1956. *On the economic theory of socialism*. University of Minnesota Press.

LaPorta, Rafael, Florencio Lopez-de-Silanes, Andrei Shleifer, and Robert Vishny. 1997. 'Trust in large organizations'. *American Economic Review 87(2)*, 333–8.

Layard, Richard. 2003. 'Happiness: Has Social Science a Clue.' Lionel Robbins Memorial Lectures 2002/3, London School of Economics, March 3–5.

Layard, Richard. 2005. *Happiness: Lessons from a New Science*. London: Penguin.

Lech, Marian. 1965. *Za króla Sasa*. Warszawa: Ksiazka i Wiedza.

Leder, Andrzej. 2013. 'Dosc tych dworkow', interview with Ewa Kretkowska, Marta Madejska, Maciej Melon, Krytyka Polityczna, September 5.

343

Leder, Andrzej. 2014. *Przesniona rewolucja. Cwiczenia z logiki historycznej*. Warszawa: Wydawnictwo Krytyka Polityczna.

Leitenberg, Laurence and Gary Goertz. 2003. 'Structure de la population active du monde en 1937: analyse comparative de soixante-et-onze pays.' *Economies et sociétés 37.1*, 75–113.

Leszczyński, Adam. 2012. 'Rzeczpospolita w gospodarce', *Gazeta Wyborcza*, 14 December.

Leszczyński, Adam. 2015a. *Skok w nowoczesnosc. Polityka wzrostu w krajach peryferyjnych 1943–1980*. Wydawnictwo Krytyka Polityczna.

Leszczyński, Adam. 2015b. 'Antyliberalizm i kolektywizm. Polityka i gospodarka od II wojny światowej do lat siedemdziesiątych na przykładzie polskich programów powojennej odbudowy', *Pamiec i Sprawiedliwosc. Pismo Instytutu Pamieci Narodowej* nr 1 (25)/2015.

Leszczyński, Adam. 2017. *Leap into Modernity. Political Economy of the Growth on the Periphery, 1943–1980*. Peter Lang International Academic Publishers.

Levits, Egils, 1998. 'Harmonization of the Legal Systems of Latvia and the European Union Community' in Talavs Jundzis (ed.), *The Baltic States at Historical Crossroads*, Riga: Academy of Sciences, Latvia.

Lewandowski, Piotr and Jan Baran, 2016. 'Labor markets and education in Poland'. Background paper for World Bank.

Lieberman, Evan S. 2002. 'Taxation Data as Indicators of State-Society Relations: Possibilities and Pitfalls in Cross-National Research.' *Studies in Comparative International Development 36(4)*, 89–115.

Lin, Justin Yifu. 2009. *Economic Development and Transition. Thought, Strategy, and Viability*. Cambridge Books. Cambridge University Press.

Lin, Justin Yifu and David Rosenblatt. 2012. 'Shifting patterns of economic growth and rethinking development', *Journal of Economic Policy Reform 15(3)*, 171–94.

Lipset, Seymour M. 1959. 'Some social requisites of democracy: Economic development and political legitimacy'. *American Political Science Review 53*, 69–105.

Lipton, David and Jeffrey Sachs. 1990. 'Creating a market economy in Eastern Europe: The case of Poland', *Brookings Papers on Economic Activity 1*, 75–147.

Litan, Robert E. 2014. *Trillion Dollar Economists: How Economists and Their Ideas have Transformed Business*. Bloomberg.

Loayza, Norman, Jamele Rigolini, and Gonzalo Llorente. 2012. 'Do middle classes bring about institutional reforms?', *Economics Letters 116*, 440–4.

Łoziński, Maja and Łoziński, Jan. 2012. *Historia polskiego smaku*, Wydawnictwo Naukowe PWN.

Lucas, Robert. 2003. 'Macroeconomic Priorities'. *The American Economic Review, 93(1)*, 1–14.

Luengnaruemitchai, Pipat and S. Schadler. 2007. 'Do Economist' and Financial Markets' Perspectives on the New Members of the EU Differ?' *IMF Working Paper No. WP/ 07/65* (Washington, International Monetary Fund).

Luttmer, Erzo F. P. and Monica Singhal. 2011. 'Culture, Context, and the Taste for Redistribution', *American Economic Journal: Economic Policy 3 (February)*, 157–79.

Mach, Bogdan. 2004. 'Intergenerational Mobility in Poland: 1972–88–94 in: Richard Breen (ed.) *Social Mobility in Europe*, Oxford University Press.

Mach, Bogdan W. 2000. 'Nomenklatura, communist party membership, and advantage on the labor market.', in: Kazimierz Slomczynski (ed.) *Social Patterns of Being Political. The Initial Phase of the Post-Communist Transition in Poland*. Warsaw: IFiS Publishers.

Mach, Zdzisław. 1998. *Niechciane miasta—migracje i tozsamosc spoleczna*. Universitas.

Mączak, Antoni. 1981. *Encyklopedia historii gospodarczej Polski do 1945 roku*. Warszawa: Wiedza Powszechna.

Mączyński, Jerzy and Dariusz Wyspiański. 2011. 'Differences on Organizational Practices and Preferred Leader Attributes between Polish Managers Studied in 2010/2011 and 1996/1997', *Journal of Intercultural Management*, 3, nr 2 | 7–18.

Maier, Charles S. 2012. 'The Travails of Unification: East Germany's Economic Transition since 1989', in: Gerard Roland (ed.) *Economies in Transition*, Palgrave Macmillan, pp. 344–63.

Malinowski, Mikolaj. 2016a. 'Little Divergence revisited: Polish weighted real wages in a European perspective, 1500–1800', *European Review of Economic History, 20(3)*, 345–67.

Malinowski, Mikołaj. 2016b. 'Market conditions in preindustrial Poland, 1500–1772.' *Economic History of Developing Regions 31.2-3*, 253–76.

Malinowski, Mikolaj. 2017. 'Economic consequences of anarchy; Legal state capacity and market integration in early modern Poland', draft paper, September.

Malinowski, Mikolaj and Stephen Broadberry. 2017. 'Living standards in the long-run: The place of Central, East and South-East Europe in the Divergence debate'. In: M. Morys (ed.), *The Economic History of Central, East and South-East Europe, 1800 to the present day*. Routledge.

Malinowski, Mikołaj and Jan Luiten van Zanden. 2015. 'National income and its distribution in preindustrial Poland in a global perspective', Working Papers 0076, European Historical Economics Society (EHES).

Malinowski, Mikołaj and Jan Luiten van Zanden. 2017. 'Income and its distribution in preindustrial Poland.' *Cliometrica 11(3)*, 375–404.

Mandes, Slawomir and Maria Rogaczewska. 2013. 'I don't reject the Catholic Church - the Catholic Church rejects me': How Twenty- and Thirty-somethings in Poland Re-evaluate their Religion'. *Journal of Contemporary Religion 28(2)*, 259–76.

Maseland, Robbert. 2013. "Parasatical cultures? The cultural origins of institutions and development", *Journal of Economic Growth 18(2)*, 109–36.

Marshall, Monty G., Keith Jaggers, and Ted Robert Gurr. 2011. 'Polity IV Project: Dataset Users' Manual'. Center for Systemic Peace: Polity IV Project.; data from http://www.systemicpeace.org/polity/polity4x.htm.

Mateju, Petr. 1996. 'Winners and Losers in the Post-Communist Transformation: The Czech Republic in Comparative Perspective,' *Innovation 9(3)*.

Mateju, Petr. 2000, 'Mobility and Perceived Change in Life Chances in Postcommunist Countries,' in: Birdsall and Graham (eds.) *New markets, new opportunities? Economic and social mobility in a changing world*, Brookings Institution Press, Washington DC, pp. 267–90.

Mavridis, Dimitri and Palma Mosberger. 2016. 'Income Inequality and Incentives .The Quasi-Natural Experiment of Hungary, 1914-2008', paper presented at 'the IOS/APB/ EACES Summer Academy on Central and Eastern Europe, Tutzing; University of Verona.

Mazzucato, Mariana. 2015. *The Entrepreneurial State*. Public Affairs.

McCleary, Rachel and Robert Barro. 2006. 'Religion and Economy', *Journal of Economic Perspectives 20(2)*, 49–72.

McCloskey, Deirdre. 2006. *The Bourgeois Virtues: Ethics for an Age of Commerce*. University of Chicago Press.

McCloskey, Deirdre. 2010. *Bourgeois Dignity: Why Economics Can't Explain the Modern World*. University of Chicago Press.

McCloskey, Deirdre. 2016. *Bourgeois Equality: How Ideas, Not Capital or Institutions, Enriched the World*, University of Chicago Press.

McEvedy, Colin and Richard Jones. 1978. *Atlas of World Population History*, Penguin.

Milanovic, Branko. 2010. *The Haves and the Have-Nots: A Brief and Idiosyncratic History of Global Inequality*, Basic Books, New York.

Milanovic, Branko. 2016a. *Global Inequality: A New Approach for the Age of Globalization*. Harvard University Press.

Milanovic, Branko. 2016b. 'There is a trade-off between citizenship and migration. *Financial Times*, April 20.

Milanovic, Branko. 2017a. 'Rising capital share and transmission into higher interpersonal inequality', voxeu.org, May 16.

Milanovic, Branko. 2017b. 'Increasing capital income share and its effect on personal income inequality', in: Heather Boushey, Brad de Long, Marshall Steinbaum (eds.), *After Piketty: The agenda for economics and inequality*, Harvard University Press, 235–59.

Milanovic, Branko and Lire Ersado. 2012. 'Reform and Inequality During the Transition: An Analysis Using Panel Household Survey Data, 1990–2005,' in: Gérard Roland (ed.) *Economies in Transition: The Long-Run View*. Houndmills, United Kingdom: Palgrave Macmillan.

Milanovic, Branko, Peter Lindert, and Jeffrey G. Williamson (2010) 'Pre-Industrial Inequality', *The Economic Journal 121(551)*.

Mills, Rodney H. Jr 1965. 'The Spanish 'Miracle': Growth and Change in the Spanish Economy, 1959–65'. The Board of Governors of the Federal Reserve System, Washington DC, November 9.

Millward Brown. 2008. 'A Portrait of the Affluent in Poland', 11 July.

Ministry of Foreign Affairs. 2013. 'Raport o sytuacji Polonii i Polaków za granicą 2012'. Poland's Ministry of Foreign Affairs, January.

Ministry of Regional Development. 2013. 'Wpływ polityki spójności na rozwój społeczno gospodarczy Polski w latach 2004–2015 w świetle wyników badań makroekonomicznych'. 10 June.

Mokyr, Joel. 1990. *The Lever of Riches: Technological Creativity and Economic Progress* Oxford University Press.

Mokyr, Joel. 2016. *Culture of Growth: The Origins of the Modern Economy*. Princeton University Press.

Molinas, César. 2013. *Qué hacer con España*. Destino.

Morawski, Wojciech. 2011. *Dzieje gospodarcze Polski*. Warsaw: Difin.

Mundell, Robert A. 1995. 'Great contractions in transition economies'. First Dubrovnik Conference on Transition Economies. 8–9 June.

Murrell, Peter. 1996. 'How far has the transition progressed?', *Journal of Economic Perspectives 10(2)*, 25–44.

Murrell, Peter. 2003. 'The relative levels and character of institutional development in transition economies', in: Nauro Campos and Jan Fidrmuc (eds.) *Political Economy of Transition and Development: Institutions, Politics and Policy*. Kluwer, Boston, Dordrect and London.

Myck, Michał and Mateusz Najsztub. 2016. 'Distributional Consequences of Tax and Benefit Policies in Poland: 2005-2014.' CenEA Working Paper Series (2), 1–38.

NBP. 2015. 'Household Wealth and Debt in Poland: Pilot Survey Report 2014.' National Bank of Poland, Warsaw.

NBP. 2016. 'Obywatele Ukrainy pracujacy w Polsce: raport z badania'. National Bank of Poland.

Newell, A. and B. Reilly. 2000. 'The Gender Wage Gap in the Transition from Communism: Some Empirical Evidence', *William Davidson Institute Working Paper No. 305*.

Niederhut, Jens. 2006. 'Doświadczenia pracowników administracji i instytucji NRD, uprawnionych do podróży służbowych na Zachód', in: Sandrine Kott, Marcin Kula and Thomas Lindenberger *Socjalizm w życiu powszednim. Dyktatura a społeczeństwo w NRD i PRL*. TRIO, Zentrum für Zeithistorische Forschung Potsdam, Warszawa, pp. 198–9.

Nguyen, Ha and Jaramillo, Patricio A. 2014. 'Institutions and Firms' Return to Innovation: Evidence from the World Bank Enterprise Survey'. *World Bank Policy Research Working Paper No. 6918*.

Nolan, Brian, Max Roser, and Stefan Thewissen. 2016. 'GDP per capita versus median household income: what gives rise to divergence over time?', *INET Oxford Working Paper* no. 2016–03.

Noland, Marcus. 2005. 'Religion and Economic Performance'. *World Development 33(8)*, 1215–32.

North, Douglass C. 1990. *Institutions, Institutional Change, and Economic Performance*. Cambridge University Press, New York.

North, Douglass C. 1991. 'Institutions'. *The Journal of Economic Perspectives, 5(1)*, 97–112.

North, Douglass C. 1993. 'Economic Performance through Time'. Nobel Prize lecture. From: http://www.nobelprize.org/nobel_prizes/economic-sciences/laureates/1993/north-lecture.html.

North, Douglass C. 1994. 'Economic Performance Through Time', *The American Economic Review 84(3)*, 359–68.

North, Douglass C. 1997. 'The Contribution of the New Institutional Economics to an Understanding of the Transition Problem', WIDER Annual Lectures, 1 (March), The United Nations University World Institute for Development Economics Research (WIDER), Helsinki.

North, Douglass. 2002. 'Understanding Economic Change and Economic Growth'. Distinguished Lectures Series, No. 7, Kozminski University, Warsaw.

North, Douglass. 2005. *Understanding the Process of Economic Change*. Princeton: Princeton University Press.

Novokmet, Filip, Thomas Piketty, and Gabriel Zucman. 2017. *From Soviets to Oligarchs: Inequality and Property in Russia, 1905–2016*. No. w23712. National Bureau of Economic Research.

Nunberg, Barbara. 1999. *The State After Communism: Administrative Transitions In Central And Eastern Europe*. Washington, DC: World Bank.

Nunn, Nathan. 2012. 'Culture and the Historical Process'. *NBER Working Papers 17869*, NBER.

OECD. 1992. *Poland, OECD Economic Surveys*. Paris.

OECD. 2012. *Looking to 2060: Long-Term Growth Prospects for the World*. Organisation for Economic Cooperation and Development.

OECD. 2016a. *Education at a Glance 2016: OECD Indicators*. OECD Publishing. Paris.

OECD. 2016b. *PISA 2015 Results (Volume 1). Excellence in Equity and Education*. Paris: OECD.

OECD. 2016c. *Survey of Poland*. Paris: OECD.

OECD. 2016d. *Skills Matter: Further Results from the Survey of Adult Skills*, OECD Skills.

OECD. 2016e. *Regions at a Glance*. Paris: OECD.

OECD. 2016f. *Policy Priorities for Making Poland a More Inclusive and Knowledge-Based Economy*. Paris: OECD.

OECD/World Bank. 2016. 'The squeezed middle class in OECD and emerging countries – myth and reality', OECD Headquarters, Paris, 1 December, 2016, Issues Paper.

Ogilvie, Sheilagh and A.W. Carus. 2014. 'Institutions and Economic Growth in Historical Perspective' in: *Handbook of Economic Growth*, Volume 2A, Elsevier.

Olson, Mancur. 1982. *The Rise and Decline of Nations*. London: New Haven.

Orłowski, Witold M. 2010. *W pogoni za straconym czasem. Wzrost gospodarczy w Europie Środkowo-Wschodniej, 1950–2030*. Warszawa: Polskie Wydawnictwo Ekonomiczne.

Ormerod, Paul. 1994. *The Death of Economics*. Faber and Faber.

Osęka, Piotr. 2011. 'Znoje na wybojach', *Polityka*, 21 July.

Ostrom, Elinor. 2005. 'Doing Institutional Analysis: Digging Deeper than Markets and Hierarchies,', in: Claude Menard and Mary M. Shirley (eds.) *Handbook of New Institutional Economics*. Dordrecht, Netherlands: Springer.

Ostrom, Elinor. 2010. 'Beyond Markets and States: Polycentric Governance of Complex Economic Systems,' *American Economics Review 100*, 641–72.

Ostry, Jonathan, Andrew Berg, and Charalambos Tsangarides. 2014. 'Redistribution, Inequality, and Growth', *IMF Staff Discussion Note SDN/14/02*, International Monetary Fund, April.

Paldam, Martin and Gert Tinggaard Svendsen. 2001. 'Missing social capital and the transition in Eastern Europe.' *Journal for Institutional Innovation, Development and Transition, 5*.

Pamuk, Şevket. 2007. 'The Black Death and the origins of the 'Great Divergence'across Europe, 1300–1600.' *European Review of Economic History 11.3*, 289–317.

Paredes, Evelio, Grigoli, Francesco and Di Bella Gabriel. 2016. 'Inequality and Growth: a Heterogeneous Approach'. *IMF Working Paper No. 16/244*, December.

Parente, Stephen L. and Edward C. Prescott. 2005. 'A Unified Theory of the Evolution of International Income Levels', in: Aghion, Philippe and Steven N. Durlauf (eds.) *Handbook of Economic Growth.* Amsterdam: Elsevier.

Pasek, Jan Chryzostom. 1690 (2004). *Pamietniki.* Wydawnictwo Zielona Sowa.

Pescatori, Damiano Sandri, and John Simon. 2014. 'Debt and Growth: Is There a Magic Threshold?', *IMF Working Paper WP/14/34*, February.

Piatkowski, Marcin. 2009. 'The Coming Golden Age of New Europe,' *Center for European Policy Analysis Report Nr 26*, October.

Piatkowski, Marcin. 2011a. "How the Polish Banking Sector Has Survived the Global Crisis". Kwartalnik Nauk o Przedsiebiorstwie, 2011/4, Warsaw School of Economics, pp. 24–9.

Piatkowski, Marcin. 2011b. 'Post-Crisis Prospects and a New Growth Model for the EU-10,' *Center for European Policy Analysis Report Nr 33*, April, Washington DC.

Piatkowski, Marcin. 2012. "State Commercial Banks in Action during the Crisis: The Case of Poland (PKO Bank Polski)", background paper for the Global Financial Development Report 2013. Rethinking the Role of the State in Finance. The World Bank, September.

Piatkowski, Marcin. 2013. 'Poland's New Golden Age: Shifting from Europe's Periphery to Its Center', *World Bank Policy Research Working Paper, Working Paper Series nr 6639*.

Piatkowski, Marcin. 2014. 'The Warsaw Consensus: The New European Growth Model' in: Grzegorz W. Kolodko (ed.) *Management and Economic Policy for Development*, Nova Science Publishers.

Piatkowski, Marcin. 2015a. 'Four ways Poland's state bank helped it avoid recession', Brookings Future Development blog, June 12.

Piatkowski, Marcin. 2015b. 'Chińskie tańsze, niemieckie lepsze? Czas zbudować 'Drugą Gdynię', *Gazeta Wyborcza*, November 25.

Piatkowski, Marcin and Mariusz Jarmuzek. 2008. 'Zero corporate income tax in Moldova: Tax Competition and its Implications for Eastern Europe.' *IMF Working Paper 8/203*, International Monetary Fund, August.

Piatkowski, Marcin and Natasha Kapil. 2015. 'From Imitating to Innovating'. Brookings Future Development blog. January 8.

Pickett, Kate and Richard Williamson. 2011. *The Spirit Level: Why Equality is Better for Everyone.* Penguin.

Piketty, Thomas. 1995. 'Social mobility and redistributive politics.' *The Quarterly journal of economics 110.3*, 551–84.

Piketty, Thomas. 2014. *Capital in the twenty-first century.* Cambridge: Harvard University Press.

Piketty, Thomas, Emmanuel Saez, and Gabriel Zucman. 2016. 'Distributional National Accounts. Methods and Estimates for the United States'. *NBER Working Paper No. 22945.* December.

Pinker, Steven. 2011. *The Better Angels of Our Nature: Why Violence Has Declined.* Penguin Books.

Pinto, Brian. 2014. *How Does My Country Grow? Economic Advice Through Story-Telling.* Oxford University Press.

References

Pinto, Brian, Marek Belka, and Stefan Krajewski. 1993. 'Transforming State Enterprises in Poland: Evidence by Manufacturing Firms'. *Brookings Papers on Economic Activity*, no. 1. Washington: Brookings Institution.

Pistor, Katharina. 2001. 'Law as a Determinant for Equity Market Development: The Experience of Transition Economies.' In: Peter Murrell ed., *Assessing the Value of Law in Transition Economies*. Ann Arbor: University of Michigan Press.

Plakans, Andrejs. 1995. *The Latvians: A Short History*. Hoover Institution Press.

Popov, Vladimir. 2007. 'Shock therapy versus gradualism reconsidered: Lessons from transition economies after 15 years of reforms'. *Comparative Economic Studies, 49*, 1–31.

Pritchett, Lant and Larry H. Summers. 2014. 'Asiaphoria Meets Regression to the Mean', *NBER Working Paper 20573*, October.

Putnam, Robert. 1993. *Making Democracy Work*. Princeton University Press.

PWC. 2017. 'The World in 2050. The Long View How will the global economic order change by 2050?' PWC, February.

Raiser, Martin. 1997. 'Informal institutions, social capital and economic transition: reflections on a neglected dimension'. *EBRD Working Paper* No. 25, August.

Raiser, Martin, Christian Haerpfer, Thomas Nowotny, and Claire Wallace. 2001. 'Social capital in transition: a first look at the evidence', *EBRD Working Paper* No. 61, February.

Rajan, Raghuram and Arvind Subramanian. 2011. 'Aid, Dutch Disease, and Manufacturing Growth.' *Journal of Development Economics 94(1)*, 106–18.

Ransom, Roger L. and Richard Sutch. 2001. *One Kind of Freedom: The Economic Consequences of Emancipation*, 2nd Edition. New York: Cambridge University Press.

Reding, Viviane. 2012. 'Why we need a United States of Europe now', speech at the Centrum für Europarecht an der University Passau, 8 November.

Reinhart, Carmen M. and Kenneth S. Rogoff. 2009. *This Time Is Different: Eight Centuries of Financial Folly*. Princeton, NJ: Princeton University Press.

Reinhart, Carmen M. and Kenneth S. Rogoff. 2010. 'Growth in a Time of Debt'. *NBER Working Paper No. 15639*, January.

Rhee, Alaina P, Allan Dizioli, Anna Ilyina, Christian Ebeke, Daria Zakharova, Faezeh Raei, Gil Mehrez, Haonan Qu, Lone Engbo Christiansen, Nadeem Ilahi, and Ruben V. Atoyan. 2016. 'Emigration and Its Economic Impact on Eastern Europe', *Staff Discussion Notes* No. 16/7. International Monetary Fund. July 20.

Richter, Tomas. 2010. 'Tunnelling: The Effect - and the Cause - of Bad Corporate Law', *Columbia Journal of European Law, 17(23)*, Winter 2010/2011.

Ridley, Matt. 2010. *The rational optimist: How prosperity evolves*. New York: Harper.

Robles, Adrian and Grigoli, Francesco. 2017. 'Inequality Overhang', *IMF Working Paper* No. 17/76, March.

Rodrik, Dani. 2007. 'The Real Exchange Rate and Economic Growth: Theory and Evidence.', John F. Kennedy School of Government, Harvard University, July.

Rodrik, Dani. 2008. 'Normalizing Industrial Policy'. *Commission on Growth and Development Working Paper;* no. 3. Washington, DC: World Bank.

Rodrik, Dani. 2013. 'Unconditional convergence in manufacturing'. *Quarterly Journal of Economics 128(1)*, 165–204.

Rodrik, Dani. 2015. *Economics Rules: The Rights and Wrongs of the Dismal Science.* Norton, New York.

Rodrik, Dani, Arvind Subramanian, and Francesco Trebbi. 2004. 'Institutions Rule: The Primacy of Institutions over Geography and Integration in Economic Development,' *Journal of Economic Growth V9(2),* 131–65.

Roland, Gerard. 2000. *Transition and Economics: Politics, Markets and Firms.* MIT Press.

Roland, Gerard. 2014. 'Transition in historical perspective' in: Aslund, Anders and Simeon Djankov (eds.), *The Great Rebirth: Lessons from the Victory of Capitalism over Communism.* Peterson Institute for International Economics.

Roland, Gerard and Thierry Verdier. 1999. 'Transition and the output fall', *The Economics of Transition 7(1), 1–28,* March.

Roland, Gérard and Thierry Verdier. 2003. 'Law Enforcement and Transition'. *European Economic Review, 47()4,* August.

Romer, Paul M. 2008. 'Economic growth' in: David Henderson (ed.) *The Concise Encyclopedia of Economics.* Liberty Fund.

Rose-Ackerman, Susan. 1999. 'Political corruption and democracy.', *Connecticut Journal of International Law, 14,* 363.

Roser, Max, Stefan Thewissen, and Brian Nolan. 2016. 'Incomes across the Distribution'. *Published online at OurWorldInData.org.* Retrieved from: https://ourworldindata.org/incomes-across-the-distribution/[Online Resource].

Rosés, Joan R. and Nikolaus Wolf. 2008. 'Prosperity and depression in the European economy and during interwar years (1913–1950): an introduction.', unpublished paper.

Rubin, Jared. 2017. *Rulers, Religion, and Riches: Why the West Got Rich and the Middle East Did Not.* New York: Cambridge University Press.

Rutkowski, Jan. 1998. 'Welfare and the labor market in Poland: social policy during economic transition', *World Bank Technical Paper,* No. 417, September.

Sachs, Jeffrey. 1993. *Poland's Jump to the Market Economy.* MIT Press.

Sachs, Jeffrey. 1994. 'Shock Therapy in Poland: Perspectives of Five Years'. The Tanner Lectures on Human Values delivered at University of Utah, April 6 and 7.

Sandbu, Martin. 2015. *Europe's Orphan. The Future of the Euro and the Politics of Debt.* Princeton University Press.

Sandbu, Martin. 2017. 'Leapfrogging to universal basic income', Financial Times, June 7. *Europe's Orphan. The Future of the Euro and the Politics of Debt.* Princeton University Press.

Sedlacek, Tomas. 2011. *Economics of Good and Evil: The Quest for Economic Meaning from Gilgamesh to Wall Street.* Oxford University Press.

Sen, Amartya. 1999. *Development as Freedom.* Anchor.

Scheidel, Walter. 2017. *The Great Leveler: Violence and the History of Inequality from the Stone Age to the Twenty-First Century.* Princeton University Press.

Schulz, Kathryn. 2011. *Being Wrong: Adventures in the Margin of Error.* Ecco, HarperCollins Publishers.

Schwartz, S. H. 1994. 'Beyond Individualism/Collectivism: New Cultural Dimensions of Values' in Uichol K. et al, eds., *Individualism and Collectivism: Theory, Method, and Applications.* Sage Publications: 85–119.

Semuels, Alana. 2016. 'Why So Few American Economists Are Studying Inequality'. *The Atlantic*, September 13.

Sharma, Ruchir. 2016. *The Rise and Fall of Nations: Forces of Change in the Post-Crisis World*. W.W. Norton & Company.

Shiller, Robert J. 2017. 'Narrative economics.' *The American Economic Review 107.4*, 967–1004.

Shleifer, Andrei. 2012. 'Seven lessons from post-communist transition'. CASE No. 03/2012. February.

Skidelsky, Robert and Skidelsky, E. 2012. *How much is enough: Money and the good life*. Other Press.

Skodlarski, Janusz. 2013. *Historia gospodarcza*. Wydawnictwo Naukowe PWN.

Słomczyński, Kazimierz M. and Goldie Shabad. 1996. 'Systemic transformation and the salience of class structure in East Central Europe', *East European Politics and Societies 11.1*,155–89.

Smith, Adam. 1776. *The Wealth of Nations*. London: W. Strahan and T. Candell.

Smolar, Aleksander. 2009. 'Self-limiting Revolution: Poland 1970-89', in: Adam Roberts and Timothy Garton Ash (eds.). *Civil Resistance and Power Politics: The Experience of Non-violent Action from Gandhi to the Present*. Oxford University Press.

Snyder, Timothy. 2012. *Bloodlands: Europe between Hitler and Stalin*. Basic Books.

Solow, Robert. 1966. 'The Capacity to Assimilate an Advanced Technology,' in: Nathan Rosenberg (ed.), *The Economics of Technological Change*, Harmondsworth: Penguin.

Solow, Robert. 2007. 'The Last 50 Years in Growth Theory and the Next 10.' *Oxford Review of Economic Policy 23(1)*, 3–14.

Sowa, Jan. 2012. *Fantomowe cialo krola. Peryferyjne zmagania z nowoczesna forma*. Kraków: Universitas.

Soysal, Yasemin Nuhoglu, and David Strang. 1989. 'Construction of the First Mass Education Systems in Nineteenth-Century Europe'. *Sociology of Education, 62(4)*, 277–88.

Spence, Michael, Patricia Clarke Annez, and Robert M. Buckley (eds). 2009. 'Urbanization and Growth'. *Commission on Growth and Development*. Washington DC: World Bank.

Stevenson, Betsey and Justin Wolfers. 2013. 'Subjective Well-Being and Income: Is There Any Evidence of Satiation?' *American Economic Review, Papers and Proceedings 101(3)*, 598–604, May.

Stiglitz, Joseph. 1999. 'Whither Reform? Ten Years of the Transition', Keynote Address, World Bank Annual Bank Conference on Development Economics.

Stiglitz, Joseph. E. 2002. *Globalization and Its Discontents*. WW Norton & Co.

Stiglitz, Joseph, Amartya Sen, and Jean Paul Fitoussi. 2008. 'Report of the Commission on the Measurement of Economic Performance and Social Progress.' Commission on the Measurement of Economic Performance and Social Progress, Paris.

Stola, Dariusz. 2010. 'A country with no exit? International Migrations form Poland, 1949–1989.' English summary. Polish Institute of National Remembrance.

Stola, Dariusz. 2016. 'Patterns of the evolution of the communist regime: the case of international mobility from Poland'. *Divinatio 42–43, spring-summer*.

Stöllinger, Roman. 2016. 'Structural Change and Global Value Chains in the EU', *The Vienna Institute for International Economic Studies Working Paper 127*, July.

Sturis, Dionisios. 2017. *Nowe zycie. Jak Polacy pomogli uchodzcom z Grecji*. Warsaw: Wydawnictwo W.A.B.

Supruniuk, Miroslaw. 2011. *Uporządkować wspomnienia: nieautoryzowane rozmowy z Jerzym Giedroyciem*. Toruń: Towarzystwo Przyjaciół Archiwum Emigracji.

Sylwester, Kevin. 2003. 'Income Inequality and Population Density 1500 AD: A Connection'. *Journal of Economic Development 28(2)*, December.

Szelenyi, Istvan, Daniel Treisman, and Edmund Wnuk-Lipinski, eds. 1995. *Elites in Poland, Russia, and Hungary: Change or Reproduction?* Warsaw: Polish Academy of Sciences.

Tabellini, Guido. 2010. 'Culture and Institutions: economic development in the regions of Europe'. *Journal of the European Economic Association 8(4)*, 677–716, June.

Taleb, Nassim. 2005. *Fooled by Randomness: The Hidden Role of Chance in Life and in the Markets*. Random House.

Taleb, Nassim. 2006. *The Black Swan: The Impact of the Highly Improbable*. Random House.

Taleb, Nassim. 2012. *Antifragile: Things That Gain from Disorder*. Random House.

Tamanaha, Brian Z. 2015. 'The Knowledge and Policy Limits of New Institutional Economics on Development.' *Journal of Economic Issues 49(1)*, 89–109.

Tanzi, Vito. 2006. 'Public Finances and Long-Term Economic Growth: Toward a Warsaw Consensus' in: *Fiscal Policy and the Road to the Euro*, National Bank of Poland, pp. 267–80.

Tazbir, Janusz. 1967. *Państwo bez stosów. Szkice z dziejów tolerancji polskiej*. Warszawa.

Tazbir, Janusz. 2007. *Historia Polski. Polska 1586–1821. Tom 6*. Warszawa. Wydawnictwo PWN.

Tazbir, Janusz. 2013. *Kultura szlachecka w Polsce. Rozkwit, upadek, relikty*. Wydawnictwo Nauka i Innowacje.

Tetlock, Philip E. 2005. *Political Judgment: How Good Is it? How Can We Know?*, Princeton University Press.

Thaler, Richard H. and Shlomo Benartzi. 2007. 'Save More Tomorrow™: Using Behavioral Economics to Increase Employee Saving.' *International Library of Critical Writings in Economics 204*, 131.

Thum, Gregor. 2003. *Uprooted: How Breslau Became Wroclaw during the Century of Expulsions*. Princeton University Press.

Thurow, Lester C. 1984. 'The Disappearance of the Middle Class'. *The New York Times*, 5 February.

Toborowicz, Jerzy. 2017. 'Behavioral economics and its applications in public policy' PhD thesis, unpublished. Kozminski University.

Tomkiewicz, Jacek. 2017. *Dynamika i struktura dochodow w warunkach globalizacji*. Warszawa: Wydawnictwo Naukowe PWN.

Tornell, A. 1997. 'Economic growth and decline with endogenous property rights'. *Journal of Economic Growth 2*, 219–50.

Treisman, Daniel. 2012. 'Twenty Years of Political Transition', in: Gérard Roland (ed.) *Economies in Transition: The Long-Run View*. London: Palgrave Macmillan.

Treisman, Daniel. 2014a. 'The Political Economy of Change After Communism' in Anders Aslund and Simeon Djankov (eds) *The Great Rebirth: Lessons from the Victory of Capitalism over Communism*. Institute for International Economics.

Treisman, Daniel. 2014b. 'Income, Democracy, and Leader Turnover'. *American Journal of Political Science 59(4)*, 927–42.

Tschierschky, Siegfried. 1932. 'Étude sur le nouveau régime juridique des ententes économiques (cartels etc.) en Allemagne et en Hongrie'. Préparée pour le Comité économique; Section des Relations économiques, Geneve.

Turnock, David. 2006. *The Economy of East Central Europe, 1815–1989. Stages of Transformation in a Peripheral Region*. London: Routledge.

Tycner, Adam. 2014. 'Lobbysci II RP', *Rzeczpospolita*, 25 April.

United Nations DESA. 2015. 'World Population Prospects: The 2015 Revision, Key Findings and Advance Tables'. Working Paper No. ESA/P/WP.241, Department of Economic and Social Affairs.

Van Ark, Bart and Marcin Piatkowski. 2004. 'Productivity, Innovation and ICT in Old and New Europe', *International Economics and Economic Policy 1 (2–3)*, 215–46.

Van Wijnbergen, Sweder and Nina Budina. 2001. 'Inflation Stabilization, Fiscal Deficits and Public Debt Management in Poland.' *Journal of Comparative Economics 29*, 293–309.

Varga, Janos and Jan In't Veld. 2009. 'A model-based assessment of the macroeconomic impact of EU structural funds on the new Member States,' European Economy—Economic Papers 2008–2015 371, European Commission.

Veblen, Thorstein. 1899. *The theory of the leisure class: An economic study in the evolution of institutions*. Macmillan.

Volcker, Paul. 2009. 'Paul Volcker: Think More Boldly', *Wall Street Journal*, December 14.

Vonyo, Tamas. 2016. 'War and socialism: why eastern Europe fell behind between 1950 and 1989'. *Economic History Review 00(0)*, 1–27. https://pseudoerasmus.files.wordpress.com/2017/01/vonyo-2016.pdf

Vonyo, Tamas and Alexander Klein. 2017. 'Why Did Socialism Fail? The Role of Factor Inputs Reconsidered'. *The University of Warwick Working Paper Series* No. 276, May.

Wade, Nicholas. 2014. *A Troublesome Inheritance: Genes, Race and Human History*. New York: Penguin Books.

Walicki, Andrzej. 1991. *Trzy patriotyzmy. Trzy tradycje polskiego patriotyzmu i ich znaczenie współczesne*. Warszawa; Res Publica.

Wallerstein, Immanuel. 1974. *The modern world-system: Capitalist agriculture and the origins of the European world-economy in the sixteenth centenary*. Academic Press.

Wasilewski, Zygmunt. 1934. 'Na widowni'. *Myśl Narodowa*. April 15, p. 233.

Weber, Max. 1905/2002. *The protestant ethic and the 'spirit' of capitalism and other writings*. New York: Penguin Books.

WHO. 2015. 'Poland: Alcohol Consumption, Levels and Patterns'. World Health Organization.

Williamson, John (ed.). 1990. *Latin American Adjustment: How much has Happened*. Washington DC; Institute for international Economics.

Williamson, John. 2004. 'A Short History of the Washington Consensus', paper commissioned by Fundación CIDOB for a conference 'From the Washington Consensus towards a new Global Governance,' Barcelona, September 24–25, 2004.

Wnuk, Marcin, Barbara Purandare, and Jerzy Marcinkowski. 2013. 'Struktura spozycia alkoholu w Polsce w ujeciu historycznym'. *Probl Hig Epidemiol 94(3)*, 446–50.

Wójtowicz, Anna and Grzegorz Wójtowicz. 2009. *Dlaczego nie jesteśmy bogaci. Dystans gospodarki polskiej do zachodnioeuropejskiej*. Warszawa.

Wolek, Tomasz. 1997. 'Tadeusz Mazowiecki. Polityk Zgody' in: *Rodem z 'Solidarnosci'. Sylwetki tworcoe NSZZ 'Solidarnosc'*. Warszawa: Stowarzyszeni Archiwum Solidarnosci i Niezalezna Oficyna Wydawnicz, 1997.

World Bank. 1996. World Development Report 1996: From Plan to Market. World Bank, Washington, DC.

World Bank. 2002a. *Transition: The First Ten Years. Analysis and Lessons for Eastern Europe and the Former Soviet Union*. World Bank, Washington, DC.

World Bank. 2002b. *Building Institutions for Markets. World Development Report 2002*. World Bank, Washington, DC.

World Bank. 2006. *World Development Report 2006: Equity and Development*. World Bank, Washington, DC.

World Bank. 2008. *The Growth Report: Strategies for Sustained Growth and Inclusive Development*. World Bank, Washington, DC.

World Bank. 2011. 'Europe 2020. Fueling Growth and Competitiveness in Poland Through Employment, Skills and Innovation'. Nina Arnhold, Itzhak Goldberg, Natasha Kapil, Marcin Piatkowski and Jan Rutkowski. World Bank, Washington, DC, March.

World Bank. 2012. *China 2030: Building a Modern, Harmonious, and Creative High-Income Society*. World Bank, Washington, DC.

World Bank. 2013a. *Turn Down the Hear: Climate Extremes, Regional Impacts, and the Case for Resilience*. World Bank, Washington, DC.

World Bank. 2013b. 'The Status of Contract Enforcement in Poland'. World Bank, Washington, DC.

World Bank. 2013c. 'Toward a Stronger Insolvency Framework in Poland". World Bank, Washington, DC, April.

World Bank. 2014. *Poland: Saving for Growth and Prosperous Aging*. World Bank.

World Bank. 2015a. *World Development Report: Mind, Society and Behavior*. Washington DC: World Bank.

World Bank. 2015b. *Competitive Cities for Jobs and Growth. What, Who and How*. Washington DC: World Bank.

World Bank. 2016a. 'Toward an Innovative Poland: The Entrepreneurial Discovery Press and Business Needs Analysis'. Washington DC: the World Bank.

World Bank. 2016b. 'EU Regular Economic Report - Growth, Jobs and Integration: Services to the Rescue'. The World Bank. Fall.

World Bank. 2016c. Doing Business 2017. Equal Opportunity for All. The World Bank.

World Bank. 2017a. Lessons from Poland, Insights for Poland: A Sustainable and Inclusive Transition to High-Income Status. Washington, D.C.: World Bank Group.

World Bank. 2017b. Poland - Systematic Country Diagnostic: Toward a Strategic, Effective, and Accountable State. Washington, D.C.: World Bank Group.

World Bank. 2017c. *World Development Report 2017 Governance and the Law*. World Bank, Washington, DC.

Wyczański, Andrzej. 1973. *Polska w Europie XVI stulecia*. Tom 253 serii wydawniczej Omega.

Wysokinska. Agnieszka. 2011. 'Invisible Wall: Role of Culture in Long-Term Development', mimeo.

Wysokinska, Agnieszka. 2016. 'Institutions or Culture? Lessons for Development from Two Natural Experiments of History', mimeo.

Zagórski, Krzysztof. 1978. 'Social mobility in socio-demographic regions in Poland,' in Z. Mlinar and H. Teune [eds.] *The Social Ecology of Change: From Equilibrium to Development*. London: Sage.

Żarnowski, Janusz. 2007. 'The Polish Intelligentsia since 1944. Social Structure and Social Roles', *Acta Oeconomica Pragensia 7*, 472–80.

Zatonski, Witold, Hannia Campos, and Walter Willett. 2008. 'Rapid Declines in Coronary Heart Disease Mortality in Eastern Europe Are Associated with Increased Consumption of Oils Rich In Alpha-Linolenic Acid'. *European Journal of Epidemiology 23(1)*, 3–10.

Zimmerman, Paul. 2014. 'Cultural Tradition and Cultural Change in Postcommunist Poland: A Secondary Data Analysis'. Diss. Phoenix, Arizona: ProQuest LLC.

Zingales, Luigi. 2013. 'Preventing Economists' Capture', in: Daniel Carpenter and David Moss (eds.) *Preventing Regulatory Capture: Special Interest Influence and How to Limit it*. Cambridge University Press.

Znaniecki, Franciszek. 1935. *Ludzie teraźniejsi a cywilizacja przyszłości*. Warszawa.

Suggested Further Reading

Aiyar, S., R. Duval, D. Puy, Y. Wu, and L. Zhang. 2013. 'Growth Slowdowns and the Middle-Income Trap', IMF Working Paper No 13/71, Washington: International Monetary Fund.

Barro, Robert. 1996. *Getting it Right: Markets and Choices in a Free Society*. Cambridge: MIT Press.

Bloom, Nicholas and John Van Reenen. 2010. 'Why Do Management Practices Differ across Firms and Countries?', *Journal of Economic Perspectives 24(1)*, 203–24.

Boni, Michal (eds). 2011. 'Mlodzi 2011'. Poland's Prime Minister's Chancellery.

Broadberry, Stephen and Bishnupriya Gupta. 2004. 'Monetary and Real Aspects of the Great Divergence Between Europe and Asia, 1500–1800', mimeo. 6 August.

Brunarska, Zuzanna, Malgorzata Grotte, and Magdalena Lesinska. 2012. 'Migracje obywateli Ukrainy do Polski w kontekscie rozwoju społeczno-gospodarczego: stan obecny, polityka, transfery pieniężne'. *CMR Working Papers 60/118*, Centre of Migration Research, Warsaw University, December.

Bukowski, Adam. 2011. 'Przegląd publikacji z historii gospodarczej na łamach'Explorations in Economic History' w latach 2001–2010', in: Rafał Matera and Andrzej Pieczewski (eds.). Przegląd badań nad historią gospodarczą. Wydawnictwo Uniwersytetu Łódzkiego, Łódź 2011, pp. 225–35.

Carone, Giuseppe, Denis, Cecile, Mc Morrow, Kieran, Mourre, Gilles, and Roeger, Werner. 2006. 'Long-Term Labour Productivity and GDP Projections for the EU25 Member States: A Production Function Framework'. https://ssrn.com/abstract= 930421 or http://dx.doi.org/10.2139/ssrn.930421.

Clark, Gregory. 2007. A Farewell to Alms: A Brief Economic History of the World. Princeton University Press.

DeLong, Bradford J. and Barry Eichengreen. 1993. 'The Marshall Plan as a Structural Adjustment Programme,' in Rüdiger Dornbusch, Wilhelm Nölling, and Richard

Layard, eds., *Postwar Economic Reconstruction: Lessons for Eastern Europe*. London: Anglo-German Foundation for the Study of Industrial Society.

Erikson, Robert, John Goldthorpe, and Lucienne Portocarero. 1979. 'Intergenerational Class Mobility' in Three Western European Societies.' *British Journal of Sociology 30(4)*, 15–41.

Geodecki, Tomasz, Jerzy Hausner, Aleksandra Majchrowska, Krzysztof Marczewski, Marcin Piatkowski, Grzegorz Tchorek, Jacek Tomkiewicz, and Marzena Weresa. 2013. 'Competitive Poland. How To Advance in The World's Economic League?'.

Gerschenkron, Alexander. 1962. *Economic backwardness in historical perspective, a book of essays*, Belknap Press of Harvard University Press, Cambridge, MA.

Gros, Daniel. 2014. 'From Transition to Integration: The Role of Trade and Investment'. In: Anders Åslund and Simeon Djankov (eds) *The Great Rebirth: The Victory of Capitalism over Communism*. Washington: Peterson Institute for International Economics.

Hofstede, Geert. 1991. *Cultures and Organizations: Software of the Mind*. London: McGraw-Hill.

Inglot-Brzek, Elzbieta. 2012. 'The Demographic Changes and the Evolution of Higher Education System in Poland', mimeo.

Jacob, William. 1826. Report on the Trade in Foreign Corn and on the Agriculture of the North of Europe. London, Ridgway.

Kochanowicz, Jacek. 2006. *Backwardness and Modernization: Poland and Eastern Europe in the 16th–20th Centuries'*, Aldershot.

Koepke, Nikola and Joerg Baten. 2005. 'The Biological Standard of Living in Europe During the Last Two Millennia,' *European Review of Economic History 9–1*, 61–95.

Koepke, Nikola and Jörg Baten. 2008. 'Agricultural Specialization and Height in Ancient and Medieval Europe', *Explorations in Economic History 45, 127–46*.

Kolodko, Grzegorz W. 1992. 'Transition from Socialism and Stabilization Policies: The Polish Experience', in: Michael Karen and Gur Ofer, eds., *Trials of Transition: Economic Reform in the Former Communist Block*. Boulder, Col.: Westview, pp. 129–50.

Kolodko, Grzegorz W. 1999. 'Ten Years of Postsocialist Transition: the Lessons for Policy Reforms'. *Policy Research Working Paper*, No. 2095, The World Bank, Washington, DC.

Kolodko, Grzegorz W. 2002. *Globalization and Catching-up In Transition Economies*. Rochester, NY and Woodbridge, Suffolk, UK: University of Rochester Press, pp. 105.

Kolodko, Grzegorz W. 2005. *The Polish Miracle. Lessons for the Emerging Markets*, co-author and editor. Burlington, England and Aldershot, VT, USA: Ashgate.

Kolodko, Grzegorz W. 2007. 'Institutions, Policies and Economic Development', in: George Mavrotas and Anthony Shorrocks, eds., *Development: Advancing Core Themes in Global Economics*. New York: Palgrave Macmillan, pp. 531–54.

Kolodko, Grzegorz W (ed.). 2011. *20 years of Transformation: Achievements, Problems and Perspectives*, co-author and co-editor. New York: Nova Science, pp. 292.

Kolodko, Grzegorz W. 2013. 'The Great Transformation 1989–2029', in: Paul Hare and Gerard Turley, eds., *Handbook of the Economics and Political Economy of Transition*. London and New York: Routledge, pp. 456–67.

Kolodko, Grzegorz W. 2014. 'The New Pragmatism, or Economics and Policy for the Future', *Acta Oeconomica 64(2), 139–60*.

Kolodko, Grzegorz W. 2014. *Whither the World: The Political Economy of the Future*, Houndmills: Palgrave Macmillan, Hampshire: Basingstoke, Vol. I, pp. XI + 224 & Vol. II, pp. VI + 226.

Kolodko, Grzegorz W. and Michal Rutkowski 1991. 'The Problem of Transition from a Socialist to a Free Market Economy: The Case of Poland', *The Journal of Social, Political and Economic Studies 16(2)*.

Lucas, Robert. 1988. 'On the mechanics of economic development'. *Journal of Monetary Economics 22(1)*, 3–42.

Maddison, Angus. 2008. 'The west and the rest in the world economy: 1000–2030'. *World Economics 9(4)*, 75–99.

Morris, Ian. 2010. *Why the West Rules—For Now: The Patterns of History, and What They Reveal About the Future*. Farrar, Straus & Giroux.

Raiser, Martin. 2001. 'Trust in Transition,' *EBRD Working Paper*, No. 39.

Rajan, Raghuram. 2010. *Fault Lines: How Hidden Fractures Still Threaten the World Economy*. Princeton University Press.

Rodrik, Dani. 2002. 'After Neoliberalism, What?', Remarks at the BNDES Seminar on 'New Paths of Development', Rio de Janeiro, September 12–13.

Rodrik, Dani. 2014. 'When Ideas Trump Interests: Preferences, Worldviews, and Policy Innovations,' *Journal of Economic Perspectives 28(1)*, 189–208.

Schadler, Susan, Adrian Mody, Abdul Abiad, and David Leigh. 2006. 'Growth in the Central and Eastern European Countries of the European Union', *IMF Occasional Paper* 252.

Shleifer, Andrei and Daniel Treisman. 2014. 'Normal Countries: The East 25 Years after Communism'. *Foreign Affairs*, Fall/Winter.

Sztompka, Piotr. 1993. Civilizational incompetence: The trap of post-communist societies. *Zeitschrift für Soziologie 22(2)*, 85–95.

Tanzi, Vito and Ke-young Chu, eds. 1998. *Income Distribution and High-Quality Growth*. Cambridge, MIT Press.

UN Economic Commission for Europe. 2014. *Economic Statistics*. Vienna.

Van Zanden, Jan Luiten. 1999. 'Wages and the Standard of Living in Europe, 1500–1800', *European Review of Economic History, August 3(2)*, 175–97.

Van Zanden, Jan Luiten et al. (eds.). 2014. *How Was Life?: Global Well-being since 1820*. OECD Publishing.

Williamson, John. 2008. 'Exchange Rate Economics'. *Commission on Growth and Development Working Paper* No. 2. Washington, DC: World Bank.Wolff, N. 2009. 'Agriculture and economic development in Poland, 1870–1970', in: Pedro Lains, Vicente Pinilla (eds.) *Agriculture and Economic Development in Europe Since 1870*. Routledge: London-New York.

Wyczański, Andrzej. 2001. *Szlachta polska w XVI wieku*. Warszawa.

Zagórski, Krzysztof. 1983. 'Social mobility into post-industrial society.' Paper presented to the meeting on general issues of stratification and mobility, ISA Research Committee on Social Stratification, Amsterdam.

Index